Biosocial Mechanisms of Population Regulation

CONTRIBUTORS

Reuben M. Baron, Professor and Director, Social Psychology Program, University of Connecticut at Storrs

John J. Christian, Professor of Biology, State University of New York at Binghamton

Mark Nathan Cohen, Associate Professor of Anthropology, State University of New York at Plattsburgh

Lee C. Drickamer, Associate Professor of Biology and Coordinator of the Bronfman Science Center, Williams College

Yakov M. Epstein, Associate Professor of Psychology, Rutgers, the State University of New Jersey

Jonathan Freedman, Professor of Psychology, Columbia University

Fekri A. Hassan, Assistant Professor of Anthropology, Washington State University

Robert A. Karlin, Assistant Professor of Psychology, Rutgers, the State University of New Jersey

Harold G. Klein, Associate Professor of Biology, State University of New York at Plattsburgh

Richard B. Lee, Professor of Anthropology, University of Toronto

James A. Lloyd, Associate Professor of Reproductive Medicine and Biology, University of Texas Medical School at Houston

Roy S. Malpass, Associate Professor of Behavioral Science, State University of New York at Plattsburgh

L. David Mech, U.S. Fish and Wildlife Service, Patuxent Wildlife Research Center, Laurel, Maryland

Jane M. Packard, Department of Ecology and Behavioral Biology, University of Minnesota

Thomas Richie, School of Medicine, University of Pennsylvania

Suzanne Ripley, Visiting Assistant Professor of Anthropology, Columbia University

Donald Stone Sade, Professor of Anthropology, Northwestern University

M. Farooq Siddiqi, Lecturer, Department of Geography, Aligarh University

Charles H. Southwick, Professor of Biology and Chairman, Department of EPO Biology, University of Colorado

Robert H. Tamarin, Associate Professor of Biology, Boston University

Henry Taylor, Resident Physician, Baltimore City Hospital

H. Jane Teas, Harvard School of Public Health

C. Richard Terman, Professor of Biology, Laboratory of Endocrinology and Population Ecology, College of William and Mary

BIOSOCIAL MECHANISMS OF POPULATION REGULATION

Edited by Mark Nathan Cohen,
Roy S. Malpass, and Harold G. Klein
Foreword by G. Evelyn Hutchinson

YALE UNIVERSITY PRESS
New Haven and London
1980

Published with assistance from the foundation established in memory of Philip Hamilton McMillan of the Class of 1894, Yale College.

Designed by James J. Johnson
and set in Times Roman type. Printed in the United States of America by Edwards Brothers, Inc., Ann Arbor, Michigan.

Published in Great Britain, Europe, Africa, and Asia (except Japan) by Yale University Press, Ltd., London. Distributed in Australia and New Zealand by Book & Film Services, Artarmon, N.S.W., Australia; and in Japan by Harper & Row, Publishers, Tokyo Office.

Library of Congress Cataloging in Publication Data

Main entry under title:

    "Papers . . . originally written for an interdisciplinary symposium . . . held on the Plattsburgh campus of the State University of New York in the spring of 1978."

    Includes bibliographies and index
    1. Animal populations—Congresses. 2. Population—Congresses. 3. Crowding stress—Congresses. I. Cohen, Mark Nathan. II. Malpass, Roy S. III. Klein, Harold G.
    QH352.B56   591.5′24   79–19023
    ISBN 0–300–02399–5

CONTENTS

FOREWORD

The study of the demography of literate cultures in western Europe began in the seventeenth century and started to produce theoretical ideas almost immediately. The interests of the earlier workers were mainly economic and sociological. In spite of evolution by natural selection being fundamentally a demographic process, biologists did not turn their thoughts to the creation of a really comparative science of population until the present century. This may have been to some extent due to the unreasonable antithesis that developed between biometricians and mendelians shortly after the rediscovery of Mendel's work.* Both classical demography based on official censuses and biological demography, largely developed experimentally, are now lively areas of science.

A very complicated area of investigation lies between these two types of endeavor. The present volume deals with a part of this intermediate territory. It tells, often with great distinction, the workers on human societies much of what they need to know about the population biology of nonhuman mammals. It also shows how the debatable problems that arise in the study of crowding in modern human societies may bear on the ecology of man and so on the biological problems of birth and death. That difficulties and contradictions appear to arise is not only inevitable but promising. An unresolved problem is the most likely initial disguise for a really important discovery.

The last few papers deal with questions having evolutionary significance. Though important to the student of man, for whom they are

---

*See particularly [C. H. Waddington]. 1971. Individual paradigms and population paradigms. *Times Literary Supplement* 70:1309–10.

primarily written, they are also highly significant to anyone concerned with evolutionary biology. They deal basically with the mode of origin of optimal reproductive rates, which always puts some sort of strain on the operation of natural selection. These papers can and should set the biologist thinking. We are shown that the physiological spacing of births is a real phenomenon in some human populations though its exact mechanism is still not clear. We are also made to see that infanticide by males in langurs is a very different phenomenon from the infanticide by females in man. We are given an adaptive interpretation of the case of the langurs, in terms of maintenance of polymorphism. The authors who discuss these matters, however, keep the obvious secret of the human case to themselves, wishing no doubt to stretch our minds. Since any kind of spacing equivalent to a given removal of infants by infanticide is done at less cost in resources, infants being expensive to make, a given economy, achievable by either method, will result, in the long run, in rather more resources being available to the mothers in families in which physiological spacing occurs than when infanticide is practiced. Provided the social structure permits the advantage to be reaped primarily within the family, the expectation of survival and further reproduction should be greater in the offspring of females using spacing than those using infanticide, though both these methods might be more efficient than unrestrained fertility. A pure kind of K-selection would in fact be occurring, which if everything worked out right, which it seldom does, should replace infanticide by a physiological method of family limitation.

All evolutionists should read the book, if only for the pleasure of seeing what they can catch when they throw in their lines.

16 May 1979   *G. Evelyn Hutchinson*

INTRODUCTION

The papers in this volume were originally written for an interdisciplinary symposium on the topics of "crowding," "density-dependence," and "population regulation" held on the Plattsburgh Campus of the State University of New York in the spring of 1978. The conference was convened on the basis of our perception that, although these concepts were in general use in all three of the disciplines (anthropology, social psychology, and biology) which we represent, and although they were being used in intuitively similar ways in each discipline, they were nonetheless poorly understood and often poorly communicated between disciplines. It was our hope to promote dialogue between the disciplines and, through dialogue, to promote common usage and fruitful conceptual interchange.

We were concerned primarily with generating a comparative analysis of the responses organisms make to the increasing density of conspecifics (or to some function of that density).* This focus led us to concentrate heavily on what might be referred to as endogenous mechanisms of population regulation—mechanisms of *self*-regulation.

*Density effects in population dynamics are ill-defined and little understood. Measures of density are useful so long as one bears in mind that the density of a population is merely the researcher's crude measure of an aggregation of individuals of the population. The significance of density levels to the members of a population may be quite variable, depending upon the nature of the sensory-perceptual systems of the species, the basic social behavior of the species, and other factors such as the phase of reproductive physiology of the individuals. Various authors in this volume note that density per se is not the key factor in regulating populations, and they address their presentations to the mechanisms by which density translates into the behavioral and physiological events involving individuals of a population and leading to regulation of the population or at least to changes in the behavior and health of individuals. Collectively, these papers should provide the reader with a better perspective on the meaning of population density as it applies to the social behavior of various species.

However, it was not, and is not, our intention to argue for the primacy of self-regulation over exogenous regulatory mechanisms (predation, parasitism, and resource scarcity) as the means by which most populations are controlled. Nor was it our presumption that such systems of self-regulation are common to all animal populations. (In fact, an informal consensus of the participants in the symposium, pre-selected in large part for their interest in internal regulation, was that there is enormous variation both among species and among habitats in the relative importance of self-regulation; that mechanisms of self-regulation at some level are probably fairly common among animal species; but that for most species they may only rarely come into play in periods when exogenous forces do not first intervene.) Whatever the balance in nature, it was our intention to focus on intraspecific regulatory mechanisms, with emphasis on understanding their possible application to human populations.

To the extent that self-regulation actually characterizes various species in nature, either as a by-product of selection for individual fitness or as a more direct consequence of kin (or even group?) selection, we might expect that the regulatory mechanisms would be fairly closely adapted to a particular environment. Therefore, as with other locally selected traits, we would expect mechanisms and systems of population regulation to be fairly specific to particular populations or species rather than displaying marked phylogenetic continuity. Moreover, as a result of the history of local selective pressure, we might expect the regulatory system of each local population to be something of a pastiche, a complex of feedback loops evolved at different periods and therefore operating through many different body systems and responding to varied features of the internal and external environment. Nonetheless, we believe that evolutionary theory suggests that there should be more continuity among species (and particularly between man and other mammals) in the perception and processing of density-related information and in the repertoire of responses to that information than the separate disciplines currently recognize. We held the symposium in the belief that both homologous and analogous features of density-perception and population regulation could be recognized and in the belief that each discipline could benefit from greater exposure to the theories, methods, and data manipulated by the others in analyzing common problems.

The conference was specifically designed to assemble scientists concerned with population regulation from four different perspectives, each with access to a different body of data and with a different set of theoretical biases: (1) those scientists studying density-dependent effects in laboratory situations or in controlled populations, primarily of rodents; (2) those making longitudinal observations on population trends and behavior in free-living populations, primarily of primates and other large mammals; (3) those studying human responses to crowding and density under controlled conditions or in situations "controlled" through statistical manipulation of census data; and (4) those interested in the evolution of density-dependent responses and population regulation in our own species and in studies of human population trends over time.

In an attempt to promote explicit comparisons among the various studies, we requested that various participants evaluate the density-dependent responses of their subject populations in terms of a three-part conceptual model. We asked, first, that they identify the antecedents of such responses, the environmental cues to which organisms respond, or the density-related parameters which they appear to measure. (See appendix 1 for a proposed check list of such cues.) We asked, second, that they evaluate what was known about the mechanisms, the neural or hormonal pathways, by which this environmental information was processed by the organism. We asked, third, that they consider the repertoire of responses available to the organism and the pattern of choice among responses exhibited in various circumstances. (For a proposed list of such responses see appendix 2.)

In proposing this tripartite division, we anticipated considerable difficulty in describing, let alone comparing, the various mechanisms of processing (the second category), and our pessimism was well founded. Pieces of a system for hormonal processing of density-related data are discussed, most notably in the paper by Christian; but we are far from understanding how the system he describes is integrated into the more general repertoire of processing strategies available to any organism, and even farther from gaining a comparative approach to such processing in different species.

We were, however, surprised and disappointed by our collective inability to describe either the range of cues to which organisms of any species responded or the range of responses evidenced. In the papers which follow it will be clear that *some* cues and *some* responses can be identified for *some* populations of *some* species under *some* conditions.

But even with the best-studied species and populations we are far from being able to characterize the range of cues or the repertoire of responses available to a population or species, much less to elucidate how particular patterns of cues and of responses are related. In sum, we are disappointingly far from being able to characterize or summarize species-specific patterns from which meaningful evolutionary comparisons can be made.

We retain our sense that this is an important and attainable goal, and it is our hope that the papers in this volume which provide no more than a scattering of partial responses will stimulate efforts to fill in the data necessary before more reliable comparisons can be made. In any case the juxtaposition of scholars from various fields points up a number of general issues of scientific method and theory. It is these issues, generated by the interdisciplinary nature of the conference itself, which we wish to address here. Some more specific issues and problems are discussed in footnotes to individual papers. Otherwise we defer to Professor Hutchinson and to the individual reader in the elucidation of the themes and problems that emerge through comparison and contrast of the papers.

It is important to note, first, that the papers bring to light problems of interdisciplinary communication that must be solved before a truly evolutionary perspective across species and disciplines can be accomplished. Collectively, the papers are striking for the comparisons and contrasts they draw, but also for those they do not. The reader will be struck in many cases not so much by the correspondence between papers as by the lack thereof. In part, of course, this is merely a sampling problem; the conference was, necessarily, only a partial sampling of existing scholarship. More important, there is significant sampling error within the fields of study themselves. Sheer limits of time and money, particularly on studies which involve field observation of wild populations, mean that data samples are poor, the range of conditions observed or tested is likely to be limited, and results therefore will only occasionally be comparable—especially if each field is inclined to use its limited resources in ways dictated by its own intellectual history rather than by efforts at comparison.

If some such problems are the result of random sampling or purely historical biases, however, others are deeply rooted in the necessary structure of research and will therefore be intractable. The major problem both with the conference format and with the literature at large is that differences of methodology often parallel taxonomic distinctions among subject populations. This may result from historical divergence of disciplines, but it is often rooted in the practical necessities of research design. Whatever its source, the result is that it is often difficult to distinguish the divergent properties of subject populations from the properties of specific research designs. One such problem concerns the relative tractability or intractability of different species to different kinds of manipulation. Thus, for example, studies of controlled populations (cf. Lloyd, Terman, this volume) are most commonly concerned with rodent populations for reasons of size, time, and expense; whereas studies of free-ranging populations are commonly of larger animals (primates or carnivores—cf. Sade, Southwick et al., Packard and Mech, this volume) for reasons of visibility. Contrasts drawn may thus reflect either the conflicting outcomes of the two research designs (discussed more fully below) or the attributes of various taxa.

A second related problem, and one which is critical for our purposes, concerns differential access which human scientists have to the behaviors of different species. Consider the apparent contrast between primate and rodent populations. Primate studies are relatively rich in the details of behavior of individual organisms and their individual social histories; the rodent studies typically report only aggregate behavior: group totals, percentages, and occasionally (as in some experiments described by Lloyd) the interactions of crudely defined demographic classes or other subgroups of the population. One possible interpretation of this difference is that primates in fact display greater individual sophistication in their interactions, a hypothesis compatible with their near-human status and flattering to our self-image. Another possibility is that this difference simply represents the fact that primates, but not rodents, are large enough and slow enough to be observed individually. A third possibility is that as primates ourselves we are sensitive to the social interactions of other primates in a manner that we cannot extend to rodents. (One result of this difference, in terms of the paradigm outlined above, incidentally, is that primatologists can at least respond to the problem of identifying cues for behavior even if they cannot identify the full range; rodent specialists profess almost complete ignorance. We know very little about what constitutes crowding in the eyes—or noses or whiskers—of rodents.)

A third related problem is that categories of action as commonly represented in the literature are not comparable across disciplines. And often it may be, in fact, that no such comparability can be established. One example is that studies of human crowding (cf. Karlin, Epstein, Freedman, this volume) are often setting-specific in a way, and to a degree, that animal studies are not. The setting-specific nature of human crowding studies is perhaps necessitated by a peculiarly human subdivision and categorization of usable space, but it may also reflect the fact that we are sensitive to human subdivisions and not to those of animals. Perhaps other animal populations make such fine distinctions but we do not recognize them. (What is the rodent equivalent of crowding in mass transit or of a shortage of bathrooms?) Whichever explanation we select, however, we are still faced with the problem of comparing setting-specific data on human groups with more general estimates of density and crowding afforded elsewhere in the literature.

A fourth problem may be that we have difficulty controlling such comparisons with regard to the scale of density or crowding which is being observed. It is not clear, for example, that any instance of human crowding cited in this volume either in history or experiment is strictly analogous to levels of crowding which produce stress in laboratory rodents. (Indeed a major weakness of the social-psychology literature on human crowding may be that it focuses heavily on special settings within the sparsely populated and relatively affluent United States rather than looking at instances of extreme density or scarcity of resources.) But this problem is circular, because until we have better access to the density-perceiving and processing structures of the various species there will be no means for structuring densities of comparable scale, if in fact "density" can be made comparable even then.

Despite these and other very serious limitations on communication between the fields, the juxtaposition of approaches in this volume does suggest a number of ways in which the various methods and disciplines can benefit from exposure to one another. The contrast between studies of laboratory and of free-ranging populations is probably the most basic, but also the most widely recognized and widely discussed. Laboratory studies have the advantage of controlling for most variables, with the result that specific responses to specific situations can be carefully defined and easily replicated. Moreover, test situations can be systematically varied to check the effects of specific changes in experimental design. In particular, the manipulation of laboratory conditions can permit us to approach what might be called the psychophysics of crowding—to determine the nature of the mathematical function relating increments in absolute density or some other measurement of crowding to the type and magnitude of the response. By gradually increasing the density of an experimental situation we can determine which responses intensify gradually (and by what mathematical function of density or other quantifiable cues) and which responses appear to be triggered by specific thresholds of crowding. Laboratory studies can thus produce relatively clean and concrete results. On the other hand, by the very fact of controlling variables, laboratory studies lose much of their accuracy as a means of predicting actual behavior in the wild. Their ability to reconstruct the actual balance among various modes of regulation (the pattern of "intercompensation" of regulatory mechanisms) or the balance between density-dependent regulation and density-independent influences in nature is quite limited, since, by design, a limited number of responses is studied *in vacuo*. Equally important is the possibility that responses that emerge in laboratory situations may in fact be of relatively minor consequence in nature.

Studies of free-living populations presumably have the advantage of dealing with a "natural" mix of environmental factors and of regulatory systems. But there are important disadvantages: (1) the particular stimuli triggering particular responses are relatively difficult to unravel; (2) conditions are hard to manipulate for subtle variations; and (3) observations are difficult to replicate. In this case, a far richer sense of natural intercompensation of regulatory mechanisms may be obtained, but the high cost of studies and the difficulty of replication make this pattern hard to describe in any systematic fashion. In fact one of the things that emerges from these studies (cf. papers by Sade, Southwick, Packard and Mech) is a sense of just how particularistic each study must be. We are far from obtaining a coherent general picture and certainly have not attained a quantification of anything like a species-general pattern of regulation.

One of the major themes that emerges from the contrast between controlled and free-ranging population studies is the dialogue concerning the relative importance of different mechanisms of regulation; the importance of endogenous as compared to exogenous regulatory mechanisms; and even the very prevalence of density-dependent regulation per se as contrasted with the incidence of density-independent events. Laboratory studies (cf. Lloyd, Terman, this volume) tend to present a picture of populations well regulated and largely self-regulated by endocrine-mediated responses to social interactions to conspecifics. (For an exhaustive description of the mechanisms involved, see the paper by Christian.) Because food, predation, and disease are not allowed to act as limiting factors, exogenous controls appear unimportant, and since random environmental events are prevented from impinging, equilibrium states are readily observed. In contrast, studies of free-ranging populations (including historical and evolutionary reconstructions of the history of the human population) seem to place a much stronger emphasis on the interaction between a population and its food, its predators, or its parasites (see papers by Packard and Mech, Cohen, Lee, Ripley, Hassan). The question emerges how often social self-regulation occurs in nature, and how often, when it occurs, social regulation is still an indirect reflection of variations in exogenous factors such as food supply. Moreover, when observations in sufficient depth and detail are possible (see Southwick et al.) it becomes evident that the actual population history of any species is a complex mix of homeostatic tendencies and of disruptive influences of the environment. If one accepts the assumption that species in nature tend to evolve toward equilibrium with their food supplies, there is still reason to question how often an equilibrium state is achieved before environmental conditions are altered. To what extent do populations actually achieve, rather than strive toward, the kind of asymptotic values observed in laboratories? The same question may be phrased differently: in the evolution of equilibrium by natural selection what is the ratio of populations or even whole ecosystems that fail to those that survive? Of the populations observable in any system at any point in time, how many are on the way to destruction or crippling loss by reasons of inadequate homeostasis? Several papers in the volume call attention to the apparent inadequacy of regulatory mechanisms among modern human populations. But just how unusual is this?

The bringing together of animal specialists and human social psychologists emphasized further contrasts in method and theory. Experiments on human subjects often utilize the subjects' own verbal self-report of feelings and responses. This adds a richness of appreciation of responses not available to the animal experimenters. It also adds, however, a potential source of error, since both subject and experimenter may be misled by expressed feelings that are at odds with actual behavioral responses. Similarly, studies on human subjects have the advantage that the experimenter begins with a basic sensitivity to the human beings. Certainly the summation by Christian provides a number of specifically testable propositions which can be carried over into the human crowding studies. Moreover, the rodent experiments and, more generally, observations on animal population dynamics may provide the concrete observations necessary to assist social scientists and historians in distinguishing significance among the myriad patterns of self-report and cultural bias inherent in our interpretations of ourselves.

The juxtaposition of animal- and human-oriented researchers (particularly those with an interest in the human population of evolutionary time) was also intended to focus our attention on a number of questions of theoretical and practical significance concerning the potential for self-regulation within our own species. The single most important theme of the conference involved our attempts to identify continuities and discontinuities between man and nonhuman animals. It was partly for this reason that the group was structured to include discussion both of primates (which provide a phylogenetic basis for understanding human patterns) and of wolves (whose habits of social predation make them a likely basis for interpreting human social evolution).

We have recently been challenged by the sociobiologists to recognize the existence of continuities between nonhuman and human behavior and to recognize the existence of genetic programs underlying human behavior. The field of natural population regulation would appear to be an excellent testing ground for such ideas because population regulation is an aspect of behavior closely linked with population biology and the ecology of the species, areas where social sciences are relatively likely to concede the possibility of biological/genetic determinants. The possible biological basis of population-regulatory systems in human populations is debated in the series of papers with which the book closes (Cohen, Hassan, Lee, Ripley).

The comparison of human and nonhuman populations is also suggested by the recognition of the stress syndrome (see Christian) and the apparent absence of a similar mechanism (at least in response to crowding) among human beings (see Freedman, Karlin, Epstein), a problem that has been debated in a number of places since the early 1970s. The question must be raised whether human populations have developed cognitive mechanisms, perhaps associated with the evolution of symbolic behavior, which mediate effectively between objective densities and perceived crowding. This subject was debated during

same range of environmental cues that are likely to be significant
the subject, particularly in studies done without crossing cultu
boundaries; but he has the disadvantage that because he is person;
sensitive to those cues he is far more likely to add personal biases
the interpretation of subjective responses. The animal studies have
advantage of providing affectively neutral, concrete behavior or ph
iological responses to concrete experimental situations. Their dis
vantage lies in our inability to define accurately the range of poter
stimuli and the level of sensory discrimination available to nonhui
subject species. Animal experiments are strongly biased in the se
that they begin by presuming sensitivity to the range of stimuli '
which we are familiar, and they progress beyond this bias only to
extent that specific experiments succeed in demonstrating specific
ferences in discriminatory capabilities between ourselves and spe
groups of subject animals. (The histories of attempts to understanc
feeding behavior of sharks and the homing behavior of pigeons
good examples of the need to go beyond human sensory metapho;
understanding other species.)

One result is that the literature on human crowding (cf. papel
Karlin, Epstein, Freedman) provides a range of subtle variation
definitions of crowding unknown to the animal experimenters w
might well be taken by the latter as models for further experim
design. For example, the setting-specific nature of many of the
chologists' experiments (and some of their results) referred to a
suggests modifications of some of the animal experiments design
determine what activities or phases of the life cycle are particu
sensitive to density. Similarly, psychologists' discussions of the
ous *ways* in which density contributes to crowding not only su
further discriminatory experiments but also offer a framework in v
the effects of social organization on density sensitivity (apparent
nonhuman populations discussed) might be explained. "Control'
"manning theory" (cf. Baron, Karlin, Epstein) may help explai
example, how density and social rank interact.*

Conversely, the animal experiments suggest a number of sp
physiological and behavioral responses which should be evaluat(

---

*An introduction to the Barker-Wicker theory of manning, with related findings, is p1
in A. W. Wicker, *An introduction to ecological psychology* (Monterey, California: Brool
1979).

the conference, but other than a set of exploratory hypotheses offered by Baron no sense of these mediating mechanisms was developed.

The comparison of animal and human data was also suggested by a problem that has emerged in anthropology in recent years resulting from assumptions about the prevalence of population homeostasis that were popular in the last decade. In the 1960s anthropology went through a period of what might be called "optimism"; a period of neo-functionalist analysis of human social systems which purported to demonstrate the homeostatic role of various behaviors and which took for granted that effective density-dependent regulation was the rule (V. C. Wynne-Edwards's influence, coming in the midst of this period was far more profound and long-lasting in anthropology than in biology itself). In the last several years some of the comfortable optimism about homeostasis has been challenged, but there remains, in anthropology, a lack of perspective on the balance of homeostatic success and failure debated in the biological world.

Finally, the juxtaposition of laboratory and short-term studies with studies having an evolutionary perspective emphasizes a different set of contrasts. Evolutionary studies have a potential methodological advantage over both laboratory and short-term natural observations: the ability to focus on naturally defined "significant" events. Unlike studies in the laboratory, which must structure variables in advance, and unlike studies of natural groups, which encompass a bewildering array of events, the long-term perspective of the evolutionary studies permits scientists at least to attempt to recognize which environmental factors and which systems of regulation are actually of major importance to the ecology of a given species. Hence the papers by Cohen, Hassan, Lee, and Ripley are able to debate the possibility of factoring out both elements of the environment and whole regulatory systems as insignificant to the overall history of the species. On the other hand, the disagreement among these papers indicates the degree to which such studies are limited by the indirect methods that must often be employed and the degree to which the studies are dependent on accurate short-term observations.

The evolutionary studies have one other important advantage: they call attention to the role of previous evolutionary history as well as of contemporary adaptive patterns as a determinant of contemporary structure and behavior. Synchronic studies are always in danger of overestimating the degree to which specific patterns are designed for, and successful at, adapting to the contemporary environment (witness the "optimism" of anthropology alluded to above).* One interesting theme in several of the papers is the extent to which previous adaptive histories and the time lag between altered circumstances and evolutionary adjustment may affect a species' ability to regulate itself successfully or may dictate the manner in which such regulation comes to be achieved. The problem of time lag may be particularly great among human beings (as some of these papers stress), because of the potential for rapid technological change, but such a maladaptation is an interesting possibility which should be given greater attention in the systematic study of other species as well.

A brief note on the structure of the volume: In order to facilitate comparisons among the studies and among the various species and disciplines they represent, we have taken the liberty of adding footnotes. These operate on two levels. First, they call attention in a mechanical way to treatment of the same theme by more than one author, in order to assist the reader in finding and comparing complementary or conflicting treatments of particular subjects. Second, on a more creative but more speculative level, they attempt to suggest areas where the data or concepts of one discipline might profitably be compared with those of another or where the work in one field suggests new possibilities for research in another. Unless otherwise specified, author-citations in the notes refer to papers in this volume.

Acknowledgments

The conference which these papers represent was held under the aegis of the Faculty of Arts and Science of the State University College, Plattsburgh, N.Y., and was sponsored by the George H. Hudson Fund of the college, the Plattsburgh Student Association, and the Wenner Gren Foundation for Anthropological Research. We wish to thank Philip Clarkson, Robert Moll, Jaimie Trautman, Lita Osmundsen, Sheila Payne, Charles Ricker, and Richard Currier for their assistance in organizing the conference and in preparing the resulting manuscripts. The volume was prepared

---

*Compare the recent critique of sociobiology offered by R. C. Lewontin, Sociobiology as an adaptationist program, *Behavioral Science* 24 (1979):5–14.

while the senior editor was a fellow of the Center for Advanced Study in the Behavioral Sciences, Stanford, California.

M.N.C.
R.S.M.
H.G.K.

Appendix I: *Potential Environmental Signals of "Density" or Antecedent Conditions for Responses by Individual Organisms Which Contribute to Population Regulation*

1. Resource Scarcity or Abundance
    a) Nutrient scarcity or abundance
        absolute level of caloric (or other specific nutrient) intake
        ratio of caloric (or other specific nutrient) intake to output
        balance or ratio of specific nutrients to one another
        distribution of caloric intake (other nutrients?) over time
        number of sensory messages indicating availability of nutrients over time
            from each of the major senses
        frequency with which other activities are interrupted or deferred for food
            quest
        frequency of competitive interactions for food
    b) Raw material scarcity or abundance
        access to building material, etc.
    c) Abundance or scarcity of space
        average space or distance between organisms
        average distance to nearest organism
        availability of unoccupied alternative space
        percentage of time (critical times?) when unoccupied space is accessible
        availability of "preferred" or "significant" spaces (e.g. nesting sites, bathrooms)
        frequency of competition for space or preferred or significant space
        average or minimum distance maintainable from perceived dangers
        frequency with which barriers to free, normal, necessary, or desired patterns of movement are encountered
        availability of "privacy"
        organism's ability to bound and/or structure available space
    d) Abundance or scarcity of social resources
        access to social roles ("overmanning")
        access to other organisms as scarce resources
        frequency/intensity of competition for social resources
2. Interactions with Conspecific Organisms
        Frequency of sensory inputs per unit time (for each of the major senses)

Number of different organisms from which inputs received per unit time
Number of inputs requiring altered attention structure per unit time
Number of inputs containing specific communication or message
Number of inputs from higher ranking organisms (or from members of other specific social categories, e.g. infants)
Duration of episodes of information
Duration of intervals between episodes
Frequency with which inputs disrupt particular activities (e.g. mating)
Frequency of inputs concerning the interaction of two or more other organisms
Randomness or predictability of sensory load
Length and amplitude of fluctuations in sensory load
Percentage of sensory load initiated by other organisms or otherwise outside control of individual
Percentage of sensory load received in specific settings
Percentage of sensory inputs signaling abnormal/pathological interactions or presence of abnormal/pathological individuals
Bulk accumulation of inputs
Ratio of sensory outputs received by different sensory modes

3. Extra-specific Relations
Parasite infestations per unit time
Parasite infestations perceived per unit time
Predator encounters per unit time
Predator encounters perceived per unit time
Probability of death or significant damage from predator or parasite action per unit time

4. Higher Order, or More Deeply Processed, Variables
Decision control
Outcome control
Environmental quality
Changes in subjective expected utility of actions or environments due to density variation
Increased variance in means-ends relations or probabilities (uncertainty, perceived loss of control)

Appendix II: *Outcomes (Individual Reactions, Responses)*

1. Mental Adjustments without Corrective Action
Cognition, habituation, conditioning
Readjustment of goal expectations
Flexibility in using means to maintain control
Compression of territories (elastic disc hypothesis)

2. Physiological Responses
Nutritional infertility (critical body fat hypothesis)
Anovulation due to endocrine system failure

Delayed or irregular sexual maturation

Suppression of spermotogenesis or male sexual function

Suppression of sexual signals or reception to signals

Gonadal regression

Fertilization failure

Prenatal mortality (non-implantation, abortion, embryo resorption)

Lactogenic failure

Infectious disease susceptibility (suppression of immunochemistry and disease resistance)

Non-infectious stress disease syndrome

3. Overt Behavioral Responses

Agonistic behavior

Territoriality

Dominant-subordinate interaction

Dispersal, presaturation, and saturation

Outmigration

Niche modification

Temporal changes in activity patterns

Abortion and contraception

Alterations in sexual interactions

Maternal failure in nest-building and nursing

Infanticide

4. Genetic-Evolutionary Phenomena

Short-term genetic changes in populations (vole cycles)

Long-term genetic changes in populations (coevolution and genetic feedback)

Individual selection and group selection

Biosocial Mechanisms of Population Regulation

1

INTERACTION OF SOCIAL STRUCTURE AND REPRODUCTION IN POPULATIONS OF MICE

James A. Lloyd

The social structures of populations of mice have an impact on their growth in that social rank, territoriality, age composition, and levels of aggression affect levels of natality and mortality in these populations. Each element affects reproduction at many levels. The study of large freely growing populations of mice has provided a model for asking questions regarding the dynamics of interactions of social structure and reproductive response. A large body of evidence relates social inter-actions to endocrine reproductive response in populations of mice.* Studies of smaller groups have been utilized to address specific ques-tions arising from studies of the larger populations. A discussion of our current understanding of these questions is the framework on which this paper is built. These questions include: (1) What is the relationship of territoriality to natality? (2) How may social rank affect reproduction? (3) What is the relationship of aggression to mortality, particularly infant mortality? (4) How does age composition affect the territorial system? (5) How does available space affect population growth? (6) How do social interactions affect physiological responses involved in reproduction? (7) How does social structure change as population size increases? Two species of mice, the house mouse (*Mus*

Editors' Note: Lloyd's emphasis on social structure (as opposed to absolute density) and the experiments he describes should be compared to discussions by the social psychologists on social factors mediating human responses to density and to discussions of social regulation of fertility in other populations. Cf. discussions by Sade and by Southwick et al. on populations of rhesus monkeys, and by Packard and Mech on wolf populations. The endocrine mechanisms to which Lloyd refers are discussed more fully by Christian.

musculus)* and the deermouse (*Peromyscus maniculatus bairdii*), will be examined.†

Social Structure and Reproduction in House Mice

Territories that are defended by individual males are a major component of social structure in house mouse populations (Davis 1958; Anderson 1961; Crowcroft and Rowe 1963; Rowe and Redfern 1969; Anderson and Hill 1965; Reimer and Petras 1967; Vessey 1967; Lloyd and Christian 1969; Oakeshott 1974; Lloyd 1975a, 1975b; Poole and Morgan 1976). Territoriality has been associated in house mice with the establishment of breeding groups (Rowe and Redfern 1969; Reimer and Petras 1967; Lloyd and Christian 1969; Poole and Morgan 1976). With increasing density, territorial systems may be replaced by hierarchies, with one animal assuming dominance over an entire population. In a study of two freely growing populations, the interaction of territoriality and births and the interaction of aggression and infant mortality were demonstrated. In the first population, as the territorial system collapsed, births fell and population growth stopped. In the second instance, the territorial system was maintained with increased aggression, triggering movement of breeding females and massive mortality of the young, stopping reproduction. In the population in which the territorial system collapsed one dominant male took over. Breeding females remained with that dominant male. In both populations 30% of the females accounted for all of the litters born (Lloyd 1975a).‡

*The house mice (*Mus musculus* L) were taken from a colony originally derived from wild house mice in Bethesda, Maryland, 25 years ago. These mice have been outbred as a laboratory colony.

†*Editors' Note:* Compare the studies of Lloyd on population regulation in mice with the study of wolves (Packard and Mech) or of monkeys (Sade) with respect to the relative kinds of data obtained. Differences in the practicability of working with these three kinds of animals are reflected in the differences in research techniques. Research on mice emphasizes large numbers of anonymous individuals experimentally manipulated under laboratory conditions. Wolf research has profitably used radio-telemetry techniques which allow the marking and following of known individuals and their social groups in a natural environment. Monkeys, typically, can be observed and followed on a direct basis as individuals.

‡*Editors' Note:* The relation between hierarchical structures, aggression, and the cessation of breeding is discussed further by Christian. Parallel observations are offered on wolf populations by Packard and Mech and on rhesus monkey populations by Sade.

The utilization of space can also be considered in relating social structure to population. Petrusewicz (1957) demonstrated that by relocating established populations in new cages, further population growth occurred irrespective of the size of the new cage, suggesting that changes in the social structure of the populations had led to further growth. There is some indication that space may affect ultimate population size as well as the rate of increase, particularly during the initial phases of a population's growth, but empirical data on this issue remain to be gathered (Christian et al. 1971). Mice in confined freely growing populations do not utilize all the space available to them, irrespective of population size. In all our studies there have always been areas of cages as well as nest sites which have remained unused (Lloyd 1975a). Some have shown that mice will not always disperse from a smaller area into a larger one (Warne 1947; Eibl-Eibesfeldt 1950; Young et al. 1950; Southwick 1955a; Davis 1958; Anderson 1961; Terman 1962; Reimer and Petras 1967). In our laboratory three separate populations were established in cages measuring 1.32 m in length and .66 m in width. Each of the cages had two levels. A population was established in one level of each cage with two sibling females and one sibling male. The populations were allowed to expand until growth ceased, when the remaining level of the cage was opened. In all three instances there was no further growth in the populations, even though the space available to them was doubled in size.

In addition to space, age composition may affect population growth. Proximity of adult males has an inhibitory effect on the sexual maturation of young males (Terman 1965; Vandenbergh 1967; Lombardi and Vandenbergh 1977; McKinney and Desjardins 1973) and it is possible that as the ratio of adults to juveniles increases in populations, juveniles do not mature.* Eventually, as fertility declines the entire population ages, further reducing fertility. The level of infant mortality in a population may be related to levels of aggression, and as juveniles mature, increased fighting as the young adults challenge older territorial males may adversely affect infant survival (Southwick 1955a). In other instances a population may have aged to the point where there is a very rigid territorial system, and new space is not utilized simply because none of the animals are able to move about

*Editors' Note: Factors affecting maturation rates and their consequences for population growth are discussed further by Christian and by Drickamer. Parallel observations on wolf populations are offered by Packard and Mech.

freely. At the time space was increased in the three populations mentioned above, each of the populations had a different age composition. In the first population all the animals were over 100 days old. The territorial system was very rigid, with infrequent and limited movement of animals and frequent fights at the boundaries of territories. After the space available to this population was doubled in size, nothing happened; no mice moved into the new space, no new territories were formed, and no further reproduction occurred. The second population had a large cohort of young adults when space was doubled. Young males moved into the new space and formed new territories. When space was doubled, the population size was 40 mice. Two months after the space was increased in this population, 40 mice were born within 1 week. However, none of these mice survived to weaning, hence this population did not grow either. Levels of aggression were very high in the population as younger males fought frequently with older territorial males. In the third population the birth rate had dropped to zero after 240 days, and at 280 days cage size was doubled. The ratio of juveniles to adults was 1:6 when space was doubled. During the next 100 days there was no further reproduction in this population. Earlier in this population's history, when growth was very rapid, the ratio of juveniles to adults was 1:1. These studies suggest that space, per se, is not the major factor influencing population size, but that multiple influences affect population growth. Possibly, if space is increased as population growth is slowing but before it has stopped, further population growth may be stimulated by additional space. More work is needed on the effect of manipulation of space on growth in populations of different size.

Overt aggression, as well as the proximity of aggressive animals, may also affect population growth, through effects on infant mortality. Brown (1953) showed that as density rose in house mouse populations, aggression increased, resulting in disturbances of parturient females and increased infant mortality. Similar effects of aggression on infant mortality have been reported by Southwick (1955a, 1955b). Adding chlorpromazine to drinking water reduced aggression in a population of mice, with subsequent reduction of infant mortality (Vessey 1967). In our studies a sevenfold increase in aggression in one population resulted in a redistribution of breeding females followed by increased infant and adult mortality, producing not only a halt in population growth, but an actual decline (Lloyd 1975a). Observed increases in infant mortality in populations of mice have been attributed to nest disturbances resulting from the increased fighting (Brown 1953; South-wick 1955a), or to disturbances of lactation and maternal care resulting from the proximity of fighting males (Christian et al. 1965; Lloyd and Christian 1969; Lloyd 1975a). An interesting observation in our stud-ies has been that in populations at low densities several dams and their litters shared single nest sites, yet most of the young survived even though the nest sites were "crowded." As densities of these populations rose, even single litters alone with their dams in a nest site did not survive.

Some time ago it was established that social strife within a popu-lation could adversely affect lactation, with subsequent adverse effects on the survival of progeny (Christian and Lemunyan 1958). It has also been hypothesized that the proximity of fighting males may impinge upon endocrine systems, resulting in inhibition of lactation (Lloyd and Christian 1969).* In our laboratory a study was undertaken to deter-mine the effects of proximity without tactile contact of various social groups upon lactation of dams and survival of litters in house mice. The experiments were carried out in cages .43 m by .58 m. A wire mesh barrier divided each cage, permitting animals on either side of the barrier to be in visual, auditory, and olfactory contact with each other without physical contact. Seven different social environments were created, consisting of a lactating female with a litter on one side of the wire barrier and various combinations of mice on the other side. Social groups opposite the lactating females and their litters consisted of no mice, another female with a litter, the male that had inseminated the female, a strange male, three adult females, three adult males that had been castrated during the first week of life, and three intact adult males. There were 25 replicates of each of the social groups. The fe-males were placed in the cages when they were visibly pregnant. At term the social environments were established on the side of the barrier opposite all the nursing dams. To standardize litter size, all litters were culled to four mice on the day of delivery. Mice in each of the cages were observed daily for an hour in the morning and an hour in the afternoon.

Data were recorded on the amount of time spent on the nests and

*Editors' Note: The impact of density-related social factors in lactation and maternal care is also discussed by Christian. The possible implications of this for human demography are largely unexplored in this volume either in the papers on contemporary human crowding or in the papers on human prehistory, even though lactation and nursing behavior are discussed extensively in the latter (cf. papers by Cohen and Lee).

the number of fights occurring in the social groups. Data were also recorded on the number of litters surviving and the number of individual mice surviving within each litter. Surviving pups were weaned at 21 days of age and their weights were recorded. If only one pup in a litter survived to weaning, the litter was recorded as having survived. The percentage of litters surviving, the percentage of mice surviving, and the mean body weights of mice at weaning were calculated for each group. Percentage of litters surviving opposite each social group was lower than in litters housed alone with their dam (table 1.1). However, the most striking loss of litters and pups occurred among litters opposite three intact adult males and opposite three castrate males. Using a z-test for differences in proportions (Dixon and Massey 1969) percentages of entire litters surviving among mice opposite three intact males and three castrate males were found to be significantly lower ($p < .004$ and $p < .04$, respectively) than among litters nursed by solitary dams. The percentages of individual mice surviving among litters opposite three adult males and three castrate males were also significantly lower ($p < .0001$ and $p < .015$, respectively) than among litters nursed by solitary females. Most of the deaths of pups occurred within the first day or two after birth, and the stomachs of intact dead pups were empty. If mice survived the first 5 days, they generally lived to reach weaning age of 21 days. The mean weight of mice at weaning did not differ among the groups nor did the amount of time the dams spent nursing differ in the various groups (table 1.2). Levels of fighting

Table 1.1.   Litter Survival among House Mice Exposed to Different Social Environments during Nursing

Social environment	Percent litters surviving	Percent mice surviving	Mean number surviving mice per litter ± standard error
Female	88	85	3.4 ± .26
Female: mate	80	76	3.0 ± .33
Female: female	76	75	2.9 ± .26
Female: strange male	70	72	2.6 ± .35
Female: 3 females	71	70	3.0 ± .35
Female: 3 castrate males	68	59	2.4 ± .28
Female: 3 intact males	60	47	2.2 ± .39

Table 1.2. Amount of Time Lactating Dams Exposed to Different
Social Environments Spent on Nests

Social environment	Mean number of minutes on nest/observation hour ± standard error
Female	43.13 ± 1.58
Female: mate	38.67 ± 1.29
Female: female	36.64 ± 1.15
Female: strange male	40.31 ± 1.49
Female: 3 females	37.57 ± 1.51
Female: 3 castrate males	38.07 ± 1.36
Female: 3 intact males	40.65 ± 2.25

Table 1.3. Level of Fighting in Social Environments Opposite
Lactating Dams and Their Litters

Social environment	Mean number of fights per observation hour ± standard error
Female: 3 females	1.07 ± .43
Female: 3 castrate males	8.11 ± 1.29
Female: 3 intact males	33.05 ± 8.63

were highest among the intact males and lowest among the groups of
three females (table 1.3).

A second study to determine the effects of social stress on the development of the mammary glands of lactating females was carried
out. In this second study procedures were as before, but only two social groups were studied and the tests were terminated after 6 days.
Dams were sacrificed on day 6 or on the day when they lost all of their
litter, whichever came first. At sacrifice the dams were weighed, anes-
thetized, shaved, and skinned. The skin was stretched on a board and
with the blunt end of a scalpel the mammary gland was scraped from
the skin and weighed on a Mettler balance. Mammary gland weight as
a percent of body weight was calculated. Percentage of litters surviving
among those exposed to fighting males was significantly lower ($p <$
.001) than in those raised alone with their dams (table 1.4). The percentage of pups surviving in each litter was also significantly lower ($p
< $ .001) in the mice exposed to the fighting males (table 1.4). Daily

Table 1.4.   Survival of Nursing Mice Proximal to Fighting Males

	Percentage of litters surviving
Nursing litters proximal to fighting males	20
Litter and dam alone	86.7 ($z = 3.66$)

	Percentage of pups surviving/per litter
Nursing pups proximal to fighting males	18.3
Pups and dam alone	86.4 ($z = 7.43$)

Table 1.5.   Comparison of Mean Daily Pup Weights of Nursing Pups Proximal to Fighting Males with Pups and Dam Alone

Day postpartum	*Mean pup weight (gr) ± standard error of pups proximal to fighting males*	*Mean pup weight (gr) ± standard error of pups with dam alone*
1	1.43 ± .027	1.53 ± .034
2	1.42 ± .041	1.57 ± .043
3	1.39 ± .084	1.68 ± .072
4	1.50 ± .206	1.91 ± .147
5	1.90 ± .291	2.44 ± .182
6	2.42 ± .291	2.72 ± .220

mean weights of pups next to fighting males were lower than for those pups alone with their dams (table 1.5). A two-way analysis of variance for cell frequencies showed that mean experimental pup weights were significantly lower than mean control pup weights ($p < .05$) and that there was a significant difference between experimentals and controls in mean weights from day to day ($p < .05$). As in the previous experiment, there were no significant differences in the time the dams spent on the nest (table 1.6). Weights of mammary glands from mice exposed to fighting males were significantly lower ($p < .05$) than were those of mice alone with their litters (table 1.7). The results of these experiments clearly indicate that the proximity of fighting males can adversely affect lactation and result in the deaths of young.* However,

*Editors' Note: This effect could have been mediated through a number of sensory-perceptual pathways. See Drickamer for studies of the effects of pheromones and Terman for studies of the effects of tactile sensation on various aspects of reproduction in mice and monkeys.

Table 1.6.   Comparison of Mean Time Spent on Nest by Dams Proximal to Fighting Males with That by Dams Alone

	Mean time on nest (min) observation hour ± standard error
Dams proximal to fighting males	49.86 ± 2.33
Dams alone	48.42 ± 2.84

Table 1.7.   Comparison of Mammary Gland Weights as a Percent of Body Weights of Dams Proximal to Fighting Males with Dams Alone

	Mean mammary gland weight as a percent of body weight ± standard error
Dams proximal to fighting males	4.65 ± .40
Dams alone	5.79 ± .33

the mechanisms of action affecting lactation in this situation are not clear, and further studies are in progress to measure prolactin levels in lactating females subjected to social stress.

Social rank of animals may also be related to reproduction in that hormonal activity may affect, or in turn be influenced by the position of an animal in a social hierarchy. Cause-and-effect relationships are not always clear, but gonadal and pituitary hormones involved in reproduction may be affected by social interactions (Lloyd 1975b). Adrenal response, which may in turn affect the action of reproductive hormones, is also influenced by social interactions (Christian 1971). Evidence from both field and laboratory studies indicates that as populations grow, increased social pressure impinges on the hypothalamic-pituitary-adrenal axis, producing increased adrenal cortical activity which may inhibit gonadotropins and gonadal hormones and result in decreased natality. Inhibition of sexual maturation, fetal resorption, interruption of estrus, and breakdown of lactation and maternal care are typical manifestations of adverse endocrine responses seen in populations as density increases (Christian et al. 1965; Christian 1971; Lloyd 1975a).

No study has yet compared levels of androgens in territorial and nonterritorial mice in freely growing populations. However, studies on the relationship of androgens to aggression and social rank have been extensive. Testosterone has been shown to be required for the initiation and maintenance of aggression in mice (Frederickson 1950; Bronson and Desjardins 1971; Davidson and Levine 1972; McKinney and Desjardins 1973; Barkley and Goldman 1977b). Earlier studies suggested that since testes and sexual accessory size decreased with descending social rank in mice, it might be expected that circulating levels of testosterone would be related to social rank (Lloyd 1971; Oakeshott 1974). However, recent attempts to correlate transient plasma levels of testosterone with social rank have produced variable results. Several investigators were unable to demonstrate a positive correlation between social rank and levels of circulating plasma testosterone in male mice (Bartke et al. 1973; Barkley and Goldman 1977a; Selmanoff et al. 1977b). However, it has been shown that hyperphysiological doses of testosterone given to male mice in silastic implants had a positive effect on levels of aggression, demonstrating that aggression is influenced by circulating titers of testosterone (Selmanoff et al. 1977a).

Levels of plasma testosterone in relation to rank in adult male house mice have been examined in our laboratory. Mice were isolated at weaning and upon reaching 60 days of age were placed in groups of four mice for 3 hours, 1 day, 3 days, 6 days, and 14 days. Ten groups of four mice were run at each of the time intervals. Blood was taken by decapitation, placed in 6- by 50-mm borosilicate glass culture tubes and allowed to clot at room temperature for 4–8 hours. Tubes were stored at 4°C for 12–16 hours and then spun at 2,500 rpm for 20 minutes at 4°C. Serum was removed and stored at − 20°C until assayed. Assay for testosterone was performed according to Tcholakian et al. (1974). The samples for the dominant animals and the subordinate animals were pooled for each time interval. A pool of 10 control samples was run with each of the time-interval groups. There were no significant differences in the levels of plasma testosterone between dominant and subordinate mice in the 3-hour, 1-day, or 3-day time intervals, but among mice held in groups for 6 days and 14 days, significantly higher levels of plasma testosterone occurred in the dominant mice (table 1.8).

In a second study adult mice were placed in paired encounters for various times. The mice were placed two to a cage, with each mouse on the opposite side of a wire mesh barrier. Once a day, at the same time of day, the barriers were raised between the pairs and the mice were allowed to interact until the dominance of one mouse was estab-

Table 1.8.   Plasma Testosterone Levels in Dominant and Subordinate
Male House Mice Grouped Four per Group for Various Time
Intervals

Length of time in group		Plasma T ng% ± standard error
3 hours		
Dominant		340.24 ± 42.62
Subordinate		350.78 ± 37.84
Controls		569.31 ± 4.15
1 day		
Dominant		321.47 ± 15.55
Subordinate		430.39 ± 27.69
Controls		313.02 ± 19.93
3 days		
Dominant		306.21 ± 10.54
Subordinate		334.80 ± 10.19
Controls		422.98 ± 23.68
6 days		
Dominant	$>p<.05$	428.94 ± 12.65
Subordinate		291.47 ± 16.83
Controls		478.84 ± 13.25
14 days		
Dominant	$>p<.001$	593.28 ± 5.08
Subordinate		384.04 ± 3.48
Controls		332.76 ± .51

lished or for 30 minutes, whichever came first. Mice were held in pairs for 1 hour, 1 day, 7 days, and 14 days. At sacrifice, plasma samples were not pooled but were prepared for individual assay. As in the preceding study, there were no significant differences in the levels of plasma testosterone between dominant and subordinant mice held for short periods of time. Plasma levels of testosterone were significantly higher in the dominant mice held for 7 days but not in those in the 14-day group (table 1.9). As with other investigators, the results of measurements of testosterone in our laboratory have shown a high degree of variation. It has been indicated that a source of this variation in measurements made on single samples may be due to the pulsatile nature of the release of testosterone into blood (Bartke et al. 1973). Although many studies indicate that androgens are in some way related to the initiation and maintenance of dominant social rank, single samples of plasma taken from a mouse at a particular time may not provide an accurate measure of testosterone release in a given social situation over an extended time.

Gonadotropins have also been shown to respond to social stimuli in

Table 1.9.   Plasma Testosterone Levels in Dominant and Subordinate
Mice Paired for Various Time Intervals

Length of time in pairs	*Plasma T ng% ± standard error*
30 min	
Dominant	244.9 ± 38.3
Subordinate	307.9 ± 20.8
Controls	328.0 ± 31.1
24 hours	
Dominant	355.2 ± 81.4
Subordinate	203.5 ± 24.3
Controls	453.8 ± 148.3
7 days	
Dominant	$>p<.005$ $\Big\{$ 447.8 ± 101.4
Subordinate	108.7 ± 32.4
Controls	349.3 ± 127.5
14 days	
Dominant	974.7 ± 333.2
Subordinate	1129.3 ± 275.2
Controls	917.5 ± 270.1

groups of animals. In paired encounters of CF-1 mice, exposure of
mice to fighter mice suppressed gonadotropins in the subordinate mice
(Bronson and Eleftheriou 1963; Eleftheriou and Church 1967; Eleftheriou and Church 1968). Grouping previously isolated CF-1 male
mice, four per cage, for 1 hour resulted in declines of 19% in plasma
follicle-stimulating hormone (FSH) and of 94% in plasma-luteinizing
hormone (LH). In mice held for several days, FSH levels returned to
baseline levels in the dominant animals, but levels of FSH in the subordinate animals and levels of LH in both dominant and subordinate
animals remained suppressed after a 15-day period (Bronson 1973).
Much more work needs to be done on the relationship of gonadotropins
to aggression in mice, but these studies support the concept that social
stress can affect gonadotropin levels, which might ultimately have an
effect on reproduction (Christian et al. 1965; Christian 1971).

Social Interactions and Reproduction in Populations of Deermice

Social structures of freely growing populations of deer mice are dis-
tinctively different from those of house mice. Unlike the house mouse,
deer mice do not form and defend territories (Terman 1968; Hill 1977).

Delineations of dominant and subordinate animals in confined populations of deer mice are more subtle than in the house mouse. Social
interactions of *Peromyscus* are typified by a relatively low frequency
of aggression (King 1957) and it has been observed that dominant and
subordinate mice frequently share the same nest site (Hill 1977). Apparently, mutual avoidance by individuals functions as a mechanism
for dispersion in space rather than the aggressive defense of clearly
defined territories (Hill 1977). However, a distinctive feature of social
organization in deer mice is the caching of food in specific places
(King 1957).

Studies in our laboratory have produced some interesting results
with respect to the relationships of social structure and population
growth in *Peromyscus maniculatus bairdii*. Two separate populations
of *P. m. bairdii* were established, managed, and observed according to
procedures previously described (Lloyd 1975a). The populations were
established on the same day in the same room under identical conditions of housing, temperature, and light control. The first population
was initiated from descendants of a strain of *P. m. bairdii* (Bar
Harbor strain) that originated at Bar Harbor and had been in laboratories for many years. The second population was begun from the offspring of mice recently trapped at a field station (Letterkenny strain).*
After a little over 1 year the Bar Harbor strain achieved a population
size of 113 mice and then subsequently declined to 87 mice, until the
population was terminated at 450 days (table 1.10). After somewhat
over 3 months the Letterkenny strain reached a population size of 16
mice and essentially stabilized at that point until it was terminated at
460 days (table 1.11). In both populations the mice formed a food
cache. In each cage a nest site was chosen as a storage bin. Food
consisted of Purina laboratory mouse chow and dried wheat, barley,
oats, and corn. The food was scattered about throughout each cage.
Within 2 hours after food was introduced into either population, every
morsel had been gathered up and carried to the cache. In each population the cache was guarded by a female. Individual mice were free to
go to the cache and eat, but any mice carrying food away from the

*The Letterkenny field station is located in south-central Pennsylvania and is an army ord-
nance depot on what was originally farmland. The *Peromyscus* live in grassy fields and in wood
lots on the depot, a typical habitat for this species in North America. The Bar Harbor strain was
from Jackson Memorial laboratory in Bar Harbor, Maine. These *Peromyscus* have been maintained over the last 30 years as an outbred colony in the Jackson laboratories.

Table 1.10. Levels of Activity in a Freely Growing Population of
Peromyscus bairdii (Bar Harbor strain)

Number of animals over 21 days of age	Day of population	Mean percentage of total number of mice active per observation hour ± standard error
3	1–129	21.00 ± 27.19
4	130–153	13.63 ± 14.89
5	154–176	21.87 ± 16.45
7	177–227	21.32 ± 27.53
23	228–260	16.76 ± 8.49
30	261–270	14.27 ± 7.39
36	271–300	15.73 ± 7.45
52	301–322	17.85 ± 6.81
76	323–344	15.00 ± 5.76
94	345–356	14.30 ± 6.22
105	357–376	12.42 ± 4.35
113	377–399	20.20 ± 7.71
87	400–450	19.62 ± 10.40

Table 1.11. Levels of Activity in a Freely Growing Population of
Peromyscus bairdii (Letterkenny strain)

Number of animals over 21 days of age	Day of population	Mean percentage of total number of mice active per observation hour ± standard error
3	1–75	39.49 ± 41.40
8	76–101	20.32 ± 20.21
16	102–185	23.41 ± 17.68
15	186–217	25.77 ± 15.99
14	218–284	39.36 ± 21.50
13	285–350	33.84 ± 18.69
12	350–360	42.00 ± 20.52
16	361–435	30.92 ± 15.66
15	436–460	31.67 ± 19.56

cache were immediately pursued by the guardian and a "tug-of-war" would ensue in which the guardian would try to pull the piece of food from the mouth of the other. Frequently, a chase would ensue with the guardian obtaining the food. Sometimes the food would be dropped and momentarily ignored, but it would eventually be picked up. The mice formed burrow systems underneath the layers of sawdust and nesting materials covering the floor of the cage, and frequently the mouse stealing the food would disappear into a burrow. In the wild strain this system of food hoarding persisted throughout the entire history of the population, but in the laboratory strain the hoarding system collapsed after 7½ months, when the population had reached a size of 23 mice. Food was left scattered about in the cage and mice fed openly anywhere in the cage. The food hoard was never reestablished in this population. In neither population was there any evidence of territoriality.

Mice moved freely about anywhere in the cage and it was difficult to discern any rank order. The mice moved very quickly, suddenly darting from place to place. Aggressive encounters were infrequent and very brief, with two mice nipping each other frontally and then quickly flying apart and running off. The activity of mice in both populations was highly variable, with no particular pattern being evident for any time of the day. During some observation periods as many as 75–100% of the total population would be active, whereas during other observation periods there were no mice active. The numbers active were highly variable at the same time of day from one day to the next. Overall, the mean percentages of mice active at different population sizes, while showing some variation, were not significantly different in either population (tables 1.10 and 1.11). However, the percentages of the total population active in the Letterkenny strain were consistently somewhat higher than those of the Bar Harbor strain.

Conclusions

In reviewing studies of the relationship of social structure and reproduction in populations of mice, it quickly becomes apparent that no single element of social structure is responsible for the regulation of population growth, but that multiple influences interact in a complex fashion in each population. It is also clear that each species has its own unique organization of social structure and that very different aspects of social structure may be critical in specific instances. Hence, in one case population growth may be regulated through the mediation of a territorial breeding system, while in another arrangements surrounding access to food may be critical. In each case the primary factor interacts with lesser ones in ways that are characteristic and unique for each population. Thus, social factors may influence reproductive responses so that endocrine activity related to natality may be the primary force affected and a population will experience a decline in births. In other instances the effect may be primarily on infant mortality, or, in many cases, an equal impact is felt on both natality and mortality. These studies suggest that the availability of food and space and absolute numbers of animals in and of themselves are not necessarily the primary factors in the kinetics regulating population growth. Access to and utilization of space and food are very much influenced by many components of social organization, and the impact of the quantities of these resources may be overriden. Similarly, the overall effects of density are very much influenced by the nature and frequencies of social interactions. Elements of social structure such as age composition may exert important influences on the biological forces of natality and mortality through their effects on sexual maturation, territorial systems, and levels of aggression. An overall conclusion from these studies is support of the concept that social structures of populations have a major influence on the regulation of population growth through the interaction of endocrine responses and reproductive behavior, but that individual species manifest these interactions in unique and individualistic ways. However, in spite of species variations, the current cumulative body of evidence from a number of studies lends support to the concept that the interplay of numbers of animals plus the quantity and quality of social interactions can operate via effects on reproductive endocrine responses to regulate population size by inhibiting growth at many different levels.

Acknowledgments

Thanks to Dr. Robert Tcholakian for technical assistance and advice with assays of testosterone and to Dr. H. Edward Grotjan, Jr., for assistance with statistical analyses.

This work was supported by U.S. Public Health Service Grant HD-0096 and NICHD Grant 5P50-HD-08338.

References

Anderson, P. K. 1961. Density, social structure and nonsocial environment in house mouse populations and the implications for regulation of numbers. *Trans. N.Y. Acad. Sci.* 23:447–51.

————, and Hill, J. L. 1965. *Mus musculus*: experimental induction of territory formation. *Science* 148:1753–55.

Barkley, M. S., and Goldman, B. D. 1977a. A quantitative study of serum testosterone, sex accessory organ growth and the development of internal aggression in the mouse. *Horm. Behav.* 8:208–18.

————, and Goldman, B. D. 1977b. The effects of castration and silastic implants of testosterone on intermale aggression in the mouse. *Horm. Behav.* 9:32–48.

Bartke, A.; Steele, R. E.; Mustro, N.; and Caldwell, B. V. 1973. Fluctuations in plasma testosterone levels in adult male rats and mice. *Endocrinology* 92:1223–28.

Bronson, F. H. 1973. Establishment of social rank among grouped mice: relative effects on circulating FSH, LH, and corticosterone. *Physiol. Behav.* 10:947–51.

————, and Desjardins, C. 1971. Steroid hormones and aggressive behavior in mammals. In *The physiology of aggression and defeat*, ed. B. E. Eleftheriou and J. P. Scott, pp. 43–63. New York: Plenum Press.

————, and Eleftheriou, B. E. 1963. Adrenal responses to crowding in *Peromyscus* and C57BL/10j mice. *Physiol. Zool.* 36:161–66.

Brown, R. Z. 1953. Social behavior, reproduction and population changes in the house mouse (*Mus musculus*). *Ecol. Monogr.* 23:217–40.

Calhoun, J. B. 1962. Population density and social pathology. *Sci. Am.* 206:139–48.

Christian, J. J. 1971. Population density and reproductive efficiency. *Biol. Reprod.* 4:248–94.

————, and Lemunyan, C. D. 1958. Adverse effects of crowding on reproduction and lactation of mice and two generations of their progeny. *Endocrinol.* 63:517–29.

————; Lloyd, J. A.; and Davis, D. E. 1965. The role of endocrines in the self-regulation of mammalian populations. *Recent Prog. Horm. Res.* 21:501–78.

————; Lloyd, J. A.; Goldman, D. E.; and Davis, D. E. 1971. An empirical formula for the growth of some vertebrate populations. *Curr. Mod. Biol.* 4:26–34.

Crowcroft, P., and Rowe, F. P. 1963. Social organization and territorial behavior in the wild house mouse (*Mus musculus* L.). *Proc. Zool. Soc. Lond.* 140:517–31.

Davidson, J. M., and Levine, S. 1972. Endocrine regulation of behavior. *Ann. Rev. Physiol.* 34:375–408.

Davis, D. E. 1958. The role of density in aggressive behavior of house mice. *Anim. Behav.* 6:207–10.

Dixon, W. J., and Massey, F. J., Jr. 1969. *Introduction to statistical analysis*. New York: McGraw-Hill.

Eibl-Eibesfeldt, I. 1950. Beitrage zur Biologie der Haus und der Ahrenmaus nebst einigen Beobachtungen an andere Nagern. *Z. Tierpsychol.* 7:558–87.

Eleftheriou, B. E., and Church, R. L. 1967. Effects of repeated exposure to aggression and defeat on plasma and pituitary levels of luteinizing hormone in C57BL/6J mice. *Gen. Comp. Endocrinol.* 9:263–66.

————, and Church, R. L. 1968. Levels of hypothalamic luteinizing hormone-releasing factor after exposure to aggression (defeat) in C57BL/6J mice. *J. Endocrinol.* 42:347–48.

Frederickson, E. 1950. The effects of food deprivation upon competitive and spontaneous combat in C57 black mice. *J. Psychol.* 29:89–100.

Hill, J. L. 1977. Space utilization of *Peromyscus*: social and spatial factors. *Anim. Behav.* 25:373–89.

King, J. A. 1957. Intra and inter-specific conflict of Mus and Peromyscus. *Ecology* 38:355–57.

Lloyd, J. A. 1971. Weights of testes, thymi, and accessory reproductive glands in relation to rank in paired and grouped mice (*Mus musculus*). *Proc. Soc. Exp. Biol. Med.* 137:19–21.

———— 1975a. Social structure and reproduction in two freely-growing populations of house mice (*Mus musculus* L.). *Anim. Behav.* 23:413–24.

————. 1975b. Social behavior and hormones. In *Hormonal correlates of behavior*, ed. B. E. Eleftheriou and R. L. Sprott, pp. 185–204. New York: Plenum Press.

Lloyd, J. A., and Christian, J. J. 1969. Reproductive activity of individual females in three experimental freely growing populations of house mice (*Mus musculus*). *J. Mammal.* 50:49–59.

Lombardi, J. R., and Vandenbergh, J. G. 1977. Pheromonally induced sexual maturation in females: regulation by the social environment of the male. *Science* 196:545–46.

McKinney, T. D., and Desjardins, C. 1973. Intermale stimuli and testicular function in adult and immature house mice. *Biol. Reprod.* 9:370–78.

Oakeshott, J. G. 1974. Social dominance, aggressiveness and mating success among male house mice (*Mus musculus*). *Oecologia* 15:143–58.

Petrusewicz, K. 1957. Investigation of experimentally induced population growth. *Ekol. Pol. Ser. A.* 5:281–309.

Poole, T. B., and Morgan, H. D. R. 1976. Social and territorial behaviour of laboratory mice (*Mus musculus* L.) in small complex areas. *Anim. Behav.* 24:476–80.

Reimer, J. D., and Petras, M. L. 1967. Breeding structure of the house mouse (*Mus musculus*) in a population cage. *J. Mammal.* 48:88–89.

Rowe, F. P., and Redfern, R. 1969. Aggressive behavior in related and unrelated wild house mice (*Mus musculus* L.). *Ann. Appl. Biol.* 64:425–31.

Selmanoff, M. K.; Abreu, E.; Goldman, B. D.; and Ginsberg, B. E. 1977a. Manipulation of aggressive behavior in adult DBA/2/Bg and C57BL/10/Bg male mice implanted with testosterone in silastic tubing. *Horm. Behav.* 8:377–90.

————; Goldman, B. D.; and Ginsberg, B. E. 1977b. Serum testosterone, agonistic behavior, and dominance in inbred strains of mice. *Horm. Behav.* 8:107–19.

Southwick, C. H. 1955a. The population dynamics of confined house mice supplied with unlimited food. *Ecology* 36:212–25.

Southwick, C. H. 1955b. Population characteristics of house mice living in English Corn ricks: density relationships. *Proc. Zool. Soc. Lond.* 131:163–75.

Tcholakian, R. K.; Chowdhury, M.; and Steinberger, E. 1974. Time of action of oestradiol-17ß on luteinizing hormone and testosterone. *J. Endocrinol.* 63:411–12.

Terman, C. R. 1962. Spatial and homing consequences of the introduction of aliens in semi-natural populations of prairie deermice. *Ecology* 43:216–23.

————. 1965. A study of population growth and control exhibited in the laboratory by prairie deermice. *Ecology* 46:890–95.

————. 1968. Population dynamics, In *Biology of Peromyscus*, ed. J. A. King, pp. 412–50. Special publication #2, American Society of Mammalogists.

Vandenbergh, J. G. 1967. Effect of the presence of a male on the sexual maturation of female mice. *Endocrin.* 81:345–48.

Vessey, S. 1967. Effects of chlorpromazine on aggression in laboratory populations of wild house mice. *Ecology* 48(3):367–76.

Warne, M. C. 1947. A time analysis of certain aspects of the behavior of small groups of caged mice. *JCPP* 40:371–87.

Young, H.; Strecken, R. L.; and Emlen, J. T. Jr. 1950. Localization of activity in two indoor populations of house mice (*Mus musculus*). *J. Mammalogy* 31:403–10.

2

BEHAVIOR AND REGULATION OF GROWTH IN LABORATORY POPULATIONS OF PRAIRIE DEERMICE

C. Richard Terman

Study of the dynamics of populations has occupied the attention of animal ecologists for many years. Providing significant impetus to these studies was the publication in 1942 of Charles Elton's *Voles, mice and lemmings*. Interest centered on the Norway lemming, the varying hare, the Arctic fox, the snowy owl, and voles of various species because of the great fluctuations known to occur in their population numbers. The Norway lemming (*Lemmus lemmus*), for example, is not only firmly established in the folklore of the region, but also gained worldwide notoriety because every 3–4 years its populations increased to tremendous numbers and they entered upon a mass emigration, moving over the countryside like a tidal wave, consuming the crops in their path and being followed and preyed upon by hawks, cats, dogs, and other predators. Elton presents documentary evidence in his book that in November 1868 a steamer traveling up the Trondheim Fjord took 15 minutes to pass through a shoal of swimming lemmings.

My interest in population phenomena was whetted by such information and the realization that species of animals generally do not increase to an abundance excessive for their habitats and that consequently controlling influences are implied. Populations of most species are regulated prior to levels that would be suicidal for them, at which mass starvation or mass mortality from other causes may occur. The specific mechanisms of regulation appear to vary, but three basic forces are natality, mortality, and movements (immigration or emigration). Although it is evident that these forces influence populations, factors governing their actions are not so evident. For example, predation, disease, and starvation obviously result in removal of individuals from populations. Data are accumulating, however, implicating influences developed intrinsically in each population which may act to control growth via other means. This chapter presents information from studies of prairie deermouse populations that suggest these influences.

For the past several years, I have been studying the characteristics of control of growth in laboratory populations of prairie deermice (*Peromyscus maniculatus bairdii*). The deermouse is a small brown mouse, many species of which occur across North America. Further, there are more than 60 subspecies of the species *Peromyscus maniculatus* (Hooper 1968). Data available from natural population studies of this mouse and of the Genus *Peromyscus* indicate that irruptions rarely occur and that populations are regulated within a rather narrow range of variability (Terman 1966). Deermice thus appear to be sensitive to factors regulating population growth and, as such, seem appropriate for studies of population regulation.

I will begin by summarizing some of the basic information we have obtained over several years and then I will draw attention to our more recent findings, which suggest (1) that behavior is basically involved in the regulation of population growth and that regulation is not a function of density per se; (2) that laboratory populations respond differentially to controlling influences; (3) that intrinsic population organization and communication are involved in the mechanisms of regulation;* and (4) that tactile cues are primary factors inhibiting the reproductive development of young born into laboratory populations.†

Experimental Studies of Population Dynamics—Basic Information

Detailed descriptions of the procedures and materials used in establishing and maintaining experimental populations have been published previously (Terman 1965, 1969) and will only be briefly described here. Populations were founded by one male and one female from four different litters born into a laboratory colony in which sib matings were not permitted. Following weaning (21 days), young were introduced

---

Editors' Note: These findings parallel the observations of Lloyd, of Drickamer, and of Christian suggesting that social factors as well as density are involved in population regulation among rodents and that such social factors are idiosyncratic to individual populations. Compare the observations of Sade on rhesus monkeys and of Packard and Mech on wolves.

†*Editors' Note:* The importance of tactile cues among rodents is further discussed by Drickamer. Their importance for the measurement of human crowding is discussed by Epstein and by Karlin.

into circular pens enclosing 20 ft² of floor space covered with a layer
of wood shavings. Eight nest boxes were arranged in a circular pattern
in each closure, and food and water were present in excess at all times.
Lighting was programmed for approximately 12 hours (0200 to 1345)
of bright light (four 150-watt bulbs) and 12 hours of dim light (four
15-watt bulbs). There was a 15-minute period of darkness at the end
of each bright and dim phase of the cycle. The mice of each population
were examined periodically (once every other week), at which time
pregnancies and births were recorded, newborn were marked, and spatial distribution was noted.

Control animals of known age were reared in isolated bisexual pairs
from weaning (21 days) until killed at varying ages in excess of 90
days. Young born to these mice were removed at birth and discarded,
to eliminate the effects of increased density.

All animals were killed with ether and weighed, the peritoneal cav-
ity was opened, and the whole animal was placed in 10% formalin.
Selected organs were subsequently cleaned of fat, lightly blotted, and
weighed to the nearest .01 mg.

Under the conditions mentioned above, one might expect an "ex-
plosion" of growth, particularly since pairs of deermice housed in individual cages can produce a litter of from five to eight young every
25 days and protection from predation, disease, and environmental
fluctuation was provided. Such uncontrolled growth did not occur,
however, as illustrated in figure 2.1, which presents the growth curves
of four populations. The number of animals is plotted against the number of days since the populations were assembled. Each of the triangles
or quadrilaterals records the birth of a litter, the female parent, and the
number of young born and surviving 10 days. Dashed triangles refer
to litters known to be born even though the young were never found.
Information obtained from the analysis of such growth curves is presented briefly as follows:

1. *Control of population growth distinct.* Each population reached
an asymptote (stopped growing) which was clearly discernible, the criterion being no young born or surviving during a period of 15 weeks
subsequent to the birth of the last surviving litter. This period was
sufficient for surviving young of previous litters to reach an age at
which they would normally be reproductively mature (Clark 1938).
The time between founding populations and cessation of their growth
varied from 6 to 18 months (Terman 1965).

2. *Asymptote of long duration.* Not only was growth control dis-

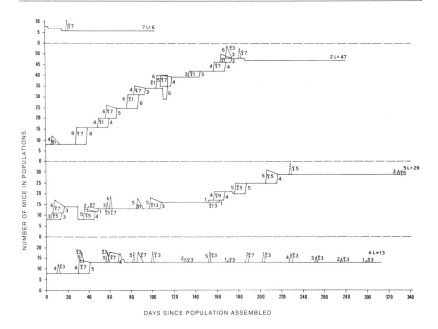

DAYS SINCE POPULATION ASSEMBLED

Figure 2.1.   Growth curves of four populations. Litters are represented by triangles or quadrilaterals. The female parents and the numbers of young born and surviving 10 days
are indicated.

tinct, but once achieved, it was of long duration. We have not routinely
maintained populations more than 300 days following cessation of
growth. However, it is extremely rare for young to be born or to survive in a population during this time period.

3. *Asymptote variable.* Although the populations were maintained
under identical conditions, the number of animals present in each when
growth was curtailed varied widely. Some populations stopped growing at less than 10 animals while others grew to more than 60. Clearly,
those factors determining population control were not influenced consistently by numbers per se.

4. *Mechanisms of control.* Control of population growth was
achieved either by *cessation of reproduction* (most frequent) or by *failure of the young to survive.* Mortality of young was typically due to
abandonment by their mothers.

5. *Reproductive attributes of animals.* Those influences producing
control of population growth have drastic effects on the reproductive
attributes of the component animals. For example, the weights of the
reproductive organs (ovaries, uteri, testes, seminal vesicles, bacula) of

population animals were significantly smaller than those of control mice maintained as bisexual pairs ($p <$ .001, table 2.1). An average of only two females reproduced, even though each population averaged five or more times that many. In addition, the mice born into the populations were inhibited in reproductive function and, as a consequence, *less than 10% of the females reaching at least 100 days of age reproduced* (Terman 1965, 1969, 1973b) *and the others remained in a pre-pubertal state for life.* However, when these reproductively inhibited mice were removed from the populations and paired with proven mates, reproductive recovery of both males and females occurred very rapidly (more than 50% reproduced within 30 days of such manipulation and more than 75% within 80 days, Terman 1973a). This rapid recovery of reproductive function once the mice were removed from their populations indicates that the mechanism of inhibition does not involve permanent pituitary or gonadial alteration and points to a mechanism that although chronic, is dynamic.

To obtain further information on the reproductive physiology of population and control females, the ovaries of these animals were serially sectioned at 7–10 μm and stained with haematoxylin and eosin.

Table 2.1.   Comparisons of Body (g) and Reproductive Organ (mg) Weights of Population and Control Deermice

	Control		*Population*		
	n	*Mean ± SE*	*n*	*Mean ± SE*	*p*
Males					
Body weights	44	16.05 ± .31	7(62)	15.63 ± 1.22	NS
Testes	52	202.24 ± 6.45	7(61)	69.98 ± 20.22	
(paired)					<.001
Vesicular	51	151.89 ± 10.06	7(61)	27.59 ± 14.87	
glands					
(paired)					<.001
Baculum	37	.635 ± .03	7(42)	.181 ± .05	<.001
Females					
(nonparous)					
Body weights	25	14.93 ± .39	7(36)	13.58 ± .39	NS
Ovaries	35	7.01 ± .62	7(39)	2.04 ± .25	
(paired)					<.001
Uterus	28	25.14 ± 2.49	7(37)	6.09 ± .13	<.001

Notes: *n* refers to the number of population mean weights; the number of animals contributing to the means is indicated in parentheses.
NS, probability of calculated *t* value greater than .05

Table 2.2. Comparisons of Mean Number of Atretic Follicles and Mean
Diameters of Largest Follicles in Ovaries from Population and
Control Deermice

Comparisons	Number of ovaries	Number of atretic follicles:		Number of ovaries	Diameter of follicles[a]	
		mean ± SE	*p*		*mean ± SE*	*p*
All females						
Control	38	20.85 ± 2.44		44	55.64 ± 1.77	
			<.001			<.001
Population offspring	57	48.03 ± 2.81		78	40.73 ± .69	
Nonparous females						
Controls	31	19.31 ± 2.47		39	54.72 ± 1.83	
			<.001			<.001
Population offspring	54	48.63 ± 2.93		75	39.78 ± .87	

[a]Follicle size is measured in eyepiece micrometer units.

For each ovary, the numbers of atretic follicles in the middlemost section of the middle and plus or minus one row of sections were counted. The two largest maturing follicles in each ovary were measured with an ocular micrometer at $100\times$ magnification. The data obtained were presented in detail in Terman (1973b), but a modified presentation in table 2.2 shows that population animals have significantly more atretic follicles and significantly smaller follicles of maximum size than do control mice.

6. *Prediction of the numerical level of growth control.* We know of no way at present to predict at the time a population is founded when growth will stop, because the factors producing such growth control are still imperfectly understood.*

Behavior and Population Regulation

Populations are not merely aggregates of animals. With the foregoing basic information on growth regulation of laboratory populations in mind, I would like next to present evidence to support the suggestion

Editors' Note: For further discussion of known mechanisms contributing to the cessation of growth in rodent populations see Lloyd, Christian, and Drickamer.

that behavioral factors are involved in the phenomena observed and that populations may be regarded as entities that respond to intrinsic pressures to limit their growth.

Variable Asymptote Levels—Similar Physiological Effects. Although the numbers of animals in each asymptotic population varied widely (10–60 animals), the reproductive rates, the weights of the reproductive organs and other physiological measurements (progesterone and coritcosterone levels) were similar between populations (Terman 1965, 1969, 1973b; Albertson et al. 1975; Sung et al. 1977). These and other data suggest that growth regulation was in response to stimuli that were intrinsically developed and was not a function of the numbers of animals present in each population per se (Terman 1973b). These findings suggest that differences in the behavior of the animals comprising each population may be responsible for cessation of growth at different numerical levels, other factors being equal.

Social Behavior and Organization. At present we have no definitive information regarding the behaviors that stimulate growth regulation intrinsically in each population. Social behavior would seem to be of importance, and it is logical to assume that aggressive behavior might be directly involved. A description of the behavioral characteristics of one series of populations (Terman 1974) indicates that the development of a social organization among the males took place during the first days after founding the populations and involved a few active animals which differed among themselves in dominance and sexual behavior. Very little overt aggressive behavior took place, and that which did occur was expressed toward only a few individuals. Fighting accompanied the initial social organization, which, once accomplished, appeared to be stable for long periods of time. Furthermore, the records of aggression indicate that 44% of all aggressive interactions were noted during the first 7 days subsequent to founding the populations, and there was no increase in aggression as asymptote was approached. A more extensive examination needs to be made of social behavior in populations as they grow to asymptote.

Food Hoarding. One of the most obvious behavioral changes in populations growing toward asyptote (Terman 1974) was the development of food hoarding. Food hoarding involved removal by the mice of pellets from the central food hopper. The pellets were transferred to or "hoarded" in a location within the enclosure, typically a nestbox. A founding female was the first and most consistent hoarder, although other mice in each population sporadically participated in the hoarding.

The hoard was not defended, and other mice were permitted to eat the food as long as they remained at the site of the hoard. But if food was removed from the site of the hoard to be eaten elsewhere, the mouse so doing was immediately chased by one of the hoarders, and the food was taken away and returned to the hoard. If, during this process, the chased mouse returned to the hoard with the food, there was no further interference from the hoarder-guardian and the food could be consumed at the site of the hoard.

The relationship between hoarding activity and cessation of population growth is not clear. Among the populations exhibiting consistent hoarding, a Spearman rank correlation coefficient (r_s) of .8482 ($p <$ .05) was calculated between size of population at asymptote and the day subsequent to founding at which hoarding began. Thus, the larger populations also began hoarding after greater intervals subsequent to founding. The differences in numerical levels of populations at asymptote may have reflected influences stimulating hoarding behavior. Establishment and maintenance of the hoard appeared to be an effort to spatially organize the population with respect to the hoard and location of food consumption. While food consumption decreased significantly subsequent to the start of consistent hoarding in the populations, there is no evidence that any of the mice were physically prevented from eating. Further, the body weights of the hoarders were not significantly different from those of nonhoarders. Hoarding behavior, beginning as it generally does prior to population asymptote, may indicate increasing intraspecific competition or social pressure correlated with changing social or physiological relationships or both. The correlation between latency of hoarding and population numbers at asymptote is suggestive of such interactions.

Another study of hoarding (Rice 1972) has generally confirmed these findings. In addition, the following pertinent information was obtained. Generally, the nestbox nearest the food hopper became the site of the hoard. Only food pellets were hoarded, not wooden pellets, cotton balls, or 1-day-old young. Young from outside the population were retrieved to nestboxes other than the hoard sites. Typically, a specific animal established the hoard, the location of which was related to proximity to the feeder. Once established, the hoard appeared to act as a cue to which other animals continued to carry food, and removal of all the food pellets from the site disrupted the behavior, resulting in relocation and a longer time to complete the hoarding of additional

Table 2.3.   Selected Organ Weights and Percentage of Female Deermice
Ovulating Relative to the Mechanism of Population Growth
Regulation

	Mechanism of population growth control				
	Cessation of reproduction		*Death of offspring*		
	n	*Mean ± SE*	*n*	*Mean ± SE*	*p*
Males					
Body weights	41	14.62 ± .38	21	17.03 ± .70	<.005
Testes (paired)	40	43.92 ± 4.97	21	87.25 ± 13.83	<.005
Vesicular glands					
(paired)	40	7.16 ± 2.56	21	38.72 ± 10.97	<.005
Baculum	29	0.33 ± .02	13	0.51 ± .04	<.001
Females (nonparous)					
Body weight	23	13.80 ± .35	13	13.70 ± .24	NS
Ovaries (paired)	24	1.79 ± .16	15	2.45 ± .25	<.05
Uterus	23	4.38 ± .42	13	7.67 ± 1.83	<.05
Number ovulating		1 of 24		11 of 16	<.001

Notes: Weights were of mice born into the populations and greater than 90 days of age.
NS, probability of calculated *t* value greater than .05.

food. Hoarding behavior is clearly a major phenomenon occuring in the population, but its significance to growth regulation is still not clear.

Intrinsic Population Differences Related to Mechanisms of Growth Regulation. As mentioned previously, population growth is controlled either by cessation of reproduction or by mortality of young. Marked differences were noted when reproductive rates and selected organ weights were compared relative to the mechanisms of growth control exhibited by the populations. Table 2.3 presents these comparisons as modified from Terman (1973b). The males from populations regulated by complete cessation of reproduction had significantly smaller testes, vesicular glands, bacula, and body weights than those from populations regulated by failure of young to survive. Similarly, females from the former populations had significantly smaller ovaries and uteri and significantly fewer ovulations than those from the latter. These differences occurred in spite of the fact that variations in the numerical levels of the populations at asymptote were unrelated to the mechanism of control. Further, in spite of these differences in ovulation rate and re-

Table 2.4. Population Cues: Comparisons of the Body (g) and
Reproductive Organ (mg) Weights of Freely Ranging and
Caged Population Deermice

	Freely ranging		*Caged*		
	n	*Mean ± SE*	*n*	*Mean ± SE*	*p*
Nonparous females					
Ovaries	8(55)	5.73 ± .70	8(51)	11.03 ± .79	<.001
Uteri	8(53)	17.61 ± 3.74	8(51)	30.31 ± 5.29	<.1
Adrenals	8(47)	2.57 ± .10	8(45)	2.62 ± .05	NS
Body (g)	8(56)	12.32 ± .36	8(53)	14.29 ± .64	<.025
Total females					
Ovaries	8(66)	5.80 ± .69	8(68)	10.87 ± .66	<.001
Adrenals	8(56)	2.58 ± .09	8(60)	2.65 ± .04	NS
Males					
Testes	8(61)	180.75 ± 19.80	8(70)	265.75 ± 11.24	<.01
Vesiculars	8(62)	75.12 ± 13.53	8(68)	132.87 ± 9.23	<.01
Adrenals	8(56)	2.67 ± .14	8(61)	2.88 ± .10	NS
Body (g)	8(66)	15.04 ± .54	8(71)	16.75 ± .44	<.05

Notes: *n* refers to the number of population mean weights; the number of animals contributing
to the means is indicated in parentheses.
NS, probability of calculated *t* value greater than .05.

productive organ weights, less than 10% of the females reproduced in
the populations, again not in a pattern directly related to the mechanisms of control. These data indicate that the populations were intrinsically different, and they provide strong evidence that the mechanism
of control was not a function of density per se but is perhaps reflective
of differences in intrapopulation communication.

Evidence of the Importance of Tactile Cues. We have recently obtained evidence that tactile contact between animals is involved in
maintaining the reproductive inhibition observed among animals in the
experimental populations (Terman 1979). Eight populations were
founded by releasing four males and four pregnant females into our
standard enclosures with food and water in surplus. Young born into
these populations were reared as bisexual pairs in "no-contact" cages
within the enclosures, where they received visual, auditory, and olfactory stimuli from the populations but could not be touched by any
population animal. Their sibs remained freely ranging in the populations. The results (table 2.4) indicate that maintaining young born into
the populations in the wire no-contact cages from 21 to 150 days of
age resulted in their developing significantly larger reproductive organs

than did their freely ranging sibs. Thus, tactile cues received from population animals appear to be of primary importance in inhibiting reproductive development and function in freely ranging animals.

Discussion

Behavior is basically involved in the regulation of growth of laboratory populations of prairie deermice. The relation between behavior and control of growth is not clear, although data are accumulating from both laboratory and field studies of several species of *Peromyscus* which suggest such a relationship (Bendell 1959; Sadlier 1965; Healy 1967; Fordham 1971; Rintamaa et al. 1976). Behavioral factors have frequently been implicated in studies of population regulation in other species as well (Christian 1961, 1971a, 1971b; Christian and Davis 1964; Wynne-Edwards 1966; Flowerdew 1972; Chitty 1970; Krebs 1970a, 1970b). Data from studies of natural island populations of bank voles (*Clethrionomys glareolus*) suggest that where emigration is restricted, both sexual maturation of young females and reproductive function of mature females may be inhibited by social interactions associated with the spatial structure of the population (Bujalska 1970, 1971, 1973, 1974; Bujalska and Gliwicz 1968; Gliwicz et al. 1968; Petrusewicz et al. 1968; Walkowa 1971). Consequently, the population may not attain the density permitted by the carrying capacity of the habitat, but is stabilized at a lower density.

The mechanism(s) by which behavior influences reproductive physiology and population control is at this point unclear, although Christian (1963, 1971a, b; Christian et al. 1964, 1965) has hypothesized a pituitary-adrenal-gonadal endocrine feedback response to population density and social interaction which may produce reproductive inhibition. Christian has emphasized the importance of sociobiological phenomena by suggesting that populations at asymptote, regardless of their numerical levels, are influenced by a similar number of units of "social pressure," each unit relating to a differing number of animals. Social pressure may be defined as the sum total of negative interactions among individuals within a population. Furthermore, a significant amount of evidence for some of the physiological mechanisms involved has been accumulated.*

*Editors' Note: For further discussion see Christian.

The data presented in this chapter suggest that factors which control population growth may produce physiological effects directly related to the approach of a population to asymptote and not to the numbers of animals present per se. Thus, density may be relative to social factors, and we should think of the numbers of animals in a population in a qualitative as well as a quantitative sense. Further, I have suggested that laboratory populations should be regarded as entities distinct from each other. Mechanisms of control thus appear to develop intrinsically within each population, involving communication through one or more of the senses of touch, smell, sight, hearing, and taste. My data suggest that tactile cues received from population animals (not necessarily overt aggression) may be of major importance in producing the reproductive inhibition observed.* These stimuli may be received in the ventral part of the brain (the hypothalamus). The hypothalamus is involved in controlling the pituitary gland, the master gland of the endocrine system, which influences the development of reproductive capacity. Normal release of hormones concerned with the maturation of the reproductive organs may be prevented. We are continuing to explore the complete system, including the behavioral patterns triggering the response and the neural and endocrinological mechanisms producing regulation in laboratory and in natural populations. For all persons interested in such studies, however, it is important to remember that populations of small mammals, at least, are not merely aggregates of animals but social entities of varying complexity involving behavioral organization and communication among individuals.

Acknowledgments

These studies were supported by U.S. National Institutes of Health Research Grants MH-08289, HD-04787, HD-08906, and Research Career Development Award HD-07391. Facilities and supplies have also been provided by the College of William and Mary, Williamsburg, Virginia.

Editors' Note: See Drickamer concerning the necessity of tactile contact among female mice in the production of a urinary pheromone which causes delayed sexual maturation in these animals.

References

Albertson, B. D.; Bradley, E. L.; and Terman, C. R. 1975. Plasma progesterone concentration and ovarian histology in prairie deermice (*Peromyscus maniculatus bairdii*) from experimental laboratory populations. *J. Reprod. Fertil.* 43:407–14.

Bendell, J. F. 1959. Food as a control of a population of white-footed mice, *Peromyscus leucopus noveboracensis. Can. J. Zool.* 37:173–209.

Bujalska, G. 1970. Reproduction stabilizing elements in an island population of *Clethrionomys glareolus. Acta Teriol.* 15:381–412.

———. 1971. Self-regulation of reproduction in an island population of *Clethrionomys glareolus* (Scherber, 1780). *Ann. Zool. Fenn.* 8:91.

———. 1973. The role of spacing behavior among females in the regulation of reproduction in the bank vole. *J. Reprod. Fertil. Suppl. 19*, 465–75.

———. 1974. The influence of natality and mortality on the dynamics of numbers of a population of *Clethrionomys glareolus.* (Abst.) *Proc. 1st Int. Congr. Ecol.*

———, and Gliwicz, J. 1968. Productivity investigation of an island population of *Clethrionomy glareolus* (Schreber, 1780). III. Individual growth curve. *Acta Teriol.* 13:427–33.

Chitty, D. 1970. Variation and population density. *Symp. Zool. Soc. Lond.* 26:327–33.

Christian, J. J. 1961. Phenomena associated with population density. *Proc. Natl. Acad. Sci. U.S.A.* 47:428–49.

———. 1963. Endocrine adaptive mechanisms and the physiologic regulation of population growth. In *Physiological mammalogy*, vol. 1, ed. W. B. Mayer and K. G. VanGelder, pp. 189–353. New York: Acad. Press.

———. 1971a. Population density and reproductive efficiency. *Biol. Reprod.* 4:248–94.

———. 1971b. Population density and fertility in mammals. In *The action of hormones: genes to population*, ed. P. P. Foa, pp. 471–98. Springfield, Ill.: Thomas.

———, and Davis, D. E. 1964. Endocrines, behavior and population. *Science* 146:1550–60.

———; Lloyd, J. A.; and Davis, D. E. 1965. The role of endocrines in the self-regulation of mammalian populations. *Recent Prog. Horm. Res.* 12:501–78.

Clark, F. 1938. Age of sexual maturity in mice of the genus *Peromyscus. J. Mammal.* 19:230–34.

Elton, C. 1942. *Voles, mice and lemmings. Problems in population dynamics.* Oxford: Clarendon Press.

Flowerdew, J. R. 1972. The effect of supplementary food on a population of wood mice (*Apodemus sylvaticus*). *J. Anim. Ecol.* 41:553–66.

Fordham, R. A. 1971. Field populations of deermice with supplemental food. *Ecology* 52:138–46.

Gliwicz, J., Andrezejewski, R.; Bujalska, G.; and Petrusewicz, K. 1968. Productivity investigation of an island population of *Clethrionomys glareolus* (Schreber, 1780). I. Dynamics of cohorts. *Acta Theriol.* 13, 23:401–13.

Healy, M. C. 1967. Aggression and self-regulation of population size in deermice. *Ecology* 48:377–92.

Hooper, E. T. 1968. Classification. In *Biology of Peromyscus*, Spec. Publ. 2, Am. Soc. Mammal., ed. J. A. King, pp. 27–69.

Krebs, C. J. 1970a. Genetic and behavioral studies in fluctuating vole populations. Proc. Adv. Study Inst. Dyn. Number Pop. (Oosterbeek, 1970), pp. 243–56.

———. 1970b. Microtus population biology: behavioral change associated with population cycle in *M. ochrogaster* and *M. pennsylvanicus*. *Ecology* 51:34–52.

Petrusewicz, K., Andrezejewski, R.; Bujalska, G.; and Gliwicz, J. 1968. Productivity investigation of an island population of *Clethrionomys glareolus* (Schreber, 1780). IV. Production. *Acta Theriol.* 13, 26:435–45.

Rice, L. Z. 1972. A study of food hoarding in freely growing laboratory populations of prairie deermice. Unpublished M.A. thesis, College of William and Mary. 46 pp.

Rintamaa, D. L.; Mazur, P. A.; and Vessey, S. H. 1976. Reproduction during two annual cycles in a population of *Peromyscus leucopus noveboracensis*. *J. Mammal.* 57:593–95.

Sadlier, R. M. F. S. 1965. The relationship between agonistic behavior and population changes in the deermouse, *Peromyscus maniculatus* (Wagner). *J. Anim. Ecol.* 34:331–52.

Sung, P. K.; Bradley, E. L.; and Terman, C. R. 1977. Serum corticosterone concentrations in reproductively mature and inhibited deermice (*Peromyscus maniculatus bairdii*). *J. Reprod. Fertil.* 49:201–06.

Terman, C. R. 1965. A study of population growth and control exhibited in the laboratory by prairie deermice. *Ecology* 46:890–95.

———. 1966. Population fluctuations of *Peromyscus maniculatus* and other small mammals as revealed by the North American Census of small mammals. *Am. Midl. Nat.* 76:419–26.

———. 1969. Pregnancy failure in female prairie deermice related to parity and social environment. *Anim. Behav.* 17:104–08.

———. 1973a. Recovery of reproductive function by prairie deermice from asymptotic populations. *Anim. Behav.* 21:443–48.

———. 1973b. Reproductive inhibition in asymptotic populations of prairie deermice. *J. Reprod. Fertil. Suppl. 19*, 457–63.

———. 1974. Behavioral factors associated with cessation of growth of laboratory populations of prairie deermice. *Res. Popul. Ecol.* 15:138–47.

———. 1979. Inhibition of reproductive development in laboratory populations of prairie deermice (*Peromyscus maniculatus bairdii*): influence of tactile cues. *Ecology*. In press.

Walkowa, W. 1971. The effect of exploitation on productivity of laboratory mouse populations. *Acta Teriol.* 16:295–328.

Wynne-Edwards, V. C. 1966. Regulations in animal societies and population. In *Regulation and control in living systems*, ed. H. Kalmus, pp. 397–421. New York: Wiley.

3

SOCIAL CUES AND REPRODUCTION:
RODENTS AND PRIMATES

Lee C. Drickamer

This volume focuses on three major categories of topics: (1) potential environmental signals of "density" which may contribute to population regulation, (2) mechanisms by which animals process these information signals, and (3) the actual outcomes or observed mechanisms of population control. Within the first category, subtopics include resource scarcity and abundance, extraspecific relations such as those with predators or parasites, and interactions with conspecifics (social behavior). The last subcategory is the focus of this chapter.

A variety of social behaviors have been hypothesized as contributing to population regulation in mammals. Among these are the epidiectic displays proposed by Wynne-Edwards (1962): organisms use a variety of displays and other means of communication to signal to one another regarding population numbers in relation to available resources. His hypothesis claims that these signals are mediated through physiological pathways, as yet not clearly delineated, and this leads to a stabilizing control of organism numbers with respect to available food, shelter, and so on. In other studies of population cycles of rodents, Chitty (1967) and Krebs (1964) have theorized that changes in levels of aggression occur during such cycles. As the number of animals in an area increases, there is increased mutual interference which leads to a reduced rate of increase due to lowered reproduction, deaths, and emigration. This, in turn, leads to selection for more aggressive animals, which ultimately brings about lower population levels and a decline in numbers and once again increases in population size are initiated.

Two major social behavior processes have received only cursory attention with respect to population regulation in mammals: (1) factors

37

that alter the timing of estrus in females, and (2) factors that influence synchronization of mating season activity between males and females.

In calculating changes in population size, three types of parameters are generally considered: natality, mortality, and immigration/emigration. A fourth parameter, sometimes considered as a part of natality, is generation time. With shorter generation times, more animals enter the pool of potential contributors to reproduction per unit time period, which increases population growth. Conversely, with longer generation times, fewer animals are entering the reproductive pool and growth will be slower or the population may decline. Two other critical points should be made regarding generation time. For species that mate as soon as they are sexually mature, the generation time will be equivalent to the age at puberty. For species that are monogamous, the generation time for both males and females will be important, whereas in species that are more promiscuous, with one male servicing several or more females, only the generation time for females will be critical in relation to changes in population size and growth. In addition to influencing the timing of first reproduction, the same or similar factors may also affect the timing of estrous cycles in adult female mammals. Accelerating or delaying the estrous cycles of adults could also greatly influence changes in population size by affecting the number of potential and actively reproductive females present in the population.

Interactions between males and females and their reactions to external factors leading to synchronization of mating can be important in both a short-term and a long-term sense. The immediate coordination of reproduction has been studied extensively in the ring dove (see Lehrman 1964, 1965). In ring doves there are complex interactions involving both the internal states of the birds and various external cues that govern the progression from mating through fledging of young squabs. Synchronization of the activities of both members of the pair is essential for successful reproduction. For species that are seasonal breeders, synchronization of reproductive condition at the onset of the mating season may also involve complex interactions between the animals and reactions to various external factors in the environment. It is this latter type of long-term synchrony that will be examined here.

This chapter will examine studies on rodents and primates which involve social cues that influence the timing of estrous cycles and synchronization of breeding and thus potentially contribute to population regulation.* I am using "social cues" here in a broad sense to include interactions among conspecifics as well as any signs or products from the animals that might be received by animals of the same species via various sensory modes which may exert a direct effect or may affect the physiology of conspecifics.

Factors Affecting Estrus

The discussion of social factors that influence the timing of estrous cycles will be divided into three parts: (1) influences on puberty in rodents, (2) influences on estrous cycles in adult rodents, and (3) comments on estrous cycles in primates. Considerably more research on this topic has been reported for rodents than for primates from both laboratory and field investigations; perhaps the types of studies that have been conducted using rodents can suggest problems for future investigations of similar phenomena in primates.

Puberty in Rodents

The timing of sexual maturation in rodents can be accelerated or delayed by social factors. This conclusion is supported by data from both laboratory experiments and field investigations. Extensive work on social factors affecting puberty has been conducted using laboratory stocks of house mice (*Mus musculus*).

Acceleration. Vandenbergh (1967) was the first to report that caging a young female mouse with an adult intact male led to an earlier age for first vaginal estrus when compared with control females caged alone. This finding was confirmed by Kennedy and Brown (1970) and Fullerton and Cowley (1971). Additional studies have shown that acceleration of female sexual maturation can be effected by a pheromone

Editors' Note: The actual endocrine pathways underlying some of the effects described below by Drickamer are discussed further by Christian. Effects of social cues on sexual maturation and estrous among laboratory rodents are also discussed by Terman and by Lloyd. Similar effects among rhesus monkeys and among wolves are suggested by the studies of Sade and of Packard and Mech. Lee, Cohen, and Ripley also debate factors regulating the onset and periodicity of ovulatory cycles in human females, but there is a striking lack of overlap between those factors considered in the human studies and those factors considered in the study of animal populations. Particularly noteworthy is the lack of concern for nutritional effects in the animal studies and for social inhibition or facilitation of female fertility in the human studies.

contained in the excreted and bladder urine of intact but not castrated males (Vandenbergh 1969a; Cowley and Wise 1972; Vandenbergh 1973; Colby and Vandenbergh 1974; Drickamer and Murphy 1978). On the average, first estrus occurs 6–8 days earlier in young females caged with a male than for females housed alone, and 3–5 days earlier for young females exposed to intact male urine. Unpublished data from my laboratory, involving mating puberal females with proven males, confirm that the young mice reaching first estrus are in fact ovulating at the time of the first cycle and can conceive and bear litters.

The pheromone that leads to accelerated sexual development has been partially characterized (Vandenbergh et al. 1975; Vandenbergh et al. 1976). The compound is associated with the protein component of the urine; an active fraction obtained by dialysis and sequential ultrafiltration followed by chromotography has yielded results which indicate that the compound is a peptide of molecular weight 860. The androgen dependency of the pheromone has been confirmed by Lombardi et al. (1976).

Other social cues are also implicated in the acceleration of puberty in young females by males. Drickamer (1974a, 1975) demonstrated that the presence of an adult neonatally androgenized female would accelerate sexual maturation of young females, although not to the same degree as the presence of an adult intact male. Combining the presence of an androgenized female and urine from intact males containing the pheromone produced an acceleration equivalent to that obtained when an intact male was present. Further investigations of synergistic social cues in male-induced puberty (Bronson and Maruniak 1975) verified that the important secondary cue was tactile contact between the young female and male. So, two social cues are important for male-induced acceleration of puberty in young females.

Several studies which are similar to those described above for laboratory house mice have been reported for other rodents. Hasler and Nalbandov (1974) reported that vaginal opening was accelerated in weanling voles (*Microtus ochragaster*) caged with adult males relative to caging females with either littermate males or nonlittermate weanling males. Accelerated vaginal opening has also been reported for young female collared lemmings (*Dicrostonyx groenlandicus*) caged with adult males and compared to single females caged alone (Hasler and Banks 1975a). Vandenbergh (1976) has shown that weanling female rats caged with adult males attain first vaginal estrus 9 days ear-

lier than weanling females caged individually without a male. Drickamer (1979) has recently shown that acceleration of puberty via either
the presence of an adult male or urine from adult males occurs in laboratory stocks of wild *Mus musculus*. Acceleration of puberty has not
yet been investigated in any free-living natural populations of rodents.

   Delay. In 1944 Andervont observed that young female mice caged
separately attained first vaginal estrus earlier than mice caged in groups
of eight. This finding was confirmed in recent years by Vandenbergh
et al. (1972) and Drickamer (1974b). On the average, female mice in
groups reach puberty 4–7 days later than do control females caged
alone. This delay phenomenon also involves a urinary pheromone;
when singly caged weanling females are treated with urine from
grouped females, the isolates reach puberty at the same age as if they
were part of the group. Additional experiments (Drickamer 1974b)
demonstrated that tactile contact among freely interacting females in
groups is necessary for production of the delay pheromone.

   The maturation-delaying pheromone is present in the excreted and
bladder urine of grouped females and is also found in the bladder urine
of singly caged mice (McIntosh and Drickamer 1977). Apparently,
something happens to the pheromone in singly caged mice between the
bladder and excretion. Singly caged test females treated with bladder
urine, containing the pheromone, homogenized with urethras from singly caged females reach puberty at the same age as controls. It appears
that the urethras or associated glands of singly caged females produce
a substance that deactivates the maturation-delaying pheromone contained in bladder urine. No reported attempts have yet been made to
isolate or chemically identify the delay pheromone.

   A number of investigators have reported delays of or a complete
inhibition of puberty in free-living laboratory or natural populations of
rodents, including *Microtus pennsylvanicus* (Christian 1971), *Mus
musculus* (Christian 1956, 1968; Southwick 1958; Crowcroft and
Rowe 1957), *Microtus agrestis* (Clarke 1955), and *Peromyscus maniculatus* (Terman 1965, 1969). Zejda (1961, 1967) found that young
bank voles (*Clethrionomys glareolus*) born into dense populations
failed to reach puberty in the season of their birth, but did mature the
next year when densities were lower. Kalela (1957) recorded large
differences in the proportion of young voles (*Clethrionomys rufocanus*) attaining puberty in different years, depending upon the stage
of the population cycle. In years of high density few voles attained

puberty, but in years of low population density a great majority of young voles reached sexual maturity.

Estrous Cycles in Rodents

Two effects similar to the acceleration and delay of puberty in female laboratory mice have been reported for adult females; these involve induction of estrus and the occurrence of anestrus.

Several investigators (e.g., Whitten 1958, 1959; Marsden and Bronson 1964) demonstrated that the estrous cycles of female mice were shorter in the presence of a male than when males were absent. Later studies (Whitten et al. 1968; Bronson and Whitten 1968) have confirmed this effect and demonstrated that an airborne pheromone contained in the urine of intact males is responsible for inducing estrus in females. The pheromone is present in the excreted and bladder urine of intact male mice, but is absent in castrated males, indicating that either production or excretion of the pheromone is dependent upon testicular androgens.

More recently, Chipman and Albrecht (1974) have shown that urine from preputialectomized male mice was significantly less effective in inducing estrus in adult females than was urine from males with preputials intact. Urine from preputialectomized males did not differ from urine excreted by castrated males in inducing estrus. In another investigation published at about the same time (Colby and Vandenbergh 1974), results indicated that preputialectomy did not affect the puberty-accelerating pheromone contained in intact male urine. This difference between the effects of preputialectomy suggests that there may be two separate pheromones, one that induces estrus in adult females and a second pheromone that accelerates puberty in young females. Parsimony and the similarity of the effects of these pheromones indicates that they could be the same chemical; further investigations confirming the existence of two distinct pheromones is needed to clarify this issue.

As with the social stimuli accelerating puberty in young female rodents, there have been some studies of induction of estrus in rodents other than laboratory mice. Hasler and Banks (1975b) reported that caging female collared lemmings (*Dicrostonyx groenlandicus*) with adult intact males induced estrus. Estrus was also induced when the male was simply caged next to the female and was not present in the same cage, suggesting the presence of a pheromone. Similarly, the induction of estrus occurs in wild house mice (*Mus musculus*) when females are caged with adult males. For prairie voles (*Microtus ochragaster*) a 72-hour exposure to an intact male was maximally effective in inducing estrus (Hasler and Conaway 1973).

In terms of inhibition of estrus, Whitten (1958) reported that when female laboratory mice were caged in groups of 30, the mice became anestrus and some remained so for as long as 40 days. This effect also appears to be dependent upon a pheromone; the effects of grouping on estrous cycles can be imitated by housing single females in cages recently soiled by groups of females (Champlin 1971). Kimura (1971) has shown that ovariectomized female mice have a reduced capability for suppressing estrous cycles. That ovarian hormones are involved in suppression of estrus has been confirmed by Clee et al. (1975). They reported that by using implants of estradiol they could reactivate the ovariectomized female mouse's ability to suppress estrus in group-caged conspecifics. These findings differ from recent data in my laboratory (Drickamer et al. 1978). For the maturation-delaying pheromone we found that excreted or bladder urine from grouped ovariectomized female mice produced the same delays in puberty relative to singly caged females as did urine from intact grouped females. These data, together with the two reports mentioned previously, suggest that there are two pheromones excreted by females which affect the estrous cycles of other females, one which delays the onset of puberty that is not dependent upon ovarian hormones and a second which is dependent upon ovarian hormones and suppresses estrous cyclicity in adult females. As with the male pheromone(s), additional experiments are necessary to confirm the existence of two separate pheromones.

The occurrence of anestrus in adult female rodents with conditions of increased density has been reported for house mice (*Mus musculus*; Christian 1971), deermice (*Peromyscus maniculatus*; Terman 1965), and meadow voles (*Microtus pennsylvanicus*; Pasley and McKinney 1973). In cases where populations are found with females in anestrus it may not be possible to determine whether these females have never exhibited estrus (puberty inhibited) or have experienced one or more estrus cycles and are now inhibited. So, for example, studies cited earlier by Southwick (1958) and Kalela (1957) report on females in anestrus in natural populations; these may be young that have not matured or adult females that have returned to anestrus.

Primates

There are currently no data on primates which are comparable to the investigations discussed above for rodents regarding social factors affecting puberty or estrous cycles in adults. Two studies on rhesus monkeys (*Macaca mulatta*) suggest further work, and more detailed experimental analysis could be productive. Sade et al. (1976) reported that for free-ranging rhesus macaques at Cayo Santiago Island off Puerto Rico, higher-ranking genealogies were growing faster than middle- or low-ranking genealogies. (Since it has been impossible, until the recent application of modern biochemical techniques, to determine paternity, and because the social structure of the species is based on female groups which remain stable while males shift groups, genealogies are based on female lineages.) Data from another Puerto Rican free-ranging rhesus colony at La Parguera (Drickamer 1974c) indicate that young female rhesus born to high-ranking females reach sexual maturity significantly sooner than do females born to middle- or low-ranking mothers. Together these studies suggest that some, as yet undetermined, social factors may affect sexual maturation of young females differentially, depending upon the mother's rank. Detailed behavioral observations of rates of interaction between these prepuberal females and, for example, adult males, might reveal that young daughters of high-ranking female parentage interact more with males. Such a finding could be evidence for social acceleration of puberty, analogous, in overall effect, to the phenomena already recorded for rodents.

Mating Synchrony

A second social behavior process that could be a factor in regulating population size is the mating synchrony of the two sexes. Synchrony of males and females in reproduction might be important in those species which reproduce throughout the year, but would be of critical significance in species that mate seasonally. Recall that I am dealing with synchrony here in a longer time-sense perspective with reference to animals of both sexes attaining breeding condition at the onset of a mating season.

Reproductive coordination of the sexes can be accomplished in several ways. Both sexes may respond to external features of the environment, such as climatic conditions or vegetation, which act as triggers affecting their endocrine systems and behavior. In addition, the behavior patterns and communications exhibited by one or both sexes could influence members of the opposite or even the same sex. Thus, the internal state of each animal, its behaviors, and the external features of the environment are interwoven in a complex network of feedback loops. Social processes that affect reproductive synchrony will be discussed first for rodents and then for primates.

Rodents

There has been only one experimental study conducted on reproductive synchrony in rodents (Vandenbergh 1977). Male golden hamsters (*Mesocricetus auratus*) were housed in isolation under short-daylength conditions to induce testicular regression. When these males were exposed to receptive females no gonadal recrudescence occurred, but when the males were exposed to long daylengths *and* either sexually receptive females or cages soiled by these females significant recrudescence occurred. These findings suggest that the interaction of social stimuli and photoperiod can facilitate reproductive coordination of the two sexes. Also, some form of chemical stimulation from the female may be involved.

Because so many rodents are seasonal breeders it is clear that considerable additional investigation is needed regarding reproductive synchrony in a variety of rodent species. As the study mentioned above clearly illustrates, it is often the interaction of social stimuli and other factors such as climate which brings about the return to reproductive condition for each new breeding season. It will also be important to look for synchrony from both the male and female points of view.

A variety of social cues may bear investigation as social variables affecting synchrony. Studies of short-term coordination may provide some suggestions. Ultrasonic vocalizations have been reported to be important factors in mate finding, mate selection and courtship in hamsters and rats (Floody and Pfaff 1977; McIntosh et al. 1978). In addition to the Vandenbergh (1977) study, reports of laboratory mice (Caroom and Bronson 1971), laboratory rats (Gawienowski et al. 1975; Gawienowski et al. 1976) and hamsters (Macrides et al. 1977) all report on odor cues from males which act as attractants for females. Contact-type social cues may also play a role in long-term synchrony just as they do in courtship and related activities (Doty 1974; Parker and Pearson 1976).

Primates

Many primate species are seasonal breeders; that is, they mate only at a discrete period of each year. Representatives of most major primate groups show a seasonal rhythm, including prosimians (lemurs) (Petter-Rousseaux 1964), new world monkeys (squirrel monkey) (Baldwin and Baldwin 1971), and old world monkeys (macaques, baboons, and cercopithecus monkeys) (Southwick et al. 1965; Devore and Hall 1965; Struhsaker 1967). Data on seasonal breeding in primates have been summarized by Michael and Zumpe (1976). Because they are seasonal, males and females of these various primate species must synchronize their endocrine and behavioral conditions for successful mating to take place.

Several authors (e.g., Baldwin 1970) have gathered evidence to suggest that part of the coordination occurs through responses of both sexes to environmental factors. From his observations Baldwin concluded that male and female squirrel monkeys (*Saimiri*) may respond to increased rainfall prior to the onset of mating. He also asserts that behavior patterns and communication exhibited by males and females may affect each other in the synchronization process. Climatic changes have also been implicated as a factor affecting reproductive cyclicity in rhesus monkeys (*Macaca mulatta*); both rainfall and subsequent changes in vegetation are suggested as possible environmental factors (Vandenbergh and Vessey 1968; Vandenbergh 1971).

Several experimental studies have been performed using rhesus monkeys to test endocrine coordination. Vandenbergh (1969b), working in the nonbreeding season, made observations on caged macaques. Sexually inactive males paired with females artificially brought into estrus showed increased interest in the females, as evidenced by higher rates of grooming and lowered levels of aggression and by the end of 2 weeks of pairing, some males showed complete copulatory behavior.

The capability of females to induce changes in the hormonal condition and behavioral responses of potential male mates was further tested in the free-ranging rhesus colony at La Parguera, Puerto Rico (Vandenbergh and Drickamer 1974). In one free-ranging social group, two ovariectomized females were brought into estrus in the nonbreeding season with implants of estradiol benzoate. Observations revealed that within 8–10 weeks the male sex skin color had reddened (an indication of heightened levels of circulating testosterone), there was increased grooming between males and females, and sexual behavior increased, even though the normal mating season was still several months away. Other social groups in the colony, which served as controls, did not show similar changes. Interestingly, in the subsequent birth season untreated females in the experimental group delivered infants significantly sooner than did females in control groups.

This last observation suggested that either the females in artificial estrus or the males whose sexual activity increased were, in turn, inducing changes in untreated females in the experimental group. In a follow-up investigation (Vandenbergh and Post 1976) intact females were paired, during the nonbreeding season, with males given implants of testosterone propionate. Observations of these animals revealed only minor effects on sexual behavior by females and no detectable changes in ovarian cycles. So, sexual activity by males apparently did not induce changes in females. Presumably the untreated females in the experimental group in the study by Vandenbergh and Drickamer (1974) were influenced by the treated females and not by the males.

In a separate series of studies on rhesus monkeys carried out at the Yerkes Primate Center Field Station in Georgia, various social and environmental variables have been implicated as factors influencing plasma testosterone levels in males (Rose et al. 1972; Bernstein et al. 1974; Gordon et al. 1976). Seasonal breeding in the male rhesus was correlated with increased levels of plasma testosterone. All of the following factors were found to affect male testosterone levels: (1) age, (2) daily rhythms, (3) access and/or proximity to females, (4) seasonal (climatic) rhythms, (5) social rank, and (6) outcomes of agonistic encounters. Thus, both social and environmental parameters apparently interact in a complex manner affecting the male hormone levels.

Finally, several investigations have reported on the possibility that female rhesus monkeys communicate their sexual status and possible receptivity by pheromones from the vaginal tract (Michael and Keverne 1968, 1970; Curtis et al. 1971). These investigations deal with short-term synchrony and male attraction to the female; the males are already sexually active. However, their findings raise the question of whether the same (or similar) stimuli acting over a longer time period might be involved in the long-term synchrony of males and females at the onset of a new breeding season. It should be noted, however, that attempts to replicate the findings by Michael and colleagues cited above have proven unsuccessful in at least one other laboratory (Goldfoot et al. 1976). Nevertheless, the nature of the stimuli involved in endocrine coordination for each mating season remains to be investigated. Only when such studies are completed for both rodents and primates will it be possible to assess ways in which this synchrony can be disrupted, naturally or artificially, thus affecting population growth.

Conclusions

Studies of population regulation must be governed by at least two caveats: (1) no one mechanism of population control is likely to be operative across a very wide range of animal species, and (2) for each animal species several regulatory mechanisms are operative, forming a system of checks and balances. It has been my intention in this review to explore social behaviors involved in affecting the timing of estrus and synchronization of reproduction in mammals, two factors which heretofore have been given minor attention by investigators and theoreticians concerned with population regulation.

It appears from the studies cited here that in both rodents and primates these social factors could influence population size both directly and indirectly. The exact nature of the cues that are important and the mechanisms by which these cues are processed may differ, but both factors affecting estrus and influences on endocrine coordination could be parts of a general model for population regulation that would be applicable to both rodents and primates. Because I have limited my comments, particularly on factors affecting puberty and estrus, to females, this information will be applicable only to those species in whose social systems it is the females that are critical for population control.

Acknowledgment

The rodent research in my laboratory was supported in part by USPHS Grant No. HD-08585 from the National Institutes of Health. I am indebted to Dr. John Vandenbergh under whose auspices I spent thirteen months studying primates at the La Parguera, Puerto Rico, facility of the Caribbean Primate Research Center supported by USPHS Grant No. MH-19837 from the National Institutes of Mental Health.

References

Andervont, H. B. 1944. Influence of environment on mammary cancer in mice. *J. Natl. Cancer Inst.* 4:579–81.

Baldwin, J. D. 1970. Reproductive synchronization in squirrel monkeys (*Saimiri*). *Primates* 11:317–26.

———— and Baldwin, J. I. 1971. Squirrel monkeys (*Saimiri*) in natural habitats in Panama, Columbia, Brazil and Peru. *Primates* 12:45–61.

Bernstein, I. S.; Rose, R. M.; and Gordon, T. P. 1974. Behavioral and environmental events influencing primate testosterone levels. *J. Hum. Evol.* 3:517–25.

Bronson, F. H., and Maruniak, J. A. 1975. Male-induced puberty in female mice: evidence for a synergistic action of social cues. *Biol. Reprod.* 13:94–98.

————, and Whitten, W. K. 1968. Oestrous-accelerating pheromone of mice: assay, androgen-dependency, and presence in bladder urine. *J. Reprod. Fertil.* 15:131–34.

Caroom, D., and Bronson, F. H. 1971. Responsiveness of female mice to preputial attractant: effects of sexual experience and ovarian hormones. *Physiol. Behav.* 7:659–62.

Champlin, A. K. 1971. Suppression of oestrus in grouped mice: the effects of various densities and the possible nature of the stimulus. *J. Reprod. Fertil.* 27:233–41.

Chipman, R. K., and Albrecht, E. D. 1974. The relationship of the male preputial gland to the acceleration of oestrus in the laboratory mouse. *J. Reprod. Fertil.* 38:91–96.

Chitty, D. 1967. The natural selection of self-regulatory behavior in animal populations. *Proc. Ecol. Soc. Aust.* 2:51–78.

Christian, J. J. 1956. Adrenal and reproductive responses to population size in mice from freely growing populations. *Ecology* 37:258–73.

————. 1968. The potential role of the adrenal cortex as affected by social rank and population density on experimental epidemics. *Am. J. Epidemiol.* 87:255–64.

————. 1971. Population density and reproductive efficiency. *Biol. Reprod.* 4:248–94.

Clarke, J. R. 1955. Influence of numbers on reproduction and survival in two experimental vole populations. *Proc. R. Soc. Lond. Ser. B* 144:68–85.

Clee, M. D.; Humphreys, E. M.; and Russell, J. A. 1975. The suppression of ovarian cyclical activity in groups of mice, and its dependence on ovarian hormones. *J. Reprod. Fertil.* 45:395–98.

Colby, D. R., and Vandenbergh, J. G. 1974. Regulatory effects of urinary pheromones on puberty in the mouse. *Biol. Reprod.* 11:268–79.

Cowley, J. J., and Wise, D. R. 1972. Some effects of mouse urine on neonatal growth and reproduction. *Anim. Behav.* 20:499–506.

Crowcroft, P., and Rowe, F. P. 1957. The growth of confined colonies of the wild house mouse (*Mus musculus* L.). *Proc. Zool. Soc. Lond.* 129:359–70.

Curtis, R. F.; Ballantine, J. A.; Keverne, E. F.; Bonsall, R. W.; and Michael, R. P. 1971. Identification of primate sexual pheromones and the properties of synthetic attractants, *Nature* 232:396–98.

DeVore, I., and Hall, K. R. L. 1965. Baboon ecology. In *Primate behavior*, ed. I. DeVore, pp. 20–52. New York: Holt, Rinehart and Winston.

Doty, R. L. 1974. A cry for the liberation of the female rodent: courtship and copulation in *Rodentia*. *Psychol. Bull.* 81:159–72.

Drickamer, L. C. 1974a. Contact stimulation, adrogenized females, and accelerated sexual maturation in female mice. *Behav. Biol.* 12:101–10.

———. 1974b. Sexual maturation of female house mice: social inhibition. *Devel. Psychobiol.* 7:257–65.

———. 1974c. A ten-year summary of reproductive data for free-ranging *Macaca mulatta*. *Folia Primatol.* 21:61–80.

———. 1975. Contact stimulation and accelerated sexual maturation of female mice. *Behav. Biol.* 15:113–15.

———. 1979. Acceleration and delay of first estrus in wild stocks of *Mus musculus*. *J. Mammal.* 60:215–16.

———, and Murphy, R. X. 1978. Female mouse maturation: effects of excreted and bladder urine from juvenile and adult males. *Devel. Psychobiol.* 11:63–72.

———; McIntosh, T. K.; and Rose, E. 1978. Effects of ovariectomy of production of a maturation-delaying pheromone by grouped female house mice. *Horm. Behav.* 11:131–37.

Floody, O. R., and Pfaff, D. W. 1977. Communication among hamsters by high-frequency acoustic signals: III. Responses evoked by natural and synthetic ultrasounds. *J. Comp. Physiol. Psychol.* 91:820–29.

Fullerton, C., and Cowley, J. J. 1971. The differential effect of the presence of adult male and female mice on the growth and development of the young. *J. Genet. Psychol.* 119:89–98.

Gawienowski, A. M.; Orsulak, P. J.; Stacewicz-Sapuntzakis, M.; and Joseph, B. M. 1975. Presence of sex pheromone in preputial glands of male rats. *J. Endocrinol.* 67:283–88.

———; Orsulak, P. J.; Stacewicz-Sapuntzakis, M.; and Pratt, J. J. 1976. Attractant effect of female preputial gland extracts on the male rat. *Psychoneuroendocrinology* 1:411–18.

Goldfoot, D. A.; Kravetz, M. A.; Goy, R. W.; and Freeman, S. K. 1976. Lack of effect of vaginal lavages and aliphatic acids on ejaculatory responses in rhesus monkeys: behavioral and chemical analyses. *Horm. Behav.* 7:1–27.

Gordon, T. P.; Rose, R. M.; and Bernstein, I. S. 1976. Seasonal rhythm in plasma testosterone levels in the rhesus monkey (*Macaca mulatta*): a three-year study. *Horm. Behav.* 7:229–43.

Hasler, J. J., and Banks, E. M. 1975a. The influence of mature males on sexual maturation in female collared lemmings (*Dicrostonyx groenlandicus*). *J. Reprod. Fertil.* 42:583–86.

———, and Banks, E. M. 1975b. The influence of exteroceptive factors on the estrous cycle of the collared lemming (*Dicrostonyx groenlandicus*). *Biol. Reprod.* 12:647–56.

———, and Conaway, C. H. 1973. The effect of males on the reproductive state of female *Microtus ochragaster*. *Biol. Reprod.* 9:426–36.

————, and Nalbandov, A. V. 1974. The effect of weanling and adult males on sexual maturation in female voles (*Microtus ochragaster*). *Gen. Comp. Endocr.* 23:237–38.

Kalela, O. 1957. Regulation of reproductive rate in subarctic populations of the vole *Clethrionomys rufocanus*. *Ann. Acad. Sci. Fenn. Ser. A.* 34:1–60.

Kennedy, J. M., and Brown, K. 1970. Effects of male odor during infancy on the maturation, behavior, and reproduction of female mice. *Devel. Psychobiol.* 3:179–89.

Kimura, T. 1971. Modifications of the oestrous cycle in mice housed together with normal or ovariectomized females. *Sci. Pap. Coll. Gen. Educ. Univ. Tokyo* 21:161–66.

Krebs, C. J. 1964. The lemming cycle at Baker Lake, Northwest Territories during 1959–62. *Act. Inst. N. Am. Tech. Pap. 15.*

Lehrman, D. S. 1964. Control of behavior cycles in reproduction. In *Social behavior and evolution among vertebrates*, ed. W. Etkin, pp. 143–66. Chicago: Univ. of Chicago Press.

————. 1965. Interaction between internal and external environments in the regulation of the reproductive cycle of the ring dove. In *Sex and Behavior*, ed. F. A. Beach, pp. 355–380. New York: Wiley.

Lombardi, J. R.; Vandenbergh, J. G.; and Whitsett, J. M. 1976. Androgen control of the sexual maturation pheromone in house mouse urine. *Biol. Reprod.* 15:179–86.

Macrides, F.; Johnson, P. A.; and Schneider, S. P. 1977. Responses of the male golden hamster to vaginal secretion and dimethyl disulfide: attraction versus sexual behavior. *Behav. Biol.* 20:377–86.

McIntosh, T. K., and Drickamer, L. C. 1977. Excreted urine, bladder urine, and the delay of sexual maturation in female house mice. *Anim. Behav.* 25:999–1004.

————; Barfield, R. J.; and Geyer, L. A. 1978. Ultrasonic vocalizations facilitate sexual behavior of female rats. *Nature* 272:163–64.

Marsden, H. M., and Bronson, F. H. 1964. Estrous synchrony in mice: alteration by exposure to male urine. *Science* 144:1469.

Michael, R. P., and Keverne, E. B. 1968. Pheromones in the communication of sexual status in primates. *Nature* 218:746–49.

————, and Keverne, E. B. 1971. An annual rhythm in the sexual activity of the male rhesus monkey, *Macaca mulatta*, in the laboratory. *J. Reprod. Fertil.* 25:95–98.

————, and Zumpe, D. 1976. Environmental and endocrine factors influencing annual changes in sexual potency in primates. *Psychoneuroendocrinology* 1:303–13.

Parker, G. A., and Pearson, R. G. 1976. A possible origin and adaptive significance of the mounting behaviour shown by some female mammals in oestrus. *J. Nat. Hist.* 10:241–45.

Pasley, J. N., and McKinney, T. D. 1973. Grouping and ovulation in *Microtus pennsylvanicus*. *J. Reprod. Fertil.* 34:527–30.

Petter-Rousseaux, A. 1964. Reproductive physiology and behavior of the Lemuroidea. In *Evolutionary and genetic biology of primates*, ed. J. Buettner-Janusch, pp. 91–132. New York: Academic Press.

Rose, R. M.; Gordon, T. P.; and Bernstein, I. S. 1972. Plasma testosterone levels in the male rhesus: influences of sexual and social stimuli. *Science* 178:643–45.

Sade, D. S.; Cushing, K.; Cushing, P.; Dunlaif, J.; Figueroa, A.; Kaplan, J.; Lauer, C.; Rhodes, D.; and Schneider, J. 1976. Population dynamics in relation to social structure on Cayo Santiago. *Yearb. Phys. Anthropol.* 20:253–62.

Southwick, C. H. 1958. Population characteristics of house mice living in English cornricks: density relationships. *Proc. Zool. Soc. Lond.* 131:163–75.

———; Beg, M. A.; and Siddiqi, M. R. 1965. Rhesus monkeys in North India. In *Primate behavior*, ed. I. DeVore, pp. 111–59. New York: Holt, Rinehart and Winston.

Struhsaker, T. T. 1967. Behavior of vervet monkeys (*Cercopithecus aethiops*). *Univ. Calif. Publ. Zool.* 82:1–74.

Terman, C. R. 1965. A study of population growth and control exhibited in the laboratory by prairie deermice. *Ecology* 46:890–95.

———. 1969. Weights of selected organs of deermice (*Peromyscus maniculatus bairdi*) from asymptotic laboratory populations. *J. Mammal.* 50:311–20.

Vandenbergh, J. G. 1967. Effect of the presence of a male on the sexual maturation of female mice. *Endocrinology* 81:345–49.

———. 1969a. Male odor accelerates female sexual maturation in mice. *Endocrinology* 84:658–60.

———. 1969b. Endocrine coordination in monkeys: male responses to the female. *Physiol. Behav.* 4:261–64.

———. 1971. Reproductive adaptations in macaques. In *Advances in reproductive physiology*, ed. M. W. H. Bishop, pp. 103–18. London: Logos Press.

———. 1973. Acceleration and inhibition of puberty in female mice by pheromones. *J. Reprod. Fertil. Suppl. 19*, 411–19.

———. 1976. Acceleration of sexual maturation in female rats by male stimulation. *J. Reprod. Fertil.* 46:451–53.

———. 1977. Reproductive coordination in the golden hamster: female influences on the male. *Horm. Behav.* 9:264–75.

———, and Drickamer, L. C. 1974. Reproductive coordination among free-ranging rhesus monkeys. *Physiol. Behav.* 13:373–76.

———, and Post, W. 1976. Endocrine coordination in rhesus monkeys: female responses to the male. *Physiol. Behav.* 17:979–84.

———, and Vessey, S. H. 1968. Seasonal breeding of free-ranging rhesus monkeys and related ecological factors. *J. Reprod. Fertil.* 15:71–79.

———; Drickamer, L. C.; and Colby, D. R. 1972. Social and dietary factors in the sexual maturation of female mice. *J. Reprod. Fertil.* 28:397–405.

———; Whitsett, J. M.; and Lombardi, J. R. 1975. Partial isolation of a pheromone accelerating puberty in female mice. *J. Reprod. Fertil.* 43:515–23.

———; Finlayson, J. S.; Dobrogosz, W. J.; Dills, S.S.; and Kost, T. A. 1976. Chromatographic separation of puberty accelerating pheromone from male mouse urine. *Biol. Reprod.* 15:260–65.

Whitten, W. K. 1958. Modification of the oestrous cycle of the mouse by external stimuli associated with the male. *J. Endocrinol.* 17:307–13.

————. 1959. Occurrence of anoestrus in mice caged in groups. *J. Endocrinol.* 18:102–07.

————; Bronson, F. H.; and Greenstein, J. A. 1968. Estrus-inducing pheromone of male mice: transport by movement of air. *Science* 161:584–85.

Wynne-Edwards, V. C. 1962. *Animal dispersion in relation to social behavior.* New York: Hafner Press.

Zejda, J. 1961. Age structure in populations of the bank vole, *Clethrionomys glareolus. Zool. Listy* 10:249–64.

————. 1967. Mortality of a population of *Clethrionomys glareolus* Schreb. in a bottomland forest in 1964. *Zool. Listy* 16:221–38.

4

ENDOCRINE FACTORS IN POPULATION REGULATION

John J. Christian

There is little doubt that in many species of mammal increases in population density or social strife* evoke a series of behavioral and endocrine responses that ultimately serve to control and limit population growth. The body of evidence supporting this statement is too large to cover completely here. In addition, recent major discoveries in endocrinology and neuroendocrinology bear significantly on our understanding of population regulation. Therefore, this review is limited largely to new results, pertinent recent advances in endocrinology, and work that has not been reviewed recently. For coverage of earlier work and for support of undocumented statements in this account, the reader is referred to one or more of several reviews (Christian 1961, 1971a,b, 1975, 1978; Christian et al. 1965).

Hypothalamic-Pituitary-Adrenocortical (HPA) Responses to Population Density

Increased HPA activity usually accompanies increased density or low social rank in either static or freely growing confined populations of

Editors' Note: Christian's repeated reference to social strife as evoking endocrine responses is one indication that nonhuman animals, like people, respond to the nature of the social environment rather than to density per se (cf. the debate between Freedman and Baron). Lloyd and Terman treat this theme explicitly with regard to populations of laboratory rodents, but the importance of social organization as a mediator of density-dependent responses is evident in other animal studies as well. Christian's reference to social strife invites comparison to a number of themes that emerge in the analysis of human perception of crowding. His reference to low social rank (below) suggests specifically comparison to the concepts of *manning* and *control* discussed by Baron and Epstein and Karlin.

mice, rats, voles, tree shrews, and rhesus monkeys. For example, increased cortisol secretion was consistently associated with low social rank and fear in rhesus monkeys (Chamove and Bowman 1976), confirming the results of earlier studies (Sassenrath 1970; Sassenrath et al. 1969). Genetically determined differences in aggressiveness may influence the magnitudes of the responses.

Adrenal weight is still a useful indicator of adrenocortical (AC) responses to changes in density or to social rank provided that allowances are made for certain morphological variations (Christian and Davis 1964), and a positive correlation between AC secretion and adrenal weight has been established for the same or related species, as in the case of California ground squirrels (*Spermophilus beecheyi*), house mice, Norway rats, voles (*Microtus* sp.), lemmings (*Lemmus*), and several other species. The use of weight avoids the severe problems, such as acute responses to handling and disturbance of the population, inherent in measuring levels of corticoids in the blood of members of a population. *In vitro* incubation of the adrenal glands, with and without ACTH, circumvents these problems, but it has its own limitations in time and expense. The recent development of techniques for measuring corticoids in the urine of mice may circumvent some of these problems (Kley et al. 1976). Nevertheless, one of these procedures must be used when adrenal weight does not reflect AC Function. For example, adrenal weight is not a valid index of AC responses to density or social strife in gerbils (*Meriones unguiculatus*), prairie deermice (*Peromyscus m. bairdii*), or white-footed mice (*Peromyscus leucopus*) in the laboratory. "Crowded" gerbils had lighter adrenals than do paired animals, but cortisol (F) secretion was increased (Hull et al. 1976). Similarly, adrenal weight was decreased while secretion of corticosterone (B) was significantly increased in deermice from experimental populations (Sung et al. 1977). Similarly, ACTH increased secretion of progesterone, F, and B without changing adrenal weight in *P. leucopus* (Ogle 1974). These results may apply to some other species of cricetines, such as the cotton rat, *Sigmodon hispidus* (Green 1964), in which adrenal weight failed to respond to increased density. Sex steroids often affect adrenal weight. Estrogens increase adrenal weight in females of many species, including voles, an effect that becomes apparent at puberty. This effect is due to the action of estrogens on the adrenals, on hepatic enzymes, and on binding of circulating corticoids. Androgens increase adrenal weight in some other species, such as *Peromyscus leucopus, P. maniculatus*, and *Mesocricetus auratus* (Christian 1964; Gaskin and Kitay 1970). However these effects are rather constant percentage-wise after puberty and do not interfere with the use of adrenal weights if data from mature and immature and both sexes are treated separately.

The responses of adrenal weight to increased density in *P. leucopus* are not always predictable. Some respond with an increase in adrenal weight, whereas others do not (Southwick 1964). The difference depends on behavioral factors. Adrenal weight increased with density in freely growing confined populations of *Peromyscus leucopus*, but not in *P. m. bairdii* (Terman 1969; Christian 1975).

The AC responses to changes in density in mammals from natural populations are largely consistent with those above, with some notable exceptions. B secretion in *P. m. bairdii* was related to behavioral characteristics of the population and to changes in density, but not linearly (Andrews et al. 1975a). In some other natural populations, adrenal weight was correlated with density in *P. m. bairdii* of both sexes and in female *P. leucopus*, but not in male *P. leucopus* (Christian 1971b, 1975). Adrenal weight in the males was correlated with breeding activity, but *not* with reproductive function per se. This relationship resembles that in *Microtus pennsylvanicus*, in which adrenal weight in mature males reflects the intensity of social strife (Christian 1975, 1978). Recent studies support earlier work indicating that adrenal secretory activity is positively correlated with density in lemmings (*Lemmus trimicronatus*) (Andrews et al. 1975b). To and Tamarin (1977) found a significant positive correlation between adrenal weight and population size in *Microtus breweri* of both sexes, but only for female *M. pennsylvanicus*. The failure to find such a correlation in male *M. pennsylvanicus* is unexplained. Despite the significant correlation between density and adrenal in these two species, particularly females, the authors concluded that AC activity and related physiological responses could not explain population cycles, since the populations of *M. breweri* were noncyclic, at least during the 4 years of the study. This conclusion is tenable only if one believes that "cycles" are unique and their dynamics differ from those of other populations of small mammals. There is no evidence to support this view. On the contrary, data from North America and Eurasia indicate that cycles reflect the same population dynamics that operate elsewhere, but the amplitude of their changes in numbers is magnified by characteristics of the environment. An irruption of *Microtus montanus* in California is of interest in this regard. The irruption occurred primarily in extensive and relatively uniform cultivated lands, while smaller, isolated cultivated lands and natural habitats of the voles were less affected (Murray 1965). Frank (1957) also noted that irruptions of *M. arvalis* occur regularly only on the open, continuous steppes. These results are consistent with other observations on the occurrence of irruptions of cycles relative to the nature of the habitat (Christian 1970). *M. pennsylvanicus* is "cyclic" in northeastern Pennsylvania, with densities ranging from at least 200 to 1 or less per acre, but the last two peaks were separated by 6 years. Cycles of lemmings, voles, or other species exhibit considerable variability in the between-peak interval. The length of the interval is undoubtedly a function of a number of ecological factors and possibly the amplitude of the preceding peak. In any case, a single 4-year study is insufficient to conclude that a species is "non-cyclic."

Snowshoe hares (*Lepus americanus*) secreted high levels of cortisol (F) in a year of peak density, but whether or not this reflected high density is uncertain (Fevold and Drummond 1976). European rabbits (*Oryctolagus cuniculus*) respond to increased density (or decreased space) with increased adrenocortical activity (Myers et al. 1971), but their patterns of steroid secretion have not been studied in relation to density. Rabbits switch from secreting predominantly B to secreting predominantly F with prolonged stimulation by ACTH (Krum and Glenn 1965; Fevold 1968, 1969; Ganjam et al. 1972; Slaga and Krum 1973). Since F is a more potent glucocorticoid than B, the change in secretory pattern may have profound physiological and pathological effects on the rabbits and their populations. Hares may similarly alter the pattern of corticoid secretion, but their steroidogenesis is somewhat different from that of rabbits (Fevold and Drummond 1976), which leaves open the question of the significance of F secretion by hares in a peak year.

The studies described above indicate that changes in AC activity are positively correlated with density (via behavioral mechanisms) in many species, but that adrenal weight may be a poor indicator of cortical function in some species.

The Nature of ACTH
The last few years have seen major advances in our knowledge of adrenocorticotropins (ACTH), brought about by the development of

highly sensitive, specific radioimmune assays (RIA) and immunocytochemical techniques. Until relatively recently, ACTH was considered to be a single 39 amino acid compound with minor variations
between species. The steroidogenic activity of ACTH apparently re-
sided in N-terminal 24 amino acid sequence, and this fragment was
believed to be the smallest with full potency, but it is more readily
broken down *in vivo* than is the natural compound. However, many
smaller fragments of ACTH stimulate steroidogenesis *in vitro* if they
contain the 4–10 amino acid sequence of $_{1-39}$ACTH (Schwyzer 1977).
The differences in their potencies *in vivo* reflect the ease with which
they are degraded. ACTH and some of these smaller fragments with
the ACTH 4–10 amino acid sequence have marked effects on behavior,
particularly on the acquisition and maintenance of conditioned-avoidance responses (de Wied 1977). These effects are most evident following intraventricular injection.

The discovery that there are at least four molecular forms of ACTH
was another notable advance. Orth et al. (1970, 1973) first found a
larger form of ACTH with an apparent molecular weight of about
7,800 in cells of a functional murine pituitary tumor. Since then three
forms of ACTH and a precursor molecule have been found in the pituitaries of a number of species (Coslovsky et al. 1975; Mains and
Eipper 1975, 1976; Eipper and Mains 1975; Eipper et al. 1976; Eipper
and Mains 1977; Mains et al. 1977; Lee and Lee 1977; Roberts and
Herbert 1977a,b). These three are "little" (sACTH), "intermediate"
(iACTH), and "big" (bACTH), with molecular weights of about 4,-
500, 13,000 (Mr 6,700), 23,000, and 31,000, respectively. They occur, apparently with minor variations between species, in the pituitaries of mice, rats, cattle, dogs, rabbits, and man, but iACTH was not
found in sheep (Lee and Lee 1977). Hamsters may lack sACTH, but
this is still uncertain (Coslovsky and Yalow 1974; Orth and Nicholson
1977). Intermediate and big ACTH occur in the pituitaries as glycoproteins which contain the 1–39 peptide sequence of ACTH (Eipper et al.
1976; Eipper and Mains 1977; Lee and Lee 1977; Orth and Nicholson
1977; Roberts and Herbert 1977a,b). Intermediate ACTH is a glycosylated polypeptide with a molecular weight of $6,700 \pm 600$ (Eipper
and Mains 1977). An oligosaccharide chain is probably bonded cova-
lently to the ACTH polypeptide in the 29–31 residue sequence. Intermediate and $_{\alpha 1-39}$ACTH have equal biological activity on a molar basis.

The prevalence of these forms of ACTH in the pituitary varies with
species. Little ACTH accounts for more than 90% and iACTH about

5% of the ACTH activity in bovine pituitaries. However, in cells of murine pituitaries and functional murine pituitary tumors, iACTH accounts for about 25% of the total ACTH bioactivity (Eipper and Mains 1975).* However, when the murine tumors are incubated and the medium extracted, iACTH accounted for about 80% of the ACTH bioactivity. There was little or no sACTH. Big ACTH accounted for about 5% of the bioactivity in the pituitary, pituitary tumor, and incubation medium. The absence of a significant amount of sACTH from the medium has not been fully explained. However, its absence has a number of potentially important implications. As a general rule, the longer peptides are more resistant to degradation *in vivo*. Since the pituitary contains proteolytic anzymes that can destroy ACTH, sACTH may be broken down in the pituitaries of mice, whereas the larger forms may be resistant to enzymatic degradation are are secreted. In any event, the results suggest that the glycosylated iACTH may be the most important form in mice, rats, and possibly a number of other species. If so, it might explain why it takes relatively large amounts of injected sACTH (natural porcine, ovine, or synthetic $_{\beta1-24}$ACTH) to stimulate secretion of physiological levels of corticosteroids in mice (Christian et al. 1965; Ungar 1965). If iACTH proves to be the normal ACTH secreted by the pituitary of *Peromyscus*, it could explain why injected $_{\alpha1-39}$ACTH (sACTH) occasionally has erratic effects on their adrenals (Christian unpublished). More research is needed on the importance of iACTH in those species whose populations are most commonly studied.

Opioid Peptides

The discovery of a natural opiate receptor in the brains of mice (Pert and Snyder 1973) led to the discovery of a number of natural peptide ligands for these binding sites with potent opioid activity, particularly if injected intraventricularly (Hughes 1975; Hughes et al. 1975; Terenius and Wahlström 1975a,b; Bajusz et al. 1976; Guillemin et al. 1976; Jacquet and Marks 1976; Lazarus et al. 1976; Ling et al. 1976; Li and Chung 1976; Székely et al. 1977; Hollósi et al. 1977; Urca et al. 1977). These peptides fall into two general categories: the penta-

---

*These pituitary tumors synthesize the same forms of ACTH as do normal pituitaries and in the same proportions, and have the advantage of making available large amounts of tissue for extraction.

peptide enkephalins, found mainly in the brain, or the larger peptidic endorphins, found mainly in the pituitary. The enkephalins apparently are neurotransmitters within the brain, whereas endorphin in the brain may modulate neuronal function (Bloom et al. 1977; Watson et al. 1977). All of these opioid peptidic sequences are contained in 61–91 amino acid sequences of β-lipotropin (LPH), a 91 amino acid peptide isolated from the pituitaries of several species (Li et al. 1965a,b) which is a prohormone for the endorphins and enkephalins (Lazarus et al. 1976; Mains et al. 1977; Roberts and Herbert 1977a,b). The enkephalins are 61–65 LPH. The endorphins share the same LPH (61–65) sequence as the enkephalins at their N-terminus, but are larger fragments of LPH (61–91). α, γ, δ, and β-endorphin have the same sequences respectively as 61–76, 61–77, 61–87, and 61–91 LPH (Bloom et al. 1976; Bradbury et al. 1976; Cox et al. 1976; Li and Chung 1976; Guillemin et al. 1976; Ling et al. 1976). β-Endorphin is the principal endorphin found in the pituitary. However, α-endorphin appears to be an artifact of extraction (Rossier et al. 1977). These natural opioids will undoubtedly prove to have important effects in modulating behavior and behavioral homeostasis. However, even their opioid activities differ from peptide to peptide (Wei et al. 1977). None has much effect when administered peripherally, but more are potent when administered more directly to the CNS. β-Endorphin is 10–30 times more potent than morphine (Loh and Li 1977; Székely et al. 1977), binds competitively with morphine to opioid binding sites, and its action is antagonized by the opiate antagonist naloxone. While the potency of these compounds in a general way increases with increasing molecular length and resistance to enzymatic degradation (Bradbury et al. 1976; Goldstein and Cox 1977; Li et al. 1977; Lord et al. 1977; Rónai et al. 1977), their potencies vary considerably with certain amino acid sequences (Bradbury et al. 1976) and molecular configuration (Horn and Rodgers 1976). The relative potencies of these peptides also vary with different binding sites (Hughes et al. 1975; Lord et al. 1977).

Like ACTH, β-endorphin and LPH are found in all the cytoplasmic secretory granules of the AP corticotropes and in the parenchymal cells of the intermediate lobes of the pituitaries (Pi) of mice, rats, sheep, cattle, pigs, and rhesus monkeys (Pelletier et al. 1977; Bloom et al. 1977; Labella et al. 1977). Endorphins and LPH also are found in discrete areas of the brain (Bloom et al. 1977). However, the endorphins in the pituitary and brain may not be identical, although the existence in the brain of an endorphin smaller than β-endorphin might be artifactual (Rossier et al. 1977). β-Endorphin and ACTH are secreted simultaneously and in parallel from the pituitary in response to acute systemic stress or to chronic adrenalectomy, and the secretion of both is blocked by dexamethasone (Guillemin et al. 1977). Thus, endorphin and ACTH share identical regulatory mechanisms. It takes high pharmacological doses of β-endorphin administered peripherally to produce analgesia, despite the fact that only .5 μg injected into the brain produces analgesia (Guillemin et al. 1977). Because of this difference, it was suggested that β-endorphin, like other pituitary hormones, may reach the brain via retrograde circulation (Oliver et al. 1977). However, levels of endorphin in the brain did not parallel those in the peripheral circulation; so its role in peripheral circulation is unknown. On the other hand, brain opioids increase in response to acute stress with an accompanying decrease in responsiveness to pain (Madden et al. 1977; Grevert and Goldstein 1977).

The 31K ACTH in mice is the common precursor of LPH, endorphins, and of the various forms of ACTH as follows (Mains et al. 1977; Roberts and Herbert 1977a,b):

$$\text{β-endorphin}(_{61-91}\text{βLPH})(3.5\text{K})$$

$$\text{β}_{1-91}\text{LPH}(11.7\text{K})$$

$$_{1-60}\text{βLPH} \;\rightarrow ?$$

C-terminus

$$\text{β}1-260\text{R}(31\text{K "ACTH"})$$

N-terminus

$$\text{iACTH}(6.7\text{K}) \text{ "glycosylated" } \alpha_{1-39}\text{ACTH}$$

$$\alpha_{1-160}\text{ACTH}(23\text{K})$$

$$\alpha_{1-39}\text{ACTH}(4.5\text{K})$$

The 23K ACTH was shown to be a transient biosynthetic intermediate. Intermediate and little ACTH are formed separately from 23K ACTH.

ACTH in the Intermediate Lobe of the Pituitary

Twenty years ago Miahle-Voloss (1958), Rochefort et al. (1959), and Smelik (1960) reported that the intermediate lobe of the pituitary (Pi)

contained and secreted ACTH in response to psychogenic ("neurogenic," "emotional") stress.* These results have been confirmed using
more sensitive techniques (Dellman et al. 1973; Moriarty and Moriarty
1975; Moriarty et al. 1975). The Pi contains about one tenth of the
total pituitary ACTH bioactivity, but its concentration is greater than
that in the AP (Kraicer et al. 1973; Mains and Eipper 1975). There is
no iACTH in the Pi of mice. Little ACTH accounts for about 75% of
the ACTH bioactivity of the Pi and bACTH accounts for the rest
(Mains and Eipper 1975). Endorphins are also found in all cellular
elements of the Pi (Bloom et al. 1977). In contrast to ACTH in the
AP, ACTH in the Pi does not respond to adrenalectomy, blood levels
of corticoids, systemic stress, hypothalamic corticotropin-releasing
factor (CRF), or to ether (Gosbee et al. 1970; Kastin et al. 1971; Greer
et al. 1975; Moriarty and Moriarty 1975; Moriarty et al. 1975; Kraicer
1976; Fischer and Moriarty 1977). These treatments all stimulated
ACTH release from the AP, whereas psychogenic stress (flashing light
and bell), which caused a significant decrease in bioactive ACTH in
the Pi, failed to stimulate ACTH release from the AP (Moriarty and
Moriarty 1975). The control of ACTH in the Pi is clearly independent
of that of the AP. The Pi is richly supplied with serotonergic, dopa-
minergic, noradrenergic, and cholinergic nerve endings and has direct
synaptic input from neurones from the hypothalamus (Mains and Eipper 1975; Kraicer 1976). Denervation of the neurointermediate lobe
prevents the secretion of ACTH from the Pi (Kraicer 1976). The secretion of ACTH from Pi cells is stimulated primarily by acetylcholine
and inhibited by dopamine, although other monoamine neurotransmitters in large doses have inhibitory or stimulatory actions (Kraicer and
Morris 1976; Fischer and Moriarty 1977; Kraicer 1977). Lowry et al.
(1977) claimed that ACTH in the Pi serves only as a precursor for
αMSH with CLIP (the remainder of the ACTH molecule after the
MSH has been cleaved off) as a by-product, and cited the fact that the
Pi *in vitro* failed to incorporate amino acids into ACTH. Since this
procedure involved denervation of the gland, and no monoamine
stimulants were provided, the observed results are not surprising. In a
similar vein, Greer et al. (1975) concluded that the Pi does not secrete
functionally significant amounts of ACTH, since it did not respond to

---

Editors' Note: See Freedman for a reference to the production of "stimulus overload" by
high density in human beings. Also see Epstein for a discussion of psychophysiological measures
of "arousal" in human beings under crowded, stressful conditions.

ether, adrenalectomy, or a tourniquet on the leg. However, none of these is a psychogenic stimulus, so that the functional significance of ACTH from the Pi was not tested. In the light of more recent evidence, these claims seem to be questionable.

These results are important when considering ACTH-AC responses to social strife and increased population density. Since the release of ACTH in response to psychogenic stimuli is controlled by direct neural input from the brain, and apparently is independent of CRF and negative feedback controls, it may explain why AC responses to psychogenic stimuli reach and are sustained at high levels. The ultimate importance of ACTH from the Pi in the mediation of AC responses to social strife and changes in density must be established, but it seems clear that it may be important. Furthermore, ACTH from the Pi may reach the brain via retrograde circulation in the long portal vessels, since the levels of ACTH in the portal plasma were greatly reduced by removal of the posterior and intermediate lobes of the pituitary (Oliver et al. 1977).

A number of years ago, Bronson and Clarke (1966) reported that the pelage of adrenalectomized *Peromyscus maniculatus* maintained on NaCl turned dark gray, blackish, or even black in three to six months. Since ACTH from the Pi is unresponsive to adrenalectomy or corticoids, the source of the increased MSH and ACTH responsible for the increased pigmentation must have been from the AP. These results suggest that the AP, and not the Pi, is the major source of MSH activity in this species.

ACTH in the Anterior Pituitary

The major features of the regulation of ACTH secretion from the AP are fairly well known and are covered in textbooks, reviews, and in the proceedings of a recent conference on ACTH (*Ann. N.Y. Acad. Sci.* 297:1–664, 1977). The secretion of ACTH from the AP and its regulation are the topics usually covered in accounts on the subject, since it has been only recently that ACTH from the Pi has been the subject of intensive research. Therefore, discussion of AP, together with ACTH and its regulation, will be omitted here.

However, a question that has arisen frequently with regard to the HPA system and the chronic psychogenic stress accompanying increased density is whether or not there is adaptation to these stresses with an accompanying decline in HPA activity. Data from a variety of populations have suggested that this is not the case. Experimental evidence supports this conclusion.

There is a triphasic pattern of ACTH secretion in response to a wide variety of chronic stimuli (Knigge et al. 1959); Henkin and Knigge 1963; Dallman et al. 1972, 1974; Dallman and Jones 1973). First there is a rapid rise of ACTH to high levels, followed by a prolonged (several hours to two days) return to basal or subbasal levels, and finally a return to sustained high levels. The magnitude and duration of the response are determined by the intensity and duration of the stimulus (Kendall et al. 1972). The initial rise of CRF-ACTH is probably limited by a rate-sensitive (derivative) negative feedback inhibition of CRF release by rising levels of glucocorticoids acting primarily at the hypothalamus (Sato et al. 1975; Abe and Critchlow 1977). This is a fast feedback that probably acts by producing neuronal membrane stabilization (Jones and Hillhouse 1976). The decline following the initial rise probably is produced by a slower negative feedback, which acts in proportion to the circulatory levels of corticoids and probably inhibits the synthesis and release of CRF (Sato et al. 1975; Abe and Critchlow 1977; Jones and Hillhouse 1976). These mechanisms do not explain the termination of the depressed phase and the return to high levels of CRF and ACTH secretion, although a fall in circulating levels following decreased ACTH secretion may remove feedback inhibition. However, the second sustained rise is not inhibited by the consequent rise in corticoids. Other changes must occur in the system, such as changes in the sensitivity of pituitary corticotropes to stimulation by CRF (Brattin and Portanova 1975). However, there is no adaptation to repeated or continued exposure to the same stress and no decrease in response to a second stressor except during the initial rapid rise in corticoid levels (Cook et al. 1973, 1974; Cook and Olson 1973; Dallman and Jones 1973; Riegle 1973; Nemeth et al. 1975; Sakellaris and Vernikos-Danellis 1975; Sakakura et al. 1976). Rather than adaptation, there is sensitization of the system to subsequent stimulation lasting for several days after a stimulus, so that the response to a second stimulus is faster and of equal or greater magnitude than the initial response. In addition, stimulation of the adrenal cortex by ACTH apparently increases the sensitivity of the cortex to subsequent stimulation (Stark et al. 1963; Kolanowski et al. 1975). The second increase in ACTH secretion is sustained for as long as the stimulus persists. However, animals may adapt behaviorally rather than physiologically to some initially stressful situations, such as handling, confinement, and transfer to another cage through learning that the procedures are not harmful. This would not be the case for many noxious physical and psychogenic stimuli.

The kinds of stimuli that stimulate increased HPA activity can be conveniently grouped and summarized as follows:

1. *Reduction or removal of negative feedbacks.* Unilateral or bilateral adrenalectomy (the former temporarily), various drugs that interfere with corticoid synthesis. These effects may be acute or chronic.

2. *Pharmacological.* Agents acting directly on central neural tracts, primarily in the hypothalamus, to prevent normal neural function. Ether is an outstanding example of this group. May be acute, repeated, or chronic.

3. *Psychogenic (neurogenic, emotional).* Involve neural pathways to the intermediate pituitary. Neural stimulation of ACTH release from the Pi apparently is unaffected by corticoid feedback systems and is unresponsive to CRF. Possibly some of these stimuli may also produce increased ACTH secretion from the AP via stimulation of CRF release. These distinctions have not been evaluated, nor has there been sufficient investigation of the responses to psychogenic stress, since the apparent role of the Pi has been established, as well as the failure of AP corticotropes to respond to the same stimuli. The stimuli may be acute, repeated, or chronic, and may include restraint, immobilization, photic or acoustic stress, handling, defeat, group caging, and other situations or procedures that evoke fear or apprehension. Some of these procedures may have a physical component as well.

4. *Systemic stress.* Acts by stimulating increased secretion of CRF.

(a) *Through neural pathways to the hypothalamus* to stimulate the secretion of hypothalamic CRF (H-CRF). Intact neural tracts to and through the hypothalamus are required for stimuli to be effective. Stimuli include electric shock, acute hemorrhage, physical trauma such as fracture of a leg, laparotomy, stretching the gut, and histamine. May be acute, repeated, or chronic.

(b) *Humoral transmitter mechanism.* Tissue CRF (T-CRF) arising peripherally stimulates the AP directly. Its action would be subject to corticoid negative feedback inhibition only to the extent that the response of the pituitary is inhibited. T-CRF is apparently released into the peripheral circulation following severe, extensive trauma or conditions resulting in tissue hypoxia (Egdahl 1960; Witorsch and Brodish 1972; Lymangrover and Brodish 1973; Brodish 1977). T-CRF differs from H-CRF in that it acts later after the initial insult and for a longer period.

Clearly, the CNS is important in the regulation of the HPA system, and its role has been actively investigated in recent years. However, a discussion of its role will be omitted here.

Effects on Disease and Mortality

Increased density with increased social strife may increase mortality either by decreasing host resistance to infectious disease and parasitism or by inducing disease directly through increased HPA activity (Christian 1963, 1967, 1968, 1976; Christian et al. 1965). With increased density, particularly in lower-ranking individuals, decreased host resistance should be anticipated. It is well known that adrenal glucocorticoids inhibit inflammation, granulation, phagocytosis, migration of cells into areas of inflammation, healing, and every stage of the immune response, including antibody formation (Melby 1977). Thymocytes and thymus-dependent small lymphocytes, the cells primarily involved in cell-mediated immunity, are most affected by corticosteroids. Increases in density or low social rank have been shown to have similar effects (Christian et al. 1965; Christian 1968). Patterns of disease under these circumstances are usually quite different than those seen in typical epidemics. The principal effect of increased density is to decrease host resistance to most pathogens, in contrast to the typical epidemic spread of a single virulent pathogen through a population. However, with decreased resistance of a population, a number of pathogens may be involved in different individuals or different segments of a population, although this does not rule out the possibility of an epidemic in a population with reduced resistance. The experiments of Topley, Wilson, Greenwood, and their colleagues on herd immunity and epidemiology in mice are fascinating illustrations of changes in host resistance of this sort (Wilson and Miles 1961; Christian 1968). Several more recent experiments demonstrate these facts. Antibody titers to *Salmonella typhimurium* vaccine in mice were inversely related to density of mice, and significantly fewer responded at high than at low density (Edwards and Dean 1977). At the highest densities, 30–40 mice per cage, the number of deaths of nonimmunized mice increased significantly after challenge with virulent *S. typhimurium*. In experiments on the relationship between density and resistance to parasitism by *Microphallus pygmaeus* in male and female mice, a standard number of metacercaria were given to mice housed one, two, four, or six per cage (Brayton and Brain 1974). The number of retained parasites and adrenal weight increased, while body weight and weights of the reproductive organs, preputials, thymus, and spleen decreased in males. The number of parasites in females changed similarly, but changes in organ weights were less marked.

One of the features of high density is the persistence of certain effects after the population declines. Chandra (1975) has shown that reduced caloric intake results in impairment of immunological mechanisms in rats, and the F_1 and F_2 progeny of underfed dams have impaired antibody formation. Considering that lactation and/or maternal care may be inadequate at high densities, particularly in low-ranking animals (Calhoun 1950; Christian and LeMunyan 1958; Christian et al. 1965; Lloyd this volume), it is not surprising that high density has prolonged adverse effects on resistance to disease in the progeny for more than one generation. Large litters also result in decreased nutrition of its members, therefore producing the same effects. Similar effects with stunting of the offspring probably occur in *Microtus pennsylvanicus* as well (see below). Large litters are characteristic of the attainment of peak densities (Christian 1978), so that large litters may contribute to the long-lasting effects of high density on a population. Density- or rank-induced changes in host resistance of this sort probably explain the changes in "quality" and decreases in viability that Chitty observed in populations of voles (Chitty 1952, 1954). A point that is frequently forgotten is that populations early in their decline phase following a "high" actually are at their maximum effective density.

Increased pituitary-adrenocortical activity associated with increased density or social strife can produce disease directly. Renal glomerulosclerosis was probably an important cause of mortality in a population of woodchucks at high density (Christian 1963, 1976; Christian et al. 1965). The prevalence, incidence, and severity of this disease was reduced by reducing social strife through changing the structure of the population. ACTH, including synthetic β_{1-24}ACTH, produces an apparently identical disease in woodchucks, intact and adrenalectomized mice, Australian brush-tailed possums and hairy rats, but not in laboratory rats, rabbits, *Microtus*, or *Peromyscus*

(Christian et al. 1965; Christian 1967, 1976). However, the prevalence of a similar renal disease in *Peromyscus leucopus* was greatly increased in a natural population at very high density compared to these mice from populations of lower density (Christian 1979). Recently, Geller (1978) has found that the prevalence and severity of renal pathology was greater in dispersing than in nondispersing *Microtus pennsylvanicus*. Other investigators have reported a similar relationship between renal disease and density in Norway rats and tree shrews (Andrews et al. 1972; von Holst 1972).

Increased density (social strife) can also cause hypertension. Blaine (1973) found arterial blood pressure significantly increased in *M. pennsylvanicus* from an experimental population at asymptotic density. Increased density also results in increased blood pressure in mice and can probably be attributed to psychological factors (Henry and Cassel 1969; Ely and Henry 1974). Increased secretion of sodium-retaining mineralocorticoids whose secretion is controlled by ACTH may induce the hypertension in these circumstances (Nowaczynski et al. 1975; Fraser et al. 1976). These steroids are 11-deoxycorticosterone (DOC) and 18-hydroxy-11-deoxycorticosterone (18-OH-DOC), both of which have been implicated in the etiology of hypertension. 18-OH-DOC is particularly interesting because, like DOC and corticosterone (B), its secretion by the adrenal fasciculata-reticularis is under the control of ACTH, but, unlike the others, it has no negative feedback inhibitory effect on ACTH secretion, and finally, it circulates in the free, unbound, active form (Kraulis et al. 1973; Nowaczynski et al. 1975; Fraser et al. 1976).

Clearly, there are a number of mechanisms that can result in increased infectious and noninfectious disease at increased densities and thus increase mortality.

Changes in Splenic Weight

The spleen is important in resistance to disease, and is an active hematopoietic tissue in rodents. It filters blood and removes senescent cells from the circulation by phagocytosis. The spleen responds to antigenic stimulation, especially particulate antigens, with a series of specific immune responses that result in the production of antibodies and produces lymphocytes and antibody-synthesizing plasma cells. Lymphoid tissue comprises the white pulp and is concentrated around arterioles and in nodules that are divided into T(hymus) and B(ursa) dependent areas. Germinal centers develop in the nodules. Because of the duality of splenic function, changes in weight may reflect different functions. It may enlarge in response to acute systemic infections, due in part to hyperplasia of myeloid and lymphatic cells and in part to congestion by erythrocytes. It can also enlarge as a result of hyperplasia of hematopoietic elements in response to anemia. On the other hand, increased glucocorticoids may drastically reduce the lymphoid tissue. Changes in splenic weight are the net result of relatively independent changes in different tissues of the spleen. There may be a marked increase in one tissue and a simultaneous decrease in another. For example, there may be a marked increase in hematopoietic tissue in response to anemia resulting from wounding and a marked decrease in lymphatic elements due to increased adrenocortical activity as a result of social strife (Rapp and Christian 1963; Blaine and Conaway 1969). The increased splenic hematopoiesis in these experiments involved all cellular elements of the blood. Blaine and Conaway (1969) suggested that the increased adrenocortical activity also resulted from wounding, but this interpretation was probably incorrect, since adrenocortical activity increases with descending rank and increased density with or without wounding (Christian 1959) or without physical contact between the animals (Bronson and Eleftheriou 1965). This will become more evident below. Splenic hypertrophy occurs in subordinate voles in the laboratory under similar circumstances (Clarke 1953).

Chitty (1958) observed splenic hypertrophy in natural populations of voles (*Microtus agrestis*) that appeared to be related to certain phases of population growth. The hypertrophy, associated with peripheral reticulocytosis and anemia, was due to marked congestion and hyperplasia of hemapoietic tissue, although there was a reduction in lymphoid elements. Further study indicated that the anemia, reticulocytosis, and splenic enlargement were greater in September and December than in March or May (Newson and Chitty 1962). Similar changes occurred in *Clethrionomys glareolus* in summer, but not in winter (Newson 1962). The changes were unrelated to reproductive status or age. Subsequent studies indicated that parasitemia might account for the blood destruction, anemia, compensatory splenic hematopoiesis, congestion, and splenic enlargement (Baker et al. 1963).

Splenic weights have been analyzed for 984 voles (*Microtus pennsylvanicus*) for 8 years from a population in southcentral Pennsylvania (LKY) and 297 voles for 10 years from a population in northeastern

Pennsylvania (PV), although data for the last 2 years of each study are still incomplete. Some of the data on reproduction, adrenal weights, and density of these populations have been published (Christian and Davis 1964, 1966; Christian 1971a,b,c, 1975, 1978). The PV population in five fields was trapped at irregular intervals through 1973, after which each field was sampled at least monthly. The southcentral population occupied 3,600 acres with a cover of tender grasses, clover, and other herbs (Snyder 1960; Davis et al. 1964; Christian and Davis 1966; Ludwig 1976). Details of trapping in 1959 through 1961 have been published (Christian and Davis 1966). No trapping was done in 1962–64. A more intensive monthly program of trapping began in March 1965 using about 400 traps for one or two nights. In October 1965 the trap effort was increased to a minimum of 1,200 traps for two nights monthly through 1970. Trapping was on a different, but similar and contiguous area each month so that no area was trapped more than once a year. In addition, there were two 400 and two 200-trap live-trapping grids.

Several relationships between splenic weight and body weight were examined in order to use all the splenic weights in a sample. The logarithms of splenic weight on body weight gave the best linear fits, the most uniform variances, and the highest correlation coefficients. The regressions calculated from these data included both sexes and all ages (table 4.1). The increase in splenic weight with respect to body weight was appreciably greater in the LKY than in the PV population. The

Table 4.1.   Regressions of Splenic Weights or Logarithms of Splenic Weights on Body Weight and on Population Indices (Means of Samples Used for Regressions on Population Indices) for PV and LKY Populations of *Microtus pennsylvanicus*

Splenic wt. vs. body wt.:
   LKY: ln spl. wt. = 3.074 + .053 body wt., g, $n = 984$, r = .41, $p < .0001$
   PV: ln spl. wt. = 3.709 + .0284 body wt., g, $n = 297$, $r = .48$, $p < .0001$

Splenic wt. vs. population indices
   Arithmetic: LKY: spl. wt. = 125.5 + .32 Pi, $n = 47$, $r = .016$
                      PV: spl. wt. = 93.2 − .038 Pi, $n = 11$, $r − .14$
   Logarithmic: LKY: ln spl. wt. = 4.605 + .00046 Pi, $n = 44$, $r = .031$
                       PV: ln spl. wt. = 4.517 − .00056 Pi, $n = 11$, $r = − .165$

Note: Difference in n for population indices due to omission of zero values for logs.

LKY spleens were generally larger and reached much greater individual values with many exceeding 400 mg, and some approaching 2 g, whereas only one 957-mg spleen from PV exceeded 400 mg. These differences occurred even though the maximum size of the LKY population was less than one fourth of that at PV (92 vs. 452 voles per 1,000 trap nights), and a higher proportion of the PV voles were captured in years of relatively high density. However, whether or not the *relative* densities of the two populations differed is not known, even though their numerical densities differed.

The splenic weight of each vole was adjusted for body weight using the regressions of logarithms of splenic weight on body weight. The means of these values were determined for each sample, and a number of comparisons were made within and between populations.

There was no difference in relative splenic weights between mature males and females in the PV population, but those of immature voles were greater than in adults ($p < .001$ for males and $p < .01$ for females). There was no difference in relative splenic weights between immature male and female voles. Similar comparisons have not been made yet for the LKY voles.

Neither arithmetic nor logarithmic values for splenic weight (the mean of the logarithms of relative spleen weights) were related to population size in either population (table 4.1). The fact that LKY voles had heavier spleens than those from the PV population, despite lower densities, supports this conclusion.

Splenic weight did not vary significantly with time of year and in the LKY population, for which there were more data for every month, the combined mean relative splenic weights for May through August did not differ from those for November through March ($t = .99$, 38 d.f.) (table 4.2). The data for the PV population have not yet been examined from this point of view.

Splenic weight was uncorrelated ($r = .034$) with severity of

Table 4.2. Means of the Mean Sample Means of Splenic Weight vs. Time of Year for the LKY Population of Voles

	Jan.–Feb.	Mar.–Apr.	May–June	July–Aug.	Sept.–Oct.	Nov.–Dec.
Mean	128.9	126.3	123.2	106.6	136.1	134.1
Std. error	18.4(7)	11.0(12)	7.2(11)	16.4(9)	13.1(8)	19.0(7)

Note: *n* is in parentheses.

wounding from fighting (including animals without wounds). In fact, the mean relative weight of the spleens from voles in April and early May from the PV population, when all males were wounded (Christian 1971c), was 74.25% of reference values for animals of their size, well below that of many other samples without wounding from either population. The mean relative splenic weight for severely scarred males (grades 4 and 5) was 70.5 ± 23.1, while it was 78.7 ± 9.4 for lightly scarred voles (grades 1 and 2). The fact that relative splenic weight was the same in male and female voles, although the latter were rarely wounded, supports this conclusion.

Since relative splenic weight was less in mature than in immature female voles, it is unlikely the pregnancy or lactation per se affected splenic weight. However, splenic weight in late vs. early pregnancy was examined for both populations. Splenic weights of pregnant voles were greater in the LKY than in the PV populations, and in both populations those with embryos less than 15 mm long had higher relative spleen weights than those with larger embryos (table 4.3). Clearly, splenic weight is not greater in females in late pregnancy than in those in early pregnancy.

In summary, splenic weight in meadow voles from two populations did not vary with sex, season, density, or degree of injury due to fighting, but did vary with maturity and stage of pregnancy, and was different in the two populations. The reason for the difference cannot be explained, although ectoparasites might be a factor: trombiculid mites, possibly vectors for blood parasites of *Microtus*, were very abundant in the LKY area, but were absent from PV.

Table 4.3. Mean Relative Splenic Weights and Their Standard Errors for All Visibly Pregnant Female *Microtus* Relative to the Length (CR) of the Embryos

Population	n	<15mm CR	n	>15 mm CR	Significance of differences between sp. wts. re embryo size
LKY	138	116.0 ± 6.6	47	83.3 ± 9.9	$t = 2.75, p < .01$
PV	38	81.1 ± 6.9	12	44.0 ± 4.8	$t = 4.42, p < .001$

Significance of differences between populations:

	176	$t = 3.66$	59	$t = 3.57$
		$p < .001$		$p < .002$

Reproduction

Natality is the only major positive input into the population equation. The other major force—mortality—is negative, with only the amplitude of negativity changing. The third force—movement—is usually negative in natural populations of small mammals, although it can be positive (immigration), particularly in unsaturated environments.

The intensity of reproduction is determined by genetic, physiological, and environmental factors, so that productivity in the long run balances mortality and movement, often by direct compensatory mechanisms. However, in shorter time periods, such as a single year or only a few years, there may not be a balance, and populations may fluctuate rather strikingly. Mortality appears to be a relatively constant factor in that life expectancies of small mammals vary little—no more than a month or two—at different times of the year. To slow and limit the rate of population growth, mortality must affect an increasing proportion of the population (i.e., it will be density-dependent), and it also must increasingly exceed the rate of recruitment. However, there are few, if any, quantitative data demonstrating that mortality is density-dependent in a population. Obviously, if breeding ceases, mortality will exceed recruitment and result in a decline in a population. However, such evidence as there is suggests that mortality follows a negative exponential curve and therefore affects a constant proportion of the population and therefore acts in density-independent fashion. Mortality generally seems to lag behind natality. Predation, a particular form of mortality, may account for the loss of enormous numbers of animals, but experiments indicate that predation seldom controls and limits population growth (see Christian 1979), although it may act in density-dependent fashion to prolong periods of low density following population peaks. In fact, the population of prey more often regulates the populations of predators. Reproductive rate and its changes seem to be the most important variable leading to fluctuations in populations of small mammals in temperate and subarctic regions with adequate precipitation. Therefore, the balance of this paper will discuss changes in reproductive function in response to environmental factors, particularly population density. However, some basic aspects of reproduction in *Microtus pennsylvanicus* will be covered first.

Factors in Reproduction of *Microtus pennsylvanicus*

Litter Size vs. Maternal Size. When population density reached its maximum size in the PV population, the mean number of embryos per gravidum reached a maximum of 6.95 ± .42 ($n = 22$) and females also were larger at this time. The mean gravidal size was significantly larger by at least one than those at any other time (Christian, 1978). The number of embryos per gravidum varied significantly with maternal body weight for females from the PV population for 1966 through 1975 (fig. 4.10).

Gravidal size = 2.59 + .062 (maternal wt., g), $n = 157$

Thus, gravidal size increases by an average of one embryo for each increase of 16 g in maternal weight.

Pup Size vs. Litter Size. Data on the realtionship of pup weight at 10 and 21 days after birth to litter size were obtained from our laboratory colony of *M. pennsylvanicus*, although the data are limited. The following equations were obtained (weight in grams):

At 10 days of age: Pup wt. = 8.78 − .33 (litter size), $n = 42, p < .05$

At 21 days of age: Pup wt. = 20.88 − 1.15 (litter size), $n = 32, p < .02$

Pup weight decreases significantly as litter size increases in voles, as in house mice and rats. If the relationship continues to follow the pattern in rats, voles from large litters may be permanently stunted. An increase in litter size from 4 to 7, the mean size at peak density (Christian 1978), results in a 21% decline in pup weight. Stunting of this sort may explain in part the smaller sizes of voles for 1 year or more after peak densities, and, since the voles are smaller, may also partly explain reduced litter sizes.

Pup Weight vs. Maternal Weight. From the regressions for pup weight on litter size and for gravidal size on maternal weight, the following relationships can be derived:

Pup wt. at 10 days = 7.93 − .02 (maternal wt.)

Pup wt. at 21 days = 17.9 − .71 (maternal wt.)

Constancy of Gravidal Size. The number of viable embryos *in utero* closely reflects litter size at birth, since there is only a slight, statistically insignificant, decrease in gravidal size between the time pregnancy is first visible and birth (fig. 4.1). This is true for all densities in both populations and at all times from April to October for which sufficient data are available:

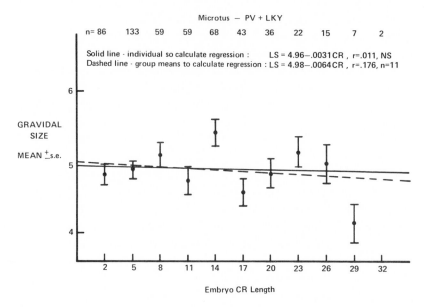

Figure 4.1.   Gravidal size in *Microtus pennsylvanicus* versus embryo crown-rump length in 3-mm intervals. The number of gravida in each sample is shown at the top. Regressions of gravidal size on embryo size were calculated for individual values ($n =$ 533) and for means of embryo sizes ($n = 11$). The data from northeastern Pennsylvania (PV) and southcentral Pennsylvania (LKY) were combined since there was no difference between the two. These data and those in figure 1.3 indicate that there is not a significant loss of partial gravida in these *Microtus*.

April and May: gravidal size $= 5.32 - .0087$ (crown-rump length); $n = 9, r = .146$
June: gravidal size $= 5.28 - .0044$ crown-rump length; $n = 10, r = -.976$
Aug.–Oct: gravidal size $= 4.96 - .0057$ crown-rump length; $n = 10, r = -.072$
Gravidal size did not vary with parity in these populations, although parous voles usually had only one prior litter, and rarely three or more; so variation with parity would have very little effect on gravidal size, productivity, and population growth.

Thus, the loss of partial gravida *in utero* is small, and is consistent with the 1.8% resorption rate reported by Hamilton (1941) in *M. pennsylvanicus*.

Loss of Entire Gravida. In contrast to the low losses of partial gravida, the loss of whole gravida is high. Plotting the number of gravida against embryo length reveals a striking, apparently exponential, decline in the number of viable gravida as embryonic size increases in *Microtus pennsylvanicus*, *Peromyscus leucopus*, and *Peromyscus maniculatus* (figs. 4.2 and 4.3). It can be shown that embryonic crown-rump length increases approximately linearly with time, with a small

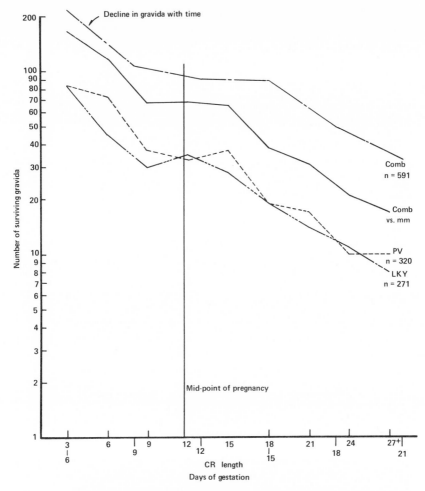

Figure 4.2. Logarithms of the number of gravida in a given 3-mm interval of embryo crown-rump (CR) length plotted against embryo length for *Microtus pennsylvanicus* from the PV and LKY populations, separately and combined, and the combined data plotted against day of gestation. Clearly, the decline in the number of gravida as CR length or day of gestation increases is approximately exponential. The equivalence of days of gestation and embryo size were extrapolated from Hoffmann (1958), Rugh (1968), and Ozdzenski and Mystkowska (1976). Either the CR length was measured directly (80 for PV and 139 for LKY) or it was derived from the maximum uterine swelling diameter by subtracting 2 mm. The latter practice was derived from instances when both measurements were made. Uterine swellings less than 2 mm in diameter were simply called very early pregnancy. Hoffmann (1958), Mallory and Clulow (1977), Layne (1968), and others indicate that the blastocyst implants late on day 4 of gestation in *Microtus* and *Peromyscus*. Increased vascularity and swelling of the uterus can be detected grossly at this time. Data from these and other sources indicate that embryo length increases linearly with day of gestation. The cube root of embryo weight also is linear with CR length of the embryo. The time scale obviously could be shifted somewhat without altering the nature of the conclusions based on these data.

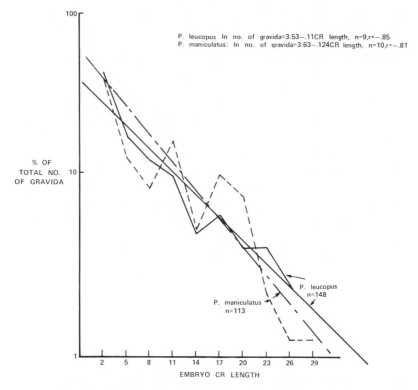

Figure 4.3.   Logarithms of the percentages of gravida in each size category of embryos plotted
against embryo size for *Peromyscus leucopus* and *Peromyscus maniculatus*. The
data from several populations are pooled. The decline in the number of gravida is
approximately exponential with embryo size. Thus, the greatest losses occur before
mid-term, which is at an embryo size of about 8–10 mm CR. The percentages of
the losses that occur before a length of 8 mm is reached is 74% for *P. leucopus* and
54% for *P. maniculatus*, although the total losses to term, estimated to be when an
embryo size of 26 mm is reached, are about the same (92–95%), so more are lost
in late pregnancy in *P. maniculatus*. However, birth may occur in many instances
before the embryos reach this size. Presumed losses in species other than *Microtus*
are largely conjecture and must be regarded as such since there are no data to
establish a relation between time and embryo size. However, extrapolating from
data for other species one arrives at figures for loss of gravida of roughly the same
magnitude.

increase in slope beginning about day 16 (Hoffman 1958; Rugh 1968;
Ozdzenski and Mystkowska 1976; Mallory and Clulow 1977; and present data). Using these various data, equivalence of embryo size and
day of gestation can be determined (fig. 4.2). In addition, the time-

length equivalence allows further analyses in terms of length alone. The data for *Microtus* are adequate for further examination, but are not adequate for *Peromyscus*.

Variation with Duration of Pregnancies. These apparent losses of young *in utero* might be accounted for in several ways: (1) loss of females due to death or movement, (2) loss of whole gravida, (3) changes in trappability of females as pregnancy advances, or (4) some combination of these. Also, there may be a variation in the size at which pups are born. Data of Mallory and Clulow (1978) indicate that pups are born when they reach a crown-rump (CR) length of 28–29 mm. However, we find young *in utero* up to 33 mm CR. A change in the number of females captured due to pregnancy is unlikely, since the ratios of pregnant and parous voles to the total number of females are almost identical to those for mature to immature males (table 4.4). There is no evidence that pregnant *M. pennsylvanicus* alter their patterns of movement until near term or after the young are born (Madison, 1978). The "rates" of loss are nearly the same in two quite different localities (fig. 4.4):

LKY: ln no. of gravida = 4.480 − .087 CR length
PV: ln no. of gravida = 4.696 − .092 CR length

Hoffman (1958) shows similar losses for *Microtus montanus* from the Sierra Nevadas. If predation were the primary cause, differences between localities and times might be expected. Furthermore, there is a close similarity in the loss of gravida with respect to embryo size in the three different species. If the numbers of gravida are expressed as percentages to adjust for differences in total numbers, the regressions of the logarithms of the numbers of gravida on embryo size are fairly similar for *P. maniculatus*, *P. leucopus*, and *M. pennsylvanicus*:

M. pennsylvanicus: ln percent of gravida = 3.53 − .091 CR length
P. leucopus: ln percent of gravida = 3.53 − .112 CR length
P. maniculatus: ln percent of gravida = 3.63 − .124 CR length

The decline in the number of viable gravida with increasing embryo size for *Microtus*, using the data from both populations, is as follows:

ln no. gravida = 5.305 − .091 CR length

Gravidal losses apparently vary somewhat with density, but the differences are not great at least for the present data. Data from the LKY population from April through June of years with moderately high densities (1959, 1960, 1966) were compared with those for the same months of years of low density (1961, 1967–69) (fig. 4.5). The

Table 4.4. Combined Data from LKY and PV Populations on Reproductive Function for Spring and Summer

	Total voles	Total females	Both sexes: total immat.	Mature Total	No. preg. and parous	No. preg.	No. parous	No. lactating	Immat. per preg. female	Immat. per parous female	Immat. per lactating female	Immat. per mat. female
								Mature Females				
15 April–12 May	492	222	45	209	181	158	45	28	.28	1.00	1.61	.22
15 May–30 June	667	350	263	246	212	167	150	81	1.57	1.75	3.25	1.07
July	359	168	130	122	97	66	71	36	1.97	1.83	3.61	1.07
August	178	110	46	91	82	65	56	33	.71	.82	1.39	.51
Total	1,696	850	484	668	572	456	322	178	1.06	1.50	2.72	.72

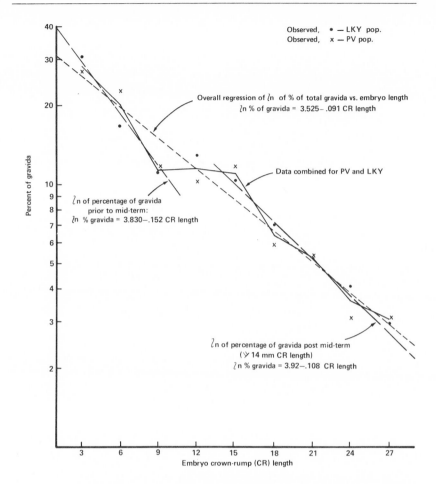

Figure 4.4.   Logarithms of the percentages of the gravida in each size category plotted against
3-mm intervals of embryonic CR length for *Microtus* from PV and LKY. Percentages are used to make the data from the two populations comparable. Regressions,
as shown, were fitted for the combined data from the two populations. The overall decline in numbers is approximately exponential, but the decline through day
10 is faster than that after day 16. There appears to be little loss between days
10 and 16.

differences in survival of gravida are slight although a vertical life table
indicates a significant difference (fig. 4.6). However, the survival of
gravida to birth was significantly lower in decreasing than in peak or
increasing populations of *Microtus pennsylvanicus* at PV and vicinity
(Geller 1978).

Because of the similarity of the overall data for *Microtus* from PV

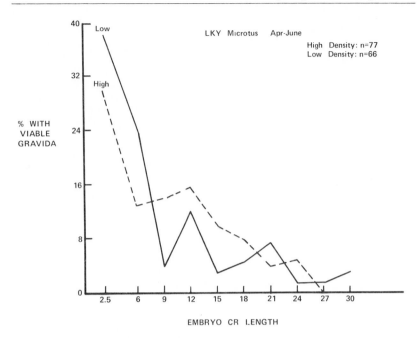

Figure 4.5.   Decline in the number of gravida (as percentages of the whole sample for each
category of density) with respect to embryo size for years of low density and years
of moderately high density from the LKY population of *Microtus*. The losses early
in pregnancy are apparently greater at low than at higher density, whereas the
reverse seems to be true for the second half of pregnancy.

and LKY, the data on gravida were combined and examined further.
The number of gravida at days 20 and 21 of gestation were only 15%
of the number in initial numbers (fig. 4.2). However, since the rest of
the data were grouped into 3-day intervals, adjusting the number for
the last 2 days accordingly gives 49.5 gravida—the same number as in
the preceding 3-day interval. Thus, only 23% of the initial 219 gravida
presumably survived to birth. Of the 169 gravida lost, 75% were lost
prior to midterm and the remaining 25% were lost between days 11
and 17. Figure 4.7 illustrates the high rate of loss during the first half
of pregnancy in terms of embryo length.

Life tables based on embryo length show that the expectancies of
survival to larger sizes or to birth are similar for both the PV and LKY
populations, regardless of whether the data for all females are used or
only the data from April through June for all years. Thus, the differences in survival to term, such as with differences in density, are

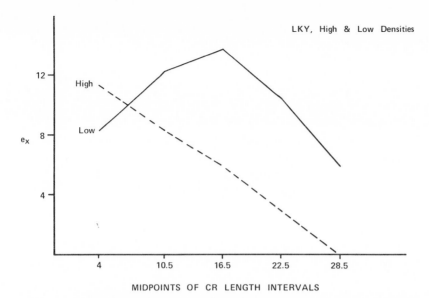

LKY, High & Low Densities

MIDPOINTS OF CR LENGTH INTERVALS

Figure 4.6. Life tables were constructed from the data plotted in figure 4.5, and remaining life
expectancy, e_x is plotted against embryo size. Survival of gravida was better at low
than at higher densities, despite the fact that the difference in the actual numbers of
gravida surviving was not great (fig. 4.2). The decline in e_x is approximately linear
with increasing embryo size at the higher densities, indicating a more uniform rate
of loss with respect to embryo size.

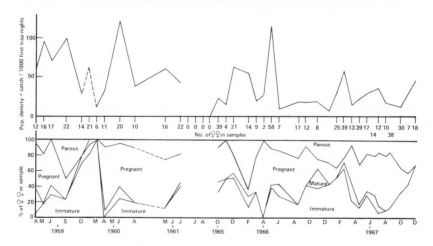

Figure 4.7. History of the LKY population for 1959–61 and 1965–67 in terms of relative density and percentages of the females in different categories of reproductive activity
for each sample. The apparent minor peak in population size in January 1960 had
to be due either to movement or to response to bait, since it would be impossible
to explain by reproduction.

small, but must be very significant for population growth and decline. A more meaningful interpretation of these data might be possible if samples were large enough for constructing age-specific life tables, since the gravida of young females may have somewhat different survival than those of older voles. However, the fact remains that gravidal loss must be great in all age groups; furthermore, the prevalence of lactation was lowest in April and early May, when all females were large and had overwintered (table 4.4).

The only reasonable explanation for these data seems to be that losses of whole gravida are extremely high in natural populations of this species, regardless of density, season, social factors, or other environmental variables. Clearly, changes in food cannot be a factor, because of the uniformity of the losses regardless of season, locality, and species, whether granivores or herbivores. Also, the losses are the same for pregnant nulliparous voles as for pregnant, parous, lactating, or nonlactating voles. In general, these data are consistent with the high percentage of parous, nonlactating females in these populations, as well as with the proportion of immature to mature voles captured during spring and early summer, the only period when inhibition of maturation is not a complicating factor (table 4.4). The number of immature voles captured cannot provide a reliable quantitative estimate of the number of young born, but it does give a crude relative indication. Losses of young obviously cannot be considered further because the appropriate data are not available. However, the numbers of parous females that are lactating may give a better indication of the number of litters actually born (table 4.4). An average of 52.5% of the parous females were lactating during the height of the spring breeding season, but this is an overestimate, since it is difficult to detect placental scars of past pregnancy in pregnant uteri beyond the first few days after implantation. Probably considerably fewer than 50% of the parous females were lactating. In many parous females, the mammae were prelactational with no evidence of lactation, suckling, or recent birth. Many of these females undoubtedly reflected the loss of entire gravida. These data suggest that a minimum of 50% of the gravida were lost *in utero*.

The number of pregnant females lost due to mortality (mainly predation) or emigration during the 17 days of visible pregnancy can be estimated on the basis of a mean life expectancy of 3 months for these voles during the snow-free portion of the year, and the fact that declines in the numbers of these voles generally follow a negative exponential curve (Christian 1971b). A total of 27 of the 219, or 12–13%, of the pregnant voles in the original cohort were estimated to have been lost during the 17 days of implantation. This number accounts for 16% of the losses, and even twice this number would leave over half of the losses unaccounted for. The higher figure may be more nearly correct, since females nursing pups are more subject to predation than are other mature females (Madison 1978). Nevertheless, mortality or predation cannot account for the majority of losses of viable gravida. Postimplantation disruption of pregnancy by the presence of a strange male may account for part of the losses of whole gravida in wild voles and mice (Kenney et al. 1977), and increased levels of ACTH and adrenal glucocorticoids accompanied by decreased secretion of gonadotropins may explain other losses (Christian 1975). However, further research is required for any conclusions to be drawn with regard to the causes of this natural intrauterine mortality.

Inhibition of Reproduction

Partial or complete inhibition of reproductive function is a common correlate of increased density, or subordinate social rank, in natural and experimental populations. In this regard, increased density depresses reproductive function as it does many other kinds of stress. Aggressive interactions result in diminished secretion of gonadotropins and increases adrenocortical activity (Bronson et al. 1973). These responses are much more pronounced in subordinate than in dominant animals.*

In experimental populations of mice, reproductive function is inversely related to the logarithm of population size (Christian 1971a). In snowshoe hares the reproductive rate is inversely related to population size. The seasonal pattern of secretion of pituitary gonadotropins parallels changes in litter size; and reproductive function and pituitary gonadotropins decrease with increasing density, at least during the increasing phase of the population (Davis and Meyer 1973). Inhibition

*Editors' Note: The inhibition of reproductive function through a combination of density and subordinate social rank is discussed for wolf populations by Packard and Mech and for populations of rodents by Terman and by Lloyd. The same phenomenon in primates is discussed by Sade and may be implied in the conclusions of Southwick et al. Possibly in contrast is Freedman's conclusion that among human beings there is no evidence of comparable density-related inhibition of reproductive function.

of reproductive function is a graded response that may involve all levels of reproductive function from maturation and gametogenesis through lactation. The stage of the reproductive process at which the inhibition becomes evident may also be a graded response, probably reflecting the degree of inhibition of gonadotrophin secretion. At peak densities, there may be total inhibition of reproductive function in voles, lemmings, and mice of all ages, but at lower densities inhibition of maturation may be the primary effect, usually accompanied by inhibition of growth, whereas mature animals are only partially affected.* In addition, the degree of inhibition varies with social rank within a population. The dominant animals may be unaffected, whereas the degree of inhibition may increase as rank decreases, so that the lowest ranking animals may experience total inhibition. The degree of inhibition also varies with species, sex, season, maturity, and probably other factors.

In natural populations, the responses to changes in population size may be seen on an annual or multiannual basis; that is, each year as numbers increase during the breeding season, the effects may be reflected by inhibition of maturation or even of adult reproductive function. Over a number of years, the maximum densities in each year often vary greatly, particularly in "cyclic" species, with the result that in years of peak densities there may be complete cessation of reproductive function, whereas in years of low densities the young may continue to mature throughout the breeding season. The length of the breeding season also reflects these differences in numbers. In years of high density, the breeding season may be very short, whereas at low densities it may extend well into autumn (Christian 1961). Whether or not breeding in late autumn or winter reflects differences in density is unclear. Winter breeding may simply reflect survival of small numbers of mature voles into winter from the preceding breeding season and intensive enough sampling to catch them.

Reproductive Function in the LKY and PV Populations of Microtus. Figure 4.7 illustrates the changes in the relative abundance of fe-

Editors' Note: The inhibition of growth and maturation by social constraints in populations of wolves is discussed by Packard and Mech. The same phenomenon among laboratory rodents is discussed by Terman and by Lloyd. Observations by Sade on differential rates of maturation in dominant and subordinate lineages of rhesus monkeys should also be noted. The human literature in this volume is silent on this point although possible nutritional effects on sexual maturation are discussed by Cohen.

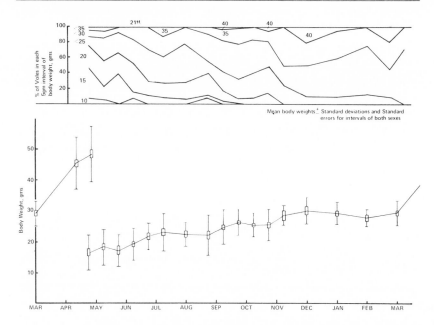

Figure 4.8.   (*Top*) Numbers of immature voles from the PV population in various categories of body weight with years and sexes combined. (*Bottom*) Mean body weights and their standard deviations and standard errors for immature voles from the population. These data illustrate the inhibition of growth (and maturation) that begins in July and continues until the following March.

males in each general reproductive category for 6 years in the LKY population of *Microtus pennsylvanicus*. In 1959 densities were generally higher in spring than in the following year, although the numbers were apparently somewhat greater in June 1960. The percentage of pregnant females in the spring of 1960 indicates that breeding intensity was much greater than in the same period in 1959. The high prevalence of pregnancy presumably led to the sharp peak in numbers in June 1960. In all years there was an increase in the number of immature voles from April to June, followed by a decline in July, reflecting the maturation of immature voles and their entry into the population. At the same time, additional young were being produced, and the numbers of immature voles rose steadily from July or August until, by late autumn or winter, they comprised the bulk of the population. The time of the start of this increase in 1959–60 was in part a function of the times of sampling, but from 1965 on (there were *no* voles captured from March through September in 1965), sampling was frequent and

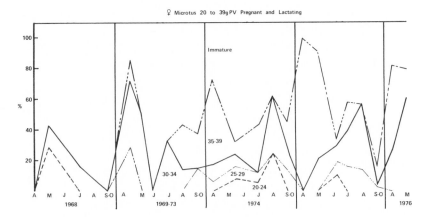

Figure 4.9.   Percentages of female voles from the PV population weighing 39 g or less which
were either sexually inactive (immature) or pregnant and/or lactating in samples
collected from 1968 to 1976.

intensive enough to provide accurate dates for the beginning of the
accumulation of immature voles. The data indicate that the accumulation of inhibited immature voles began much earlier in 1967 than in
1966; also, the number of pregnant voles remained higher in 1967 than
in 1966. Rapid growth of immature voles stopped at between 25 and
35 g and increased very slowly thereafter until March–April, when
rapid growth and maturation resumed.

Similar retardation of growth occurred in the PV populations (fig.
4.8) and in other populations and species of *Microtus* (Barbehenn
1955; Martinet and Meunier 1969; Martinet et al. 1971; Brown 1973;
Worth et al. 1973). There were pregnant voles in the LKY population
during late autumn or winter in every year for which data are available
except 1967 (fig. 4.7). The magnitude and timing of the events, including the duration and termination of the breeding season and productivity of the population, are functions of density (Christian 1961,
1971b). The effects of density are greatest on the younger members of
the population, as indicated by inhibition of maturation and the numbers becoming productive in the year of their birth (fig. 4.9). When
densities are low, young *Microtus* may reach sexual maturity at a very
early age and have low body weights. The differences between annual
densities are most conspicuous after June, although they may be seen
earlier. These differences are shown most clearly by the numbers of

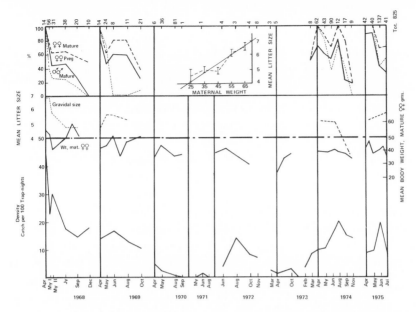

Figure 4.10. History of the PV population of *Microtus* from 1968 to July 1975 (data are not complete yet for August 1975 through 1976). The relative densities are given at the bottom, average weights of mature females and average gravidal size are shown above the density. At the top are graphs showing the percentages of mature males and females in the samples. Sample sizes are given across the top. Numbers of pregnant females were too small from 1970 through 1972 to plot gravidal sizes and percentages of mature voles. The inset shows litter size, based on gravidal size (see the text for a justification for using gravidal size), plotted against maternal weight for 157 females from the PV population. Gravidal size = 2.59 + .062 (maternal wt., g). Data for LKY voles have not yet been similarly analyzed.

females in the 20- to 39-g range of body weights that are pregnant or are parous. Inevitably, there is some confounding with those exhibiting inhibited growth, but it is minimized if only sexually mature voles are considered. Figure 4.9 illustrates data on voles of this size from the PV population. The PV population reached a peak density of more than 200 voles per acre in 1968 (Christian, 1978; Geller, 1978) (fig. 4.10). The years 1974 and 1975 may have been aborted peak years, although maximum densities reached on the study area were less than half of those reached in 1968. Numbers declined sharply in 1976. Sampling was more frequent and more intensive in 1974–75 than in preceding years. Densities were too low in 1970 through 1973 to provide meaningful samples. Figures 4.9 and 4.10 illustrate how few voles reached maturity in 1968 in contrast to 1974 and 1975. The question raised by these and similar data from other populations of small mammals is how changes in density bring about these differences in reproduction and growth.

Mechanisms of Inhibition of Reproduction and Growth

Aggression. Increased density apparently acts by increasing the number of aggressive encounters between sexually mature or pubertal voles, although there are differences between the sexes in the way they respond to changes in population status (Christian 1978). Aggressive behavior, together with numbers of animals, elicits increased hypothalamo-hypophyseal-adrenocortical activity and inhibition of reproductive function, particularly maturation and growth. Aggressive behavior, especially if there is no physical combat, acts as a psychogenic stress, stimulating increased ACTH secretion in subordinate animals. If physical combat is also a factor, it probably acts in addition as a systemic stress. Aggressive behavior in house mice, and probably in male voles, depends on circulating levels of androgens and on postnatal and pubertal exposure to androgens (Barkley and Goldman 1977a,b; Vom Saal et al. 1976). In natural populations young male voles are not involved in aggressive encounters until there is significant secretion of testosterone, as indicated by enlargement of the seminal vesicles (Christian 1971c). Experiments with house mice have supported this conclusion (McKinney and Desjardins 1973; Barkley and Goldman 1977b). However, once mature levels of testosterone and aggressive behavior are attained, additional androgens will not increase aggression and may even decrease it (Grunt and Young 1953; Bevan et al. 1957; Leshner 1975; Barkley and Goldman 1977a). In conformance with these results, Turner and Iverson (1973) found an annual cycle of intraspecific aggression in *M. pennsylvanicus* in which increased aggression coincided with the breeding season and sexual activity. Other factors may affect aggressive behavior and hence the level of aggression in a population. The pineal may modulate aggressive behavior and affect dominance relationships, apparently acting through effects on the reproductive system (McKinney et al. 1975). The acquisition and retention of fear-motivated conditioned-avoidance responses to attack and defeat are facilitated by ACTH (de Wied 1977), and ACTH may also reduce aggression in subordinate animals (Leshner et al. 1973; Poole and Brain 1974, 1975). The fact that significant amounts of ACTH have been found in parts of the brain may be related to these effects (Krieger et al. 1977; Pacold et al. 1978).

Interspecific aggression may elicit the same behavioral and endocrine responses as intraspecific aggression. Female *P. leucopus* are aggressive toward, and dominant over, *M. pennsylvanicus* (Rowley and Christian 1977). The effects of other species would probably be greatest when the population of one species is high and expanding.

Cross-System Feedback Inhibition of Reproductive Function. ACTH stimulates increased steroidogenesis by the adrenal, which results in increased secretion of glucocorticoids, 18-hydroxycorticoids, adrenal androgens, estrogens, and progesterone (Shaikh and Shaikh 1975). The androgens, estrogens, and progesterone may act as feedback inhibitors of gonadotrophin secretion (Christian et al. 1965; Andrews et al. 1975b; Ogle 1977). In addition, ACTH inhibits reproductive function directly without the mediation of the adrenals in house mice, *Peromyscus*, and rats (Christian et al. 1965; Jarrett 1965; Pasley and Christian 1972; Ogle 1977). ACTH also inhibits reproductive function in intact voles (*M. pennsylvanicus*) and in grasshopper mice (*Onychomys leucogaster*) (Pasley and Christian 1971; McKinney and Pasley 1974). This action of ACTH is mediated by opiate receptors in the CNS, since naloxone, an opiate antagonist, blocks ACTH-induced reproductive inhibition (Yasukawa et al. 1978). Methionine enkephalin significantly decreases LH secretion by decreasing LRH secretion from the hypothalamus and increases secretion of growth hormone (GH) and prolactin (Bruni et al. 1977; Muraki et al. 1977). Since opiates have similar effects, endogenous endorphins may also inhibit reproduction. Any stress that stimulates increased ACTH and endorphin secretion may inhibit reproductive function through the action of either or both substances at opioid-binding sites.

The effects of density and of ACTH in inhibiting reproductive function vary with species. Their actions on laboratory rats, although real, are considerably less than those on female house mice, whereas their effects in *Peromyscus* and *Microtus* of both sexes are profound, with the former apparently more sensitive than the latter. Terman and his colleagues (Terman 1968, 1969, 1973; Thomas and Terman 1975) have demonstrated that increased density profoundly depresses reproductive function in *Peromyscus maniculatus* and for prolonged periods after the mice have been removed from the population.

Other forms of chronic psychogenic stress or psychogenic stress with a systemic component, such as immobilization, similarly inhibit reproductive function by markedly suppressing LH and FSH secretion (Euker and Riegle 1973; Blake 1975; Taché et al. 1976; Gray et al. 1977). Secretion of GH is also inhibited (Taché et al. 1976).

The effects of social subordination, density, and immobilization presumably act, at least in part, through the hypothalamus and intermediate pituitary to release ACTH. However, the adrenal cortex responds to immobilization with increased synthesis and secretion of corticosterone in the absence of the pituitary, although the magnitude of the response is about one tenth of that in intact rats (Ventura et al. 1977). Either there is an extrapituitary source of ACTH that responds to psychogenic stress, or the response of the adrenal cortex is neurally mediated. There is evidence for both, but their roles have not been clarified. Compensatory adrenal hypertrophy (CAH) is neurally mediated (Dallman et al. 1977), and there are significant amounts of bioactive ACTH in amygdala of the rat brain (Pacold et al. 1978), but whether or not it enters the peripheral circulation in significant amounts is unknown.

*Inhibition of Maturation-accelerating Pheromones.** Social subordination, or the presence of pregnant or lactating females, suppresses the activity of the androgen-dependent urinary pheromone in male mice, which accelerates maturation of females (Lombardi and Vendenbergh 1977). Therefore, the social environment may inhibit maturation. Since subordination also increases ACTH, adrenal androgen, and presumably endorphin secretion, ACTH and related peptides may mediate the inhibition of the pheromone. If this is the case, naloxone should inhibit the block.

The foregoing discussions suggest that there are several mechanisms that can inhibit reproductive function, that opioid receptors probably are involved, and that endorphins may be a factor. Increased secretion of adrenal androgens also can inhibit maturation by acting at the hypothalamus to inhibit LRH release or at the pituitary to inhibit gonadotropin release (Varon and Christian 1963; Duckett et al. 1963). Additional mechanisms may also be involved.

Changes in Hypothalamic Sensitivity to Inhibitory Feedbacks. (1) *Effect of maturity.* Early studies of the effects of increased density on

---

Editors' Note: Maturation accelerating pheromones in rodents and primates are discussed further by Drickamer.

reproduction suggested that immature mice or voles were more sensitive to reproductive inhibition than are mature animals. The difference could be explained either by differences in social rank or by a difference in sensitivity to negative feedbacks, but the latter seemed to be the more likely and more important. There was evidence to support this view, but more recent evidence clearly demonstrated the much greater sensitivity of the hypophyseal-hypothalamic system in immature than in mature animals to inhibition of gonadotropin release by sex steroids (Negro-Vilar et al. 1973).

(2) *Increased density.* Group caging increases the sensitivity of female rats to inhibition of reproductive function by ACTH (Cohen and Mann 1979). The ACTH delayed maturation, presumably by acting on the hypothalamus to inhibit the release of LRH.

(3) *Photoperiod and the pineal gland.* Decreased photoperiod renders the hypothalamus more sensitive to feedback inhibition of gonadotropin secretion by sex steroids. Significantly smaller amounts of testosterone or estrogen are required to inhibit LH secretion in rats and hamsters in short than in long photoperiods (Hoffmann and Cullin 1976; Tamarkin et al. 1976b; Turek 1977b). Similarly, there is an annual rhythm of sensitivity in ewes to inhibition of LH secretion by estrogen, with the greatest sensitivity during the annual period of diestrus, March to September, and the least during the breeding season, from October to February (Legan et al. 1977). Female rats maintained under constant-light conditions also exhibit an annual rhythm in sensitivity to inhibition of reproductive function by ACTH (Cohen and Mann 1979). Rats raised on short days (L:D 8:16) in February were by far the most sensitive to the inhibitory action of ACTH on maturation, while those raised in August under the same conditions of photoperiod were the least sensitive. The degree of sensitivity varied with season between these two limits. However, they were more sensitive at all times than rats raised on long days (L:D 14:10). The latter exhibited no seasonal change in response to ACTH.

Seasonal reproduction in many mammals is either regulated by changes in length of daily photoperiods or photoperiod plus endogenous annual rhythms. In *Phodopus, Mesocricetus, Microtus, Clethrionomys, Peromyscus,* and probably many other species of small mammals, increasing daily photoperiod stimulates reproductive function, whereas decreasing photoperiod inhibits it. Photoperiod achieves these effects by stimulating or inhibiting the secretion of gonadotropins. For example, LH levels in *Microtus agrestis* rise during the breeding season in nature or on long photoperiods in the laboratory (Worth et al. 1973). Evidently, the critical length of daily photoperiod is 12.5 hours, since daily periods of light longer than this stimulate and those shorter inhibit reproductive function (Breed and Clarke 1970; Turek et al. 1976a). These data suggest that the breeding season in photoperiodic small mammals should begin around March 21 and end about September 21, depending to some extent on latitude and other environmental variables. By and large this normally seems to be true, for example, in *Peromyscus* in temperate environments, and at low or moderate densities, but *Microtus* often continues to breed into October or even November, and some large, mature individuals may breed at any time (fig. 4.9), suggesting that changing photoperiod is not the sole determinant of the breeding season in these voles. Also, spermatogenesis either may begin or recommence in late November or early December in *Peromyscus leucopus* (Christian, unpublished).

In the laboratory, alfalfa harvested late in the season, short photoperiods, and high temperature (33°C) combine to inhibit reproduction and growth in *Microtus arvalis*, whereas long photoperiods, early alfalfa and lower temperature (5°C) stimulate reproductive activity (Martinet 1966; Martinet and Meunier 1969; Martinet et al. 1971). However, these results fail to explain the marked variations in the length of the breeding season, the inhibition of growth and maturation of young that occurs early in the breeding season in some years, or the persistence of breeding into late autumn, well after food supplies have been repeatedly frozen, in *Microtus*, *Clethrionomys*, and sometimes in other species (fig. 4.7; Kalela 1957; Clarke and Forsyth 1964; Mysterud et al. 1972; Larsson et al. 1973). The correlation between food and reproduction and growth is poor in these circumstances. In addition, deprivation of light alone caused a marked inhibition of growth and reproductive function in *Microtus montanus* (Vaughan et al. 1973), while long daily photoperiod (L:D 18:6) accelerated growth compared to short days (L:D 6:18) (Petterborg 1978). Body growth of *Phodopus sungorus* was also significantly greater in long (16:8) than in short (8:16) photogperiods. Finally, photoperiod has very little effect on reproductive function in collared lemmings (*Dicrostonyx groenlandicus*) (Hasler et al. 1976), although the population dynamics of this species are essentially the same as those of other lemmings and voles (Krebs

1964). These results suggest that decreasing photoperiod alone can account for inhibition of growth, although other factors may be involved in certain circumstances. A variety of stressful stimuli, including psychogenic stress, inhibit secretion of GH, and there seems to be a reciprocal relationship between GH and ACTH in rodents (Kokka et al. 1972; Krulich et al. 1974; Seggie and Brown 1975; Rice and Critchlow 1976; Taché et al. 1976; Terry et al. 1976).

Short photoperiods inhibit the secretion of gonadotrophins, while long photoperiods increase LH secretion in voles and other species (Charlton et al. 1970; Breed and Clarke 1970; Vaughan et al. 1973; Hoffmann 1974; Roth 1974; Turek et al. 1975). The effects of photoperiod on reproduction are laregely mediated by the pineal gland (Reiter and Vaughan 1977; Klein 1978). The pineal contains a number of substances which can inhibit the secretion of gonadotropins, particularly of LH. These substances include melatonin and other indoleamines, arginine vasotocin (AVT), and a number of peptides and unidentified compounds. However, the specific roles of these substances are far from clear. Melatonin and AVT have been leading candidates for the role of an antigonadotropin. However, melatonin may be progonadotropic or antigonadotropic, depending on photoperiod, time of administration, and other factors (Hoffmann 1973, 1974; Tamarkin et al. 1976a, 1977; Turek et al. 1975, 1976a,b; Turek 1977a). Light stimulation reaches the pineal via the retina, retinothalamic tracts, the superior cervical ganglion, and from there to the pineal by noradrenergic fibers to β-adrenergic receptors on pineal cells (Klein 1978). *Microtus* has a similar system, since pinealectomy or superior cervical ganglionectomy prevented the inhibition of gonadal function by short photoperiods (L:D 6:18) (Charlton et al. 1976). The effects of short photoperiods were much more pronounced in weanling than in adult intact controls. These results support the earlier results indicating that sensitivity to inhibition of reproductive function is greater in immature than in mature voles.

(4) *Pheromones*. A number of pheromones from several sources in the same or opposite sex influence gonadotropin secretion and reproductive function, particularly maturation, in mice, deermice, and probably other species (Terman 1968; Vandenbergh 1974; Colby 1974; Drickamer 1975, 1977; Bronson 1975; Bronson and Maruniak 1975, 1976; Maruniak and Bronson 1976; Kipps and Terman 1977). How-

ever, the roles of most of these in natural populations are unknown, but it is difficult to see how some of them would have much effect under natural circumstances. However, they provide solid evidence that maturation, sexual behavior, and reproductive function can be significantly affected by olfactory stimuli. Blinding and anosmia significantly delay maturation in female rats, whereas neither procedure by itself has much effect (Reiter and Ellison 1970; Reiter et al. 1970; Rönnekleiv and McCann 1975). Pinealectomy prevented the effects of blinding and anosmia, but only blinding affected indoleamine synthesis in the pineal. Presumably, anosmia increased the sensitivity of the site of action of pineal antigonadotropic substance to this antigonadal action.*

(5) *Changes in hypothalamic sensitivity* to negative feedbacks are clearly a major factor in determining the length of the breeding season and in inhibiting maturation and growth in young mammals. Adult animals are also affected, but to a smaller degree. Hypothalamic sensitivity is greater in immature than in mature animals. It is increased by short photoperiods, increased density, endogenous seasonal rhythms, and apparently some pheromones. A combination of these factors, such as density and decreased photoperiod, may act additively to increase sensitivity to a greater degree than that produced by either factor alone, as indicated by the experiments of Cohen and Mann (1979). The secretion of ACTH, endorphins, adrenal androgens, and progesterone is increased with increased density, so that these increased negative feedback signals act on a more sensitive hypothalamus and pituitary to inhibit maturation and growth or, if density is high enough, to inhibit reproductive function completely in mature animals. However, increased density will still inhibit reproductive function partially in adults, the degree depending on the level of density. At low densities, the negative feedback signals will be at relatively low levels, and sensitization of the hypothalamus by photoperiod will not be great enough for the low levels of feedback signals to inhibit reproductive function, particularly in adults, until the daily photoperiod is less than 12.5 hours. Thus, breeding may continue into late September. Increased latitude probably amplifies reproductive function by longer

---

*Editors' Note: Pheromones influencing gonadotropin secretion and reproductive function among rodents and primates are discussed further by Drickamer.

daily photoperiods during a shorter breeding season. However, at least some lemmings are relatively unaffected by photoperiod and apparently rely mainly on an endogenous annual rhythm.

Territoriality. Population size is limited by the territorial requirements of breeding females of some species, thus automatically limiting the number of females that can breed successfully. This appears to be the case for some populations of *Clethrionomys* (Bujalska 1970, 1971) and *Peromyscus leucopus* (Metzgar 1971). Bujalska (1970) suggests that mature females holding territories prevent immature female voles from maturing. However, this limiting mechanism cannot always work, since their populations sometimes reach plague proportions (de Vos 1951; Schorger 1956; Kalela 1957; Patric 1962; Christian 1971b). Also, unseasonal breeding in some species, such as *P. leucopus* and *P. maniculatus* (Manville 1952; Sheppe 1965), suggests that density may have more of an effect on reproduction at low or average densities than we customarily suppose.

The Prolonged Effects of Increased Density

The cause of the prolonged effects of high density after a peak population has passed has been a controversial subject, and a number of explanations have been proposed. However, the primary and secondary effects of high density (social strife) on physiological function can explain this phenomenon. This topic has been reviewed recently (Christian 1971a,b, 1975, 1978), so only an abbreviated summary will be given here. Increased density and low social rank are stressful and evoke the expected endocrine responses, including the partial or complete inhibition of reproduction. The stimuli are probably mainly psychogenic.

Increased density may partially or completely inhibit lactation through suppressing gonadotropins (Calhoun 1950; Selye 1954; Chitty 1955; Christian and LeMunyan 1958; Christian et al. 1965; Lloyd, this volume). The effects of inadequate lactation may be enhanced by deficient maternal care, itself presumably due to endocrine imbalances or deficiencies. Reducing nutrition during nursing by increasing litter size causes permanent stunting of the young, delayed maturation, higher subsequent mortality rates, decreased gonadal function when adult, and increased pulmonary infections (Widdowson and McCance 1960; Widdowson and Kennedy 1962; Kennedy and Mitra 1963). Other investigators have added to the list of permanent abnormalities and deficiencies produced. Irvine and Timiras (1966) reported that maturation of the brain in rats was accelerated in large litters. However, other investigators have reported delayed and abnormal morphological, biochemical, functional, and behavioral development of the brains of rats in large litters (Dickerson and Pao 1975; Griffin et al. 1977; Nagy et al. 1977). Similar effects result from undernutrition of the dams during pregnancy and lactation (Chow and Lee 1964; Dubos et al. 1968). Progeny of underfed dams have abnormal protein metabolism (Lee and Chow 1965; Blackwell et al. 1969), delayed sexual activity (Larsson et al. 1974), increased brain catecholamines (Shoemaker and Wurtman 1971), permanent EEG abnormalities (Gramsbergen 1976), abnormal cerebellar development (Chase et al. 1971), and depressed behavioral development (Massaro et al. 1977). Maternal malnutrition during gestation has profound adverse effects on the immune system of the progeny. Caloric restriction in young rats inhibits growth, involutes the lymphoid organs, produces lymphopenia, and significantly impairs antibody formation in the F_1 and F_2 progeny (Chandra 1975). Thus, there is a spectrum of permanent abnormalities produced by inadequate nutrition during gestation and/or nursing due either to large litter size or to maternal malnutrition or both.

The effects of increased secretion of glucocorticoids in many ways parallel those of protein restriction, since glucocorticoids are antianabolic and produce a negative nitrogen balance. They also inhibit mitoses, DNA synthesis, and growth. Chronic psychogenic stress (24 hours of restraint) produced a phenomenal rise in circulating corticosterone (B) in pregnant mice with maximum levels of 733 μg/100 ml of plasma and sustained levels of 500–600 μg/100 ml, of which 10 μg was unbound (Barlow et al. 1975a). The normal level of unbound B is 2 μg/100 ml for unstressed pregnant mice. The resting level of total B in unstressed pregnant mice is about 80 μg/100 ml. These high levels of B may have profound physiological and pathological effects during pregnancy, and were significantly correlated with the development of cleft palates (Barlow et al. 1975b). Psychogenic stress during pregnancy also increases fetal mortality in rats. Therefore, high density or increased social strife would probably cause a high rate of intrauterine mortality. In fact, 10 pairs of relatively docile albino mice per cage resulted in a 70% loss of whole gravida *in utero* (Christian and LeMunyan 1958). Prenatal psychogenic stress has profound adverse effects on the behavior, particularly sexual, of the progeny (Joffe 1965;

Ward 1972; Masterpasqua et al. 1976; Allen and Haggett 1977). Crowding pregnant mice by housing them 18 per cage on days 3 and 4 of pregnancy resulted in a 44% increase in adrenal weight in the dams and in malformations in 10% of the progeny (Hamburgh et al. 1974). Maternal stress during lactation produced elevated levels of B, and increased levels of B in the progeny in response to psychogenic stress (Levine and Thoman 1969). Furthermore, AC function in adulthood was abnormal and avoidance learning was impaired. Restraint stress also increases the loss of entire gravida (Euker and Riegle 1973). Injection of pregnant animals with glucocorticoids or ACTH results in premature aging of the placenta and a variety of adverse effects on the progeny (Velardo 1957; Kivikoski et al. 1962; Laine et al. 1963; Liggins 1968; Wellmann and Volk 1972).

In addition to these effects, a hypothalamic hormone (SRIF) that inhibits the secretion of growth hormone may have unusually long-term effects consistent with those of high density (Theisen et al. 1976). If young rats (F_1) are exposed *in utero* to SRIF by treating their dams with it through days 8–20 or 13–20 of gestation, they apparently are unaffected, but the weights of their progeny (F_2) are significantly reduced at birth. This mechanism could account, at least partly, for the reduced size of mice or voles following a peak in density.

Thus, high density can have profound and long-lasting effects on several generations of the progeny of females subjected to increased social strife and density. These physiological effects can result in marked changes in the "quality" of animals during or following peak densities. Endocrine responses are probably graded and are functions of the magnitude of the stimuli of density or rank.

Conclusion

This account reviewed the endocrine responses to increased density and their effects on the individuals in a population, as well as on the population as a whole. In addition, some new directions have been indicated which may bear importantly on behavior and population regulation. Opioid receptors are involved in the action of ACTH in inhibiting reproduction. Enkephalin, therefore probably endorphins, also inhibit LH secretion. Much has been learned in the last few years about ACTH, its synthesis, its forms, and its regulation, but little is known about the actions of intermediate ACTH *in vivo*, although it is equipotent with little ACTH in laboratory assay systems. ACTH secretion in response to psychogenic stress is apparently regulated by a different control system than is anterior pituitary ACTH. Where these pieces of the puzzle will fit into the control of population growth is uncertain, but endocrine and neuroeudocrine responses to increased density are sufficient to explain the regulation of reproduction and population growth and decline in the face of continuing high or increased mortality. Also, the effects of the hormonal responses to increased density on the progeny can adequately explain the prolonged effects of high density. Large litter size may also contribute to these effects by effectively reducing nutrition in nursing young. In addition, increased density can increase mortality by decreasing host resistance to infectious disease or by inducing noninfectious disease through the endocrine responses that it evokes. The action of all these factors can be viewed as a density-dependent two-way negative feedback control system that regulates and limits population growth. The action of this system is modulated by the characteristics of the species—its social behavior and basic reproductive rate—and by environmental inputs of varying degree.

References

Abe, K., and Critchlow, V. 1977. Effects of corticosterone, dexainethasone and surgical isolation of the medial basal hypothalamus on rapid feedback control of stress-induced corticotropin secretion in female rats. *Endocrinology* 101:498–505.

Allen, T. O., and Haggett, B. N. 1977. Group housing of pregnant mice reduces copulatory receptivity of female progeny. *Physiol. Behav.* 19:61–68.

Andrews, R. V., et al. 1972. Physiological, demographic and pathological changes in wild Norway rat populations over an annual cycle. *Comp. Biochem. Physiol.* 41A:149–65.

———, et al. 1975a. Physiological consequences of experimentally altering the population structure of *Peromyscus maniculatus* in the field. *Comp. Biochem. Physiol.* 51A:785–92.

———, et al. 1975b. Physiological and demographic profiles of brown lemmings during their cycle of abundance. *Physiol. Zool.* 48:64–83.

Bajusz, S., et al. 1976. Enkephalin analogs with enhanced opiate activity (preliminary communication). *Acta Biochem. Biophys. Acad. Sci. Hung.* 11:305–09.

Baker, J. R., et al. 1963. Blood parasites of wild voles, *Microtus agrestis*, in England. *Parasitology* 53:297–301.

Barbehenn, K. R. 1955. A field study of growth in *Microtus pennsylvanicus*. *J. Mammal.* 36:533–43.

Barkley, M.S., and Goldman, B. D. 1977a. The effects of castration and silastic implants of testosterone on intermale aggression in the mouse. *Horm. Behav.* 9:32–48.

———, and Goldman, B. D. 1977b. A quantitative study of serum testosterone, sex accessory organ growth, and the development of intermale aggression in the mouse. *Horm. Behav.* 8:208–18.

Barlow, S. M., et al. 1975a. Effects of acute and chronic stress on plasma corticosterone levels in the pregnant and non-pregnant mouse. *J. Endocrinol.* 66:93–99.

———, et al. 1975b. The relation between maternal restraint and food deprivation, plasma corticosterone, and induction of cleft palate in the offspring of mice. *Teratology* 12:97–104.

Bevan, W., et al. 1957. Spontaneous aggressiveness in two strains of house mice castrated and treated with one of three androgens. *Physiol. Zool.* 30:341–49.

Blackwell, B.-N., et al. 1969. Further studies on growth and feed utilization in progeny of underfed mother rats. *J. Nutr.* 97:79–84.

Blaine, E. H. 1973. Elevated arterial blood pressure in an asymptotic population of meadow voles (*Microtus pennsylvanicus*). *Nature* 242:135.

———, and Conaway, C. H. 1969. The role of the spleen and adrenal in the anemia of subordinate fighting mice. *Physiol. Zool.* 42:334–47.

Blake, C. A. 1975. Effects of "stress" on pulsatile luteinizing hormone release in ovariectomized rats. *Proc. Soc. Exp. Biol. Med.* 148:813–15.

Bloom, F., et al. 1976. Endorphins: profound behavioral effects in rats suggest new etiological factors in mental illness. *Science* 194:630–32.

———, et al. 1977. Endorphins are located in intermediate and anterior lobes of pituitary gland, not in neurohypophysis. *Life Sci.* 20:43–48.

Bradbury, A. F., et al. 1976. The C-fragment of lipotropin: an endogenous peptide with high affinity for brain opiate receptors. *Nature* 260:793–95.

Brattin, W. J., and Portanova, R. 1975. Corticosterone modulation of pituitary responsiveness to CRF: effect of actinomycin-d and puromycin. Endocrinol. Soc. 57th Annu. Meet. Abstr. 145.

Brayton, A. R., and Brain, P. F. 1974. Effects of "crowding" on endocrine function and retention of the digenean parasite *Microphallus pygmaeus* in male and female albino mice. *J. Helminthol.* 48:99–106.

Breed, W. G., and Clarke, J. R. 1970. Effect of photoperiod on ovarian function in the vole, *Microtus agrestis*. *J. Reprod. Fertil.* 23:189–92.

Brodish, A. 1977. Tissue corticotropin releasing factors. *Fed. Proc.* 36:2088–93.

Bronson, F. H. 1975. Male-induced precocial puberty in female mice: confirmation of the role of estrogen. *Endocrinology* 96:511–14.

———, and Clarke, S. H. 1966. Adrenalectomy and coat color in deer mice. *Science* 154:1349–50.

———, and Eleftheriou, B. E. 1965. Adrenal response to fighting in mice: separation of physical and psychological causes. *Science* 147:627–28.

———, and Maruniak, J. A. 1975. Male-induced puberty in female mice: evidence for a synergistic action of social cues. *Biol. Reprod.* 13:94–98.

————, and Maruniak, J. A. 1976. Differential effects of male stimuli on follicle-stimulating hormone, luteinizing hormone, and prolactin secretion in prepubertal female mice. *Endocrinology* 98:1101–08.

————, et al. 1973. Serum FSH and LH in male mice following aggressive and nonaggressive interaction. *Physiol. Behav.* 10:369–72.

Brown, E. B. III. 1973. Changes in patterns of seasonal growth of *Microtus pennsylvanicus*. *Ecology* 54:1103–10.

Bruni, J. F., et al. 1977. Effects of naloxone, morphine and methionine enkephalin on serum prolactin, lutenizing hormone, follicle stimulating hormone, thyroid stimulating hormone and growth hormone. *Life Sci.* 21:461–66.

Bujalska, G. 1970. Reproduction stabilizing elements in an island population of *Clethrionomys glareolus* (Schreber, 1780). *Acta Theriol.* 25:381–412.

————. 1971. Self-regulation of reproduction in an island population of *Clethrionomys glareolus* (Schreber, 1780). *Ann. Zool. Fenn.* 8:91–93.

Calhoun, J. B. 1950. The study of wild animals under controlled conditions. *Ann. N.Y. Acad. Sci.* 51:113–22.

Chamove, A. S., and Bowman, R. E. 1976. Rank, rhesus social behavior, and stress. *Folia Primatol.* 26:57–66.

Chandra, R. K. 1975. Antibody formation in first and second generation offspring of nutritionally deprived rats. *Science* 190:289–90.

Charlton, H. M., et al. 1970. Hypothalamic influence on pituitary and serum levels of LH in the vole, *Microtus agrestis*. *J. Physiol. (Lond.)* 210:7P–8P.

————, et al. 1976. The effects of pinealectomy and superior cervical ganglionectomy on the testis of the vole, *Microtus agrestis*. *J. Reprod. Fertil.* 48:377–79.

Chase, H. P., et al. 1971. Intra-uterine undernutrition and brain development. *Pediatrics* 47:491–500.

Chitty, D. 1952. Mortality among voles (*Microtus agrestis*) at Lake Vyrnwy, Montgomeryshire in 1936–9. *Philos. Trans. R. Soc. Lond. Ser. B* 236:505–52.

————. 1954. Tuberculosis among wild voles: with a discussion of other pathological conditions among certain mammals. *Ecology* 35:227–37.

————. 1955. Adverse effects of population density upon the viability of later generations. In *Numbers of man and animals*, ed. J. B. Cragg and N. W. Perie, pp. 57–67. Edinburgh: Oliver & Boyd.

————. 1958. Self-regulation of numbers through changes in viability. *Cold Spring Harbor Symp. Quant. Biol.* 22:277–80.

Chow, B. F., and Lee, C.-J. 1964. Effect of dietary restriction of pregnant rats on body weight gain of the offspring. *J. Nutr.* 82:10–18.

Christian, J. J. 1959. Lack of correlation between adrenal weight and injury in grouped male albino mice. *Proc. Soc. Exp. Biol. Med.* 101:166–68.

————. 1961. Phenomena associated with population density. *Proc. Natl. Acad. Sci. U.S.A.* 47:428–49.

————. 1963. The pathology of overpopulation. *Mil. Med.* 128:571–603.

————. 1964. Effect of androgens on the adrenal glands of deer mice (*Peromyscus*). *J. Endocrinol.* 28:x–xi.

————. 1967. Effects of β^{1-24} synthetic corticotrophin on reproductive tract and kidneys of immature female mice. *Acta Endocrinol.* 55:62–70.

————. 1968. The potential role of the adrenal cortex as affected by social rank and population density on experimental epidemics. *Am. J. Epidemiol.* 87:255–64.

————. 1970. Social subordination, population density, and mammalian evolution. *Science* 168:84–90.

————. 1971a. Population density and fertility in mammals. In *The action of hormones: genes to population*, ed. P. Foa, pp. 471–510. Springfield, Ill.: Thomas.

————. 1971b. Population density and reproductive efficiency. *Biol. Reprod.* 4:248–94.

————. 1971c. Fighting, maturity and population density in *Microtus*. *J. Mammal.* 52:556–67.

————. 1975. Hormonal control of population growth. In *Hormonal correlates of behavior*, vol. 1, ed. B. E. Eleftheriou and R. V. Stott, pp. 205–74. New York: Plenum Press.

————. 1976. Pituitary in relation to renal disease. In *Hypothalamus, pituitary and aging*, ed. A. V. Everitt and J. A. Burgess, pp. 297–332. Springfield, Ill.: Thomas.

————. 1978. Neurobehavioral-endocrine regulation of small mammal populations. In *Population of small mammals under natural conditions*, Pymatuning Lab. Ecol. Spec. Publ. 5, ed. D. P. Snyder, pp. 143–58.

————. 1979. Population dynamics.

————, and Davis, D. E. 1964. Endocrines, behavior, and population. *Science* 146:1550–60.

————, and Davis, D. E. 1966. Adrenal glands in female voles (*Microtus pennsylvanicus*) as related to reproduction and population size. *J. Mammal.* 47:1–18.

————, and LeMunyan, C. D. 1958. Adverse effects of crowding on reproduction and lactation of mice and two generations of their progeny. *Endocrinology* 63:517–29.

————, et al. 1965. The role of endocrines in the self-regulation of mammalian populations. *Recent Prog. Horm. Res.* 21:501–78.

Clarke, J. R. 1953. The effect of fighting on the adrenals, thymus, and spleen of the vole (*Microtus agrestis*). *J. Endocrinol.* 9:114–26.

————, and Forsyth, I. A. 1964. Seasonal changes in the gonads and accessory reproductive organs of the vole (*Microtus agrestis*). *Gen. Comp. Endocrinol.* 4:233–42.

Cohen, I. R., and Mann, D. R. 1979. Seasonal changes associated with puberty in female rats: effect of photoperiod and ACTH administration. *Biol. Reprod.* (in press).

Colby, D. R. 1974. Regulatory effects of urinary pheromones on puberty in the mouse. *Biol. Reprod.* 11:268–79.

Cook, D. M., and Olson, J. 1973. Studies on adaptation of ACTH secretion to repeated stress. Endocrinol. Soc. 55th Annu. Meet., Abst. 318.

————, et al. 1973. The effect of acute or chronic ether stress on plasma ACTH concentration in the rat. *Endocrinology* 93:1019–24.

————, et al. 1974. Lack of adaptation of ACTH secretion to sequential ether tourniquet, or leg-break stress. *Endocrinol. Res. Commun.* 1:347–57.

Coslovsky, R., and Yalow, R. S. 1974. Influence of the hormonal forms of ACTH on the pattern of corticosteroid secretion. *Biochem. Biophys. Res. Commun.* 60:1351–56.

—, et al. 1975. Characterization of mouse ACTH in plasma and in extracts of pituitary and of adrenotropic pituitary tumor. *Endocrinology* 97:1308–15.

Cox, B. M., et al. 1976. Opioid activity of a peptide, β-lipotropin-(61–91), derived from β-lipotropin. *Proc. Natl. Acad. Sci. U.S.A.* 73:1821–23.

Dallman, M. F., and Jones, M. T. 1973. Corticosteroid feedback control of ACTH secretion: effect of stress-induced corticosterone secretion of subsequent stress responses in the rat. *Endocrinology* 92:1367–75.

—, et al. 1972. Corticosteroid feedback control of ACTH secretion: rapid effects of bilateral adrenalectomy on plasma ACTH in the rat. *Endocrinology* 91:961–68.

—, et al. 1974. Diminishing corticotrope capacity to release ACTH during sustained stimulation: the twenty-four hours after bilateral adrenalectomy in the rat. *Endocrinology* 95:65–73.

—, et al. 1977. Neural regulation of compensatory adrenal growth. *Ann. N.Y. Acad. Sci.* 297:373–92.

Davis, D. E., et al. 1964. Effect of exploitation of birth, mortality and movement rates in a woodchuck population. *J. Wildl. Manage.* 28:1–9.

Davis, G. J., and Meyer, R. K. 1973. FSH and LH in the snowshoe hare during the increasing phase of the 10-year cycle. *Gen. Comp. Endocrinol.* 20:53–60.

Dellman, H.-D., et al. 1973. Corticotrophic cells in the pars intermedia rostral zone of the mouse and rat and their relationship to neurohypophysial nerve fibers and the hypophysial portal system. In *Brain-pituitary-adrenal interrelationships*, ed. A. Brodish and E. S. Redgate, pp. 323–27. Basel: Karger.

de Vos, A. 1951. Peak populations of *Peromyscus maniculatus gracilis* in Northern Ontario, *J. Mammal* 30:462.

de Wied, D. 1977. Behavioral effects of neuropeptides related to ACTH, MSH, and βLPH. *Ann. N.Y. Acad. Sci.* 297:263–72.

Dickerson, J. W. T., and Pao, S.-K. 1975. Effect of pre- and post-natal maternal protein deficiency on free amino acids and amines of rat brain. *Biol. Neonate* 25:114–24.

Drickamer, L. C. 1975. Contact stimulation and accelerated sexual maturation of female mice. *Behav. Biol.* 15:113–15.

—. 1977. Delay of sexual maturation in female house mice by exposure to grouped females or urine from grouped females. *J. Reprod. Fertil.* 51:77–81.

Dubos, R., et al. 1968. Lasting biological effect of early environmental influences. I. Conditioning of adult size by prenatal and postnatal nutrition. *J. Exp. Med.* 127:783–800.

Duckett, G. E., et al. 1963. Effects of adrenal androgens on parabiotic mice. *Endocrinology* 72:403–07.

Edwards, E. A., and Dean, L. M. 1977. Effects of crowding of mice on humoral antibody formation and protection to lethal antigenic challenge. *Psychosom. Med.* 39:19–24.

Egdahl, R. H. 1960. Adrenal cortical and medullary responses to trauma in dogs with isolated pituitaries. *Endocrinology* 66:200–16.

Eipper, B. A., and Mains, R. E. 1975. High molecular weight forms of adrenocorticotropic hormone in the mouse pituitary and in a mouse pituitary tumor cell line. *Biochemistry* 14:3836–44.

———, and Mains, R. E. 1977. Peptide analysis of a glycoprotein form of adrenocorticotropic hormone. *J. Biol. Chem.* 252:8821–32.

———, et al. 1976. High molecular weight forms of adrenocorticotropic hormone are glycoproteins. *J. Biol. Chem.* 251:4121–26.

Ely, D. L., and Henry, J. P. 1974. Effects of prolonged social deprivation on murine behavior patterns, blood pressure, and adrenal weight. *J. Comp. Physiol. Psychol.* 84:733–40.

Euker, J. S., and Riegle, G. D. 1973. Effects of stress on pregnancy in the rat. *J. Reprod. Fertil.*34:343–46.

Fevold, H. R. 1968. Synthetic β^{2-24} -corticotropin stimulation of cortisol biosynthesis by rabbit adrenal tissue. *Steroids* 12:697–704.

———. 1969. The pathways of corticosteroid biosynthesis by homogenates of adrenal tissue from rabbits stimulated with adrenocorticotropin. *Biochemistry* 8:3433–39.

———, and Drummond, H. B. 1976. Steroid biosynthesis by adrenal tissue of snowshoe hares (*Lepus americanus*) collected in a year of peak population density. *Gen. Comp. Endocrinol.* 28:113–17.

Fischer, J. L., and Moriarty, C. M. 1977. Control of bioactive corticotropin release from the neurointermediate lobe of the rat pituitary *in vitro*. *Endocrinology* 100:1047–54.

Frank, F. 1957. The causality of microtine cycles in Germany. *J. Wildl. Manage.* 21:113–21.

Fraser, R., et al. 1976. The adrenal cortex and hypertension: some observations on a possible role for mineralocorticoids other than aldosterone. *J. Steroid Biochem.* 7:963–70.

Ganjam, V. K., et al. 1972. Changing patterns of circulating corticosteroids in rabbits following prolonged treatment with ACTH. *Endocrinology* 91:607–11.

Gaskin, J. H., and Kitay, J. I. 1970. Adrenocortical function in the hamster: sex differences and effects of gonadal hormones. *Endocrinology* 87:779–86.

Geller, M. 1978. Dynamics of three montane populations of *Microtus pennsylvanicus* in the Northeast. Doctoral dissertation, State Univ. of New York at Binghamton.

Goldstein, A., and Cox, B. M. 1977. Opioid peptides (endorphins) in pituitary and brain. *Psychoneuroendocrinology* 2:11–16.

Gosbee, J. L., et al. 1970. Functional relationship between the pars intermedia and ACTH secretion in the rat. *Endocrinology* 86:560–67.

Gramsbergen, A. 1976. EEG development in normal and undernourished rats. *Brain Res.* 105:287–308.

Gray, G. D., et al. 1977. Chronic suppression of pituitary-testicular function by stress in rats. *Fed. Proc.* 36:322 (No. 279).

Green, P. M. 1964. Density of population as a regulating factor in the reproductive potential of *Sigmodon hispidus*. Doctoral dissertation, Oklahoma State Univ., pp. 1–101.

Greer, M. A., et al. 1975. Evidence that the pars intermedia and pars nervosa of the pituitary do not secrete functionally significant quantities of ACTH. *Endocrinology* 96:718–24.

Grevert, P., and Goldstein, A. 1977. Some effects of naloxone on behavior in the mouse. *Psychopharmacology* 53:111–13.

Griffin, W. S. T., et al. 1977. Malnutrition and brain development: cerebellar weight, DNA, RNA, protein and histological correlations. *J. Neurochem.* 28:1269–79.

Grunt, J. A., and Young, W. C. 1953. Consistency of sexual behavior patterns in individual male guinea pigs following castration and androgen therapy. *J. Comp. Physiol. Psychol.* 46:138–44.

Guillemin, R., et al. 1976. Endorphines, peptides, d'origine hypothalamique et neurohypophysaire à activité morphinomimétique. Isolement et structure moléculaire de l'α-endorphine. *C.R. Acad. Sci. Ser. D.* 282:783–85.

————, et al. 1977. β-endorphin and adrenocorticotropin are secreted concomitantly by the pituitary gland. *Science* 197:1367–69.

Hamburgh, M., et al. 1974. Malformations induced in offspring of crowded and parabiotically stressed mice. *Teratology* 10:31–38.

Hamilton, W. J., Jr. 1941. Reproduction of the field mouse (*Microtus pennsylvanicus*). Cornell Univ. Agric. Exp. Sta. Mem. 237.

Hasler, J. F., et al. 1976. The influence of photoperiod on growth and sexual function in male and female collared lemmings (*Dicrostonyx groenlandicus*). *J. Reprod. Fertil.* 46:323–29.

Henkin, R. I., and Knigge, K. M. 1963. Effect of sound on the hypothalamic-pituitary-adrenal axis. *Am. J. Physiol.* 204:710–14.

Henry, J. P., and Cassel, J. C. 1969. Psychosocial factors in essential hypertension. Recent epidemiologic and animal experimental evidence. *Am. J. Epidemiol.* 90:171–200.

Hoffmann, J. C., and Cullin, A. 1976. Effect of photoperiod length on luteinizing hormone levels in estradiol-treated ovariectomized rats. *Fed. Proc.* 35:615 (abstr.).

Hoffmann, K. 1973. The action of melatonin on testis size and pelage color varies with the season. *Int. J. Chronobiol.* 1:333.

————. 1974. Testicular involution in short photoperiods inhibited by melatonin. *Naturwissenschaften* 61:364–65.

Hoffman, R. S. 1958. The role of reproduction and mortality in population fluctuations of voles. *Ecol. Monogr.* 28:79–109.

Hollósi, M., et al. 1977. Studies on the conformation of β-endorphin and its constituent fragments in water and trifluoroethanol by CD spectroscopy. *FEBS Lett.* 74:185–89.

Horn, A. S., and Rodgers, J. S. 1976. Structural and conformational relationships between the enkephalins and the opiates. *Nature* 260:795–97.

Hughes, J. 1975. Isolation of an endogenous compound from the brain with pharmacological properties similar to morphine. *Brain Res.* 88:295–308.

————, et al. 1975. Identification of two related pentapeptides from the brain with potent opiate agonist activity. *Nature* 258:577–79.

Hull, E. M., et al. 1976. Environmental enrichment and crowding: behavioral and hormonal effects. *Physiol. Behav.* 17:735–41.

Irvine, G. L., and Timiras, P. S. 1966. Litter size and brain development in the rat. *Life Sci.* 5:1577–82.

Jacquet, Y. F., and Marks, N. 1976. The C-fragment of β-lipotropin: an endogenous neuroleptic or antipsychotogen? *Science* 194:632–35.

Jarrett, R. J. 1965. Effects and mode of action of adrenocorticotrophic hormone upon the reproductive tract of the female mouse. *Endocrinology* 76:434–40.

Joffe, J. M. 1965. Genotype and prenatal and premating stress interact to affect adult behavior in rats. *Science* 150:1844–45.

Jones, M. T., and Hillhouse, E. W. 1976. Structure-activity relationship and the mode of action of corticosteroid feedback on the secretion of corticotrophin-releasing factor (corticoliberin). *J. Steroid Biochem.* 7:11–12.

Kalela, O. 1957. Regulation of reproductive rate in subarctic populations of the vole *Clethrionomys rufocanus* (Sund). *Am. Acad. Sci. Fenn. Ser. A.* 34:1–60.

Kastin, A. J., et al. 1971. Is the intermediate lobe (IML) of the pituitary gland essential for ACTH synthesis? Endocrinol. Soc. 53rd Annu. Meet., Abstr. 338.

Kendall, J. W., et al. 1972. The importance of stimulus intensity and duration of steroid administration in suppression of stress-induced ACTH secretion. *Endocrinology* 90:525–30.

Kennedy, G. C., and Mitra, J. 1963. Body weight and food intake as initiating factors for puberty in the rat. *J. Physiol.* 166:408–18.

———, et al. 1977. Postimplantation pregnancy disruption in *Microtus ochrogaster, M. pennsylvanicus* and *Peromyscus maniculatus. J. Reprod. Fertil.* 49:365–67.

Kipps, P. L., and Terman, C. R. 1977. The influence of pheromones produced by freely growing laboratory populations on the reproductive maturation of prairie deermice following prenatal and postnatal exposure. *Res. Popul. Ecol.* 18:261–66.

Kivikoski, A., et al. 1962. Postnatal development of the young of rats treated with hydrocortisone during pregnancy. *Ann. Med. Exp. Fenn.* 40:297–301.

Klein, D. C. 1978. The pineal: a model of neuroendocrine regulation. In *The hypothalamus*, ed. S. Reichlin, R. J. Baldessarini, and J. B. Martin, pp. 303–27. New York: Raven Press.

Kley, H. K., et al. 1976. Evaluation of adrenal function in mice by measurement of urinary excretion of free corticoids. *J. Steroid Biochem.* 7:381–85.

Knigge, K. M.; Penrod, C. H. and Schindler, W. J. 1959. In vitro and in vivo adrenal corticosteroid secretion following stress. *Amer. J. Physiol.* 196:579–82.

Kokka, N., et al. 1972. Growth hormone and ACTH secretion: evidence for an inverse relationship in rats. *Endocrinology* 90:735–43.

Kolanowski, J., et al. 1975. Potentiation of adrenocortical response upon intermittent stimulation with corticotropin in normal subjects. *J. Clin. Endocrinol. Metabol.* 41:453–65.

Kraicer, J. 1976. Lack of release of ACTH from the denervated rat pars intermedia *in vivo. Can. J. Physiol. Pharmacol.* 45:809–13.

———. 1977. Control of ACTH and MSH release from the pars intermedia: *in vitro* studies. In *Melanocyte stimulating hormone: control, chemistry and effects. Frontiers of hormone research*, ed. F. J. H. Tilders, D. F. Swaab, and T. B. Greidanus, vol. 4, pp. 200–07. Basel: Karger.

————, and Morris, A. R. 1976. *In vitro* release of ACTH from dispersed rat pars intermedia cells. II. Effect of neurotransmitter substances. *Neuroendocrinology* 21:175–92.

————, et al. 1973. Pars intermedia and pars distalis: two sites of ACTH production in the rat hypophysis. *Neuroendocrinology* 11:156–76.

Kraulis, L., et al. 1973. The effects of corticosterone, 18-OH-DOC, DOC, and 11β-hydroxy-progesterone on the adrenal pituitary axis of the stressed rat. *J. Steroid Biochem.* 4:129–37.

Krebs, C. J. 1964. The lemming cycle at Baker Lake, Northwest Territories during 1959–1962. *Arct. Inst. N. Am. Tech. Pap. 15* 1–104.

Krieger, D. T., et al. 1977. Presence of corticotropin in brain of normal and hypophysectomized rats. *Proc. Natl. Acad. Sci. U.S.A.* 74:648–52.

Krulich, L., et al. 1974. The effects of acute stress on the secretion of LH, FSH, prolactin and GH in the normal male rat, with comments on their statistical evaluation. *Neuroendocrinology* 16:293–311.

Krulich, L., and McCann, S. M. 1966. Influence of stress on the growth hormone (GH) content of the pituitary of the rat. *Proc. Soc. Exp. Biol. Med.* 122:612–16.

Krum, A. A., and Glenn, R. E. 1965. Adrenal steroid secretion in rabbits following prolonged ACTH administration. *Proc. Soc. Exp. Biol. Med.* 118:255–58.

Labella, F., et al. 1977. Lipotropin: localization by radioimmunoassay of endorphin precursor in pituitary and brain. *Biochem. Biophys. Res. comm.* 75:350–57.

Laine, M. J., et al. 1963. Postnatal development of the young of rats treated with ACTH during pregnancy. *Ann. Med. Exp. Fenn.* 41:531–38.

Larsson, K., et al. 1974. Delayed onset of sexual activity of male rats subjected to pre- and postnatal undernutrition. *Physiol. Behav.* 13:307–11.

Larsson, T., et al. 1973. Winter reproduction in small rodents in Sweden. *Oikos* 24:475–76.

Layne, J. N. 1968. Ontogeny. In *Biology of peromyscus (Rodentia)*, Spec. Publ. 2 Am. Soc. Mammal., ed. J. A. King, pp. 148–253.

Lazarus, L. H., et al. 1976. β-lipotropin as a prohormone for the morphinomimetic peptides endorphins and enkephalins. *Proc. Natl. Acad. Sci. U.S.A.* 73:2156–59.

Lee, C. J., and Chow, B. F. 1965. Protein metabolism in the offspring of underfed mother rats. *J. Nutr.* 87:439–43.

Lee, T. H., and Lee, M. S. 1977. Purification and characterization of high-molecular-weight forms of adrenocorticotropic hormone of ovine pituitary glands. *Biochemistry* 16:2824–29.

Legan, S. J., et al. 1977. The endocrine control of seasonal reproductive function in the ewe: a marked change in response to the negative feedback action of estradiol on luteinizing hormone. *Endocrinology* 101:818–24.

Leshner, A. I. 1975. A model of hormones and agonistic behavior. *Physiol. Behav.* 15:225–35.

————, et al. 1973. Pituitary adrenocortical activity and intermale aggressiveness in isolated mice. *Physiol. Behav.* 11:705–11.

Levine, S., and Thoman, E. B. 1969. Physiological and behavioral consequences of postnatal maternal stress in rats. *Physiol. Behav.* 4:139–42.

Li, C. H., and Chung. D. 1976. Isolation and structure of an untriakontapeptide with opiate activity from camel pituitary glands *Proc. Natl. Acad. Sci. U.S.A.* 73:1145–48.

———, et al. 1965a. Isolation and aminoacid sequence of β-LPH from sheep pituitary glands. *Nature* 208:1093–94.

———, et al. 1965b. Isolation and structure of β-LPH sheep pituitary glands. *Endocrinology* (Proc. VI Pan-Am. Congr. Endocrinol.), ed. C. Gual, Int. Congr. Ser. No. 112, pp. 349–64. Amsterdam: Excerpta Medica.

———, et al. 1977. β-endorphin: lack of correlation between opiate activity and immunoreactivity by radioimmunoassay. *Biochem. Biophys. Res. Comm.* 75:576–80.

Liggins, G. C. 1968. Premature parturition after infusion of corticotrophin or cortisol into foetal lambs. *J. Endocrinol.* 42:323–29.

Ling, N., et al. 1976. Isolation, primary structure, and synthesis of alpha-endorphin and gamma-endorphin, 2 peptides of hypothalamic-hypophysial, origin with morphinomimetic activity. *Proc. Natl. Acad. Sci. U.S.A.* 73:3942–46.

Loh, H. H., and Li, C. H. 1977. Biologic activities of β-endorphin and its related peptides. *Ann. N.Y. Acad. Sci.* 297:115–28.

Lombardi, J. R., and Vandenbergh, J. G. 1977. Pheromonally induced sexually maturation in females: regulation by the social environment of the male. *Science* 196:545–46.

Lord, J. A. H., et al. 1977. Endogenous opioid peptides: multiple agonists and receptors. *Nature* 267:495–99.

Lowry, P. J., et al. 1977. Structure and biosynthesis of peptides related to corticotropins and β-melanotropins. *Ann. N.Y. Acad. Sci.* 297:49–62.

Ludwig, J. R. 1976. Decline of a woodchuck population and the compensation for population reduction of a low-density population. Doctoral dissertation. Southern Illinois Univ.

Lymangrover, J. R., and Brodish, A. 1973. Tissue CRF: an extra-hypothalamic corticotrophin releasing factor (CRF) in the peripheral blood of stressed rat. *Neuroendocrinology* 12:225–35.

Madden, J. IV, et al. 1977. Stress-induced parallel changes in central opioid levels and pain responsiveness in the rat. *Nature* 265:358–60.

Madison, D. M. 1978. Movement indicators of reproductive events among female meadow voles as revealed by radiotelemetry. *J. Mammal.* 59:835–43.

Mains, R. E., and Eipper, B. A. 1975. Molecular weights of adrenocorticotropic hormone in extracts of anterior and intermediate-posterior lobes of mouse pituitary. *Proc. Natl. Acad. Sci. U.S.A.* 72:3565–69.

———, and Eipper, B. A. 1976. Biosynthesis of adrenocorticotropic hormone in mouse pituitary tumor cells. *J. Biol. Chem.* 251:4115–20.

———, et al. 1977. Common precursor to corticotropins and endorphins. *Proc. Natl. Acad. Sci. U.S.A.* 74:3014–18.

Mallory, F. F., and Clulow, F. V. 1977. Evidence of pregnancy failure in the wild meadow vole, *Microtus pennsylvanicus. Can. J. Zool.* 55:1–16.

Manville, R. H. 1952. A late breeding cycle in *Peromyscus. J. Mammal.* 33:389.

Martinet, L. 1966. Modification de la spermatogenèse chez le campagnol des champs

(*Microtus arvalis*) en fonction de la durée quotidienne d'éclairement. *Ann. Biol. Anim. Biochem. Biophys.* 6:301–13.

————, and Meunier, M. 1969. Influence des variations saisonnières de la luzerne sur la croissance, la mortalité et l'établissement de la maturité sexuelle chez le campagnol des champs (*Microtus arvalis*). *Ann. Biol. Anim. Biochem. Biophys.* 9:451–62.

————, et al. 1971. Seasonal variation in growth and mortality of *Microtus arvalis*. The role of photoperiodism and of vegetation upon these variations. *Mammalia* 35:38–84.

Maruniak, J. A., and Bronson, F. H. 1976. Gonadotropic responses of male mice to female urine. *Endocrinology* 99:963–69.

Massaro, T. F., et al. 1977. Early protein malnutrition in the rat: behavioral changes during rehabilitation. *Dev. Psychobiol.* 10:105–11.

Masterpasqua, F., et al. 1976. The effects of prenatal psychological stress on the sexual behavior and reactivity of male rats. *Dev. Psychobiol.* 9:403–11.

McKinney, T. D., and Desjardins, C. 1973. Postnatal development of the testis, fighting behavior, and fertility in house mice. *Biol. Reprod.* 9:279–94.

————, and Pasley, J. N. 1974. Effect of ACTH on reproductive organs of immature female northern grasshopper mice (*Onychomys leucogaster*). *J. Reprod. Fertil.* 41:467–70.

————, et al. 1975. Pineal influence on intermale aggression in adult house mice. *Physiol. Behav.* 15:213–16.

Melby, J. C. 1977. Clinical pharmacology of systemic corticosteroids. *Ann. Rev. Pharmacol. Toxicol.* 17:511–27.

Metzgar, L. H. 1971. Behavioral population regulation in the woodmouse *Peromyscus leucopus. Am. Midl. Nat.* 86:434–48.

Mialhe-Voloss, C. 1958. Posthypophyse et activite corticotrope. *Acta Endocrinol., Suppl. 35*, 1:96.

Moriarty, C. M., and Moriarty, G. C. 1975. Bioactive and immunoactive ACTH in the rat pituitary: influence of stress and adrenalectomy. *Endocrinology* 96:1419–25.

Moriarty, G. C., et al. 1975. The effect of stress on the cytology and immunocytochemistry of pars intermedia cells in the rat pituitary. *Endocrinology* 96:1426–36.

Muraki, T., et al. 1977. Effects of morphine and naloxone on serum LH, FSH, and prolactin levels and on hypothalamic content of LH-RF in proestrous rats. *Endocrinol. Jap.* 24:313–15.

Murray, K. F. 1965. Population changes during the 1957–1958 vole (*Microtus*) outbreak in California. *Ecology* 45:163–71.

Myers, K., et al. 1971. The effects of varying density and space on sociality and health of animals. In *Behavior and environment*, ed. A. H. Esser, pp. 148–87. New York: Plenum Press.

Mysterud, I., et al. 1972. On winter breeding of the wood lemming (*Myopus schisticolor*). *Norw. J. Zool.* 20:91–92.

Nagy, Z. M., et al. 1977. Undernutrition by rearing in large litters delays the development of reflexive, locomotor, and memory processes in mice. *J. Comp. Physiol. Psychol.* 91:682–96.

Negro-Vilar, A., et al. 1973. Evidence for changes in sensitivity to testosterone negative feedback on gonadotropin release during sexual development in the male rat. *Endocrinology* 93:729–35.

Nemeth, S., et al. 1975. Shortened ACTH response to trauma in repeatedly injured rats. *Horm. Metab. Res.* 7:101.

Newson, J. 1962. Seasonal differences in reticulocyte count, haemoglobin level and spleen weight in wild voles. *Br. J. Haematol.* 8:296–302.

———, and Chitty D. 1962, Haemoglobin levels, growth and survival in two *Microtus* populations. *Ecology* 43:733–38.

Nowaczynski, W., et al. 1975. Dynamic aldosterone and 18-hydroxy-deoxycorticosterone studies in labile and stable benign essential hypertension. *J. Steroid Biochem.* 6:767–78.

Ogle, T. F. 1974. Effects of ACTH on ovarian histochemistry and maintenance of pregnancy in deermice. *Biol. Reprod.* 11:288–96.

———. 1977. Modification of serum luteinizing hormone and prolactin concentrations by corticotropin and adrenalectomy in ovariectomized rats. *Endocrinology* 101:494–97.

Oliver, C., et al. 1977. Hypothalamic-pituitary vasculature: evidence for retrograde blood flow in pituitary stalk. *Endocrinology* 101:598–604.

Orth, D. N., and Nicholson, W. E. 1977. Different molecular forms of ACTH. *Ann. N.Y. Acad. Sci.* 297:27–48.

———, et al. 1970. Adrenocorticotropic hormone (ACTH) and melanocyte stimulating hormone (MSH) production by a single cell. Endocrinol. Soc. 52nd Annu. Meet., Abstr. 207.

———. 1973. ACTH and MSH production by a single cloned mouse pituitary tumor cell line. *Endocrinology* 92:385–93.

Ozdzenski, W., and Mystkowska, E. T. 1976. Stages of pregnancy in the bank vole. *Acta Theriol.* 21:279–86.

Pacold, S. T., et al. 1978. Biologically active pituitary hormones in the rat brain amygdaloid nucleus. *Science* 199:804–06.

Pasley, J. N., and Christian, J. J. 1971. Effects of ACTH on voles (*Microtus pennsylvanicus*) related to reproductive function and renal disease. *Proc. Soc. Exp. Biol. Med.* 137:268–72.

———, and Christian, J. J. 1972. The effect of ACTH, group caging and adrenalectomy in *Peromyscus leucopus* with emphasis on suppression of reproductive function. *Proc. Soc. Exp. Biol. Med.* 139:921–25.

Patric, E. F. 1962. Reproductive characteristics of red-backed mouse during years of differing population densities. *J. Mammal.* 43:200–05.

Pelletier, G., et al. 1977. Immunohistochemical localization of β-lipotropic hormone in the pituitary gland. *Endocrinology* 100:770–76.

Pert, C. B., and Snyder, S. H. 1973. Opiate receptor: demonstration in nervous tissue. *Science* 179:1011–14.

Petterborg, L. J. 1978. Effect of photoperiod on body weight in the vole, *Microtus montanus. Can. J. Zool.* 56:431–35.

Poole, A. E., and Brain, P. 1974. Effects of adrenalectomy and treatments with ACTH and glucocorticoids on isolation-induced aggressive behavior in male albino mice. *Prog. Brain Res.* 41:471–72.

Poole, A. E., and Brain, P. F. 1975. Acute influences of corticotrophin on isolation-induced fighting in male albino mice. *J. Endocrinol.* 65:35P–36P.

Rapp. J. P., and Christian, J. J. 1963. Splenic extramedullary hematopoiesis in grouped male mice. *Proc. Soc. Exp. Biol. Med.* 114:26–28.

Reiter, R. J., and Ellison, N. M. 1970. Delayed puberty in blinded anosmic female rats: role of the pineal. *Biol. Reprod.* 2:216–22.

———, and Vaughan, M. K. 1977. Pineal antigonadotrophic substances—polypeptides and indoles. *Life Sci.* 21:159–72.

———, et al. 1970. Interaction of photic and olfactory stimuli in mediating pineal-induced gonadal regression in adult female rats. *Gen. Comp. Endocrinol.* 15:326–33.

Rice, R. W., and Critchlow, V. 1976. Extrahypothalamic control of stress-induced inhibition of growth hormone secretion in the rat. *Endocrinology* 99:970–76.

Riegle, G. D. 1973. Chronic stress effects on adrenocortical responsiveness in young and aged rats. *Neuroendocrinology* 11:1–10.

Roberts, J. L., and Herbert, E. 1977a. Characterization of a common precursor to corticotropin and β-lipotropin: cell-free synthesis of the precursor and identification of corticotropin peptides in the molecule. *Proc. Natl. Acad. Sci. U.S.A.* 74:4826–30.

———, and Herbert, E. 1977b. Chracterization of a common precursor to corticotropin and β-lipotropin: identification of β-lipotropin peptides and their arrangement relative to corticotropin in the precursor synthesized in a cell-free system. *Proc. Natl. Acad. Sci. U.S.A.* 74:5300–04.

Rochefort, G. J., et al. 1959. Depletion of pituitary corticotrophin by various stresses and by neurohypophyseal preparations. *J. Physiol (Lond.)* 146:105–116.

Ronai, A. Z., et al. 1977. Differential behaviour of LPH-(61–91)-peptide in different model systems: comparison of the opioid activities of LPH (61–91)-peptide and its fragments. *FEBS Lett.* 74:182–84.

Rónnekleiv, O. K., and McCann, S. M. 1975. Effects of pinealectomy, anosmia, and blinding alone or in combination on gonadotropin secretion and pituitary and target gland weight in intact and castrated male rats. *Neuroendocrinology* 19:97–114.

Rossier, J., et al. 1977. Radioimmunoassay of brain peptides—evaluation of a methodology for assay of beta-endorphin and enkephalin. *Life Sci.* 21:847–52.

Roth, R. R. 1974. The effect of temperature and light combinations upon the gonads of male red-back voles. *Biol. Reprod.* 10:309–14.

Rowley, M. H., and Christian, J. J. 1977. Competition between lactating *Peromyscus leucopus* and juvenile *Microtus pennsylvanicus*. *Behav. Biol.* 20:70–80.

Rugh, R. 1968. *The mouse: its reproduction and development*. Minneapolis: Burgess.

Sakakura, M., et al. 1976. Studies on fast feedback mechanisms by endogenous glucocorticoids. *Endocrinology* 98:954–57.

Sakellaris, P. C., and Vernikos-Danellis, J. 1975. Increased rate of response of the pituitary-adrenal system in rats adapted to chronic stress. *Endocrinology* 97:597–602.

Sassenrath, E. N. 1970. Increased adrenal responsiveness related to social stress in rhesus monkeys. *Horm. Behav.* 1:283–97.

———, et al. 1969. Social behavior and corticoid correlates in *Macaca mulatta*. In *Proceeding of the second international congress of primatology* pp. 219–31. Basel: Karger.

Sato, T., et al. 1975. Corticosterone-induced changes in hypothalamic corticotropin-releasing factor (CRF) content after stress. *Endocrinology* 97:265–74.

Schorger, A. W. 1956. Abundance of deer mice in Tuscola County, Michigan, in 1854. *J. Mammal.* 37:121–22.

Schwyzer, R. 1977. ACTH: a short introductory review. *Ann. N.Y. Acad. Sci.* 297:3–25.

Seggie, J. A., and Brown, G. M. 1975. Stress response patterns of plasma corticosterone, prolactin, and growth hormone in the rat, following handling or exposure to novel environment. *Can. J. Physiol. Pharmacol.* 53:629–37.

Selye, H. 1954. Stress and lactation. *Rev. Can. Biol.* 13:377–84.

Shaikh, A. A., and Shaikh, S. A. 1975. Adrenal and ovarian steroid secretion in the rat estrous cycle temporally related to gonadotropins and steroid levels found in peripheral plasma. *Endocrinology* 96:37–44.

Sheppe, W. A. 1965. Unseasonal breeding in artificial colonies of *Peromyscus leucopus*. *J. Mammal.* 46:641–46.

Shoemaker, W. J., and Wurtman, R. J. 1971. Perinatal undernutrition: accumulation of catecholamines in rat brain. *Science* 171:1017–19.

Slaga, T. J., and Krum, A. K. 1973. Modification of rabbit adrenal steroid biosynthesis by prolonged ACTH administration. *Endocrinology* 93:517–26.

Smelik, P. G. 1960. Mechanism of hypophysial response to psychic stress. *Acta Endocrinol.* 33:437–43.

Snyder, R. L. 1960. Physiologic and behavioral responses to an altered sex ratio of adults in a population of woodchucks. Doctoral dissertation, Johns Hopkins School of Hygiene and Public Health.

Southwick, C. H. 1964. *Peromyscus leucopus*: an interesting subject for studies of socially induced stress responses. *Science* 143:55–6.

Stark, E., et al. 1963. Pituitary and adrenal responsiveness in rats after prolonged treatment with ACTH. *Can. J. Biochem. Physiol.* 41:1771–77.

Sung, K. P., et al. 1977. Serum corticosterone concentrations in reproductively mature and inhibited deer mice (*Peromyscus maniculatus bairdii*). *J. Reprod. Fertil.* 49:201–06.

Székely, J. I., et al. 1977. C-terminal fragment (residues 61–91) of beta-lipotropin in a natural opiate-like neurohormone of brain? *Experientia* 33:54–55.

Taché, Y., et al. 1976. Shift in adenohypophyseal activity during chronic intermittent immobilization of rats. *Neuroendocrinology* 222:325–36.

Tamarkin, L., et al. 1976a. Effect of melatonin on the reproductive systems of male and female syrian hamsters: a diurnal rhythm in sensitivity to melatonin. *Endocrinology* 99:1534–41.

————, et al. 1976b. Regulation of serum gonadotropins by photoperiod and testicular hormone in the syrian hamster. *Endocrinology* 99:1528–33.

————, 1977. Effect of melatonin administrered during the night on reproductive function in the Syrian hamster. *Endocrinology* 101:631–34.

Terenius, L., and Wahlstrom, A. 1975a. Morphine-like ligand for opiate receptors in Human CSF. *Life Sci.* 16:1759–64.

————, and Wahlstrom, A. 1975b. Search for an endogenous ligand for the opiate receptor. *Acta Physiol. Scand.* 94:74–81.

Terman, C. R. 1968. Inhibition of reproductive maturation and function in laboratory populations of prairie deermice: a test of pheromone influence. *Ecology* 49:1169–71.

————. 1969. Weights of selected organs of deer mice (*Peromyscus maniculatus bairdii*) from asymptotic laboratory populations. *J. Mammal.* 50:311–20.

————. 1973. Reproductive inhibition in asymptotic populations of prairie deermice. *J. Reprod. Fertil. Suppl. 19*, 457–63.

Terry, L. C., et al. 1976. Antiserum to somatostatin prevents stress-induced inhibition of growth hormone secretion in the rat. *Science* 192:565–67.

Theisen, C. T., et al. 1976. Prenatal SRIF: possible effects on reproduction and neurogenesis. Endocrinol. Soc. 58th Annu. Meet., Abstr. 460.

Thomas, D., and Terman, C. R. 1975. The effects of differential prenatal and postnatal social environments on sexual maturation of young prairie deermice (*Peromyscus maniculatus bairdii*). *Anim. Behav.* 23:241–48.

To, L. P., and Tamarin, R. H. 1977. The relation of population density and adrenal gland weight in cycling and noncycling voles (*Microtus*). *Ecology* 85:928–34.

Turek, F. W. 1977a. Antigonadal effect of melatonin in pinealectomized and intact male hamster. *Proc. Soc. Exp. Biol. Med.* 155:31–34.

————. 1977b. The interaction of the photoperiod and testosterone in regulating serum gonadotropin levels in castrated male hamsters. *Endocrinology* 101:1210–15.

————, et al. 1975. Melatonin: antigonadal and progonadal effects in male golden hamsters. *Science* 190:280–82.

————, et al. 1976a. Differential effects of melatonin on the testes of photoperiodic and nonphotoperiodic rodents. *Biol. Reprod.* 15:94–97.

————, et al. 1976b. Melatonin-induced inhibition of testicular function in adult golden hamster. *Proc. Soc. Exp. Biol. Med.* 151:502–06.

Turner, B. N., and Iverson, S. L. 1973. The annual cycle of aggression in male *Microtus pennsylvanicus* and its relation to population parameters. *Ecology* 54:967–81.

Ungar, F. 1965. Discussion. *Recent Prog. Horm. Res.* 21:571–72.

Urca, G., et al. 1977. Morphine and enkephalin: analgesic and epileptic properties. *Science* 197:83–86.

Vandenbergh, J. G. 1974. Social determinants of the onset of puberty in rodents. *J. Sex. Res.* 10:181–93.

Varon, H. H., and Christian, J. J. 1963. Effects of adrenal androgens on immature female mice. *Endocrinology* 72:210–22.

Vaughan, M. K., et al. 1973. Effect of ovariectomy and constant dark on the weight of reproductive and certain other organs in the female vole, *Microtus montanus*. *J. Reprod. Fertil.* 32:9–14.

Velardo, J. T. 1957. Action of adrenocorticotropin on pregnancy and litter size in rats. *Am. J. Physiol.* 191:319–22.

Ventura, M. A., et al. 1977. Corticosterone secretion after neurogenic stress in intact and hypophysectomized rats. *Experientia* 33:686.

Vom Saal, F. S., et al. 1976. Time of neonatal androgen exposure influences length of testosterone treatment required to induce aggression in adult male and female mice. *Behav. Biol.* 17:391–97.

Van Holst, D. 1972. Renal failure as the cause of death in *Tupaia belangeri* exposed to persistent social stress. *J. Comp. Physiol.* 78:236–73.

Ward, I. L. 1972. Prenatal stress feminizes and demasculinizes the behavior of males. *Science* 175:82–84.

Watson, S. J., et al. 1977. Immunocytochemical localization of methionine enkephalin—preliminary observations. *Life Sci.* 21:733–38.

Wei, E. T., et al. 1977. Comparison of the behavioral effects of β-endorphin and enkephalin analogs. *Life Sci.* 21:321–28.

Wellmann, K. F., and Volk, B. W. 1972. Fine structural changes in the rabbit placenta induced by cortisone. *Arch. Pathol.* 94:147–57.

Widdowson, E. M., and Kennedy, G. C. 1962. Rate of growth, mature weight, and life-span. *Proc. R. Soc. Lond. Ser. B* 156:96–108.

———, and McCance, R. A. 1960. Some effects of acelerating growth. I. General somatic development. *Proc. R. Soc. Lond. Ser. B* 152:188–206.

Wilson, G. S., and Miles, A. A. 1961. *Topley and Wilson's principles of bacteriology and immunity*, vol. 11, 4th ed. Baltimore: Williams & Wilkins.

Witorsch, R. J., and Brodish, A. 1972. Evidence for acute ACTH release by extrahypothalamic mechanisms. *Endocrinology* 90:1160–67.

Worth, R. W., et al. 1973. Field and laboratory studies on the control of luteinizing hormone secretion and gonadal activity in the vole, *Microtus agrestis. J. Reprod. Fertil. Suppl. 19*, 89–99.

Yasukawa, N., et al. 1978. Opiate antagonist counteracts reproductive inhibition by porcine ACTH extract. *Life Sci.* 22:1381–90.

5

DISPERSAL AND POPULATION REGULATION IN RODENTS

Robert H. Tamarin

I divide the discussion of the role of dispersal in rodent population regulation into three sections: (1) a brief general view of population regulation; (2) an assessment of the importance of dispersal in population regulation; (3) a discussion of the population cycles of voles and lemmings as a specific example of the importance of dispersal.

The Meaning of Population Regulation

The search for a general theory of population regulation has been impeded by problems of terminology; basic approach, both theoretical and practical; and types of organism studied (Lidicker 1978; Tamarin 1978b). The basic population-regulating mechanisms are (1) density-independent factors, and (2) density-dependent factors, including both (a) extrinsic factors, and (b) intrinsic factors. I will expand on these below.

A basic difference of approach by population biologists was defined by Orians (1962), who made the distinction between an evolutionary and a functional view of the study of ecology. According to Orians, evolutionary population ecologists are interested in the adaptations of organisms, whereas functional population ecologists are more interested in the proximate controls of population density. In this chapter I will concentrate on the kinds of questions that evolutionary ecologists are asking.

A controversy has existed in ecology for some time over whether density-dependent or density-independent factors regulate populations. Those interested in density-dependent control have for the most part been evolutionary ecologists, and those interested in density-independent mechanisms have for the most part been functional ecologists. Many ecologists have defined population regulation to mean control of population density by density-dependent factors (Nicholson 1933). They have eliminated a class of regulating mechanisms, most specifically the weather, by defining it out of existence. Others (Smith 1935; Andrewartha and Birch 1954) have countered this by noting that the effects of weather can be density-dependent.

As an evolutionary population biologist, I am not really interested in determining what killed a particular animal. I am more interested in trying to understand the evolutionary framework within which a species' density is confined. To be interested in the proximal cause of mortality in every species without a framework of evolutionary theory is little more than an exercise in data gathering, and it seems reasonable to look beyond the weather or the food supply of a population to determine the regulating mechanisms. Weather can certainly kill individuals, as can starvation. However, most populations of higher organisms have evolved within the framework of a given weather and resource milieu. They have thus evolved mechanisms that keep their densities below the point of exhausting the resources.

The environment will eventually limit all populations to a certain density. This limitation will come about because of climatic severity or by a lack of resources, most notably food or space. The limit to ultimate density will be different for different habitats in different areas. However, this does not mean that climate, food, or a lack of space regulates these populations. We have good evidence, at least in vertebrate populations, that organisms have evolved mechanisms to prevent the population from increasing in numbers past the point of putting the population in jeopardy of extinction. It is these mechanisms that regulate the population. We thus see territoriality and a host of other interactions causing a limitation of population density. As will be mentioned shortly, these mechanisms can evolve through individual selection.

This view should be clearly differentiated from a multifactor mechanism of population regulation which states that populations can be regulated by different factors at different times. (See Lidicker 1978 for a summary of this view.) I have not said that populations cannot be regulated by many factors; I have said that this is the wrong way to phrase the problem. Determining that density is set by feeding sites in one population and by nesting sites in another does not give us great insight into population regulation. Rather, studying the behaviors of the individuals through which these factors regulate the population density may tell us that either nest sites or feeding sites can regulate density under different circumstances. We can then make predictions in a new population that, if supported, will result in a general theory.

An evolutionary ecologist can then define the study of population regulation in higher organisms as *the study of the relevant aspects of the behavior and genetics of a species that prevent the density of the species from exceeding the carrying capacity of the environment.*

How do we know that in fact organisms have evolved these mechanisms? The answer lies in our observations of the behavioral plasticity and complexity of mammal and bird populations. Territoriality exists. Nonbreeding members of most species exist, indicating social systems that lower the reproductive output of the population. Most mammal and bird populations do not reproduce to the utmost capacity of their physiologies (Watson and Moss 1970). Evolution is the one great paradigm of modern biology. To deny its role in the regulation of density seems inappropriate.

Potential Regulation Mechanisms

1. *Density-independent factors*: Populations can certainly be wiped out by weather catastrophes (Ehrlich et al. 1972). By our definition and interests, however, we are not concentrating on these as significant regulating factors. This is not to deny evolutionary changes in populations to deal with severe weather. Some species show morphological adaptations, some hibernate or become torpid, and others migrate to avoid difficult periods of the year.

2. *Density-dependent factors*: These factors, which increase their effects as the density of the regulated population increases, can be classified into two categories:

(a) Extrinsic factors: Mortality in these cases is caused by other species or organisms, including predators, parasites, diseases, and interspecific competitors.

(b) Intrinsic factors: Mortality here is caused by behaviors of individual members of a population directed at other members of the same population. This is often referred to as self-regulation. Intraspecific competition is the overriding factor. Presumably, its action has led to many significant evolutionary developments of populations, such as territoriality and changes in many life history parameters.

There is in many cases a fine, and not necessarily significant, line between some of the intrinsic and extrinsic factors from an evolutionary point of view. For example, there is evidence, to be discussed shortly, that predation does not take a random sample of a population. Thus, those organisms that are taken by predators may be the losers in intraspecific competitive bouts. Here, then, mortality arises from an interaction of intrinsic and extrinsic mechanisms of regulation.

Let me reiterate that we are not simply looking for the cause of death of a given individual but rather the adaptations of a species. In my own study of the regulation of density in voles, field mice, and lemmings, which undergo 3- to 4-year cycles of density, I have been concentrating on genetic and behavioral aspects of these cycling species. As my work has progressed, I am more and more impressed by the importance of dispersal in population processes: its safety valve value in relieving density pressure and, possibly more important, its potential to bring about genetic changes in populations.

The Role of Dispersal in Population Processes*

Dispersal is probably a necessary part of the population processes of almost all species because all species overproduce. The species that has not overproduced has gone extinct. Dispersal—the permanent movement by an individual away from a home area—can account for quite a large proportion of the productivity of a population (Myers and Krebs 1971; Tamarin 1977a; Krebs et al. 1976). Since we know that all populations overproduce, and we know that a major fate of overproduced animals is dispersal (Hilborn and Krebs 1976; Tamarin 1977a), we can look for two major effects of dispersal on the parent population. First, dispersers can provide a "safety valve" for the population (Lidicker 1962). As density increases, some animals may choose to leave because they are intolerant to crowding. Others may be forced out by more dominant individuals. Thus, density is reduced and the population does not overshoot the carrying capacity. Second, if the dispersers are not a random sample of the population, they can

---

*Editors' Note: Compare the discussions of dispersal among rhesus monkeys by Sade and among wolves by Packard and Mech as well as the discussion of human migration patterns by Freedman and of flux in groups of Stone Age hunters by Cohen. Note particularly that the distinction which Tamarin develops between presaturation and saturation dispersers is echoed or implied in these studies.

effect changes in the gene pool of the parent population that can lead to important evolutionary changes within the parent population. We will explore these shortly.

We need to determine what advantage accrues to the disperser. We recognize that selection must be on an individual level. That is, natural selection acts on individuals, not on populations. Van Valen (1971) has suggested that dispersal is a balance between group and individual selection. He uses the term "group selection" for interdemic selection which involves the extinction of local populations. Restricted cases, where certain traits will cause the extinction of local populations which can then be recolonized by different genotypes, will result in group (interdemic) selection. Other cases besides dispersal are known, such as the T-allele case in house mice (Lewontin and Dunn 1960).

In an evolutionary sense, every disperser weighs the advantages and disadvantages in staying versus leaving. Natural selection, by definition, will favor the disperser which makes a decision that results in an advantage to itself. Most of the following arguments have been very nicely summarized by Lidicker (1975). Disadvantages occur because the animal is leaving a dependable home area. Advantages are assumed to occur because there must be the possibility of some reward for an organism to risk the disadvantages of dispersing. Let us begin with the disadvantages. It is known that animals that leave their territories or home ranges are more exposed to predation than are residents. This has been shown; for example, by Carl (1971) in arctic ground squirrels, by Errington (1963) for muskrats, and by Metzgar (1967) in a laboratory experiment with white-footed mice. Most available evidence points out the increased vulnerability to predation of nonresident animals.

By the same token, the movements that open an animal up to predation also make that animal susceptible to starvation, exposure, and all the stresses that go with those two factors. In addition, a dispersing mouse may not be able to find a mate. Thus, a disperser runs a strong risk of actual, as well as genetic, death. To a dispersing animal, however, these risks must be weighed against both the disadvantages of staying and the possible advantages of leaving. Under conditions of increased crowding, certain types of individuals run a higher and higher risk of both not breeding and not surviving. These individuals, whose Darwinian fitness is rapidly approaching zero, have the greatest potential of increasing their fitness by dispersing. This may fall gen-

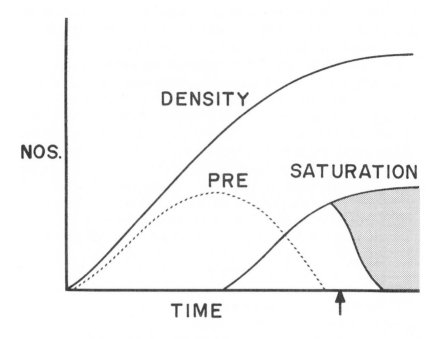

Figure 5.1.   Diagramatic representation of change in numbers (ordinate) versus time (abscissa).
Presaturation (PRE) and saturation dispersal are also shown. At the arrow, a barrier
to dispersal is introduced. The ensuing hatched area represents frustrated dispersal.
(Modified from Lidicker 1975.)

erally to an age class, such as the juvenile and subadults in a crowded
population (Boonstra 1977; Tamarin 1977a). However, the potential
gain in fitness may also fall to certain phenotypes and genotypes within
an age class (Myers and Krebs 1971).

Before listing the possible advantages to dispersers, let me present
some clarifying terminology devised by Lidicker (1975), who defined
two types of dispersal: presaturation and saturation (fig. 5.1). Saturation dispersal is the emigration of individuals from a population whose
density is near the carrying capacity of the environment. Presaturation
dispersal is the emigration of individuals from a population before that
population reaches the carrying capacity. These are more likely to be
individuals who substantially increase their fitness by leaving.

Lidicker (1975) names four types of advantages gained by dispersers: (1) *quantitative*: increased opportunities for mating; (2) *qualitative*: increased opportunity for the advantages of outbreeding, such as

heterosis;* (3) *diplomatic*: increased opportunity to avoid population crashes and predation buildup; and (4) *economic*: the more efficient use of resources. The presumption in Lidicker's terminology is that the presaturation dispersers are healthy individuals, with a high reproductive value, which gain substantially by dispersing. Saturation dispersers, on the other hand, tend to be the very young, the old, the weak, and others with an inherently low fitness which are dispersing out of desperation. They have a very slim hope of actually increasing their fitness. Both types of dispersal behavior should have evolutionary implications. Presaturation dispersal should have more of a creative evolutionary effect where individuals of relatively high fitness leave one population and play significant roles in the founding of others. Saturation dispersal should act in a more stabilizing fashion: a strong selection for those individuals best able to survive and reproduce under densities approaching the carrying capacity. As will be discussed shortly, it is the presaturation type of dispersal that may play the most significant role in population regulation.

Three aspects of dispersal are currently of prime interest to population biologists:

1. *Dispersal and population regulation.* Lidicker (1962, 1975) has suggested several models where dispersal, acting as a safety valve, can regulate, or maintain the density of a population at or below the carrying capacity.† Krebs et al. (1973) and Tamarin (1978a) have suggested models of population regulation where the dispersers are genetically different from the residents. This selective pressure is important in a genetic mechanism of population regulation. I will elaborate on this in the last section of this paper.

2. *Genetic and evolutionary implications of dispersal.* Several authors have developed mathematical models that have demonstrated that a genetic polymorphism for dispersal propensity will be maintained in a population (Van Valen 1971; Roff 1975). We thus have the theoretical framework for a genetic component of dispersal. That there actually is a genetic component to dispersal has not been documented,

---

Editors' Note: See Southwick et al., who view emigration of young adult male rhesus monkeys as a primary mechanism of gene flow between groups. See Ripley for a discussion of male infanticide in langur monkeys as a mechanism for generating genetic polymorphism.

†*Editors' Note:* However, see Packard and Mech, who state that, in addition to facilitating a population decline in dense populations, dispersal among wolves may contribute to a population increase in sparse populations.

although it has been suggested (Chitty 1970; Krebs et al. 1973; Anderson 1970). Myers and Krebs (1971) have shown that the gene pool of dispersers is different from that of residents. We await more empirical research in this area.

3. *The factors that cause individual animals to disperse.* Another area in the general study of dispersal is that of determining the motivations or cues that trigger dispersal.* Recently, Bekoff (1977) has summarized this literature and draws the following conclusions. First, behavioral interactions directly at the time of dispersal do not seem to be the triggering mechanisms. In marmots and some canids, individuals are not driven out, but leave of their own accord. Second, it is found that both aggressive and nonaggressive animals can migrate; there is no universal correlation between aggression level and dispersal propensity. In addition, aggression in the population may not be a direct predictor of social rank. Very aggressive individuals may or may not be the most dominant and may or may not make up a substantial part of the disperser group. Both Bekoff (1977) and Van Valen (1971) emphasize the potential selective advantage to parents of having their offspring disperse.

Dispersal and Population Regulation in Vole Cycles

I would like to explore further the nature of dispersal and its role in population regulation by discussing some recent research that has been done on vole cycles. Voles (the British term for field mice) and lemmings undergo regular cycles of density lasting about 3–4 years (fig. 5.2). These cycles occur in virtually all populations previously studied in the north temperate region. Among population biologists, there is no general agreement as to what causes these cycles. Nothing in the environment seems to exhibit a similar periodicity. May (1976) has provided a theoretical model of vole population regulation dependent on time lags in seasonal environments. May left open the biological, density-dependent parameters, inducing the time lags. Earlier, Schaffer and Tamarin (1973) suggested that the time lags coupled with os-

---

Editors' Note: See Sade on the diverse proximate causes of the dispersal of young males from rhesus monkey groups.

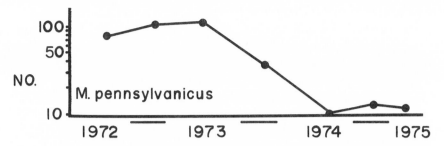

Figure 5.2. Density changes in the meadow vole, *Microtus pennsylvanicus*, at Barnstable, Massachusetts, from 1972 to 1975. Density, on a logarithmic scale, is number per 2
acres. The data points are the mean values, summed over summer and winter seasons, of the minimum number known alive. The bars represent the winter months
of November through February. These results came from a monthly live-trapping
program. (Redrawn from Tamarin 1977b.)

cillations in some environmental parameter also had the potential to
produce cycles.

Current hypotheses of vole regulation include predation (Pearson
1966), nutrient depletion (Batzli and Pitelka 1970; Schultz 1964), plant
secondary products (Freeland 1974), and the stress-related endocrine
(Christian and Davis 1964) and polymorphic behavior (Chitty 1967)
hypotheses. Krebs and Myers (1974) have summarized the literature
on this subject.

We know that dispersal is extremely important for population regulation in these species because they show what is referred to as a "fence
effect" when enclosed (Krebs et al. 1973). Krebs et al. (1969) enclosed
2-acre populations of field mice in southern Indiana and found that
mice within the fence increased to abnormally high density. Earlier
work within smaller enclosures had shown the same type of aberrant
demography (Clarke 1955; Louch 1956; van Wijngaarden 1960). The
problem was that voles intent on dispersing had nowhere to go: they
were subsequently reassimilated into the population. Lidicker (1975)
used the term "dispersal sink," which I interpret to mean the place into
which dispersers would vanish. Presumably, the fenced populations
did not have dispersal sinks. At this point, it seemed to me that the
next step in investigating the role of dispersal in vole demography was
to try to incorporate a dispersal sink into a fenced population. One way
would be to allow dispersal out of a fenced enclosure by putting in exit
doors of some type. A second way would be to include marginal habi-

tat within a fenced area. This marginal habitat would be continuously trapped out. The assumption is that any animal that would enter the marginal habitat would be a disperser. A third way to test this idea would be to look for a naturally enclosed area, such as an island, that might somehow have a dispersal sink within.

The first method, using exit outlets, has been tried with varying degrees of success by several workers (Gaines et al. 1979; Getz, Univ. Illinois, and Riggs, Univ. California—personal communications). The results of these studies have not yet been fully reported in the literature. The second method, of including dispersal sinks within a fenced enclosure, is currently under study in a project begun in the summer of 1978. My students and I included a suboptimal habitat within a fence and have continually removed all dispersers. We predict that the population within such a fence will show normal demography (i.e., cycle). All those animals that seek to disperse will be free to do so, leaving a "core" population indistinguishable from an unfenced one. Although our results are preliminary, they are encouraging. Using a method where suboptimal habitat was artificially created, Beacham (1979) has achieved similar, favorable results.

It is the third method, involving island populations, that I would like to discuss here in some detail. The beach vole, *Microtus breweri*, is endemic to Muskeget Island, off the coast of Nantucket, Massachusetts (Tamarin and Kunz 1974). The island, which is about a square mile of low-lying sand covered with beach grass (*Ammophila*), has been isolated from its neighbors for about 2000–3000 years (Wetherbee et. al. 1972; Starrett 1958). In this time speciation has taken place, although there is still some controversy about the status of the beach vole (Fivush et al. 1975). Whether or not it is a true species is not critical to our interest in its population dynamics. About one third of the island consists of suboptimal habitat: freshwater marsh, salt marsh, open dune, scrub. I believed at the outset of the study that this suboptimal habitat would satisfy the requirements of being a dispersal sink to this population, fenced in by the ocean. After 7 years of study, it appears that my original belief was a superficial view of what a dispersal sink really is. The beach vole population does not cycle (Tamarin 1977b). It has an almost flat density curve (fig. 5.3), as compared to normal cycles exhibited by mainland controls (fig. 5.2).

Analysis of movement data on Muskeget and the mainland indicates that the pattern is inherently different in the two areas (Tamarin

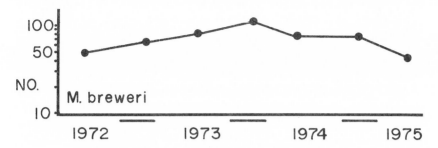

Figure 5.3.   Density changes in the beach vole, *Microtus breweri*, at Muskeget Island, Massachusetts. See the legend for Figure 5.2.

1977a). The data were gathered using "vacuum" grids, where all animals caught in a trapping period were removed; animals found on that
area the next trapping period were considered dispersers. Island movers (in the noncycling population) seemed to be predominantly saturation dispersers, whereas mainland movers (in the cycling population)
appeared to be of the presaturation type. That is, mainland dispersers
were not a random sample of the population for age category and sex
ratio, whereas on the island, dispersers were a random sample. This
indicates that dispersal on the island is "frustrated" (Lidicker 1975).
Frustrated dispersal comes about when dispersal is prevented by one
means or another—either the absence or the saturation of a dispersal
sink. We can thus draw the conclusion that Muskeget Island is acting
like a fenced population in that dispersal is not occurring in a fashion
similar to unfenced populations. We should thus be able to add Muskeget to the list of populations showing the fence effect. In a similar
manner, Sullivan (1977) studying the deer mouse, *Peromyscus*, near
Vancouver, found a lower rate of movement in island populations.

Because the beach vole does not cycle, two questions present themselves: (1) Is it true that the island does not have a dispersal sink; and
(2) Why did the island population not cycle as the mainand population
did? Regarding the dispersal sink, the simplest explanation would be
that there is no dispersal sink on Muskeget. Animals entering the suboptimal habitat can return to the favorable habitat to be reassimilated.
This is because suboptimal habitat by itself is not necessarily a dispersal sink. For suboptimal habitat to be a dispersal sink, the animals that
enter it must in some way be prevented from reentering the core population. This can happen either of two ways. The dispersers can move

on, or they can be killed in the suboptimal habitat. On Muskeget Island they cannot move on because there is nowhere else to go, assuming they do not go into the sea. They are not all killed because there is a paucity of predators on the island.

Muskeget has only two predators, both avian. A few short-eared owls (*Asio flammeus*) and marsh hawks (*Circus cyaneus*) are usually found on the island, where they occasionally breed. There are no mammalian carnivores on the island. Although there are large numbers of breeding seagulls (*Larus marinus* and *L. argentatus*) on the island, they do not prey on *Microtus*. Thus, without mammalian predators, there is not an intense predation pressure on the mice. Dispersing voles who enter suboptimal habitat can traverse it in relative safety and end up back in the core population. Unlike other species, such as ground squirrels (Carl 1971), voles will be reassimilated into the population. Ground squirrels and other rodents will prevent excess individuals from assimilating: they are killed or driven off.

Therefore, on Muskeget Island we have a population of mice that does not have a dispersal sink, exhibits frustrated dispersal, and at the same time shows aberrant demography: it does not cycle. Why does the disruption of dispersal in this isolated population lead to the absence of population cycles? Our simplest explanation is that the cycles are caused by a genetic mechanism. That is, of all the mechanisms suggested for the cause of vole cycles, the polymorphic behavior hypothesis is the one most disrupted by the alteration of dispersal (Krebs 1978). The other potential mechanisms are predation, food quality, and endocrine stress.

In this work, I am viewing predation as a means of keeping the dispersal sink functional rather than as an agent acting directly on the population.* As reviewed earlier, predators tend to take only excess individuals in a population. In more recent times, predation has been looked at more and more as a factor acting in conjunction with other agents in affecting rodent demography (Lidicker 1973; Fitzgerald 1977). That is, predation can exacerbate a decline and help maintain a low population without actually being the agent that initiates the decline. I think a reasonable view, in conjunction with our knowledge that predators tend to take nonresidents, is that predation is an impor-

Editors' Note: See Packard and Mech for a variation on the dispersal sink in wolves: dispersed wolves usually become nonreproductive lone wolves and have a decreased survival rate in dense populations. However, in sparse populations they may re-enter the breeding population.

tant agent of mortality which falls most heavily on dispersing or "excess" individuals in a population. Thus, the differences in predation between Muskeget Island and the mainland should be interpreted as an aspect of dispersal rather than as supportive of predation as a regulation mechanism in these populations.

Several hypotheses have been suggested regarding an interaction between the mice and their food that produces a cycle of nutrient quality in the plants they eat, or a cycle in toxicity (Schultz 1964; Freeland 1974). Unfortunately, there is no evidence that these mechanisms occur in temperate vole populations. However, even more compelling, if a food mechanism were regulating voles, we would expect populations on both Cape Cod and nearby Muskeget to cycle. Why should a lack of dispersal disrupt a food mechanism of population regulation? While we have been investigating the feeding habits of the beach vole (Rothstein and Tamarin 1977), we have shed no light on why a food mechanism would differ between island and mainland populations. Actually, it should work more effectively on an island where frustrated dispersal will cause numbers initially to build up higher.

Social stress causing endocrine depletion has been suggested as a mechanism of population regulation (Christian and Davis 1964). If this mechanism held, we would expect more stress in the cycling mainland populations than in the noncycling island population. Using adrenal gland weight as an indicator of stress, To and Tamarin (1977) showed that this was not the case. There was more stress measured in the island population. Thus, in these populations, stress is not associated with cycling. This leaves us only with the polymorphic behavior mechanism of Chitty (1967).

This mechanism depends upon genetic change in the population as density increases. According to Chitty (1967), there is increased social stress in a population as density increases. This social stress puts a greater value on aggressive behavior, and by a process of natural selection, the population becomes filled more and more with aggressive individuals. Presumably, a population filled with aggressive individuals is one that will be at a disadvantage: it may be too aggressive to breed, or alternatively, aggressive individuals may have reduced survival. Whatever the eventual causes of mortality, one of the potentially more important selective agents bringing about the changes in behavior is dispersal. The dispersers may very well be behaviorally different from the residents. Krebs (1970) has shown that there are behavioral changes in cycling populations, and Myers and Krebs (1971) have shown that dispersers are genetically different from residents. Therefore, preventing dispersal on Muskeget Island will halt or severely reduce genetic change in the population. With the gene pool unchanged, a genetic mechanism will not function. More of the ramifications of this island model are presented in Tamarin (1978a).

Future Work

A critical gap exists in the study of voles and many other small mammals. We need information on the precise interactions that occur in nature between individuals. By the nature of the vole, and the way we study it, we do not gather these data. That is, voles are secretive organisms that live in runways close to the ground and underground. Although most vole species are not amenable to direct observations (however, see Leuze 1976), two alternative attacks have been mounted. The first, as documented here, is the statistical approach of gathering large masses of demographic data, and from these, inferring conclusions about the interactions of individuals based on general demographic trends. The second is to bring the vole into the laboratory, where parts of its behavioral repertoire can be dissected. Newer field techniques, such as radiotelemetry, are beginning to bridge the gap to some extent (Madison 1977).

Summary

Voles undergo regular fluctuations of density, referred to as the short-term cycle. Dispersal is vital to this cycle because fenced populations do not cycle. "Normal" populations need a dispersal sink. Suboptimal habitat is not simply a dispersal sink without predation or some other agent that causes the permanent removal of dispersers from a population. When this dispersal is prevented, as on islands or within fences, the populations do not show typical demography. Of the many hypotheses currently being investigated as causing cycles, the genetic hypothesis is most supported by our analysis of dispersal. From this conclusion, and from data summarized within this paper, we can generalize the importance of dispersal to all populations of higher organisms in both its negative aspects (removal of individuals from a population) and its positive aspects (the value of dispersers in recolonization and outbreeding). Dispersal fits within a framework of density-dependent mechanisms in population regulation. I support an evolutionary view of population regulation wherein we are not merely interested in what kills animals, but in the adaptations of populations to their resources.

Acknowledgments

Larry Reich read an earlier draft of this paper and he and Fred Wasserman made helpful comments. My research on population regulation discussed here has been supported by NIH Grants HD-06621, HD-11682, and grants from the Boston University Graduate School.

References

Anderson, P. 1970. Ecological structure and gene flow in small mammals. *Symp. Zool. Soc. Lond.* 26:299–325.

Andrewartha, H., and Birch, L. 1954. *The distribution and abundance of animals.* Chicago: Univ. of Chicago Press.

Batzli, G., and Pitelka, F. 1970. Influence of meadow mouse populations on California grassland. *Ecology* 51:1027–39.

Beacham, T. 1979. Dispersal, survival, and population regulation of the vole *Microtus townsendii*. Ph.D. dissertation, University of British Columbia.

Bekoff, M. 1977. Mammalian dispersal and the ontogeny of individual behavioral phenotypes. *Am. Nat.* 111:715–32.

Boonstra, R. 1977. Predation on *Microtus townsendii* populations: impact and vulnerability. *Can. J. Zool.* 55:1631–43.

Carl, E. 1971. Population control in arctic ground squirrels. *Ecology* 52:395–413.

Chitty, D. 1967. The natural selection of self-regulatory behaviour in animal populations. *Proc. Ecol. Soc. Aust.* 2:51–78.

———— 1970. Variation and population density. *Symp. Zool. Soc. Lond.* 26:327–33.

Christian, J., and Davis, D. 1964. Endocrines, behavior, and population. *Science* 146:1550–60.

Clarke, J. 1955. Influence of numbers on reproduction and survival in two experimental vole populations. *Proc. R. Soc. Lond. Ser. B* 144:68–85.

Ehrlich, P.; Breedlove, D.; Brussard, P.; and Sharp, M. 1972. Weather and the "regulation" of subalpine populations. *Ecology* 53:243–47.

Errington, P. 1963. *Muskrat populations.* Ames: Iowa State Univ. Press.

Fitzgerald, B. 1977. Weasel predation on a cyclic population of the montane vole (*Microtus montanus*) in California. *J. Anim. Ecol.* 46:367–97.

Fivush, B.; Parker, R.; and Tamarin, R. 1975. Karyotype of the beach vole, *Microtus breweri*, an endemic island species. *J. Mammal.* 56:272–73.

Freeland, W. 1974. Vole cycles—another hypothesis. *Am. Nat.* 108:238–45.

Gaines, M.; Vivas, A.; and Baker, C. 1979. An experimental analysis of dispersal in fluctuating vole populations: demographic parameters. Ecology, in press.

Hilborn, R., and Krebs, C. 1976. Fates of disappearing individuals in fluctuating populations of *Microtus townsendii*. *Can. J. Zool.* 54:1507–18.

Krebs, C. 1970. *Microtus* population biology: behavioral changes associated with the population cycle in *M. ochrogaster* and *M. pennsylvanicus*. *Ecology* 51:34–52.

———. 1978. A review of the Chitty Hypothesis of population regulation. *Can. J. Zool.* 56:2463–80.

———, and Myers, J. 1974. Population cycles in small mammals. *Adv. Ecol. Res.* 8:267–399.

———; Keller, B.; and Tamarin, R. 1969. *Microtus* population biology: demographic changes in fluctuating populations of *M. ochrogaster* and *M. pennsylvanicus* in southern Indiana. *Ecology* 50:587–607.

———; Gaines, M., Keller, B.; Myers, J., and Tamarin, R. 1973. Population cycles in small rodents. *Science* 179:35–41.

———; Wingate, I.; LeDuc, J.; Redfield, J.; Taitt, M.; and Hilborn, R. 1976. *Microtus* population biology: dispersal in fluctuating populations of *M. townsendii*. *Can. J. Zool.* 54:79–95.

Leuze, C. 1976. Social behaviour and dispersion in the water vole, *Arvicola terrestris*, Lacépède. Ph.D. dissertation, University of Aberdeen.

Lewontin, R., and Dunn, L. 1960. The evolutionary dynamics of a polymorphism in the house mouse. *Genetics* 45:705–22.

Lidicker, W. 1962. Emigration as a possible mechanism permitting the regulation of population density below carrying capacity. *Am. Nat.* 96:29–33.

———. 1973. Regulation of numbers in an island population of the California vole, a problem in community dynamics. *Ecol. Monogr.* 43:271–302.

———. 1975. The role of dispersal in the demography of small animals. *In Small mammals: their productivity and population dynamics*, ed. F. B. Golley. Int. Biol. Prog., vol. 5. Cambridge, England: Cambridge Univ. Press.

———. 1978. Regulation of numbers in small mammal populations. In *Population of small mammals under natural conditions*, Pymatuning Lab. Ecol. Symp. 5, D. P. Snyder, ed. Ann Arbor, Mich.: Edwards Bros.

Louch, C. 1956. Adrenocortical activity in relation to the density and dynamics of three confined populations of *Microtus pennsylvanicus*. *Ecology* 37:701–13.

Madison, D. 1977. Movements and habitat use among interacting *Peromyscus leucopus* as revealed by radio telemetry. *Can. Field-Nat.* 91:273–81.

May, R. 1976. Models for single populations. In *Theoretical ecology*, R. May ed. Philadelphia: Saunders.

Metzgar, L. 1967. An experimental comparison of screech owl predation on resident and transient white-footed mice (*Peromyscus leucopus*). *J. Mammal.* 48:387–91.

Myers, J., and Krebs, C. 1971. Genetic, behavioral, and reproductive attributes of dispersing field voles *Microtus pennsylvanicus* and *Microtus ochrogaster*. *Ecol. Monogr.* 41:53–78.

Nicholson, A. 1933. The balance of animal populations. *J. Anim. Ecol.* 2:132–78.

Orians, G. 1962. Natural selection and ecological theory. *Am. Nat.* 96:257–63.

Pearson, O. 1966. The prey of carnivores during one cycle of mouse abundance. *J. Anim. Ecol.* 35:217–33.

Roff, D. 1975. Population stability and the evolution of dispersal in a heterogeneous environment *Oecologia* 19:217–37.

Rothstein, B., and Tamarin, R. 1977. Feeding behavior of the insular beach vole, *Microtus breweri*. *J. Mammal.* 58:84–85.

Schaffer, W., and Tamarin, R. 1973. Changing reproductive rates and population cycles in lemmings and voles. *Evolution* 27:111–24.

Schultz, A. 1964. The nutrient-recovery hypothesis for arctic microtine cycles. II. Ecosystem variables in relation to arctic microtine cycles. *British Ecological Society, Symposium 4*, ed. D. J. Crisp. Oxford: Blackwell.

Smith, H. 1935. The role of biotic factors in the determination of population densities. *J. Econ. Entomol.* 28:873–98.

Starrett, A. 1958. Insular variation in mice of the *Microtus pennsylvanicus* group in southeastern Massachusetts. *Diss. Abstr.* 19:917.

Sullivan, T. 1977. Demography and dispersal in island and mainland populations of the deer mouse, *Peromyscus maniculatus*. *Ecology* 58:964–78.

Tamarin, R. 1977a. Dispersal in island and mainland voles. *Ecology* 58:1044–54.

———. 1977b. Demography of the beach vole (*Microtus breweri*) and the meadow vole (*Microtus pennsylvanicus*) in southeastern Massachusetts. *Ecology* 58:1310–21.

———. 1978a. Dispersal, population regulation, and K-selection in field mice. *Am. Nat.* 112:545–55.

———, ed. 1978b. *Population regulation*. Benchmark Papers in Ecology, vol. 5. Stroudsburg, Pa.: Dowden, Hutchinson & Ross.

———, and Kunz, T. 1974. *Microtus breweri*. *Mamm. Species.* 45:1–3.

To, L., and Tamarin, R. 1977. The relation of population density and adrenal gland weight in cycling and noncycling voles (*Microtus*). *Ecology* 58:928–34.

Van Valen, L. 1971. Group selection and the evolution of dispersal. *Evolution* 25:591–98.

van Wijngaarden, A. 1960. The population dynamics of four confined populations of the continental vole *Microtus arvallis* (Pallas). *R.I.V.O.N. Meded.* 84:1–28.

Watson, A., and Moss, R. 1970. Dominance, spacing behavior, and aggression in relation to population limitation in vertebrates. In *Animal populations in relation to their food resources*, ed. A. Watson, pp. 167–218. Oxford: Blackwell.

Wetherbee, D.; Coppinger, R.; and Walsh, R. 1972. *Time lapse ecology, Muskeget Island, Nantucket, Massachusetts*. New York: MSS Information Corp.

6

POPULATION REGULATION IN WOLVES

Jane M. Packard and L. David Mech

The possibility of social regulation of wolf populations has been discussed in the literature for several years. Some of the first ecological studies of wolves indicated that their populations did not increase as rapidly as was theoretically possible, and that they reached a saturation point apparently not set by food. Subsequent captive studies demonstrated the existence of social mechanisms possibly capable of regulating population growth. However, the importance of these factors in wild populations has not been established. This paper has four objectives: (1) to evaluate the existing concept of "intrinsic limitation," (2) to propose that wolf population dynamics may be better understood by considering feedback between the prey resource and the wolf population, (3) to evaluate group selection explanations regarding evolution of "intrinsic limiting mechanisms," and (4) to propose an alternative explanation based on individual selection.

An overview of wolf biology is essential to understanding population dynamics of this species; the following summary is based on Mech (1970, 1972, 1977a). A wolf pack is a hierarchial, closed family group which maintains a territory. Wolves mate in February or March and 2 months later bear an average of five or six pups. Under good conditions, pups are full grown by autumn and accompany adults during winter. Some offspring may remain with the adults as successive litters are born; many die or disperse.

Usually, only one pair breeds in a pack, although wolves are not strictly monogamous, and several females may come into estrus within the group. Nonbreeding pack members help breeders in hunting and care of young. Wolves that disperse from packs usually wander over large areas and avoid packs (Mech and Frenzel 1971; Mech 1973 and unpublished). The mortality rate of these lone wolves is high (Mech 1977c). They do not reproduce until they are able to acquire a mate and a territory (Peters and Mech 1975).

Intrinsic Limitation

Four of the early ecological studies of wolves dealt with low populations that increased more slowly than was theoretically possible. Murie (1944) speculated that disease and intraspecific strife affected wolf mortality rates in Alaska and that productivity was reduced because only one or two females in a pack bred. In the Rocky Mountain National Parks of Canada, Cowan (1947) suggested that the low wolf density may have resulted from a disproportionate sex ratio. Intraspecific strife and low productivity were postulated as factors limiting a wolf population artifically introduced to Coronation Island, Alaska (Merriam 1964). This population showed only 10% of the growth theoretically possible. Increase of the wolf population in Alaska's Game Management Unit 13 was also comparatively slow, and Rausch (1967) cited poor pup survival, social restrictions on mating, and intraspecific strife as possible limitations.

Stable wolf populations were described in three studies. In northeastern Minnesota, the population in the Superior National Forest remained relatively stable from 1948 to 1953 (Stenlund 1955). Predator control programs and food supply were considered to be the major factors controlling wolf numbers. Stenlund also speculated that territoriality, disparate sex ratios, and a surplus of nonbreeders were important limiting factors in protected areas. On Isle Royale (Lake Superior) the wolf population remained relatively stable from 1959 to 1972, even though it was not exploited and prey populations were high (Mech 1966; Jordan et al. 1967; Wolfe and Allen 1973). Intraspecific strife and low pup productivity or survival on the island were the causes postulated for the stability.

During the same period, Pimlott et al. (1969) studied a recently protected wolf population in Algonquin Park, Ontario. This population increased and then stabilized despite an apparent abundance of food. Reviewing previous studies, Pimlott (1970, p. 66) concluded that

The density of wolf populations appears to be regulated by intrinsic mechanisms. In two areas where wolves had an abundant food supply and were completely protected, the density stabilized at a level of approximately 10 wolves per 260 square kilometers (100 square miles). Over very large areas of Canada and Alaska, the density of the wolf population rarely exceeds 10 wolves per 2,600 square kilometers (1,000 square miles) and is often much lower (Mech 1966; Pimlott 1967).

This "intrinsic limitation" concept became generally accepted (Mech 1970). When food was abundant, populations were expected to increase to the density of about 10 wolves/260 km^2 , a kind of "saturation point." Presumably at this density, social behavior would make space a limiting factor, and the population would remain relatively stable. According to this idea, the saturation point would occur at a level below where food resources would be adversely affected.

The concept of intrinsic limitation in wolves fit well with behavioral observations of captive packs. Schenkel (1947) had noted that generally only the dominant pair bred within a wolf pack. Six years of observations of the pack at Brookfield Zoo in Chicago confirmed this general rule, although there were a few exceptions (Rabb et al. 1967). Breeding was limited by strong mate preference, intrasexual and intersexual aggression, and immaturity.

Conjecture then arose as to whether the foregoing factors explained the low productivity of wolf populations in the wild (Woolpy 1968). Rabb et al. (1967), Woolpy (1968) and Fox (1971) used the terms "birth control" and "contraception" in discussing the behavioral conventions regulating breeding. To explain the high birth rate in exploited Alaskan populations (Rausch 1967), compared to the Isle Royale population, Woolpy (1968) speculated that birth control mechanisms had broken down when the social organization of the wolf population was destroyed by human hunting.

Ecological and behavioral information was integrated by Mech (1970) in a general discussion of the factors regulating pack size and number of breeding units in a population. He visualized (1) the growth of packs as regulated by social bonds and by competition for food and (2) the number of breeding units as regulated by territoriality and prey density. This theory strongly implied that upper limits of wolf populations were set by intrinsic social mechanisms.

The concept of intrinsic limitation in wolves, however, has yet to be critically evaluated. Is it accurate to speak of a saturated wolf density that is limited independently of food resources? Does intrinsic limitation mean more than just a low growth rate of the population? How does the concept relate to population adjustments in response to fluctuating food resources?

For two reasons, we believe that the concept of intrinsic limitation has become outdated in view of recent information. First, there does not appear to be a universal saturation point determined by social behavior but independent of food. Wolf populations in several areas reached almost twice the alleged saturation density of 10 wolves/260 km^2 when prey increased or became more vulnerable (Kuyt 1972; Parker 1973; Van Ballenberghe et al. 1975; Peterson 1979). In other studies, summer food was an important factor in wolf pup survival (Van Ballenberghe and Mech 1975; Seal et al. 1975), even in the presence of abundant winter prey (Peterson 1977). Second, "intrinsic limitation" focuses on the role of social behavior in limiting population growth. We believe that social behavior is also important in population declines induced by food shortage. The mechanisms involved have been described by Zimen (1976) and Mech (1977c).*

Population Regulation

We define regulation of a population as a continual adjustment of numbers to a level determined by critical resources. As vulnerable prey biomass declines, the wolf population declines. Feedback mechanisms exist that allow wolf numbers to increase as vulnerable prey biomass increases. The term "regulation" as used here describes two-way feedback between components of the predator/prey system. Prey density affects wolf numbers, and wolves affect prey populations.

This approach is an intentional departure from the "equilibrium setpoint" view of population dynamics (Murdoch 1970). Theoretically, one can describe the components and their characteristics of the system (wolf and prey densities, age structure, health, vulnerability, etc.) and we can describe the relations influencing changes among the components. From this knowledge, one could predict how any given population would change with fluctuating resources. This approach contrasts with the view that predator/prey systems tend toward equilibrium.

Editors' Note: The assumption that there is an intrinsic and constant upper limit to the population density of wolves should also be evaluated in the light of the observation by Terman that even under controlled laboratory conditions, rodent populations stabilize at irregular and unpredictable levels of density.

We adopted the concept of regulatory feedback in order to describe populations with fluctuating food resources.

The analytical questions to be asked using the concept of regulatory feedback are: (1) What events take place during adjustments in wolf populations (how do changes in resources translate into changes in reproduction, survival, and mortality)? and (2) How "tight" is the feedback between fluctuations in critical resources and population levels? The concept of tight versus loose regulation was elaborated by Murdoch (1970). A population shows tight regulation if it returns to a density determined by constant resources when displaced above or below that density. If regulation is nonexistent, a population would tend to persist at whatever level it is set, independent of fluctuations in critical resources (Murdoch 1970). Loose regulation may be identified by a lag in population change.

Eberhardt (1977) outlined a general progression of regulatory events that occur as mammalian populations encounter food shortages: (1) decreased survival of young, (2) delayed maturity, (3) reduced reproduction, and (4) increased adult mortality. In wolf populations, social behavior contributes to this same sequence of events (Mech 1977c). As a result, social behavior often seems to be the proximate cause of numerical change which is ultimately controlled by food.* We view the social factors that are independent of food as influencing the lag time, or tightness of population regulation.

Information from northeastern Minnesota and Isle Royale illustrate the feedback relations between wolf populations and their prey. The northeastern Minnesota wolf population appeared relatively stable from winter 1966–67 through winter 1968–69 (Mech 1977c). Maturing habitat, wolf predation, and a series of severe winters beginning in 1968–69 caused a drastic decline in deer numbers (Mech and Karns 1977). The wolf population increased by 32% in 1969–70, but then decreased annually until by winter 1974–75 it was less than half the 1969–70 level (Mech 1977c). Malnutrition of pups was evident from

---

Editors' Note: This is the most explicit statement in the volume concerning the interaction of social and nutritional factors in population regulation. The paucity of such statements elsewhere reflects perhaps the absence of adequate information on the relation between population and food supply for most natural populations and the more specialized nature of most controlled studies. Since the wolf is a social carnivore, it is possible that the mechanisms by which wolves adjust to their food supply would be instructive in the study of another species often portrayed as a social carnivore, early *Homo sapiens.* The contrast between the conclusions of Packard and Mech and the issues debated by Cohen, Hassan, Ripley, and Lee should be noted.

1971 through 1973, causing 30% of the wolf mortality in those years, and by 1974, the number and sizes of litters had declined (Mech 1977c).

Several behavioral, social, and ecological changes became evident in the wolf population in response to the reduced consumption rate (Mech 1977a). Intraspecific strife increased as packs trespassed into other territories on hunting trips, and in 1974 and 1975, all the natural mortality in the study population of radioed wolves was caused by other wolves (Mech 1977c).

On Isle Royale the wolf population had also been relatively stable, averaging 22 individuals for 7 years, with one breeding pack (Mech 1966; Jordan et al., 1967; Wolfe and Allen 1973). In general, pup production appeared good in years when moose calf production was high, and poor when calf production was low (Peterson 1977). A confusing situation existed from 1966 to 1969 due to the breakup of the large breeding pack, immigration of a pack from the mainland, and possible emigration of some wolves from the island. As a result, in 1969 the population was at a low of 15–17 individuals (Wolfe and Allen 1973).

The Isle Royale wolves showed an immediate behavioral response to increased moose vulnerability from 1969 to 1972. They killed more moose and utilized them less completely (Peterson 1977). The wolf population, however, showed little numerical increase until about 1972 (Peterson 1977). By 1976 the population had increased to 44 animals, and the number of breeding units from one to three (Peterson 1979). During this period, the moose population had decreased from 1,300–1,400 in 1969 to 800–900 in 1976 (Peterson 1979). Moose malnutrition was high, calves were small, and the wolf kill of calves and weak yearlings was considerable. By 1977, the wolf population declined to 34 individuals. Probably the wolves had killed the most vulnerable moose, and were again faced with a food shortage.

The preceding discussion of the northeastern Minnesota and the Isle Royale wolf populations demonstrates that (1) food supply does critically affect wolf numbers over the long term, and (2) numerical response to changes in available prey biomass may lag a few years. We hypothesize that social factors directly and indirectly affect population size. Direct effects include intraspecific strife and limitation of the number of breeding females. Social factors interact indirectly with

nutritional factors in determining which segment of the population will
be most influenced by fluctuations in food resources.

Social Factors

Territoriality and Intraspecific Strife

The theory that territoriality functions in the natural control of populations is long standing (Elton 1950). Murie (1944) was the first to
observe intraspecific strife among wolves and to comment on its potential function in population regulation. He speculated that it would
keep wolves at an optimum level in relation to prey resources. Since
then, many observations of intraspecific strife among wolves have
been recorded (Cowan 1947; Mech 1966, 1972, 1977c; Jordan et al.
1967; Mech and Frenzel 1971; Mahrenke 1971; Wolfe and Allen 1973;
Van Ballenberghe and Erickson 1973).

Extensive studies in northeastern Minnesota have shown that the
wolf population there is spatially highly structured. Reproductive
packs occupy exclusive territories, with nonreproductive lone wolves
occupying the buffer zones between territories (Mech 1972, 1973,
1977a). This spacing is maintained both by aggressive encounters and
by advertisement of a pack's presence through scent marking and
howling (Peters and Mech 1975; Harrington and Mech 1979). Such
spacing in a saturated population makes it nearly impossible for new
breeding units to become established unless major perturbations occur
in the system. In a low-density population, new breeding pairs are able
to establish territories (Mech unpublished).

If adjacent packs travel in the overlap zones between territories,
they run a greater risk of encountering each other (Wolfe and Allen
1973). While prey was abundant in northeastern Minnesota, wolves
were unlikely to kill deer in the buffer zones (Hoskinson and Mech
1976; Mech 1977a,b). However, as prey became scarce, they appeared
more likely to make kills in those areas, and to trespass into other
territories, running a greater risk of fatal encounters with neighboring
packs (Mech 1977c).

The amount of vulnerable prey biomass is probably important in
determining the size of territories. For example, after having used most
of Isle Royale for several years, the "West Pack" confined its travels

to one end of the island in 1971, when sufficient prey could be killed in that smaller area (Peterson 1979). This change seemed to fit the "elastic disc" theory of territoriality (Huxley 1934).

However, there seems to be enough flexibility in wolf consumption rates, activity levels, reproductive rates, and pack sizes that territory sizes are adjusted to food supply only within wide limits. In northeastern Minnesota, most wolf packs maintained their territories despite gross changes in deer numbers (Mech, unpublished). One wolf pack studied for 7 years occupied the same basic territory when it contained nine members as when it included only two, although size adjustments did occur along the buffer zones (Mech 1977a).

Thus, territoriality affects population size primarily by parceling a population's range into a limited number of areas, each supporting a reproductive unit. Secondarily, territoriality reduces wolf numbers through the mortality or injury that sometimes occurs when packs defend their territories.

Exclusive Breeding

Productivity of the population is regulated by the number of breeders per reproductive unit as well as the number of breeding units per area. Wolf packs sometimes contain 20–30 members, although they usually include 8–10 (Mech 1970). Nevertheless, usually only one or two females produce young each year. For example, in reviewing the research on Isle Royale, Wolfe and Allen (1973, p. 628) commented: "It has become increasingly evident during these studies that restrictions on breeding constitute an important factor in the regulation of wolf numbers on Isle Royale. Ordinarily only one or two females are actually observed to breed out of perhaps twelve females on the island."

Of 20 packs studied for from 1 to 8 years in northeastern Minnesota, Mech (unpublished) has never found evidence that more than one female in a pack bore a litter of pups. A few cases have been observed elsewhere of two females in a pack producing young in the wild (Murie 1944; R. O. Peterson, personal communication), and attempted breeding or pregnancy in more than one female in a pack has been reported in the wild (Jordan et al. 1967; Rausch 1967; Peterson 1977; Peterson and Allen 1976). However, in most such cases, extra litters probably fail to survive, as observed by Peterson (personal communication). In captive wolf packs, parallel observations have been reported (Rabb et al. 1967; Lentfer and Sanders 1973; Altmann 1974; Zimen 1975; Klinghammer et al. 1977).

The effect of a breeding system in which only one female per pack usually reproduces successfully is obvious. In larger packs, there would be several females, and if all bred, the breeding potential of the population would be much higher than it is. On the other hand, this breeding system might also allow an extra female to breed and raise young successfully if food were in abundance.

Age of Maturity

An important reproductive parameter influencing population growth is age of maturity (Cole 1954). In wolves, females usually do not mature until their second or third year. From examination of 246 pup reproductive tracts, Rausch (1967) concluded that ovulation was extremely rare in pups. In the Brookfield Zoo pack, females born after the group was established did not breed in their second year despite high social rank (Rabb et al. 1967; Woolpy 1968). Numerous other reports attest to the general rule that juvenile females rarely breed (Murie 1944; Young 1944; Lentfer and Sanders 1973; Zimen 1975).

However, under certain circumstances, the female wolf's reproductive system is capable of maturing at 10 months of age (Medjo and Mech 1976; Zimen 1975; Seal et al. 1979). This opens the possibility that ordinarily maturation is delayed through social suppression, poor nutrition, or some combination of these factors (Medjo and Mech 1976). Intriguing laboratory studies with rodents indicate that maturation may be delayed by poor nutrition or pheromones from grouped females, or may be accelerated by exposure to male urine (Vandenbergh 1973). If these effects occur in wolves, age of maturity could be a very important social factor helping to regulate wolf numbers.*

Some of the nonbreeding females observed in the wild and assumed to be socially suppressed (Wolfe and Allen 1973) may have been physiologically immature, since it is impossible in the field to reliably separate immature from mature wolves without physical examination.

Behavioral maturity may be just as important as physical maturity (Woolpy 1968). Behaviorally inexperienced young—even though

*Editors' Note: See Christian and Drickamer for further discussions of the mechanisms by which reproductive system maturation is accelerated or suppressed or delayed among rodents and primates.

physiologically mature—probably are at a serious disadvantage when competing sexually with their parents and/or older siblings. This inexperience may well explain the observations in the Brookfield Zoo pack cited above.

Dispersal

Wolves dispersing from a pack may facilitate a population decline in dense populations, and contribute to a population increase in sparse populations. In a saturated population, they are chased by resident packs (Mech 1966; Jordan et al. 1967; Mech and Frenzel 1971; Wolfe and Allen 1973) and have a decreased survival rate (Mech 1977c). They form a breeding surplus, ready to fill in openings that arise in packs (Mech unpublished). In addition, if two loners succeed in establishing a territory, they may form the nucleus of a new pack (Mech 1972, 1973; Peters and Mech 1975; Rothman and Mech 1979).

We know from the Minnesota studies that wolves may disperse at ages ranging from 9 to 28 months or more, and that some wolves born to a pack may remain with the group until at least 4.5 years of age (Mech unpublished). The effect of nutritional, social, and maturational factors on dispersal is still undetermined.

From captive studies, two types of dispersing individuals have been postulated—those which leave voluntarily, and those forced out as a result of intense sexual competition among siblings and between parents and offspring (Zimen 1976). In captivity, serious harassment of subordinate or dominant individuals, and severe dominance fights sometimes resulting in deaths, have been reported (Rabb et al. 1967; Zimen 1975, 1976; Packard et al. unpublished). Zimen (1976) postulated that dispersal may be negatively related to food availability. He found that oppression of subordinates increased and new rank relations were established as hunger increased. Low-ranking pack members were sometimes not allowed to feed. Perhaps they are more likely to leave voluntarily if hungry (Murie 1944; Mech 1970; Zimen 1976).*

Disparate Sex Ratios

Cowan (1947) was the first to suggest that "anything which upsets the 50:50 sex ratio in a monogamous species such as the wolf will exert

---

Editors' Note: Compare the discussion of two types of dispersing individuals in rodent populations provided by Tamarin as well as suggestions by Freedman that there are also individual variations among human beings in their tolerance of density-related situations and their inclination to emigrate.

profound influence upon the reproductive potential of the population."
He found a 15:10 ratio of males to females in the Rocky Mt. National
Parks of Canada, and concluded that the unbalanced sex ratio along
with natural mortality and disease were enough to hold the population
at low levels. Stenlund (1955) reported an 18:10 sex ratio in Minnesota, and agreed with Cowan.

Mech (1975) found that higher percentages of male pups were produced, or at least survived, in Minnesota wolf populations with higher
densities. As food resources declined in northeastern Minnesota, the
percentage of males in the dense population rose even further. The
importance of sex ratios in regulating populations may vary under different environmental conditions. Evidence is still scarce, but we would
expect to find the following: (1) since males tend to disperse farther
than females (Mech unpublished) in saturated populations, a prepon-
derance of dispersing males would reduce the number of lone wolves
in the local population; and (2) in populations faced with a food shortage, fewer females would result in fewer potential pairs to fill in vacant
territories created when packs break up due to territorial strife. The
degree of influence of these various social factors probably varies depending on the ecological balance between density of a wolf population and its food resources. As outlined in table 6.1, the reproductive
success of individuals in different social categories may also vary.

Interaction between Social and Nutritional Factors

Social factors may slow the growth rate of an expanding wolf population, but they do not necessarily prevent malnutrition. We propose that
social factors promote wolf population regulation in three ways: (1)
they cause the actual rate of increase of a population to be considerably
lower than the potential rate of increase; (2) they delay the numerical
response of a population to major fluctuations in vulnerable prey biomass; and (3) they result in unequal distribution of food resources
among pack members, predisposing certain segments of the population
(low-ranking individuals) to malnutrition.

Compared to populations of nonterritorial, solitary species with
comparable fecundity and mortality, wolf populations show a much
greater discrepancy between potential and realized rate of increase.
Territoriality limits the number of breeding units, and the dominance
hierarchy limits the number of breeders within each unit.

Table 6.1. Differences among Reproductive Categories of Wolves with Different Densities and Prey Resources

High density/High resources
1. Dense stable population
2. Intermediate pack conflict
3. Biders have moderate success depending on mortality due to intraspecific strife
4. Dispersers unlikely to acquire territory
5. Low proportion of breeding females

High density/Low resources
1. Declining population
2. High probability of pack conflict
3. Biders most successful since more breeding females killed in intraspecific strife
4. Dispersers unlikely to acquire territory
5. High proportion of breeding females due to low productivity and high mortality of subordinates and loners

Low density/High resources
1. Increasing population
2. Low probability of pack conflict
3. Biders less successful since death of breeder is unlikely
4. Dispersers most successful at establishing territories
5. Breeders highly successful
6. High proportion of breeding females, since dispersers establish new packs

Low density/Low resources
1. Sparse, stable population
2. Low probability of pack conflict
3. Biders less successful since death of breeder is unlikely
4. Dispersers may establish territory but not raise pups because of malnutrition
5. Intermediate to low proportion of breeding females since dispersers unlikely to breed

A lag in the numerical response to fluctuations in prey resources was apparent in the declining phase of the wolf population of northeastern Minnesota (Mech 1977c) as well as in both the increasing and declining phases of the Isle Royale population (Peterson 1979). Territoriality in a saturated population functions to buffer the decline of wolves in the initial stage of a food decline. Packs are "forced" to utilize kills more efficiently (Pimlott et al. 1969; Mech unpublished), when vulnerable prey are less available inside their territories. They can exploit previously protected prey found along the buffer zones between packs (Hoskinson and Mech 1976; Mech 1977a,b), and can switch at least temporarily to other prey (Mech 1977a).

Alternatively, a wolf population might lag behind an increase in prey if the prey remain in unhunted refuges between pack territories. Furthermore, a population may not respond to increased prey if the abundance occurs outside the pup-rearing season (Peterson 1979). Evaluation of food required for successful reproduction is very difficult (Mech 1977a), complicating clear discrimination of the role of social factors.

When food supplies become inadequate, the subsequent malnutrition of subordinate wolves has a strong social basis (Mech 1977a). Relative to a species where all females were affected equally by the nutritional deficit, productivity of wolves would not decline so rapidly because nonbreeders would perish before the reproductive capacity of breeding animals would be severely impaired (Mech 1977a,c).

In terms of predator/prey stability, the varied effects of social behavior described above would combine to produce a lag in the response of the wolf population to fluctuations in food. Such loose feedback would tend to foster predator/prey oscillations.

Earlier claims that wolf populations are limited by intrinsic social factors were partly correct, but the influence of food supply now appears to be more important than was previously recognized. The challenge for the future remains to delineate the precise conditions under which, and mechanisms by which, nutritional and social factors operate independently as well as together in regulation of wolf populations. This is one of the primary objectives of the continuing studies in northeastern Minnesota.

Acknowledgments

Our own studies included in this review were supported by the U.S. Fish and Wildlife Service, the U.S.D.A. North Central Forest Experiment Station, the Mordag Charitable Foundation, World Wildlife Fund, and New York Zoological Society. We also thank the Bush Foundation, the Wilkie Fund of the Bell Museum of Natural History, the U.S. Fish and Wildlife Service, and Varian Associates, Palo Alto, California, for supporting the senior author. The following individuals read early drafts of the manuscript and offered many helpful suggestions: D. B. Siniff, N. Flesness, D. Baird, S. H. Fritts, A. Magoun, and P. Vallkenburg.

This paper, with an additional section on the evolutionary implications of the contents, was also published with the Proceedings of the Symposium on Natural Regulation of Animal Numbers, held in Vancouver, British Columbia, in March 1978.

References

Altmann, D. 1974. Beziehunger zwischen sozialn Rangordnung und Jungen aufzucht bei (*Canis lupus l.*). *Zool. Gart.* N.F. (Jena) 44:235–36.

Cole, L. C. 1954. The population consequences of life-history phenomena. *Q. Rev. Biol.* 29:103–37.

Cowan, I. M. 1947. The timber wolf in the Rocky Mountain National Parks of Canada. *Can. J. Res.* 25:139–74.

Eberhardt, L. L. 1977. Optimal policies for conservation of large mammals, with special reference to marine ecosystems. *Environ. Conserv.* 4(3):205–12.

Elton, C. 1950. *The ecology of animals.* New York: Wiley.

Fox, M. W. 1971. *Behavior of wolves, dogs, and related canids.* New York: Harper & Row.

Harrington, F. H., and Mech, L. D. 1979. Wolf howling and its role in territory maintenance. *Behaviour* 68:207–49.

Hoskinson, R. L., and Mech, L. D. 1976. White-tailed deer migration and its role in wolf predation. *J. Wildl. Manage.* 40(3):429–41.

Huxley, J. S. 1934. A natural experiment on the territorial instinct. *Br. Birds* 27:270–77.

Jordan, P. A.; Shelton, P. C.; and Allen, D. L. 1967. Numbers turnover, and social structure of the Isle Royale wolf population. *Am. Zool.* 1:233–52.

Klinghammer, E.; Brantley, B.; and Goodman, P. 1977. The dynamics of mating behavior in two captive wolf packs: behavioral and biochemical correlates. Paper presented at the 1977 Anim. Behav. Soc. Annu. Meet.

Kuyt, E. 1972. Food habits of wolves on barren-ground caribou range. Can. Wildl. Serv. Rep. Ser. 21, Ottawa.

Lentfer, J. W., and Sanders, D. K. 1973. Notes on the captive wolf (*Canis lupus*) colony, Barrow, Alaska. *Can. J. Zool.* 51:623–627.

Mahrenke, P., III. 1971. Observation of four wolves killing another wolf. *J. Mammal.* 52:630–63.

Mech, L. D. 1966. The wolves of Isle Royale. U.S. Natl. Park Serv. Fauna Ser. 7. Washington D.C.: Govt. Printing Office.

————. 1970. *The wolf.* New York: Doubleday.

————. 1972. Spacing and possible mechanisms of population regulation in wolves. (Abstr.) *Am. Zool.* 12(4):642.

————. 1973. Wolf numbers in the Superior National Forest of Minnesota. USDA For. Serv. Res. Pap. NC–97. North Central Forest Experiment Station, St. Paul, Minn.

————. 1975. Disproportionate sex ratios in wolf pups. *J. Wildlife Manage.* 39:737–40.

————. 1977a. Population trend and winter deer consumption in a Minnesota wolf pack. In Proc. 1975 Predator Symp., ed. R. L. Phillips and C. Jonkel, pp. 55–83. Montana Forest and Conservation Experiment Station, University of Montana, Missoula.

————. 1977b. Wolf-pack buffer zones as prey reservoirs. *Science* 198:320–21.

————. 1977c. Productivity, mortality, and population trends of wolves in North-eastern Minnesota. *J. Mammal.* 58(4):559–74.

————, and Frenzel, L. D. eds. 1971. Ecological studies of the timber wolf in north-eastern Minnesota. USDA For. Serv. Res. Pap. NC–52. North Central Forest Experiment Station, St. Paul, Minn.

————, and Karns, P. D. 1977. Role of the wolf in a deer decline in the Superior National Forest. USDA For. Serv. Res. Pap. NC–148. North Central Forest Experiment Station, St. Paul, Minn.

Medjo, D., and Mech, L. D. 1976. Reproductive activity in nine- and ten-month-old wolves. *J. Mammal.* 57(2):406–08.

Merriam, H. R. 1964. The wolves of Coronation Island. *Proc. Alaska Sci. Conf.* 15:27–32.

Murdoch, W. M. 1970. Population regulation and population inertia. *Ecology* 51:497–502.

Murie, A. 1944. The wolves of Mt. McKinley. U.S. Nat. Park Serv. Fauna Ser. 5. Washington, D.C.: Govt. Printing Office.

Parker, G. R. 1973. Distribution and densities of wolves within barren-ground caribou range in northern mainland Canada. *J. Mammal.* 54(2):341–48.

Peters, R. P., and Mech, L. D. 1975. Scent-marking in wolves: a field study. *Am. Sci.* 63(6):628–37.

Peterson, R. O. 1977. Wolf ecology and prey relationships on Isle Royale. U.S. Natl. Park Serv. scientific monograph, no. 11, 210 pp.

————. 1979. The role of wolf predation in a moose population decline. In *Proc. First Conf. on Scientific Research in the National Parks*, ed. R. M. Linn, pp. 329–33. USDI Natl. Park Serv. Trans. and Proc. ser. 5.

Pimlott, D. H. 1967. Wolf predation and ungulate populations. *Am. Zool.* 7:267–78.

————. 1970. Predation and productivity of game populations in North America. Trans. IX Int. Congr. Game Biol. Moscow, pp. 53–73.

————; Shannon, J. A.; and Kolenosky, G. B. 1969. The ecology of the timber wolf in Algonquin Park. Ontario Department of Lands and Forests, Ontario.

Rabb, G. B.; Woolpy, J. H.; and Ginsburg, B. E. 1967. Social relations in a group of captive wolves. *Am. Zool.* 7:305–11.

Rausch, R. A. 1967. Some aspects of the population ecology of wolves, Alaska. *Am. Zool.* 7:253–65.

Rothman, R. J., and Mech, L. D. 1979. Scent-marking in lone wolves and newly formed pairs. *Anim. Behav.* 27:750–60.

Schenkel, R. 1947. Ausdrucksstudien an Wolfen. *Behaviour* 1:81–129.

Seal, U. S.; Mech, L. D.; and Van Ballenberge, V. 1975. Blood analysis of wolf pups and their ecological and metabolic interpretation. *J. Mammal.* 56:64–75.

————; Plotka, E.; Packard, J.; and Mech, L. D. 1979. Endocrine correlates of reproduction in the female wolf. *Biol. Reprod.* (in press).

Stenlund, M. H. 1955. A field study of the timber wolf (*Canis lupus*) on the Superior National Forest, Minnesota. Minn. Dept. Cons. Tech. Bull. 4.

Van Ballenberghe, and Erickson, A. W. 1973. A wolf pack kills another wolf. *Am. Midl. Nat.* 90(2):490–93.

————, and Mech, L. D. 1975. Weights, growth, and survival of timber wolf pups in Minnesota. *J. Mammal.* 56:44–63.

————; Erickson, A. W.; and Byman, D. 1975. Ecology of the timber wolf in Northeastern Minnesota *Wild. Mon.* 43:6–43.

Vandenberghe, J. B. 1973. Acceleration and inhibition of puberty in female mice by pheromones. *J. Reprod. Fertil. Suppl. 19*, 411–19.

Wolfe, M. L., and Allen, D. L. 1973. Continued studies of the status, socialization and relationships of Isle Royale wolves, 1967–1970. *J. Mammal.* 54:611–35.

Woolpy, J. H. 1968. The social organization of wolves. *Nat. Hist.* 77(5):46–55.

Young, S. P. 1944. The wolves of North America, Part 1. Washington, D.C.: American Wildlife Institute.

Zimen, E. 1975. Social dynamics of the wolf pack. In *The wild canids*, M. W. Fox, ed. pp. 336–62. New York: Van Nostrand Reinhold.

————. 1976. On the regulation of pack size in wolves. *Z. Tierpsychol.* 40:300–41.

7

RHESUS MONKEY POPULATIONS IN INDIA AND NEPAL: PATTERNS OF GROWTH, DECLINE, AND NATURAL REGULATION

Charles H. Southwick
with Thomas Richie, Henry Taylor,
H. Jane Teas, and M. Farooq Siddiqi

Although there has been great progress and success in primate field studies in the last 20 years, the area of primate population biology is still at an early stage of development. We have relatively few systematic census studies of primate populations over long periods, and even fewer analyses of demographic change. Our knowledge of the factors regulating primate populations is very limited, almost nonexistent.

There are some examples of long-term interest in specific primate populations, or at least cases where the same population has been studied many times. One of the best examples of the latter is the howler monkey (*Alouatta palliata*) population of Barro Colorado Island in Panama. Originally studied by Carpenter (1934) almost 50 years ago, this island population has been censused at various intervals by many different investigators. The population, which numbered about 400 animals in the early 1930s, has fluctuated from a low of just over 200 to higher levels of more than 1,000. The main problem is that these different censuses have not been coordinated nor have they been done at regular intervals. Despite the scientific interest in the howler monkey population of BCI and the substantial amount of field work on it, we still do not have an accurate picture of the interplay of factors regulating its numbers. We cannot assess the roles of disease, food supply, space, interspecific relationships, territorialism, or other aspects of social behavior in determining population size and distribution.

This paper will not attempt to review all primate literature in population ecology, but rather will be limited to three species of macaques, with emphasis on the rhesus of India and Nepal. It should be mentioned in passing that there have been some outstanding field studies of natural primate populations over periods of several years: for example, the population research on baboons by Altmann and Altmann (1970, 1974) and Kummer (1968); on colobus and vervet monkeys by Struhsaker (1975, 1976); on gibbons by Chivers (1977); on mountain gorillas by Goodall and Groves (1977) and Fossey and Harcourt (1977); and on chimpanzees by van Lawick-Goodall (1971). These and many others have made important contributions to our knowledge of primate populations, but few have concentrated on population biology or demography. Most have emphasized the study of social behavior, and most have not provided long-term data on natality, mortality, population trends, or population turnover.

In macaques, there are several studies of relatively long duration from which valuable data on population dynamics are now emerging. Examples of these are the studies on the Japanese macaque (*Macaca fuscata*) by Itani (1975), Furuya (1968), and others, which began in the 1950s; studies of the toque macaque (*M. sinica*) in Sri Lanka by Dittus (1975, 1977, 1979); the detailed work on the rhesus macaques (*M. mulatta*) of Cayo Santiago and La Parguera by Drickamer (1974), Sade et al. (1977, and this volume) and others; and the studies on the rhesus of Aligarh district in northern India by Siddiqi and Southwick (1977). This chapter will concentrate on these latter studies with references and comparisons to other macaque populations, especially those on the rhesus in Nepal by Teas et al. (1977, 1978), on the Japanese macaques in Mt. Takasaki by Itani (1975), and on toque macaques in Sri Lanka by Dittus (1975, 1977).

Background to This Study

The Aligarh rhesus studies began in 1959 with field research on the abundance and distribution of the rhesus monkey in northern India. We were particularly interested in population ecology and social behavior, and the effects of changing ecological, economic, and social conditions on rhesus populations. At this time India was strongly increasing agricultural and economic development, and the rhesus monkey population itself was being trapped at the rate of approximately 100,000 monkeys per year. Trapping for export fell substantially to only 20,000 in 1977, and stopped completely in April 1978, but the general pressures from agriculture, economic development, and human population growth still continue.

Population studies of the rhesus in India were planned with two general approaches: (1) extensive field surveys of northern India via roadside, canal bank, village, and forest surveys; and (2) an intensive population study of a limited area in Aligarh district, 130 km southeast of New Delhi. This latter study is the main subject of this paper.

The rhesus populations in Nepal were first observed by us in 1971 and 1972, with detailed ecological and behavioral studies begun in 1975. Although the main focus of this program was to analyze social behavior in relation to environmental factors, the field work also provided opportunities for census studies of untrapped rhesus populations.

Study Areas

Detailed descriptions of the study areas and field methods in India have been given by Southwick and Siddiqi (1977), and those in Nepal have been described by Teas (1978) and Taylor et al. (1978). We will review only the main features of each area here.

The rhesus groups studied in India represented most of the monkeys within Aligarh district except those in Aligarh city itself and other sizable towns nearby. This study population did not include, for example, the Aligarh temple monkeys upon which we focused early behavioral studies. Most of the groups lived in typical rural habitats, along roadsides, canal banks, near villages, or in small forest patches. At the beginning of the study, the groups varied in size from 6 to 36 individual monkeys, with an average of 17, typical of rhesus throughout the plains of northern India.

The landscape of Aligarh district is flat and intensively cultivated with crops of wheat, bajra, ragi, maize, barley, millet, rice, gram or pulse, sugarcane, and mustard. Figure 7.1 shows a group of rhesus along a roadside near Aligarh with typical agricultural landscape in the background. Mango and papaya groves are common, and native trees, including the neem, banyan, sheesham, pipal, and imle, are scattered along roadsides, canal banks, and in villages. A few small forest patches remain in the district.

Human population density is typical of the Gangetic plain, about 500 people/km². Many villages, usually 500–1,500 people, dot the countryside. Aligarh city itself has grown from 150,000 to over 300,000 people during the years of this study. Livestock populations are large, with abundant populations of cattle, water buffalo, goats, and some swine and horses. The climate is subtropical monsoon, with about 80 cm of rain, mostly occurring from June to September. Year-round agriculture is maintained by a network of irrigation canals passing through the district.

One specific location within the study area known as Chhatari-do-Raha deserves special mention because two rhesus groups there have been partially protected by local people. The monkeys at Chhatari live in and around a schoolyard compound at a rural crossroads 22 km north of Aligarh. Until 1975 both rhesus groups were protected by chowkidors (caretakers) within the school compound. The chowkidors did not permit trappers to take monkeys in or near the schoolyard, but when monkeys wandered away, the chowkidors were unable to prevent trapping. The group that lived down the roadside about 400 m from the school was subject to the most trapping, and in 1975 over half of this group was taken. Most of the rhesus groups in the study population have not been protected by local people, but recently one group living

Figure 7.1.   Rhesus monkeys along a roadside near Aligarh, showing the typical agricultural habitat of the western Gangetic plain.

near a major canal southeast of Aligarh has benefited from some local protection.

The rhesus populations in Nepal described in this paper occupy two ancient temple sites in Kathmandu valley. Kathmandu is 700 km east and slightly south of Aligarh, and the altitude is approximately 1000 m higher. One temple, Swayambhu, is a Buddhist temple on a hilltop west of Kathmandu city, and the other, Pashupati, is a Hindu temple on the eastern edge of the city. Both temple sites include surrounding parklands and agricultural fields, and the Pashupati site has small adjacent forest areas. Both temples are over 2,000 years old and represent sacred areas where people, monkeys, and other animals have interacted closely for centuries. The monkeys receive some food from worshippers and visitors, but they are largely undisturbed, and they obtain the majority of their food from natural vegetation (Marriott 1978). To our knowledge they have not been trapped or seriously molested at either location. The results and discussion section will concentrate primarily on the Aligarh data since these represent the longest series of census counts, but comparisons with the Nepalese rhesus and other macaque populations will be given.

Methods

Field censuses in India began in October 1959 with a population of 17 groups of rhesus in typical habitats of the western Gangetic basin. By 1961, these original 17 groups had increased to 22, and a regular census program was started of counting each group three times a year: (1) in March and April, just before the birth season; (2) in July and August, just after the birth season; and (3) in October and November, after the monsoon and before the winter. Such a pattern of censuses provides data on the minimum population of the year (March–April), the maximum population of the year (July–August), the number of young born, and the number of deaths or disappearances at critical times of the year (monsoon and winter). Annual mortality rates and population turnover can also be calculated. The mathematical methods for these calculations have been presented in a previous paper (Southwick and Siddiqi 1977).

Censuses in both India and Nepal were done with systematic and thorough examinations of every home range area to count all monkeys

Table 7.1. Locations, General Habitats, and Current Status of Aligarh District Groups

Group Number	Group name or location	General Habitat	Original group size October 1961	Fate of group	Recent size November 1977
1	Aligarh University farm	Rural agricultural	10	Extinct 1966[a]	15
2	Government press compound	Urban park compound	8		21
3	Cemetery group	Rural agricultural	6		8
4a	Chhatari group A	Rural agricultural	16		132
4b	Chhatari group B	Rural agricultural	33		
5	Sumera Fall jungle A	Canal bank forest	14	Extinct 1966	4
6	Sumera Fall jungle B	Canal bank Forest	19		
7	Dauthara village	Rural agricultural village	8	Extinct 1965	
8	Qasimpur canal A	Canal bank agricultural	24	Extinct 1974	
9	Qasimpur canal B	Canal bank agricultural	21	Extinct 1965	
10	Bajgarhi bridge	Canal bank and roadside	18	All trapped 1970	
11	Barautha village	Rural agricultural village	36	All trapped 1974	
12	Harduaganj	Lakeside, edge of small town	34	Extinct 1963	
13	Barauli bridge A	Canal bank and roadside	16	Extinct 1975	
14	Barauli bridge B	Canal bank and roadside	26	Extinct 1968	
15	Nanau bridge A	Canal bank and roadside	19		9
16	Nanau bridge B	Canal bank and roadside	11		33
17	Sindhauli village	Rural agricultural village	9	Extinct 1966	
18	Agra road	Rural agricultural roadside	10	Extinct 1967	
19	Delhi road school	Rural schoolyard and grove of trees	12		3
20	Satha mango grove	Rural mango grove	13	Extinct 1966	
21	Jawan village	Rural village and mango grove	14		9
		Total population	377		234

[a] The term "extinct" refers to the gradual disappearance of a group through mortality or trapping, and the date given is the year the last member or members were seen; the term "all trapped" refers to the complete trapping removal of the existing group.

present. Individuals were classified into the broad categories of infant, juvenile, and adult male and female. The groups in Aligarh district have been remarkably stable in their spatial location; with rare exceptions they have been found in the same locations each census period and accurately counted without difficulty.

Results and Discussion

From 1959 to 1962, the study population in Aligarh District increased from 337 monkeys in 17 groups to 403 in 22 groups. Table 7.1 lists the locations, habitats, original size, and fate of these groups. After July 1967, the population showed an erratic decline to a low of only 163 monkeys in 10 groups by March 1970. Twelve groups had become extinct by mortality and trapping removal; they had not simply moved out of the study area. From 1970 to November 1977 the study population increased to 234 monkeys but in only 9 groups. Within this total population, two cohorts have shown different trends. The unprotected groups declined 71% (328 to 94 monkeys) from 1961 to 1977, whereas the semiprotected population of Chhatari increased 186% (49 to 140 monkeys) in the same period (figure 7.2,, table 7.2).

These divergent trends afford the opportunity to compare the demographic traits of increasing and decreasing rhesus populations. Admittedly, the decrease is due to human factors, but this is true with many animal populations throughout the world. Later in the paper we will compare these populations with those in Nepal, which have not shown any major increase or decrease over a 4-year period.

Population Size and Structure

Tables 7.3 and 7.4 show the average population sizes, sex ratios, and some basic aspects of the age structures of the Aligarh unprotected and semiprotected (Chhatari) populations. The unprotected population showed a continuous decline throughout the 1960s from over 300 monkeys in 1961 and 1962 to less than 100 since 1974. In contrast, the Chhatari population grew from 49 to 140. The Chhatari population had more adult females per adult male (2.7 compared to 1.5), slightly more infants (27.3% compared to 24.9%), considerably more juveniles (26.9% compared to 19.2%), and more immatures within the population (54.2% compared to 44.0%). From these and other data, we con-

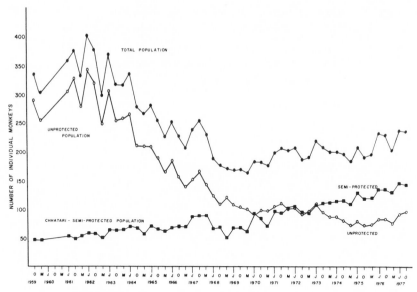

Figure 7.2. Population changes of rhesus monkeys in Aligarh District, northern India, 1959–1977.

clude as a general guideline that a macaque population should have about 50% immatures in its total population to maintain itself. Above 50%, it may be stable or increasing, depending on mortality patterns. The percent immatures of the "unprotected" population has been approaching 50% in recent years, and indeed this population has been stable or increasing slightly since 1975.

Table 7.2. Changes in Aligarh Rhesus Population, 1961–1977

Cohort of population	October 1961	October 1977	Percent change
I. Total Aligarh district population			
No. of individual rhesus	377	234	− 37.9
No. of groups	22	9	− 59.1
II. Unprotected population			
No. of individual rhesus	328	94	− 71.3
No. of groups	20	7	− 65.0
III. Semiprotected population (Chhatari-do-raha)			
No. of individual rhesus	49	140	+ 185.7
No. of groups	2	2	0

Table 7.3. Aligarh District Unprotected Population: Population Size, Sex Ratio, and Percentages of Infants and Juveniles

Year	Average total population	Adult females per adult males	Percentage infants in population	Percentage juveniles in population	Percentage immature
1959	288	—	—	—	—
1961	316	1.9	34.2	7.3	41.5
1962	314	1.7	29.3	10.9	40.2
1963	270	1.6	28.0	14.9	42.9
1964	245	1.7	27.9	16.2	44.1
1965	203	1.6	25.9	15.8	41.7
1966	168	1.5	24.8	21.0	45.8
1967	152	1.6	24.6	19.7	44.3
1968	125	1.5	25.3	19.5	44.8
1969	111	1.5	25.8	15.9	41.7
1970	97	1.3	21.6	20.6	42.2
1971	105	1.4	21.3	21.0	42.3
1972	99	1.5	24.2	15.5	39.7
1973	102	1.4	24.2	19.6	43.8
1974	86	1.2	21.3	25.2	46.5
1975	76	1.0	20.6	27.2	47.8
1976	83	1.1	19.8	30.2	50.0
1977	87	1.6	23.8	25.8	49.6
17-year average (1961–77)		1.5 ± .05	24.9 ± .9	19.2 ± 1.4	44.0 ± .6

Natality and Infant Mortality

The natality or birth rates of the unprotected population averaged 76.7% over a 17-year period, compared to 90.3% for the semiprotected population (tables 7.5 and 7.6). This is respectably high natality for both populations, and is especially remarkable for the Chhatari population. The rhesus population of Cayo Santiago averaged 78% natality in the early 1960s (Koford 1966), and that of La Parguera averaged 73% from 1964 to 1974. Both of these populations were provisioned with high-quality monkey chow. The temple populations of rhesus in Kathmandu valley, Nepal, which were provisioned with rice and local foods, averaged only 63.0% natality from 1975 through 1977 (Teas 1978). Two toque macaque populations in Sri Lanka averaged 50.8% and 68.8% natality from 1968 to 1972 (Dittus 1975).

The Chhatari population does remarkably well in a competitive agricultural environment with restricted home ranges and sparse cover.

Table 7.4. Semiprotected Population (Chhatari-do-Raha Groups): Population Size, Sex Ratio, and Percentages of Infants and Juveniles

Year	Average total population	Adult females per adult males	Percentage infants in population	Percentage juveniles in population	Percentage immature
1959	49	2.3	32.6	0	32.6
1961	52	2.7	34.0	12.6	46.6
1962	57	2.3	33.3	8.8	42.1
1963	59	2.9	29.9	16.4	46.3
1964	67	2.5	26.4	28.8	55.2
1965	64	2.5	25.9	31.1	57.0
1966	67	1.9	24.0	30.5	54.5
1967	81	1.8	22.3	36.8	59.1
1968	75	1.8	22.3	36.6	58.9
1969	62	2.1	27.3	25.7	53.0
1970	80	3.8	30.5	28.9	59.4
1971	92	3.2	26.7	28.9	55.6
1972	101	3.3	31.1	25.8	56.9
1973	105	3.6	28.7	29.9	58.6
1974	115	3.3	24.3	40.5	64.8
1975	119	3.2	24.1	37.5	61.6
1976	134	2.4	24.8	33.9	58.7
1977	137	2.5	23.4	30.7	54.1
18-year average (1959–77)		$2.7 \pm .1$	$27.3 \pm .9$	26.9 ± 2.5	54.2 ± 1.8

They are so well adapted to this environment that their reproductive success approaches the theoretical maximum. It is also interesting that the unprotected population reproduces well, but does not achieve the high level of Chhatari. The harassment and disturbances these monkeys receive from the human population seem to have some detriment on their reproductive success.

The Chhatari population has shown slightly lower infant mortality than the unprotected population, but this difference is not statistically significant. Infant mortality in both populations (15–18% per year) was higher than that of the rhesus population on Cayo Santiago (8–9%), but in the same range as that of La Parguera (17–19%) (Drickamer 1974). The infant mortality in the Aligarh populations was also less than that of the rhesus in Kathmandu (about 21% per year, according to Teas 1978), and of the toque macaques in Sri Lanka (39–47% per year, according to Dittus 1975).

Table 7.5. Aligarh District Unprotected Population: Annual Natality and Infant Mortality

| | Annual natality[a] | | Infant mortality | |
Year	Ratio	Percentage	Monsoon[b]	Annual[c]
1961	104/116	89.6	0	28.6
1962	96/121	79.3	0	31.0
1963	88/101	87.1	20.4	20.4
1964	74/89	83.1	24.3	24.3
1965	54/73	74.0	14.8	25.7
1966	44/54	81.5	9.1	30.3
1967	36/48	75.0	0	13.9
1968	31/41	75.6	12.9	12.9
1969	27/36	75.0	0	6.9
1970	16/30	53.3	0	15.0
1971	24/36	66.7	0	3.8
1972	24/36	66.7	4.2	4.2
1973	27/35	77.1	18.5	32.1
1974	19/23	82.6	10.5	10.5
1975	16/20	80.0	12.5	—
1976	18/23	78.3	5.6	11.1
1977	22/28	78.6	0	—
Average 1961–1977		76.7 ± 2.1	7.8 ± 2.0	17.7 ± 2.4

[a] Ratio and percentage of adult females producing one infant per year; live birth rate.
[b] Loss of infants from July to October.
[c] Loss of infants from end of one birth season to beginning of the next birth season.

Juvenile Loss Rates

The term "juvenile loss" rather than "juvenile mortality" is used because quite a few of the disappearances of juveniles are due to trapping rather than to mortality. The animals disappear and their fate is unknown. Evidence of dead juveniles or the remains of skeletal material is not found, however, and we conclude that the majority of juvenile disappearances were probably due to trapping removal.* Theoretically, trapping should now be greatly reduced since the ban on monkey

Editors' Note: The removal of juveniles by human trapping constitutes a form of selective predation which apparently falls most heavily on one age class of the population. This might not be the case with natural predation, which presumably would have the greatest effect on the very youngest and oldest members of the population. It would be of interest to know how this artificial predation compares with natural predation in the original habitats of this species. The reader should also note Tamarin's concept of the role of predation in population regulation, that of keeping the dispersal sink functional. In this sense, human trapping is analogous to a dispersal sink in a natural population.

Table 7.6. Semiprotected Population (Chhatari-do-Raha Rhesus Groups):
Natality and Infant Mortality

	Annual natality[a]		Infant mortality	
Year	Ratio	Percentage	Monsoon[b] (%)	Total estimated annual[c] (%)
1961	16/20	80.0	0	0
1962	21/23	91.3	19	33.3
1963	21/24	87.5	14.3	14.3
1964	16/22	72.7	6.2	6.2
1965	18/20	90.0	0	16.7
1966	17/19	89.5	5.9	5.9
1967	20/21	95.2	0	0
1968	16/20	80.0	0	43.7
1969	21/22	95.4	0	0
1970	27/27	100.0	7.4	44.4
1971	34/35	97.1	26.5	26.5
1972	34/35	97.1	8.8	11.8
1973	32/34	94.1	0	9.4
1974	27/29	93.1	0	3.7
1975	31/32	96.9	6.5	16.1
1976	37/39	94.9	0	16.2
1977	33/41	80.5	3.0	—
17-year averages (1961–77)		90.3 ± 1.9	5.7 ± 1.9	15.5 ± 3.5

[a] Ratio and percentage of adult females producing one infant per year.

[b] Loss of infants from July to October.

[c] Loss of infants from end of one birth season to the beginning of the next birth season.

exports went into effect in April 1978. Some rhesus are still trapped for biomedical research within India, however.

Juvenile loss rates varied widely from year to year, averaging 53.9% per year for the unprotected population compared to 31.5% for the semiprotected population (tables 7.7 and 7.8). This suggests that 30% juvenile removal rate will still permit population growth if natality is high, whereas a removal rate of 50% or more is excessive for population replacement on a long-term basis. In four individual years at Chhatari, the juvenile loss rate exceeded 50%, and these were years during or just after a large population increase of monkeys, suggesting that the villagers and local trappers were using trapping as a way of regulating the population. When too many monkeys are present at Chhatari, they become a nuisance and agricultural threat. At the present time the Chhatari population is considered too large by most of the

Table 7.7. Aligarh District Unprotected Population: Annual Loss Rates of
             Juveniles and Adults

Year	Percentage loss juveniles	Percentage loss adult males	Percentage loss adult females	Percentage loss total adults
1962	70.0	11.2	24.0	19.5
1963	59.4	14.5	4.4	8.4
1964	76.6	19.4	19.8	19.7
1965	65.9	29.4	27.2	28.3
1966	75.7	22.3	9.5	14.4
1967	31.4	18.4	21.7	20.6
1968	68.0	5.5	18.6	13.6
1969	57.1	35.3	26.1	30.0
1970	41.0	0	10.8	6.4
1971	50.5	13.2	2.2	7.1
1972	58.0	20.6	7.0	12.5
1973	51.4	6.1	24.7	17.5
1974	44.2	26.3	37.1	32.4
1975	22.2	8.3	16.7	12.6
1976	37.3	28.2	0	13.7
15-year averages (1962–76)	53.9 ± 4.1	17.3 ± 2.6	16.7 ± 2.9	17.0 ± 2.1

local people. The tolerance of the villagers to crop depredations and general disturbances by the Chhatari monkeys is wearing thin.

Adult Loss

The annual loss of adults averaged 17.0% in the unprotected population, compared to only 12.5% in the semiprotected population (tables 7.7 and 7.8). Again it is difficult to distinguish true mortality from trapping removal, but we feel that the majority of this is true mortality since adults are rarely trapped. Occasional remnants of adult skeletal material are found.

In the unprotected population, the loss rates of adult males and females were similar (17.3% and 16.7%), but in the protected population that of males was significantly higher than that of females (22.8% compared to 9.1%). This difference probably represents emigration of young adult males from their natal group. This is a well-known phenomenon in rhesus groups (Sade 1977) and is a primary mechanism of gene flow between groups. At Chhatari, where there are

Table 7.8.   Semiprotected Population (Chhatari-do-Raha Groups): Annual
                   Loss Rates of Juveniles and Adults

Year	Percentage loss juveniles	Percentage loss adult males	Percentage loss adult females	Percentage loss total adults
1962	75.0	32.2	0	8.8
1963	29.4	0	11.3	9.1
1964	53.3	30.0	16.7	20.6
1965	24.0	14.0	10.3	12.5
1966	32.1	0	9.5	2.9
1967	0	18.4	13.2	15.4
1968	58.1	38.2	17.9	26.6
1969	38.1	57.1	0	6.7
1970	10.0	2.5	0	0
1971	9.1	13.6	4.6	6.7
1972	57.1	43.7	5.5	17.3
1973	11.4	20.0	9.3	12.0
1974	18.2	45.1	25.7	31.6
1975	28.8	12.2	0	3.4
1976	28.0	14.6	12.3	13.9
Average (1962–76)	31.5 ± 5.5	22.8 ± 4.5	9.1 ± 2.0	12.5 ± 2.3

not many other groups within 20 km, we hypothesize that these emigrating males probably have a high mortality rate.

The higher loss rate of adult males in semiprotected groups (22.8%) than unprotected groups (17.3%) provides evidence of natural social factors regulating the number of males in rhesus groups. The unprotected groups are much smaller, averaging only 14 individuals in 1977, with only 1 to 3 adult males per group. In these small groups there is little or no agonistic pressure for subordinate males to disperse. In the larger Chhatari group, however, with 132 monkeys, there is obvious male–male aggression within the group, and this apparently serves as a dispersal stimulus for subordinate males. We believe that this group is near its socially maximum size for the space and habitat it occupies. The level of trapping and emigration that it experiences, however, seems to be properly balanced to maintain high natality and low mortality, at least for the recent past.

Annual Turnover

Annual turnover, calculated by combining age class loss rates per year with the known age structure of the population, was estimated to be

24.4% for the unprotected population and 18.4% for the semiprotected Chhatari population. These turnover rates can be compared to an estimated annual population turnover of 28.4% for the baboons of Amboseli, calculated from the data of Altmann and Altmann (1970).

Annual Population Increase

The Chhatari population increased from 49 monkeys in October 1959 to 140 in 1977, an average annual increase of nearly 6%. With complete protection and well-provisioned food supplies, macaque populations can increase at rates of 10–16% per year. For example, the rhesus population of La Parguera increased at the annual rate of 13% during its first 10 years (Drickamer 1974); that of Cayo Santiago increased at an annual rate of 16% from 1960 to 1964 (Koford 1966). The Japanese macaques of Mt. Takasaki increased from 220 in 1953 to 1,400 in 1974, an average annual increase of slightly over 10% (Itani 1975).

Similar rates of increase can occur in New World monkeys, even those which we normally think of as K-selected inhabitants of mature forest. For example, the howler monkey population of Barro Colorado Island increased from 239 in 1951 to 814 in 1959, an average annual increase of 16.4% (calculated from data in Carpenter 1962).

Thus, monkey populations can show substantial rates of increase if provided with suitable habitat, food, and protection. The Chhatari population would probably have shown higher rates of increase if totally protected and more amply provisioned, but they unquestionably would have created a serious agricultural problem.

Demographic Comparisons of Rhesus Populations

Table 7.9 summarizes a number of basic population characteristics of the two Aligarh cohorts and the Kathmandu temple populations which are totally immune from trapping. These three populations represent increasing (Chhatari), declining (Aligarh unprotected), and stable (Kathmandu) populations.

The Kathmandu populations consisted of five rhesus groups at Swayambhu and seven groups at Pashupati. They remained relatively stable over a 4-year period, averaging a total of 655 monkeys. Although the populations fluctuated annually from a low of 609 to a high of 686, they showed no consistent increase or decrease, and in 1978 they were within 2% of their level in 1975.

The highest natality or birth rate (90.3%) of the three rhesus popu-

Table 7.9. Summary of Demographic Comparisons Among the Chhatari,
Unprotected Aligarh, and Protected Kathmandu Rhesus
Populations

Population trait	Chhatari groups (semiprotected)	Aligarh (unprotected)	Kathmandu (fully protected)
Population trend	Increasing	Decreasing	Stable
Trapping removal	Slight to moderate	Heavy	None
Natality (annual birth rate)	90.3 ± 1.9	76.7 ± 2.1	63.0 ± 2.1
Percentage immature animals in total population	54.2 ± 1.8	44.0 ± .6	57.5 ± 1.4
Infant mortality per year	15.5 ± 3.5	17.7 ± 2.4	21.5 ± 4.1
Juvenile loss per year	31.5 ± 5.5	53.9 ± 4.1	17.0 ± 4.4
Adult loss per year	12.5 ± 2.3	17.0 ± 2.1	25.8 ± 6.8
Annual turnover (%)	18.4	24.4	21.2

lations in India and Nepal occurred in the Chhatari population of India,
which was subject to slight or moderate trapping. Both heavy trapping
in India and no trapping in Nepal were associated with depressed birth
rates. We propose that the birth rate is depressed in the Kathmandu
populations (63.0%) through natural biosocial mechanisms. It will,
however, require further study to determine the nature of these mechanisms. We cannot say at this time if there is a stress response to crowding or intergroup competition, a lactational delay in the resumption of
estrus, a behavioral limitation in mating success due to male competition, or a variety of other factors.* It is interesting to note also that the
natality of *M. sinica* in Sri Lanka averaged 62.8% (Dittus 1975). This
is also a population showing a stable population pattern, and one without any trapping removal.

   Another aspect of natural population regulation shown in these
comparative data is the pattern of infant mortality. The infant mortality
of the Chhatari population (15.5%) was not significantly different from
that of the unprotected population (17.7%), but both were less than

---

*Editors' Note: Note that the mechanisms listed here are discussed in this volume by
Christian, Lee, and Packard and Mech as possible regulators of population growth in other species.

that of the totally protected population in Kathmandu (21.5%). It is obvious that population regulation in the Kathmandu population occurred through increased infant mortality as well as decreased natality. Unfortunately, we do not know the causes of this mortality. Teas (1978) speculated that it occurs through a combination of infectious disease, primarily respiratory and enteric infections, and improper parental care. The Kathmandu rhesus showed less grooming of infants than most Indian populations that have been studied, and they also show considerably higher levels of aggression (Teas 1978). Certainly, the habitat in general cannot be faulted or considered deficient, since the Kathmandu habitats, in terms of vegetation, cover, water, food, and lack of human harassment, appear to be more favorable than those of Aligarh district. The vegetation of the Kathmandu temple areas is abundant and green throughout the year, and the habitat is varied with adequate space and shelter. Predation is not a significant factor. The climate is moderate with fewer extremes in temperature and drought than India. Hence, we believe that the Kathmandu rhesus populations have excellent habitat, and that their behavioral and demographic patterns cannot be attributed to limiting factors of the physical environment. Instead, we feel that these populations provide evidence of intrinsic natural population regulation.

Dittus (1975) found over 30% infant mortality in toque macaques of Sri Lanka and stated: "These data suggest that the equilibrium in the population of *M. sinica* in Polonnaruwa is achieved through lowered fertility and increased mortality in the infant and juvenile classes." A similar situation occurs in the Nepalese rhesus, except that increased mortality in Nepal occurred primarily in infants and adults rather than in infants and juveniles. Both populations can provide clues to natural biosocial mechanisms of population regulation in nonhuman primates.

Summary

Demographic data from three natural populations of rhesus monkeys in India and Nepal show significant differences in natality, mortality, and population turnover patterns. These differences are related to different population trends, which partially reflect human interactions.

The highest annual natality or birth rate (90.3%), lowest infant and adult mortality (15.5 and 12.5%, respectively), and the lowest annual turnover rates (18.4%) occurred in the Chhatari population of India, which was subjected to slight to moderate trapping removal of juveniles. This population has increased from 40 to 140 monkeys over the past 18 years, an average annual increase of 6%.

The Aligarh unprotected population, which was subjected to heavy trapping pressure and substantial human harassment, showed intermediate natality (76.7%), intermediate infant and adult mortality (17.7% and 17.0%), and higher annual turnover (24.4%). This population has shown the highest loss rate of juveniles (53.9%), clearly reflecting excessive trapping removal during the years of this study. This population has declined from 328 monkeys to 94 in the past 18 years, an average annual decline of over 6%.

The Kathmandu population, which is totally protected from trapping, showed the lowest natality (63.0%), the highest infant and adult mortality (21.5% and 25.8%), and an intermediate level of annual turnover (21.2%). This population did have the lowest loss rate of juveniles (17.0%). This population has been relatively stable over the past 4 years, changing from 686 monkeys in 1975 to 672 in 1978, a change of only 2% in 4 years. Previous observations on this population from 1971 to 1974 indicated that it had a similar size in those years, although total counts were not taken.

We believe that the Kathmandu populations demonstrate natural biosocial mechanisms of limitation in a free-living macaque population. Population regulation occurs primarily through reduced natality and increased mortality of infants and adults. Only the juveniles fare better in Nepal than in India in demographic patterns.* The Chhatari population has demonstrated a favorable level of harvest, and one that has apparently stimulated maximum natality along with minimum infant and adult mortality. The unprotected population of Aligarh has shown the detrimental effects of excessive trapping leading to long-term population decline. Collectively, these populations have provided demographic guidelines for assessing population regulation in rhesus macaques.

Editors' Note: The comparative approach which these authors employ permits a partial factoring out of exogenous population regulating or limiting factors and a partial simulation of the controlled conditions described by Lloyd and Terman. Like the study by Sade this study suggests that endogenous control mechanisms occur among "free living" primate groups when exogenous effects are minimized.

Acknowledgments

This work was begun when the senior author was a Fulbright Postdoctoral Fellow at Aligarh University. We are grateful for the cooperation and assistance of Drs. M. Babar Mirza, S. M. Alam, M. Rafiq Siddiqi, M. Azher Beg, T. N. Ananthakrishnan, M. L. Roonwal, K. K. Tiwari, R. P. Mukherjee, R. K. Lahiri, J. A. Khan, D. Lindburg, M. Neville, P. Dolhinow, M. Bertrand, J. R. Oppenheimer, F. B. Bang, T. W. Simpson, B. C. Pal, and M. Y. Farooqui. Since 1960, the field work has been supported by U.S. Public Health Service Grants RO7-AI-10048, MH-18440, and RR-00910 to Johns Hopkins University.

In Nepal, we are indebted to Professors D. R. Uprety and D. D. Bhatt; Drs. K. R. Pandey, B. Bishop, E. Snider, P. Vandegrift, and B. Marriott; Mssrs. G. Campbell, T. Acker, G. Turner, and R. Shrestha; and Ms. B. Pradhan, M. G. Smith, J. Fisher, and J. Hess. The field work in Nepal has been supported by the National Geographic Society and the Center for Field Research.

References

Altmann, S. A. 1974. Baboons, space, time and energy. *Am. Zool.* 14:221–48.

———, and Altmann, J. 1970. *Baboon ecology.* Chicago: Univ. of Chicago Press.

Carpenter, C. R. 1934. A field study of the behavior and social relations of howling monkeys. *Comp. Psychol. Monogr.* 10(2):1–168.

———. 1962. Field studies of a primate population. In *Roots of behavior*, ed. E. L. Bliss, pp. 286–94. New York: Hoeber Medical Books, Harper and Bros.

Chivers, D. 1977. The lesser apes. In *Primate conservation*, ed. H.S.H. Prince Ranier and G. Bourne, pp. 539–98. New York: Academic Press.

Dittus, W. P. J. 1975. Population dynamics of the toque monkey, *Macaca sinica.* In *Socioecology and psychology of primates*, ed. R. H. Tuttle, pp. 125–51. The Hague: Mouton.

———. 1977. The socioecological basis for the conservation of the toque monkey (*Macaca sinica*) of Sri Lanka. In *Primate conservation*, ed. H.S.H. Ranier and G. H. Bourne, pp. 237–65. New York: Academic Press.

———. 1979. A ten-years life history of wild male toque monkeys, *Macaca sinica* of Sri Lanka. VIIth Cong. Int. Primatol. Soc., Bangalore, India. Abstracts of papers, p. 99.

Drickamer, L. A. 1974. A ten year summary of reproductive data for free-ranging *Macaca mulatta. Folia Primatol.* 21:61–80.

Fossey, D., and Harcourt, S. 1977. Feeding and ranging behavior of mountain gorillas (*Gorilla gorilla berengei*) in the Virunga volcanoes region. In *Primate ecology*, ed. T. H. Clutton-Brock. London: Academic Press.

Furuya, Y. 1968. On the fission of troops of Japanese monkeys. I. Five fissions and social changes between 1955 and 1966 in the Gagyusan troop. *Primates* 9:323–50.

Goodall, A. G., and C. P. Groves. 1977. The conservation of eastern gorillas. In *Primate conservation*, ed. H.S.H. Ranier and G. Bourne, pp. 599–637. New York: Academic Press.

Itani, J. 1975. Twenty years with Mt. Takasaki monkeys. In *Primate utilization and conservation*, ed. G. Bermant and D. G. Lindburg, pp. 101–26. New York: Wiley.

Koford, C. 1966. Population changes in rhesus monkeys: Cayo Santiago 1960–64. *Tulane Stud. Zool.* 13:1–7.

Kummer, H. 1968. *Social organization of Hamadryas baboons. a field study.* Chicago: Univ. Chicago Press.

Marriott, B. 1978. A preliminary report on the feeding behavior of rhesus monkeys (*Macaca mulatta*) in Kathmandu, Nepal. *Ann. Nepal Nat. Conserv. Soc.* 2:68–72.

Sade, D. S.; Cushing, K.; Cushing, P.; Dunaif, J.; Figueroa, A.; Kaplan, J. R.; Lauer, C.; Rhodes, D.; and Schneider, J. 1977. Population dynamics in relation to social structure on Cayo Santiago. *Yearb. Phys. Anthropol.* (for 1976) 20:253–62.

Schaller, G. B. 1963. *The mountain gorilla: ecology and behavior.* Chicago: Univ. of Chicago Press.

Siddiqi, M. F., and C. H. Southwick. 1977. Population trends of rhesus monkeys in Aligarh district. In *Use of non-human primates in biomedical research*, ed. M. R. N. Prasad and T. C. Anand-Kumar, pp. 15–23. New Delhi: Indian National Sciences Academy.

Southwick, C. H., and Siddiqi, M. F. 1977. Population dynamics of rhesus monkeys in northern India. In *Primate conservation*, ed. H.S.H. Prince Ranier and G. Bourne, pp. 339–62. New York: Academic Press.

Struhsaker, T. T. 1975. *Behavior and ecology of red colobus monkeys.* Chicago: Univ. of Chicago Press.

———. 1976. A further decline in numbers of *Amboseli* vervet monkeys. *Biotropica* 8(3):211–14.

Taylor, H.; Teas, J.; Richie, T.; Southwick, C.; and Shrestha, R. 1978. Social interactions between adult male and infant rhesus monkeys in Nepal. *Primates: J. Primatol.* 19(2):343–51.

Teas, H. J. 1978. *Ecology and behavior of rhesus monkeys in Kathmandu, Nepal.* Ph.D. dissertation, Johns Hopkins University.

———; Taylor, H.; Richie, T.; and Southwick, C. 1977. Ecology and behavior of rhesus monkeys in Nepal. *Final Report to the National Geographic Society*, April 15, 1977. 103 pp.

———; Taylor, H.; Richie, T.; and Southwick, C. 1978. Behavioral ecology of rhesus monkeys in Kathmandu, Nepal. *Ann. Nepal Nature Conserv. Soc.* 2:15–20.

van Lawick-Goodall, J. 1971. *In the shadow of man.* Boston: Houghton Mifflin.

8

POPULATION BIOLOGY OF FREE-RANGING RHESUS MONKEYS ON CAYO SANTIAGO, PUERTO RICO

Donald Stone Sade

Population Dynamics of Primates

Long-term observations or repeated population surveys within the natural range of a species are required to indicate the ecological factors that limit population size among wild primates. If stationary populations are assumed or indicated by estimation of population parameters (Dittus 1975; Teleki et al. 1976), differing population densities according to habitat may suggest limiting factors (Neville 1968). Southwick's (Southwick 1960, 1967; Southwick and Beg 1961; Southwick et al. 1961a,b, 1965; Southwick and Siddiqi 1966, 1968) (very) long-term surveys in northern India show that exploitation by humans is the major factor in the decline of rhesus monkey populations. Under some circumstances exploitation by human beings and the reproductive potential of the monkeys can reach an equilibrium resulting in populations that remain stationary for a number of years (Southwick and Siddiqi 1976). The quantity of available food may be limiting in some habitats (Dunbar and Dunbar 1974, 1976; Frisch 1978; Loy 1970; Neville 1968). The quality of nutrients may become limiting under severe conditions, and may in part be responsible for the decline in the Amboseli population of baboons during a long-lasting drought (Altmann et al. 1977). These authors suggest that poor nutrition may cause delayed maturation and higher infant mortality, both of which would severely affect the reproductive potential of the population.

Some authors (Coelho et al. 1976) have claimed, however, that food resources may be present in superabundance and yet population densities remain stable at lower levels than food supply would allow. A likely factor under these conditions is the periodic outbreak of epidemic disease, which might be more severe under conditions of higher population density. Collias and Southwick (1952) suggest that this factor explains the severe drop in numbers of howling monkeys on Barro Colorado between the 1930s and 1950s.

Do characteristics of social organization distribute the effects of ecological stress unevenly through a population? Or if neither food nor epidemic disease were limiting a primate population, would factors associated with social stress come into play to reduce the rate of population increase? The concept of population regulation through social stress produced by frequent agonistic or territorial interactions and resulting in hypertrophy of the adrenal cortex and consequent increased susceptibility to infection, suppression of testicular activity, resorbtion or abortion of embryos, renal failure, and other severe physiological effects is due largely to the work of Christian, his collaborators, and followers (Anderson 1961; Andrews et al. 1972, 1975; Christian 1950, 1956, 1961, 1963, 1971; Christian et al. 1965; Pasley and Christian 1971, 1972). This work has been done largely on small rodent populations.* Additional work suggests that the suppression of growth and reproduction may also play an important part in the control of fertility in populations of rodents, beyond the severe effects of stress resulting in high mortality (Batilz et al. 1977; Vandenbergh 1971). These less severe effects may be reversible and result in the synchronization or timing of reproduction within the annual cycle as much as regulation of maximum population size. In any case, small rodent populations may increase rapidly, producing several generations in each breeding season.

Mechanisms for rapidly turning reproduction on and off in close coordination with environmental and populational factors seem to have evolved as an important part of the adaptations of these small mammals. Closely related species may emphasize or deemphasize use of these mechanisms according to reproductive strategies appropriate to their preferred habitats (Batzli et al. 1977). Can these findings be extrapolated to the primates and to human populations? These species are characterized by long life cycles, prolonged maturation, slow repro-

Editors' Note: For further discussion of the nature of these mechanisms and their effects on rodent populations, see Christian, Lloyd, and Terman. The effects of social organization in distributing the effects of ecological stress unevenly among wolf populations are discussed by Packard and Mech. And the existence of similar mechanisms is implied in the study of Indian rhesus monkeys by Southwick et al.

duction, and overlapping generations within the same social unit, and one cannot assume a priori that similar mechanisms will operate in populations where quite different reproductive strategies may be followed.*

Nevertheless, social factors affecting survival, maturation, synchronization of reproductive cycles, and physiological response to stress are known for the primates (Holst 1972; Perret 1977; Sassenrath 1969, 1970; Sassenrath et al. 1973; Vandenbergh and Drickamer 1974; Vandenbergh and Post 1976; Vandenbergh and Vessey 1966, 1968).† The basic mechanisms were in fact described for human beings (Christian 1950; Scott 1970; Scott and Eleftheriou 1968; Senay 1973).

It is likely, although not proven, that social stress produced through the dominance/subordination interactions of group-living primates has effects on the individual similar to those that have been reported for small mammals. In particular, the correlation between dominance rank and other aspects of social organization of rhesus monkeys reported below may be in part due to physiological mechanisms similar to those already documented in small mammalian populations.

Long-term observations on free-ranging rhesus monkeys living under conditions of high population density, superabundant and high-quality food supply, and a relative freedom from infectious disease provide the conclusions reported below.‡ The work is organized around characteristics of the life histories of males and females, observed since 1960 at the Cayo Santiago, Puerto Rico, colony established by C. R. Carpenter in 1938, and since 1956 managed by the NIH and the University of Puerto Rico.

The special and extreme characteristics of the colony need to be kept in mind in interpreting the conclusions of this paper:

*Editors' Note: Sade here challenges the assumption of both Cohen and Baron that the absence or insensitivity of density-dependent regulation in human beings requires special explanation. His argument parallels that of Ripley in suggesting that reproductive strategy and the need for regulatory mechanisms will depend on other specific features of lifespan and ecology and will thus be a function of specific evolutionary histories. In this context, the reader should also note Baron's discussion of the difference between animals (primates) relying heavily on visual messages about their environments and those (rodents) more heavily dependent on olfactory messages.

†Editors' Note: For a further discussion of these mechanisms see Drickamer.

‡Editors' Note: Note that the conditions described by Sade, in which there occur a minimum of exogenous population-limiting or regulating factors, parallel conditions postulated by Cohen for human populations in the Pleistocene. Sade's observations suggest that social self-regulation by groups of free-living primates at levels below the carrying capacity of resources is plausible.

1. The superabundant, artificial food supply maintains a rapidly expanding population rather than a stationary one that might be expected in the wild (Dittus 1975).

2. The water barrier surrounding the colony prevents the complete dispersal of migrants, however much they exhibit the psychological and social correlates of dispersal.

3. The population contains an excess of males, due in part to the recirculation of migrants who would disperse from a local population in the wild. In part the excess of males is due to a very high secondary sex ratio. The possible proximate causes of the latter condition are discussed elsewhere (Sade in preparation).

4. The high population density in the colony is reflected in high rates of interaction both between and within social groups.

5. The abundant, well-distributed, and constant food supply maintained in recent years probably has eliminated competition for food by animals of different social status as an important factor affecting the conclusions of this paper.

The overall effect of these special or extreme conditions may be to intensify the action of proximate social mechanisms, thus making them easier to detect, as I have suggested previously (Sade 1972a). At the same time the special and extreme conditions at Cayo Santiago make it difficult to infer ultimate causes or the adaptive significance of the patterns of population ·dynamics and social organization observed at the colony.

Obviously, only similar, long-term observations on wild populations can verify or refute the generality of the specific social mechanisms discovered at the colony, and provide the ecological information required to extend any speculation on ultimate causes.

Life Histories of Females

Dominance Relations among Females

Early studies on nonhuman primates emphasized the aggressiveness of adult males in the organization of the social group (Carpenter 1942; Hall and DeVore 1965; Koford 1965; Southwick et al. 1961a, 1965; Southwick and Siddiqi 1967). In particular, the dominance relations among the males were assumed to be important in determining group leaders, access to females, access to limited supplies of food and water, and therefore which males were more likely to survive and re-produce. Systematic studies show that in some species males formed linear hierarchies according to some criteria of success in agonistic interactions (Hall and DeVore 1965; Southwick et al. 1965). These and other studies seemed to indicate that female monkeys showed lower levels of aggressiveness and a subtler form of dominance inter-action, which made it difficult to rank them in the same manner as males (Conaway and Koford 1964; Hall and DeVore 1965; Kaufman 1965; Lindburg 1971; Southwick et al. 1965).

Several early reports from the Japan Monkey Center indicated that, to the contrary, it was possible to rank females according to some criteria of dominance, and furthermore that the rank of the female had a significant effect upon the rank of her offspring, and therefore the position of her offspring within the social group (Kawai 1958; Kawa-mura 1958).

Intensive observation of marked individual rhesus monkeys at the Cayo Santiago colony showed definitely that both adult females and juvenile male and females could be ranked in hierarchies of aggressive dominance using the same criteria by which adult males were ranked (Missakian 1972; Sade 1966, 1967). It was shown that the adult fe-males formed linear dominance hierarchies that were'very stable over periods of several years (Sade 1972a). The observations of the Japa-nese investigators, that the rank of offspring were highly correlated with and therefore determined by the rank of the mother, were abun-dantly confirmed at Cayo Santiago.

More recently, several observers have made the deliberate and suc-cessful attempt to discover whether female monkeys in the wild might also show linear dominance hierarchies, contrary to earlier reports (Dunbar and Dunbar 1977; Hausfater 1975). The idea that primate so-cieties are primarily organized around the adult males is therefore giv-ing way to the idea the adult females may form the stable and enduring aspect of the social group, except perhaps for some highly specialized species such as the hamadryas baboon (Kummer and Kurt 1963). Mon-key groups are therefore not so dissimilar after all to the social units of other mammalian species.

The Genealogy as a Unit

Observations of interactional networks of the rhesus monkey groups at Cayo Santiago indicated that subgroups within the social units were composed primarily of animals related to one another through the female line (Missakian 1974; Sade 1965, 1968, 1972b). These groups of related animals are called genealogies. The reality of the genealogically based subgroup has been demonstrated in a number of studies. Of particular importance to the present chapter is the finding that the genealogical groups rank in the dominance hierarchy of females as units (Missakian 1972; Sade et al. 1976). Therefore, it is quite correct to speak of high- and low-ranking genealogies.

Within genealogies the rank of females is also very predictable. The Japanese workers found that younger sisters tend to come to rank above their older sisters, and this observation has been repeatedly confirmed at Cayo Santiago (Kawai 1958; Kawamura 1958; Sade 1966, 1972a).

Briefly, the rank that a female infant will assume as an adult can be predicted almost perfectly in a stable group given only the information of the position of her mother in the dominance hierarchy of adult females. A very few cases of adoption of newborn infants have been observed. These indicate that the adopted female will tend to assume the rank of her foster mother. These observations indicate that the dominance rank of females is based entirely on social inheritance rather than on some genetic mechanism.

The mechanism by which juveniles acquire the rank of their mothers is not completely known. The prevailing view seems to be that the youngest offspring receives the most active aid in dominance interactions from her mother (Cheney 1977). Thus, females subordinate to the mother learn to be subordinate to her offspring, while the offspring herself gains confidence through aided victories over the losing females. This explanation may be too simple. Some observations indicate that in fights among siblings, neither elder nor younger receive the most aid from the mother (Kaplan 1977; Sade 1966). A more troublesome finding, which cannot be explained through the interventionist model, is that some young females rose to their predicted rank a number of years following the death of their mother (Sade 1972a). It may be that some imprinting-like learning occurs within the first year of life, and becomes manifest only at adolescence or later. Very numerous detailed observations on individual life histories of female rhesus monkeys at Cayo Santiago are currently being analyzed by the author and his collaborators, and by Saroj Datta at Cambridge.

Consequences of Dominance Status among Females

Reproductive Parameters in Dominance Status among Females. A cursory inspection of census information, even over a period of several years, does not seem to indicate that the dominance rank of females correlates in any profound way with their reproductive potential. In particular, high-, middle-, and low-ranking genealogies may be large or small. A more detailed analysis, however, using the life table as a tool, indicates that the reproductive potential of genealogies of different rank may be considerable. The "intrinsic rate of natural increase" (r), a reproductive parameter of considerable theoretical importance, summarizes the combined effects of age-specific rates of fertility and mortality for a population or a partition of a population. Any environmental or social factor that affects life expectancy, fertility, or age at which reproduction begins will be reflected in the value of r. Preliminary analysis of life tables from Cayo Santiago indicate that higher-ranking genealogies have a considerably higher r than do lower-ranking genealogies (Sade et al. 1976).* The main cause of the difference may be earlier successful reproduction among females of the higher-ranking genealogies (Drickamer 1974; Sade et al. 1976).

Life Expectancy and Dominance Status among Females. The effects of dominance status on longevity of females may be less profound than the effects of dominance status on their age of earliest successful reproduction. The females of the lower-ranking genealogies tend to have a lower life expectancy than those of the higher-ranking genealogies. None of the eldest females in the population were members of the low-ranking genealogies.

The differences in reproductive rates and mortality between higher- and lower-ranking genealogies are more pronounced when the rate of increase for the entire population is low than when the rate of increase for the entire population is high (Sade et al. in preparation). At Cayo Santiago low or high overall rates of increase do not necessarily correlate with the population's density, which is always high compared to wild areas. Rather, if some disturbance or stress acts on the entire

Editors' Note: The correlation of dominance and reproductive success parallels that described by Packard and Mech among wolves and recalls Christian's emphasis on rank as well as density as a factor in endocrine regulation of fertility. See Drickamer for a discussion of the possible mechanisms involved in the accelerated reproductive maturation of females in high ranking genealogies.

system, it is likely that the subordinate portions of the population will respond most strongly, being less well buffered against stress by high dominance rank.

Other workers have shown that low-ranking females may breed later, produce fewer offspring, and lose more infants than do higher-ranking females (Drickamer 1974). One study suggests that a direct reduction in fertility through harassment by higher-ranking females during the estrous cycle may be a factor (Dunbar and Dunbar 1977).

In any case, the conclusion seems clear that even in a population undergoing rapid expansion due to a superabundant source of food, there may be considerable differences in reproductive advantage among portions of the population, and that the advantages may be ordered by the hierarchy of aggressive dominance relations among the females.

Since differences in rank among females seem almost completely explained by factors of social inheritance or interaction, it does not seem necessary to suggest that differences in dominance rank among females are caused by genetic differences among them. This does not mean that the genealogy may not be genetically differentiated (Duggleby 1976; Ober 1979), but that genetic differentiation is a result, not a cause of social differences.

Origin of New Groups

There have been several episodes of group division at Cayo Santiago since 1956 (Koford 1966; Sade et al. 1976; Missakian 1973; Chepko-Sade and Sade, n.d.). The first of these may have been initiated by the sudden increase in food supply when a consistent maintenance program was started in the late 1950s. The latest episodes may have been initiated when the population density was suddenly reduced by the removal of entire large social groups. Factors internal to the groups that facilitated division may have been the sudden loss of a critical individual (Koford 1965), competition between males that accentuated already existing subgroups (Southwick et al. 1965), the recent addition of large numbers of immigrant males, or other modification of the sex ratio (Chepko-Sade, in preparation). The distribution of females into the new groups, however, has been very well analyzed (Chepko-Sade 1974, 1977; Chepko-Sade and Sade 1979), and shows again the regularity and predictability that we have come to expect from the female portion of the population. The following observations are from Chepko-Sade (1977).

Fission between Genealogies. In most cases, the parent group divided between genealogies as it fissioned into smaller daughter groups; 59 of the 68 known genealogies distributed among the daughter groups without internal divisions. Only 9 of the 68 known genealogies divided within themselves, some members going to one daughter group and some members to another. This very strong tendency for the genealogies to remain intact during group divisions is further evidence for the reality of the genealogy as a behavioral subgroup within the larger social unit.

Fission within Genealogies in Relation to Dominance Rank of Females. The nine genealogies that divided internally did not do so in a haphazard manner. Two did so between subgenealogies composed of adult females and their own offspring. In most cases these were sisters whose mother had died sometime before the fission. Each sister with her own offspring now began to act as an independent unit. In the other seven genealogies that divided internally during a group fission, the division occurred between the eldest daughter with her offspring and the rest of the genealogy, or in some cases between the eldest daughter of the eldest daughter and the rest of the genealogy. The eldest daughter and her offspring have the predictable lowest dominance rank within any genealogy and may receive the most attacks and threats that occur within the genealogy, as they are at the end of the chain of redirected aggressions. In at least one case, the eldest daughter and her family improved their dominance status by moving to the smaller daughter group. It may also be that the elder daughter has had more time to develop friendly ties with nonrelatives within the larger social group, and that these have become stronger than the intragenealogical ties.

There is some tendency for genealogies that are close together in dominance rank within the larger group to stay together in the daughter groups. In some cases this results in the lower-ranking genealogies forming the nucleus of a new social group. There are insufficient cases to say with complete certainty that the daughter group composed of formerly subordinate genealogies remains subordinate in intergroup interactions with the former dominant genealogies, but this certainly has happened in some cases. If this were a valid generalization, it would mean that the more subordinate genealogies would be the ones most likely to emigrate from the home range of the parent group and establish a new population somewhere else.

Life Histories of Males

The life histories of male rhesus monkeys are more complicated than those of females, and have not been as completely analyzed as yet from the data currently available from Cayo Santiago.

It is useful to classify males according to whether they were born into the social group in which they are presently found (natal males) or joined from other groups (nonnatal males). In the large groups that occur at Cayo Santiago, it is also convenient to classify males in another way. Central males are those who are spatially central to the social group and who interact with the females (Sade 1972b); peripheral males are those who interact mainly among themselves with occasional agonistic and rarely friendly interactions with the adults of the central group. Usually, all the males, both central and peripheral, rank in a single, linear, dominance hierarchy.

In contrast to females, males disperse from their natal groups as individuals (Drickamer and Vessey 1973; Koford 1966; Lindburgh 1969; Norikoshi and Koyama 1974; Sade 1972a; Sugiyama 1976). It is likely that every male born into a particular group will eventually disperse from that group (Drickamer and Vessey 1973). The proximate causes of the departure of males seem to be diverse. In a few cases, a male has departed following a sudden loss of dominance rank. In most cases, however, this does not seem to be a major factor in determining which males leave and when they leave. The adolescent and young adult males, who form the major portion of the migrant population, leave their natal groups apparently due to internal maturational changes rather than overt aggression on the part of more dominant animals.

The statuses that migrants achieve in the population are diverse and not simply functions of their prior statuses. That is, high-ranking animals that leave a group may achieve either high rank in the new group or remain peripheral, low-ranking, or even solitary. Conversely, low-ranking individuals may join a new group immediately as dominant, but more likely they join as peripheral animals and gradually assume a higher-ranking position over a period of several years (Boelkins and

Wilson 1972; Chepko-Sade 1974; Drickamer and Vessey 1973). The peripheral males may eventually associate with a group of females that is dispersing from a group undergoing division and become the central high-ranking males of the new group (Chepko-Sade 1974; Chepko-Sade in preparation). This process has been observed in great detail in two group divisions, and the information is currently being prepared for publication (Chepko-Sade in preparation).

What are the determinants of dominance rank among male rhesus monkeys? Koford (1963) showed that a male's dominance rank tended to correlate with his mother's rank while he was still with his natal group and therefore is presumably acquired through social factors similar to those that determine the rank of females. Among males who join from other groups, rank seems to correlate with seniority (Chepko-Sade 1974, and in preparation; Drickamer and Vessey 1973). Occasionally, individual males have shown sudden though temporary rises in dominance position at the same time as a sudden reddening of the sexual skin, indicating that a sudden testosterone surge may be involved. In general, however, the access to high-ranking positions among males may have less to do with individual differences in intrinsic physiological factors (Sade 1967) and more to do with their historical position in the social group. As with females, it may be unlikely that the differences in dominance rank among males are due to genetic differences among them.

Is there a relation between dominance status and reproduction among males? The following hypotheses are now being tested on long-term data:

1. Males of high-ranking genealogies tend to achieve high rank within their natal groups.

2. Males of high-ranking genealogies tend to remain longer with their natal groups.

3. As with females, males of high-ranking genealogies may mature at a younger age than males of low-ranking genealogies.

4. Males who are central and high-ranking may do most of the fertilizing of females, while peripheral and solitary males as a class may do a smaller proportion of breeding.

5. Socially inherited high dominance rank, rather than genetic superiority, may permit some males to reproduce earlier, and therefore greatly increase their lifetime reproductive potential in contrast to males who inherit initially low dominance rank.

Paternal Exclusions among Free-ranging Rhesus Monkeys

The above hypotheses could be tested if we could directly measure the reproductive success of males, as we can for females. A preliminary study of the possibility of directly determining paternity (Sade et al. 1977) through genetical techniques failed to reveal any association of dominance rank of male with number of infants that he might have fathered. The results are inconclusive at this time, but suggest that the dominance/subordination hierarchy among males does not result in genetical competition. The results so far suggest that males of all ranks have about equal probability of fathering young. If these results are general, which may not be the case, the function of the hierarchy may have to be interpreted in relation to processes occurring at the level of the group, as suggested below.

Christian's Theory on Dominance/Subordination among Mammals

Christian (1970) proposed a major theory regarding the function of dominance/subordination hierarchies in mammalian societies and supported the theory primarily with evidence drawn from populations of small mammals. Briefly, he suggested that dominance/subordination hierarchies defined a subordinate portion of the population that would tend to migrate under conditions of high population density, while the established, higher-ranking portion of the population remained conservatively in areas already occupied. The evolutionary potential of the species was therefore to be found in the subordinate portions of the population that would be tested in the new, perhaps less favorable regions on the periphery of the species' range. Contrary to the common notion in the literature, Christian suggested that dominance/subordination interactions did not primarily function to mediate genetic competition within the stable portion of the species' range.*

The descriptions of population dynamics in relation to social organization among rhesus monkeys presented in this paper are precisely conformable to Christian's theory in spite of the fact that the monkeys

Editors' Note: Compare the discussion of dispersal by Tamarin.

are long-lived and slow-reproducing mammals with societies composed of overlapping generations. The current tendency in biological theorizing is to reject any notion that cannot be interpreted directly in terms of interindividual competition for reproductive advantage. A healthy science requires families of alternative hypotheses and bodies of empirical data so as not to degenerate into mere philosophy. At the very least, the correspondence of these very solidly based empirical observations with Christian's theory suggest that alternative models for evolution that refer to characteristics advantageous to a population or a species, rather than only to an individual, are still viable. *

Acknowledgments

This work was supported by Grant BNS77-14882 and other grants from the NSF, and Grant MH-23809 from the NIMH, NIH, PHS. The Cayo Santiago colony is part of the Caribbean Primate Research Center, supported by a contract from the DRR, NIH, PHS to the University of Puerto Rico. The manuscript benefited from stimulating conversations between the author and Jay Kaplan on mammalian population biology. Ann Wasserman gave essential assistance in preparing the manuscript.

References

Altmann, J.; Altmann, S. A.; Hausfater, G. and McCuskey, S. A. 1977. Life history of yellow baboons: physical development, reproductive parameters, and infant mortality. *Primates* 18:315–30.

Anderson, P. K. 1961. Density, social structure, and nonsocial environment in house-mouse populations and the implications for regulation of numbers. *Trans. N.Y. Acad. Sci.* 23:447–51.

Andrews, R. V.; Belknap, R. W.; Southard, J.; Lorincz, M.; and Hess, S. 1972. Physiological, demographic, and pathological changes in wild Norway rat populations over an annual cycle. *Comp. Biochem. Physiol.* 41A:149–65.

———; Belknap, R. W.; Christiansen, E. C.; and Ryan-Kline, M. 1975. Physiological consequences of experimentally altering the population structure of *Peromyscus maniculatus* in the field. *Comp. Bioch. Physiol.* 51A:785–92.

Batzli, G. O.; Getz, L. L.; and Hurley, S. S. 1977. Suppression of growth and reproduction of microtine rodents by social factors. *J. Mammal.* 58:583–91.

Boelkins, R. C., and Wilson, A. P. 1972. Intergroup social dynamics of the Cayo Santiago rhesus (*Macaca mulatta*) with special reference to changes in group membership by males. *Primates* 13:125–40.

Editors' Note: Compare the discussion by Tamarin of group and individual selection.

Carpenter, C. R. 1942. Sexual behavior of free ranging rhesus monkeys. I. Specimens, procedures, and behavioral characteristics of estrous. *J. Comp. Psychol.* 33:113–42.

Cheney, D. L. 1977. The acquisition of rank and the development of reciprocal alliances among free-ranging immature baboons. *Behav. Ecol. Sociobiol.* 2:303–18.

Chepko-Sade, B. D. 1974. Division of Group F at Cayo Santiago. *Am. J. Phys. Anthropol.* 41:472.

———. 1977. Patterns of group splitting within matrilineal kinship groups. A study of social group structure in *Macaca mulatta*. Unpublished Master's thesis, University of Puerto Rico, Río Piedras.

———, and Sade, D. S. 1979. Patterns of group splitting within matrilineal kinship groups: a study in group structure. *Behav. Ecol. Sociobiol.* 5:67–86.

Christian, J. J. 1950. The andreno-pituitary system and population cycles in mammals. *J. Mammal.* 31:247–59.

———. 1956. Adrenal and reproductive responses to population size in mice from freely growing populations. *Ecology* 37:258–73.

———. 1961. Phenomena associated with population density. *Proc. Natl. Acad. Sci. U.S.A.* 47:428–49.

———. 1963. Endocrine adaptive mechanisms and the physiologic regulation of population growth. In *Physiological mammalogy*, Vol. 1, *Mammalian Populations*, ed. W. V. Mayer and R. G. van Gelder. New York: Academic Press.

———. 1970. Social subordination, population density, and mammalian evolution. *Science* 168:84–90.

———. 1971. Fighting, maturity, and population density in *Microtus pennsylvanicus*. *J. Mammal*, 52:556–67.

———; Lloyd, J. A.; and Davis, D. E. 1965. The role of endocrines in the self-regulation of mammalian populations. *Recent Prog. Horm. Res.* 21:501–78.

Coelho, A. M., Jr.; Coelho, L. S.; Bramblett, C. A.; Bramblett, S. S.; and Quick, L. B. 1976. Ecology, population characteristics, and sympatric association in primates: a socio-bioenergetic analysis of howler and spider monkeys in Tikal, Guatemala. *Yearb. Phys. Anthropol.* 20:96–135.

Collias, N., and Southwick, C. 1952. A field study of population density and social organization in howling monkeys. *Proc. Am. Phil. Soc.* 96:143–56.

Conaway, C. H., and Koford, C. B. 1964. Estrous cycles and mating behavior in a free-ranging band of rhesus monkeys. *J. Mammal.* 45:577–88.

Dittus, W. P. J. 1975. Population dynamics of the toque monkey, *Macaca sinica*. In *Socioecology and psychology of primates*, ed. R. H. Tuttle, pp. 125–51. The Hague: Mouton.

Drickamer, L. C. 1974. A ten-year summary of reproductive data for free-ranging *Macaca mulatta*. *Folia Primatol.* 21:61–80.

———, and Vessey, S. H. 1973. Group changing in free-ranging male rhesus monkeys. *Primates* 14:359–68.

Duggleby, C. 1976. Blood group antigens and the population genetics of *Macaca mulatta* on Cayo Santiago. II. Effects of social group division. *Yearb. Phys. Anthropol.* 20:263–71.

Dunbar, R. I. M., and Dunbar, E. P. 1974. Ecology and population dynamics of *Colobus quereza* in Ethiopia. *Folia Primatol*. 21:188–208.

————, and Dunbar, E. P. 1976. Contrasts in social structure among black-and-white colobus monkey groups. *Anim. Behav*. 24:84–92.

————, and Dunbar, E. P. 1977. Dominance and reproductive success among female gelada baboons. *Nature*, 266:351–52.

Frisch, R. E. 1978. Population, food intake, and fertility. *Science*. 199:22–30.

Hall, K. R. L., and DeVore, I. 1965. Baboon social behavior. In *Primate behavior*, ed. I. DeVore. New York: Holt, Rinehart & Winston.

Hausfater, G. 1975. Dominance and reproduction in baboons (*Papio cynocephalus*): a quantitative analysis. *Contrib. Primatol*. 7.

Holst, D. v. 1972. Renal failure as the cause of death in *Iupaia belangeri* exposed to persistent social stress. *J. Comp. Physiol*. 78:236–73.

Kaplan, J. R. 1977. Patterns of fight interference in free-ranging rhesus monkeys. *Am. J. Phys. Anthropol*. 47:279–88.

Kaufman, J. H. 1965. A three-year study of mating behavior in a free-ranging band of rhesus monkeys. *Ecology* 46:500–12.

Kawai, M. 1958. On the system of social ranks in a natural troop of Japanese monkeys. I. Basic rank and dependent rank. *Primates* 1–2:111–30.

Kawamura, S. 1958. Matriarchal social ranks in the Minoo-B troop: a study of the rank system of Japanese monkeys. *Primates* 1–2:149–56.

Koford, C. B. 1963. Rank of mothers and sons in bands of rhesus monkeys. *Science* 141:356–57.

————. 1965. Population dynamics of rhesus monkeys on Cayo Santiago. In *Primate Behavior*, ed. I. DeVore. New York: Holt, Rinehart & Winston.

————. 1966. Population changes in rhesus monkeys: Cayo Santiago, 1960–1964. *Tulane Stud. Zool*. 13:1–7.

Kummer, H., and Kurt, F. 1963. Social units of a free-living population of hamadryas baboons. *Folia Primatol*. 1:4–19.

Lindburgh, D. G. 1969. Rhesus monkeys: mating season mobility of adult males. *Science* 166:1176–78.

————. 1971. The rhesus monkey in North India: an ecological and behavioral study. In *Primate behavior: developments in field and laboratory research*, vol. 2, ed. Leonard Rosenblum. New York: Academic Press.

Loy, J. 1970. Behavioral responses of free-ranging rhesus monkeys to food shortage. *Am. J. Phys. Anthropol*. 33:263–72.

Missakian, E. A. 1972. Genealogical and cross-genealogical dominance relations in a group of free-ranging rhesus monkeys (*Macaca mulatta*) on Cayo Santiago. *Primates* 13:169–80.

————. 1973. The timing of fission among free-ranging rhesus monkeys. *Am. J. Phys. Anthropol*. 38:621–24.

————. 1974. Mother-offspring grooming relations in rhesus monkeys. *Arch. Sex. Behav*. 3:135–41.

Neville, M. K. 1968. Ecology and activity of Himalayan foothill rhesus monkeys (*Macaca mulatta*). *Ecology* 49:110–23.

Norikoshi, K., and Koyama, N. 1974. Group shifting and social organization among Japanese monkeys. *Symp. 5th Int. Primat. Soc.*, pp. 43–61.

Ober, C. 1979. Demography and microevolution on Cayo Santiago. Unpublished doctoral dissertation, Northwestern Univ.

Pasley, J. N., and Christian, J. J. 1971. Effects of ACTH on voles (*Microtus pennsylvanicus*) related to reproductive function and renal disease (35558). *Proc. Soc. Exp. Biol. Med.* 137:268–72.

————, and Christian, J. J. 1972. The effect of ACTH, group caging, and adrenalectomy in *Peromyscus leucopus* with emphasis on suppression of reproductive function. *Proc. Soc. Exp. Biol. Med.* 139:921–25.

Perret, M. 1977. Influence du groupement social sur l'activation sexuelle saisonnière chez le male de *Microcebus murinus* (Miller 1977). *Z. Tierpsychol.* 43:159–79.

Sade, D. S. 1965. Some aspects of parent-offspring relations in a group of rhesus monkeys, with a discussion of grooming. *Am. J. Phys. Anthropol.* 23:1–17.

————. 1966. Ontogeny of social relations in a group of free-ranging rhesus monkeys (*Macaca mulatta* Zimmerman). Unpublished doctoral dissertation, Univ. of California, Berkeley.

————. 1967. Determinants of dominance in a group of free-ranging rhesus monkeys. In *Social interaction among primates*, ed. S. A. Altmann. Chicago: Univ. of Chicago Press.

————. 1968. Inhibition of son-mother mating among free-ranging rhesus monkeys. *Sci. Psychoanal.* 12:18–38.

————. 1972a. A longitudinal study of social behavior of rhesus monkeys. In *Functional and evolutionary biology of primates*, ed. R. Tuttle. Chicago: Aldine-Atherton.

————. 1972b. Sociometrics of *Macaca mulatta*. I. Linkages and cliques in grooming matrices. *Folia Primatol.* 18:196–223.

————; Cushing, K.; Cushing, P.; Dunaif, J.; Figueroa, A.; Kaplan, J. R.; Lauer, C.; Rhodes, D.; and Schneider, J. 1976. Population dynamics in relation to social structure on Cayo Santiago. *Yearb. Phys. Anthropol.* 20:253–62.

Sassenrath, E. N. 1969. Neuroendocrine adaptation to the stress of group caging in *M. Mulatta*. Abstr. Proc. Am. Physiol. Soc. Meet., Aug. 1969. *The Psychologist* 12:348.

————. 1970. Increased adrenal responsiveness related to social stress in rhesus monkeys. *Horm. Behav.* 1:283–98.

————; Rowell, T. E.; and Hendrickx, A. G. 1973. Perimenstrual aggression in groups of female rhesus monkeys. *J. Reprod. Fertil.* 34:509–11.

Scott, J. P. 1970. Biology and human aggression. *Am. J. Orthopsychiatr.* 40:568–76.

————, and Eleftheriou, B. E. 1968. The physiology of fighting and defeat. *Science* 162:935–36.

Senay, E. C. 1973. General systems theory and depression. *Separation and Depression*, pp. 237–45. Washington, D.C.: AAAS.

Southwick, C. H. 1960. A population survey of rhesus monkeys in northern India: 1, Abundance, habitat distribution, and group sizes. *Bull. Ecol. Soc. Am.* 41:119–20.

————. 1967. An experimental study of intragroup agonistic behavior in rhesus monkeys (*Macaca mulatta*). *Behaviour* 28:182–209.

————, and Beg, M. A. 1961. Social behavior of rhesus monkeys in a temple habitat in northern India. *Am. Zool.* 1:262.

————, and Cadigan, F. C., Jr. 1972. Population studies of Malaysian primates. *Primates* 13:1–18.

————, and Siddiqi, M. R. 1966. Population changes of rhesus monkeys (*Macaca mulatta*) in India, 1959 to 1965. *Primates* 7:303–14.

————, and Siddiqi, M. R. 1967. The role of social tradition in the maintenance of dominance in a wild rhesus group. *Primates* 8:341–53.

————, and Siddiqi, M. R. 1968. Population trends of rhesus monkeys in villages and towns of northern India, 1959–65. *J. Anim. Ecol.* 37:199–204.

————, and Siddiqi, M. R. 1976. Demographic characteristics of semi-protected rhesus groups in India. *Yearb. Phys. Anthropol.* 20:242–52.

————; Beg, M. A.; and Siddiqi, M. 1961a. A population survey of rhesus monkeys in villages, towns, and temples of northern India. *Ecology* 42:538–47.

————; Beg, M. A.; and Siddiqi, M. R. 1961b. A population survey of rhesus monkeys in northern India: II. Transportation routes and forest areas. *Ecology* 42:698–710.

————; Beg, M. A.; and Siddiqi, M. R. 1965. Rhesus monkeys in North India. In *Primate behavior*, ed. I. DeVore. Holt, Rinehart & Winston.

Sugiyama, Y. 1976. Life history of male Japanese monkeys. *Adv. Stud. Behav.* 7:255–84.

Teleki, G.; Hunt, E. E., Jr.; and Pfifferling, J. H. 1976. Demographic observations (1963–1973) on the chimpanzees of Gombe National Park, Tanzania. *J. Hum. Evol.* 5:559–98.

Vandenbergh, J. G. 1971. The influence of the social environment on sexual maturation in male mice. *J. Reprod. Fertil.* 24:383–90.

————, and Drickamer, L. C. 1974. Reproductive coordination among free-ranging rhesus monkeys. *Physiol. Behav.* 13:373–76.

————, and Post, W. 1976. Endocrine coordination in rhesus monkeys: female responses to the male. *Physiol. Behav.* 17:979–84.

————, and Vessey, S. 1966. Seasonal breeding in free-ranging rhesus monkeys and related ecological factors. *Am. Zool.* 6:207.

————, and Vessey, S. 1968. Seasonal breeding of free-ranging rhesus monkeys and related ecological factors. *J. Reprod. Fertil.* 15:71–79.

9

HUMAN REACTIONS TO POPULATION DENSITY

Jonathan L. Freedman

It is generally accepted that most animals regulate their population. By this we mean that when the number of animals gets high relative to the amount of space, food, or other resources available, some mechanism operates to reduce the population; and also, perhaps, when the number is low, some mechanism operates to increase population. Implicit in this statement is the belief that animals respond to the existing population density. This is a necessary condition for population regulation, because it is meaningless to talk of the size of a population without references to the amount of space. Unless one is concerned about extremes, the absolute number of animals is uninteresting. At the lower extreme, we do become concerned about how many of a particular species exist on earth or in a given region because of the possibility that the animal will become extinct. Knowing that there are only 17 or 31 whooping cranes is important regardless of the amount of space they occupy, but only because we are afraid that one day there will be no more whooping cranes anywhere. At the other extreme, we are concerned about absolute numbers when the existence of too many members of a particular species threatens the environment. Knowing that there are over 4 billion humans is important for this reason. However, under most circumstances, the size of a population and the regulation of that size must be discussed in terms of how much space they occupy. Saying, for example, that there are 400 field mice in a meadow tells us little about the colony unless we add that they occupy 2 acres or 20 acres. Thus, at some level, we must deal with population in terms of the number of animals in a given space, or as it is commonly called, population density.

Nevertheless, the most important finding of research on population regulation is that animals do not seem to respond directly to the amount of space available. As noted frequently in this volume and in published papers, no behavioral or physiological reaction is related closely to density per se. Increased density is sometimes associated with enlarged adrenal glands (Christian 1975; Christian et al. 1960; To and Tamarin 1977), a decrease in the size and activity of reproductive organs (Davis and Meyer 1973; Snyder 1968), and with increased aggressiveness (Christian 1975; Southwick 1967). However, these effects are far from consistent, occurring under some circumstances and not others (e.g., Terman 1973; Sung et al. 1977); for some species and not others, for one sex and not the other (e.g., Christian 1975; Terman 1969; To and Tamarin 1977), and for some individuals and not others (e.g., Southwick and Bland 1959). Moreover, as Christian (1955) demonstrated, the effects that do occur seem to depend mainly on the number of individuals present independent of the amount of space. Similarly, although enclosed colonies of animals do regulate their populations in dramatic ways, generally reaching asymptote well below the level that the cage could maintain, this too appears to be largely independent of the area provided (Lloyd 1978; Terman 1969, 1974). Thus, the one conclusion that seems to have been reached by all of the contributors to this volume is that population density, by which I mean the amount of space available per animal, while obviously an important variable that plays a critical role in population regulation and that is associated with many behavioral and physiological effects, has no simple, one-to-one relationship with any mechanism or response that has been measured. It does have effects, but they are exceedingly complex and variable, and are not yet understood. This conclusion was based mainly on work with nonhuman animals, primarily small mammals, but it holds equally well for humans.*

Perception of the Environment

First, it should be noted that there has been relatively little work on what aspects of the environment humans perceive that relates to their responses to density. Presumably, people are aware of the distance

Editors' Note: Contrast this approach with that of Baron, who argues that human populations show greater variability in their responses to density than do other organisms.

between them and the other people who are present, and this so-called "personal space" has been shown to affect behavior (Hall 1966; Sommer 1969). However, there is no reason to believe that this is the major mediator between density and behavior, since the effects of density are by no means identical to those of personal space. People also perceive limitations on their freedom of action and interference with their activities. When density is high enough to make a particular desired activity more difficult, people do respond negatively and, of course, perform the activity less well (Heller et al. 1977). But this is a relatively rare situation, and in any case, interference cannot account for many of the effects of density, especially those that are positive rather than negative. And so on. Various factors have been suggested and none has been found to explain much of the variance in responses to density. At the moment, we know little about what aspects of the environment play a role in human responses to density. It seems likely that people respond to a wide variety of environmental factors, and the particular combination present at any given time determines how people react to changes in density.

Even less is known about how humans process the particular stimuli related to density. There has been virtually no research on this complex issue. The only suggestion has been that the response to density is mediated by many processes that include their understanding of the situation, their feelings of control, and their attributions regarding the source of any arousal they may be experiencing (Langer and Saegert 1977; Worchel and Teddlie 1976). In other words, people do not respond in simple ways to variations in density. Rather, they interpret the situation and its consequences for them, and respond accordingly. However, it should be pointed out that little research has yet supported this highly cognitive view, and there is certainly other work that indicates relatively noncognitive mechanisms at work (e.g., Freedman 1975).

Is High Density Harmful? Survey Research

Most of the research on human responses to density has focused on how variations in the amount of space available per person affect people's health, behavior, and mood. Much of the work was designed to test the initial impression that high density was harmful to people, but later work investigated more complex reactions. The research has been done by psychologists, sociologists, and geographers.

Although the question of how density affects humans has been investigated in a variety of ways, the work that is most relevant has involved people who live or work under conditions of varying density. The basic procedure in this research is to obtain measures of density of various cities, parts of cities, or individual dwelling places and to correlate these measures with indices of juvenile delinquency, mental illness, nervousness, infant mortality, life expectancy, disease rates, and a variety of other social, mental, and physical pathologies. Some of the research has used grouped data such as the crime rate for a whole city, while other studies have dealt with individuals. In addition, density has been defined in terms of number of people living per acre, people per residential acre (ignoring parks, commercial space, etc.), buildings per acre, and the square footage available per person in a dwelling. Despite the wide range of techniques and measures, and the different locations that have been studied, the results are quite consistent. With a few exceptions, the studies have not found substantial relationsips between density and any pathology once a few basic, social factors are equated. Let me describe some of the work on this issue.

Density and Crime

Stanley Heshka, Alan Levy, and I (Freedman 1975) obtained measures of the population density of all of the metropolitan areas in the United States. There are 117 such areas, ranging in size from New York with over 7 million people to Charleston, West Virginia, with about 250,-000. The densities range from as low as 40 per square mile to over 13,000. The first step was to compute correlations between density and crime rate for these areas. Overall there was a small but significant correlation ($r = .30$) that explained about 9% of the variation in crime rate. This is not a strong effect, but one that would be of some importance if it could be attributed to density. However, the next and crucial step was to equate the areas in terms of other factors, such as income level, ethnicity, and educational level. It is well established that poorer people tend to live in areas of higher density, and also that poorer people tend to commit most of the crimes on which crime rate is based. Therefore, the critical question is what happens when these other factors are controlled. The answer is straightforward and unequivocal.

With income and other social factors equated, the relationship between density and crime rate disappears. Thus, unless we want to argue that high density makes people poor rather than that poor people tend to live under high density (and similarly for the other factors), we must conclude from this analysis that density is not associated with crime.

This conclusion is further strengthened by a more detailed analysis of types of crime. If high density leads to crime, the presumption has been that it does this by making people more aggressive. Accordingly, we would expect that the relationship between density and crime would be especially strong for those crimes that involve aggressive feelings rather than those crimes that are primarily economic in nature. In particular, density should be associated with rates of murder, rape, assault—crimes against people—rather than with robbery, car theft, burglary, and other crimes that are committed primarily for economic reasons. In contrast, if it is poverty that is producing crime and at the same time causing people to live under high density, the correlation with density should be especially high for economic crimes and not high for crimes against persons. The results support the second analysis. Correlations with density are high for robbery (.46) and car theft (.45) but are not appreciable for murder (.07), rape (.12), or assault (.06). These are simple correlations with nothing else controlled. Of course, they all disappear when income level is equated. Thus, both analyses suggest that density is not a causative factor in producing crime.*

Density and Pathology

Similar results have been reported by Pressman and Carol (1971) and by Galle et al. (1974), who analyzed cities rather than metropolitan areas. This latter study looked at both density per acre and density per room, and correlated it with several measures of pathology, including suicide, alcoholism, and homicide. Again, there were substantial first-order correlations between density and each measure of pathology, but when other social factors were equated, these correlations disappeared. The only remaining correlations of any size were between density per acre and suicide and homicide, both of which were negative—the higher the density, the lower the rates of suicide and homicide. I think

*Editors' Note: For further discussions of poverty as an alternative explanation for presumed density effects see Baron and Epstein.

it would probably be a mistake to take these rather small correlations seriously, but at least the effects are not in the opposite direction. Once again, density is not shown to have any relation to pathology.

Several other studies have dealt with specific cities, comparing high- and low-density areas of each in terms of the incidence of pathology found there. Winsborough (1965) looked at Chicago, Schmitt (1957) at Honolulu, Galle et al. (1972) also at Chicago, and Freedman et al. (1975) at New York. In all these studies the correlations between density, however defined, and any of the pathologies considered are small and positive. Those people who live under higher density tend to commit more crimes, have higher rates of mental illness, higher infant mortality, and so on. In one case, Honolulu, these correlations remain even after income and education are equated. Schmitt found that with these factors controlled statistically, higher density defined in terms of population per acre was still positively related to higher crime rates. No other correlations were significant, and people per room was not asssociated with crime rate. This is the one clear instance of a negative effect of density. The other studies all found that density was unrelated to pathology once income and other social factors were equated.

Difficulties with Survey Research
However, there is some difficulty in interpreting these findings, as is shown by the differing conclusions people have drawn from the same data. For example, in their original paper, Galle et al. found substantial correlations between density per acre and density per room and a variety of indicators of pathology. But when statistical controls were put on income, education, and ethnicity, these correlations disappeared. The authors next engaged in a series of multiple correlations between four measures of density and each pathology. This procedure is of doubtful legitimacy as they used it, and even so they found only one substantial correlation. Nevertheless, they concluded that density might play a role in pathology, perhaps as the mediator by which poverty operates; that is, poverty alone has bad effects, but also poor people tend to live in crowded conditions, and this makes the effects even worse.

This conclusion has aroused considerable controversy. Several papers criticizing the statistical procedures and the conclusion have been published. Moreover, one of the original authors (McPherson 1975) has done some reanalyses of the data and now believes that the original conclusion was unwarranted. I certainly agree: both the raw data and all the analyses point to the conclusion that density plays at most a negligible role in crime or any other pathology that was measured.

Nevertheless, I should note that in all these studies, as in any correlational study that involves the use of partial correlations or stepwise multiple regressions to control for any factors, it is difficult to determine the primary relationship. That is, if density is correlated with both income and crime, and income is correlated with crime, how can one decide whether the correlation between density and crime or between income and crime is the "real" one? One way we try to do this is to see what happens when you remove the effect of each factor. When income is removed, the remaining correlation between density and crime is negligible; when density is removed, the correlation between income and crime remains substantial. This means that income and crime have some relationship over and above that contributed by density, while that is not true for density and crime with income removed. This suggests that it is income and crime that have a true relationship, with the correlation between density and crime being an artifact of the relationship between density and income. Or, in simpler terms, it is poverty that causes people to live in high-density areas and to commit crimes; density does not cause either poverty or crime. However, this conclusion is always tentative. We cannot prove it definitively with these kinds of analyses; all we can do is try to build an argument and see what seems most plausible.

More Detailed Studies

Fortunately, we have some other sources of data and other analyses that strengthen our conclusions. First, there are a few ambitious studies that use individual rather than grouped data. Some investigators have not relied on census data to obtain measures of density, nor on FBI or other reports for measures of crime rates, nor on Public Health records for measures of mental and physical illness. Instead, these intrepid souls, with a great deal of time and energy, have contacted real people, living in real houses, and explored the relationship between density and pathology using individuals as their units. For example, Booth and his colleagues (Booth 1975) did this in and around Toronto, focusing primarily on physical illness; Mitchell (1971) did the same thing in Hong Kong, with major emphasis on mental illness and stress. Both studies concluded that there were no consistent relationships between density and pathology; the few relationships that were found were exceedingly small and did not always go in the same direction. The advantage of these studies, especially Mitchell's, is that they had enough individual cases that they did not need to do statistical controls on social factors. For example, Mitchell found that among just the poorest people in Hong Kong (and they are very poor), there was no relationship between household density (and some of them were extremely crowded) and any of his measures of nervousness or stress. In other words, among those people who are in the worst shape socially, who should show the effects of high density if anyone should, there were no noticeable harmful effects. Of course, this was also true of those who were better off financially.*

Perhaps one final study along these lines might be helpful. In the study of New York mentioned above (Freedman et al. 1975), there were enough separate areas of the city that they could be divided into income levels. This meant that statistical controls were unnecessary. Rather, it was possible to look at the relationship between density and pathology within any one income level. When this was done, the results were similar to those of Mitchell. In no case was there a substantial correlation between density and any pathology. Indeed, among the very poorest people, those living under high density actually tended to commit *fewer* crimes than those who had more space. But more important, overall, for all income levels, those who lived under high and low density did not differ appreciably with regard to any pathology— social, mental, or physical (including a wide variety of diseases, infant and adult mortality, etc.). I consider this convincing evidence that density is not a causative factor in any of the pathologies studied.

I realize that many readers will be skeptical of this conclusion. Before discussing some possible explanations, let me add one bit of data that might be more persuasive or at least make it seem more plausible. Over the past 25 years, the density level in U.S. cities has decreased markedly. This is true of both population per acre (because

Editors' Note: These studies are also discussed by Epstein and by Karlin. There are some important differences in emphasis and interpretation.

there are fewer people in the cities and because some cities have expanded in area) and amount of living space per person in their dwellings (because the building boom of the 1950s and 1960s produced a huge increase in the amount of floor space available for housing, especially low-income housing). Over the same period, as we all know, the crime rate has increased sharply. Thus, density has decreased while crime rate has increased. Although this does not prove that high density is unrelated to high crime, it certainly makes it likely. In any case, it does indicate that the increase in crime is not due to an increase in density.

Is High Density Harmful? Experimental Studies

Assuming for the moment that density is not associated with any of the pathologies we have investigated, how can we explain this? Surely living under conditions of high density is a different experience from living under low density. The two conditions clearly do affect our behavior in many ways. Life in a crowded, high-density city is dramatically different from life in a low-density city or in a rural area; sharing an apartment or house that provides, say, 40 square feet per person creates demands and restrictions that do not exist when the space per person is 200 square feet. High density makes privacy more difficult to attain, makes movement more difficult, requires more sharing of resources, etc. Also, the levels of stimulation and interaction are lower under low-density than under high-density conditions. So why are there no overall effects due to density?

We do not have a definitive answer to this question, but we do have some ideas, some of which are supported by or at least consistent with the data we have collected. Studies of relatively short term exposure to different levels of density have been conducted in the laboratory and some natural settings, such as schoolyards, classrooms, and so on. Although short-term crowding of this kind differs from long-term exposure to high density, the results may be used to get some ideas as to why and how density affects people.

The work has produced two major findings. First, as with long-term situations, high density has been shown to have no overall effects on people's behavior or mood or any other psychological reactions we have studied. In experiment after experiment, people act the same under high as under low density. For example, they perform a variety of tasks as well under high- as under low-density conditions (Freedman et al. 1971; Griffitt and Veitch 1971; Paulus et al. 1976). This work has generally involved tasks that can be done alone and for which the presence of others may be distracting or otherwise interfering, but would not directly prevent the task from being performed. When the task is such that other people get in the way, there is some effect (Heller et al. 1977), of course, but even then the effects are smaller than one might think. With this limiting case, the evidence is that purely psychological effects of high density do not affect our ability to perform either simple or complex tasks.

Similarly, density has little or no overall effect on social behaviors or on the interaction of individuals. It does not affect aggressiveness or cooperativeness (Freedman et al. 1972; Stokols et al. 1973; Ross et al. 1973; Marshall and Heslin 1975) nor does it make people like each other more or less. In this context it is worth noting that the amount of space available per person has no effect on aggressiveness among children, where it might be expected to have maximal impact (Loo 1972; Smith 1973). Indeed, many different situations, subject populations, and behaviors have been observed, and there is no evidence that density produces any overall harmful, disruptive, or for that matter helpful or facilitative effects.

Complex Effects of Density

However, and this is the other major finding, high density does have substantial effects on many of the behaviors and responses just mentioned, except that these effects are complex and depend on other factors in the situation. The typical finding is that for some people, under some circumstances, high density has harmful effects, while for other people, under other circumstances, it has helpful effects. That is, virtually all of our findings indicate an interaction between level of density and some other factor or factors in the situation.

For example, several studies have suggested that males and females may differ in their response to density. All-male groups have been found to become more aggressive, more competitive, and to like each other less under high- than under low-density conditions; whereas all-female groups responded in exactly the opposite way, having more positive responses with higher density (Freedman et al. 1972; Ross et al. 1973; Marshall and Heslin 1975). One study found males performing tasks less well under high-density conditions while females performed better (Paulus et al. 1976). Other research has suggested that people who feel they have control over a situation are unaffected by high density, whereas those who feel they lack control respond badly to high density (Sherrod 1974; Langer and Saegert 1977).*

Another possible effect of high density is that it has negative effects when it clearly interferes with desired activities or behavior. This is obvious but important to remember. When the high density actually makes a given behavior more difficult (e.g., performing a task that requires considerable movement), high density not only reduces performance on the tasks but also makes people respond with negative feelings. Although this seems so obvious as to be trivial, the interesting result is that the effect is much smaller than one would expect. That is, even when the task requires movement and high density interferes with that movement, people perform almost as well as under low-density conditions, and their emotional response to the situation is only marginally more negative. Moreover, if people are given the sense that they have some control over the situation—that they can leave it or arrange it so as to prevent interference or even simply understand what is happening—they no longer respond negatively (although, of course, the behavior may still be interfered with). This suggests that people accept some of the limitations imposed by very high density without ordinarily being upset by it.

These complex effects are offered only to give some idea of the complexity of the effects we have found. For the moment, the specific factors that seem to determine how people respond to high density are probably less important than the general idea that density alone does not have overall effects on people. For example, the sex differences cited above do not always appear, sometimes reverse, and seem to be due to characteristics of the specific situation. The point is that people either adapt well or are not bothered in the first place by high density. Only when density is combined with other factors does it have consistent effects. These other factors probably include the sex of the person, background, the task that is being performed, the goals of the people in the situation, and the total context.

*See Editor's Note on page 212.

Theories of Crowding

Given these somewhat bewildering findings, we have not yet been able to construct an explanation that accounts adequately for all of them. We do have some descriptions of mechanisms that, I think, explain many of the results and may also help us understand why denstiy appears to have so little effect in the real world.

Intensification Theory

The first idea is that density operates primarily by making the other people who are present more important stimuli in the situation. With low density, the other people are less likely to impinge on the individual than with high density. Although other humans who are present are almost always important elements in the situation, with low density there may be no interaction among them, no competition for resources, no necessity of dealing with them in any way. Twenty people lying on a vast beach can arrange themselves so that they need not even look at each other, much less interact. The same 20 people sharing a tiny beach are forced to consider each other in various ways. Similarly, in a community with very low density, the people on the streets can generally walk freely without encountering obstacles imposed by the presence of others; they may meet almost no one all day long; they do not have to get out of anyone's way or be afraid that someone will bump into them; and they do not need to share parking spaces or worry about the right of way when they are driving. Increase the density of the community and all this changes. People must be constantly aware of and consider what others are doing. Thus, the idea is that as density increases, people play a greater role in the actions and reactions of others and therefore their responses to other people will be stronger or more intense. Put another way, whatever the response to other people with low density, it will be stronger with high density.

This intensification notion as it is called (Freedman 1975) is analogous to the response to any stimulus as it increases in importance. Consider our response to background music. If the music is played quietly, we may like or dislike it, but it has little effect on us; as the volume is increased, our response intensifies—becomes more positive if we like the music, and more negative if we dislike it (as least up to some limiting point where the music is unpleasant for almost everyone because it is too loud). Perhaps a better example is our response to a painting hanging in a room. If it is a small painting, it produces little effect on our response to the room as a whole. If we like the painting, it will make us like the room a little bit more; if we dislike the painting, it will slightly decrease our liking for the room. Now imagine that the painting completely fills one vast wall in the room. The painting becomes a much more important object. Whether or not we like the painting will have a major impact on our liking for the room as a whole, merely because the painting is larger and therefore more important.

The intensification explanation of density is that as people are placed in higher and higher density situations, they become more important stimulus objects for the others who are present and, accordingly, the responses to them are intensified. This implies that high density can have either good or bad effects since any response is magnified. If our reactions with low density are generally positive—we like the others, feel cooperative, enjoy their company, and so on—they should become more positive with high density; whereas if they are negative with low density, they will become more negative with high density. In fact, there is research directly supporting this prediction. When a situation is deliberately made either pleasant or unpleasant and density is varied, we find that people in the pleasant situation become more favorable with high density, while people in the unpleasant situation become more unfavorable with high density. This holds for both males and females. The real-life example of this might be a party. It is a familiar observation that having too few people for the size of the room tends to produce a dull, lifeless party and that, indeed, everyone will crowd together in one corner to make the party better. High density makes the good feelings stronger, makes the pleasant interactions more pleasant. In contrast, a subway ride, which is generally a rather unpleasant situation at any level of density, is more unpleasant under high density. Whether this holds as well for living conditions, whether a family that gets along well will get along even better under high-density conditions is unknown for the moment, but there is certainly no evidence that a house or apartment with lots of room necessarily leads to good family relations.

It is easy to see how this mechanism would account for the lack of relationships we found between density and pathology. We would expect that high density would make bad social conditions worse but good conditions better, but note that we are referring only to interpersonal, social conditions, not life in general. Poverty is obviously unpleasant, but the relations among poor people or within a poor family are not necessarily worse than among people who are better off. If someone cannot get along with those around him or feels frustrated by them, he would be expected to have some aggressive or disruptive impulses that might lead to crime, mental breakdown, or even physical illness. Anyone who feels this way would presumably feel it even more under high density. However, people who have good relations and so on would feel more of this under high density. Taking the two together, high density might increase crime for the former but reduce it for the latter (assuming that there are many causes of crime). Overall we would find no relationship between level of density and crime rate—and similarly for any other pathology we might consider.

The implication of this intensification idea is that density will have harmful effects whenever the social situation is bad to begin with, but only then. That is, high density is not bad in general or in principle but only in interaction with conditions that are bad in themselves. Clearly, this implies no overall effect of high density. However, it does mean that if we can identify social situations that are unpleasant or unhealthy for humans under low density, they will be more so under high density. One might expect, for example, that interracial strife would be intensified by high density and that we would therefore find more racial incidents in high-density areas. I know of no evidence to support this, but certainly all our intuitions and anecdotal reports indicate that this is true. In contrast, when various racial and ethnic groups are cooperating or trying to get along, it is entirely possible that high density will intensify this positive relationship. Thus, it is not surprising that in cities (with high density) we find both more racial incidents and more acceptance of deviates of various kinds, more unpleasant interpersonal relations of some kinds and more pleasant ones of other kinds, all depending not on the absolute level of density but on the underlying basic relationships among the people.

In terms of reproductive behavior, this intensification explanation makes no clear predictions except that there is no reason to expect birth rate to be affected one way or the other by density level among humans (as indeed appears to be the case).* High density should intensify feel-

Editors' Note: The apparent neutrality of density phenomena for human reproduction (which Freedman reiterates at the end of this chapter) appears to contrast with the more generally negative impact of high density (in combination with other factors) on the reproduction of other

ings of sexual attraction and liking in general, but should also increase any negative feelings. I think you could argue that rate of sexual intercourse, if it varies at all, should be higher under high density; but obviously, birth rate among humans, at least in the industrialized countries, is virtually independent of rate of sexual contact, depending almost entirely on birth control techniques of one sort or another.

The fact that infant mortality is unaffected by density means that this major control variable in population growth is independent of population density, except in so far as high density actually leads to poverty, which might then produce an increase in mortality.

Levels of Stimulation

So much for the intensification notion. A second possible explanatory idea is that people differ greatly in the level of stimulation, and in particular social stimulation, that they like best. Certainly, population density is a major factor that affects the level of social stimulation, and stimulation in general. A city is noisier, has more to see and do, contains more people with whom to interact or avoid interacting, than does a lower-density community. The higher the density, the more the stimulation, whether it be a whole community or a classroom or a home. Although it has been suggested (Milgram 1970) that high density produces stimulus overload in general—that is, that people are exposed to too much stimulation because of high density and therefore react negatively—there is no evidence to support this suggestion. As I have said, all the research shows no overall effects of high density. However, it seems plausible that some people prefer low levels of stimulation while others prefer high. By "prefer" I mean that they feel more comfortable, are happier and more productive, are less tense, and so on, under a particular level of stimulation. Those who prefer low levels would presumably do better in rural areas, low-density communities, and low-density dwellings; whereas those who like high levels would do better in cities, high-density areas, and high-density dwellings; and still others, with intermediate preferences, would do best in areas of intermediate density. Once again, this would explain why there are no overall effects of density on humans—for any given level of density, some people are responding well (it is their preferred

species as discussed by various other contributors to this volume. This contrast may support Baron's contention that human beings show greater variability in their responses to density than do other organisms.

level) while others are responding poorly. This would explain why some people love cities and others hate them; why some thrive in the country and others are bored.

I might add that there is no reason to believe that these preferences for stimulation level are simple. It is entirely possible that each person has varying preferences depending on the situation—liking high levels of stimulation sometimes and low others, high while working and low while playing, and so on. It is also possible that most people have preferences that are related to particular situations so that some general statements can be made such as that most people like high levels of stimulation at parties and when doing certain kinds of work, but low levels when at home and when doing detailed, careful work. The point is mainly that we cannot at this time make any clear statements about what level of stimulation and what level of population density is ideal for people. Moreover, it is probable that this will never be possible because the ideal level varies for different people and for different situations.

The difference between this idea and intensification is that the latter suggests a universal mechanism—all people experience an intensification of their reactions under high density—while the former suggests that reactions to density depend on individual or situational differences and there is no general mechanism other than whether the level is what is optimum for the particular combination of person and task. Note that the two ideas are by no means contradictory. It is quite possible to have the general mechanisms of intensification and also have, superimposed on it, the fact that some people generally like one level rather than another. For example, someone who is in a pleasant situation and the level of density is high will respond more pleasantly than under low density but may also dislike the high level because he prefers low levels of stimulation. The sum of these two effects would cancel in this case, whereas if he also typically liked high levels of stimulation, the two effects would sum and he would respond even more positively. Moreover, intensification deals with not only positive and negative responses, but also specific responses such as being afraid, feeling sexually attracted, and so on, which would be expected to be intensified regardless of how the person felt about optimal level of stimulation.

The implication of this individual-difference idea for population regulation is that some people will tend to thrive under high density and others under low density. If people are free to move, presumably they will migrate to their desired density levels. This is similar to Tamarin's (1978) suggestion that migration is a major mechanism of population regulation, and that those animals who migrate under high density are, in fact, different from those who do not. However, humans are not always free to migrate (because of economic or political pressures). Despite this, one would expect that as population density increased, more and more people would find that it was exceeding their optimal level and they would move, perhaps reflected in the trend in the United States to the suburbs.* I am by no means suggesting that this is the only reason why people move from the city to the suburbs. Obviously, fear of crime, financial considerations, concern about schools, and so on are strong motivations for some. The only point is that reactions to density may also play a role.

Yet there is no evidence for the moment that living under less-than-optimal levels of density affects reproductive behavior, fertility, or mortality. This remains to be investigated and, of course, depends first on locating and identifying people with varying preferences. In the extreme, this analysis suggests that there is some limiting level of density that a large percentage of people would find too high and that once reached would lead to wide-scale migration or perbaps negative responses in terms of health and social organization. However, as far as we can tell, even the exceedingly high densities of our most crowded cities—New York, Tokyo, Hong Kong, and so on—are below this hypothetical level. Thus, psychological reactions to population density would not be expected to affect migration for the foreseeable future.

Conclusions

To sum up, it appears that human responses to density are remarkably similar to those of other animals. High density is not generally harmful to people; it sometimes has negative effects, sometimes positive effects, and sometimes no effect at all. There are few, if any simple, direct effects of density. Rather, people respond to density in complex

---

*Editors' Note: Whether there is anything more than a coincidental and trivial relationship between human families moving to the suburbs because of the belief that they are better places than cities to raise children and the fact that dispersing voles and mice are often pregnant females or subadult females which become reproductively competent upon dispersal (Lidicker 1975, cited by Tamarin) is a moot point. It is at least an interesting analogy.

ways that depend on other factors in the situation. At the moment, we know of no responses to density that involve the regulation of human populations. However, variations in density do have substantial effects on people's social behavior; and these effects may indirectly determine long-range population patterns.

References

Booth, A. 1975. *Final report: urban crowding project.* Ottawa: Ministry for Urban Affairs.

Christian, J. J. 1955. Effect of population size on the adrenal glands and reproductive organs of male white mice. *Am. J. Physiol.* 181:477–80.

———. 1975. Hormonal control of population growth. In *Hormonal Correlates of Behavior,* ed. B. E. Eleftheriou and R. L. Sprott. vol. 1, New York: Plenum Press.

———; Flyger, V.; and Davis, D. E. 1960. Factors in the mass mortality of a herd of Sike deer, *Cervus nippon. Chesapeake Sci.* 1:79–95.

Davis, G. J., and Meyer, R. K. 1973. FSH and LH in the snowshoe hare during the increasing phase of the 10-year cycle. *Gen. Comp. Endocrinol.* 20:53–60.

Freedman, J. L. 1975. *Crowding and behavior.* New York: Viking Press.

———; Klevansky, S.; and Ehrlich, P. 1971. The effect of crowding on human task performance. *J. Appl. Soc. Psychol.* 1:7–25.

———; Heshka, S.; and Levy, A. 1975. Population density and pathology: is there a relationship? *J. Exp. Soc. Psychol.* 11:539–52.

———; Levy, A. S.; Buchanan, R. W.; and Price, J. 1972. Crowding and human aggressiveness. *J. Appl. Soc. Psych.* 8:528–48.

Galle, O. R.; Gove, W. R.; and McPherson, J. M. 1972. Population density and pathology: what are the relations for man. *Science* 176:23–30.

———; McCarthy, J. D.; and Gove, W. 1974. Population density and pathology. Paper presented at the Annu. Meet. Popul. Assoc. Am.

Griffitt, N., and Veitch, R. 1971. Hot and crowded: influences of population density and temperature on interpersonal affective behavior. *J. Pers. Soc. Psychol.* 17:92–98.

Hall, E. T. 1966. *The hidden dimension.* New York: Doubleday.

Heller, J. F.; Groff, B. D.; and Solomon, S. H. 1977. Toward an understanding of crowding: the role of physical interaction. *J. Pers. Soc. Psychol.* 35:183–90.

Langer, E., and Saegert, S. 1977. Crowding and cognitive control. *J. Person. Soc. Psychol.* 35:175–82.

Lloyd, J. A. 1978. Interaction of social structure and reproduction in populations of mice. Paper presented at Hudson Symp. Biosoc. Mechanisms of Popul. Regulation, Plattsburgh, N.Y.

Loo, C. M. 1972. The effects of spatial density on the social behavior of children. *J. Appl. Soc. Psychol.* 2:372–81.

McPherson, J. M. 1975. Population density and social pathology: a re-examination. *Sociol. Symp.* 141:76–90.

Marshall, J. E., and Heslin, R. 1975. Boys and girls together: sexual composition and the effect of density and group size on cohesiveness. *J. Pers. Soc. Psychol.* 31:952–61.

Milgram, S. 1970. The experience of living in cities. *Science* 167:1461–68.

Mitchell, R. E. 1971. Some social implications of high density housing. *Am. Sociol. Rev.* 36:18–29.

Paulus, P. B.; Annis, A. B.; Seta, J. J.; Schkade, J. K.; and Matthews, R. W. 1976. Density does affect task performance. *J. Pers. Soc. Psychol.* 34:248–53.

Pressman, I., and Carol, A. 1971. Crime as a diseconomy of scale. *Rev. Soc. Econ.* 29:227–36.

Ross, M.; Layton, B.; Erickson, B.; and Schopler, J. 1973. Affect, facial regard, and reactions to crowding. *J. Pers. Soc. Psychol.* 28:69–76.

Schmitt, R. C. 1957. Density, delinquency, and crime in Honolulu. *Sociol. Soc. Res.* 41:274–76.

Sherrod, D. R. Crowding, perceived control, and behavioral aftereffects. 1974. *J. Appl. Soc. Psychol.* 4:171–86.

Smith, P., and Connolly, K. J. 1973. Toys, space, and children. *Bull. Bri. Psychol. Soc.* 26:167.

Snyder, R. L. 1968. Reproduction and population pressures. In *Progress in physiological psychology*, ed. E. Stellar and J. M. Sprague, pp. 119–60. New York: Academic Press.

Sommer, R. 1969. *Personal space.* Englewood Cliffs, N.J.: Prentice-Hall.

Southwick, C. H. 1967. An experimental study of intragroup agonistic behavior in rhesus monkeys (*Macaca mulata*). *Behavior* 28:182–209.

———, and Bland, V. P. 1959. Effect of population density on adrenal glands and reproductive organs of CFW mice. *Am. J. Physiol.* 197:111–14.

Stokols, D.; Rall, M.; Plinner, B.; and Schopler, J. 1973. Physical, social, and personal determinants of the perception of crowding. *Environ. Behav.* 5:87–115.

Sung, P. K.; Bradley, E. L.; and Terman, C. R. 1977. Serum corticosterone concentrations in reproductively mature and inhibited deermice (*Peromyscus maniculatus bairdii*). *J. Reprod. Fertil.* 49:201–06.

Tamarin, R. H. 1978. Dispersal and population regulation in rodents. Paper delivered at Hudson Symp., Plattsburgh, N.Y.

Terman, C. R. 1969. Pregnancy failure in female prairie deermice related to parity and social environment. *Anim. Behav.* 17:104–08.

———. 1973. Reproductive inhibition in asymptotic populations of prairie deermice. *J. Reprod. Fertil.* 19:457–63.

———. 1974. Behavioral factors associated with cessation of growth of laboratory populations of prairie deermice. *Res. Popul. Ecol.* 15:138–47.

To, L. P., and Tamarin, R. H. 1977. The relation of population density and adrenal gland weight in cycling and noncycling voles (*Microtus*). *Ecology* 58:928–34.

Winsborough, H. H. 1965. The social consequences of high population density. *Law Contemp. Prob.* 30:120–26.

Worchel, S., and Teddlie, C. 1976. The experience of crowding: a two-factor theory. *J. Pers. Soc. Psych.* 34:30–40.

10

PHYSIOLOGICAL EFFECTS OF CROWDING ON HUMANS

Yakov M. Epstein

The past several years have witnessed a growing interest in the effects of crowding in humans. Karlin et al. (1978a) have suggested that the effects of crowding are setting specific.* These authors have differentiated between residential, transportation, and classroom settings in which crowding may occur. While, at first glance, the literature on the physiological effects of crowding may appear to offer contradictory findings, the present review will reveal a considerable degree of consistency in findings on the effects of crowding as a function of settings. This chapter will review the literature on health and physiological arousal separately for residential, classroom, and transportation settings.† It will also compare these findings with the results of studies using nonhuman subjects.

Some of the studies to be cited have been conducted in the experimental laboratory while the majority have been conducted in field settings. In many of the laboratory studies as well as in virtually all of the field studies many factors act in combination to produce the effects of crowding. While high density is perhaps the most salient factor, it rarely operates in the absence of other factors. Jonathan Freedman (1975) has conducted an invaluable series of laboratory experiments to

---

*See Editors' Note on page 225.

†*Editors' Note:* Compare Epstein's discussion of health and physiological arousal in human beings with Christian's review of endocrine mediated responses to high density by other organisms. "Arousal" as used by Epstein appears similar to Christian's "psychogenic stress." The latter, associated with high density, low social rank, or social strife, results in hypertension, infertility, kidney effects, and increased incidence of both infectious and noninfectious diseases. One noticeable difference in the two discussions is that "arousal" as used by Epstein does not appear to have consistently negative effects on fertility (as Freedman explicitly notes).

highlight the effects of high density, which operates in the absence of other factors. Simply stated, his results reveal clearly that high density per se does not lead to negative effects. However, this review will focus on the effects of crowded environments in which high density combines with other important factors. It will attempt to elucidate the conditions under which such multidetermined crowding causes negative outcomes.

Crowding in Residential Settings

The health and physiological effects of residential crowding have been studied in three major settings: homes, prisons, and college dormitories. The effects have been assessed through archival studies using the technique of ecological correlation, through interview studies, and by means of field experiments.

Ecological Correlation

The earliest studies of residential crowding used archival records of aggregate data and analyzed them with the ecological correlational technique. Easily available public information on census tract density and dwelling unit density was correlated with other public data, such as infant mortality, hospital admissions, and psychiatric impairment. Attempts were made to control statistically the influence of a variety of demographic variables, such as income, education, and ethnicity. The results of these studies are inconsistent, sometimes showing that crowding has negative effects and at other times failing to show that it does. Numerous investigators have found a positive relation between density and health-related measures. Winsborough (1965) found a positive relation between density and infant deaths. Schmitt (1966) found positive relationships with death rate, mental illness, tuberculosis, and venereal disease. Galle et al. (1972) found positive associations with mortality and fertility.

Additionally, Factor and Waldron (1973), using data from Chicago, found a positive relation between density and mental hospital admissions; although at a more global level, using the overall density of countries matched for per capita GNP and health care facilities as the unit of analysis, these investigators found no realtion between crowding and mortality. In earlier epidemiological studies, Hollingshead and Redlich (1958) and Lantz (1953) found a positive correlation between population size of a town and the rate of mental illness. Levy and Herzog (1974), studying the population of The Netherlands, found some positive and some negative relationships between density and health-related measures. Using persons per room as a measure of density, they found positive correlations with mental hospital admissions, and with numbers of accidental deaths but negative correlations with nonaccidental deaths and general hospital admissions. When these investigators used numbers of persons per acre as their measure of density, correlations with nonaccidental deaths and with general hospital admissions were positive. In a more recent study (1978), these investigators found health deficits associated with crowding among residents of Chicago. Using numbers of persons per room as a measure of density, they found positive correlations with deaths associated with heart attacks, cancer, stroke, respiratory disease, homicide, and cirrhosis of the liver. Additionally, they found that high density was related to increased use of drugs, alcoholism, and higher rates of tuberculosis. Further, using number of people per acre as the measure of density, these researchers found positive correlations with death due to cancer, stroke, and heart disease, as well as positive correlations with hospital emergencies and child deaths. In a study of residents of Manila, Marsella et al. (1970) found a positive correlation between number of persons per household and anxiety and skin eruptions. Finally, Ward (1975) found a positive correlation between number of persons per room in Chicago census tract areas and number of mental hospital admissions.

There are a number of methodological problems with many of these studies which render their findings ambiguous. This can be illustrated by considering two studies mentioned above which produced opposite findings. Ward (1975) reanalyzed the Galle et al. (1972) data using a different criterion for defining poverty, which was subsequently used for purposes of statistical control. Galle et al. had considered people earning less than the median income within a neighborhood as impoverished and concluded that crowding rather than poverty accounted for the lowered level of fertility and higher mortality rate. However, when Ward defined poverty as income less than $3,000 per year, she found that the mortality and fertility effects were attributable to poverty rather than to density.*

A slightly different approach representing a different way to control

*See Editors' Note on page 193.

for some of the possible confounds in the usual correlational study of crowding can be found in a study conducted by Freedman et al. (1975). Rather than statistically partialing out the effects of income and ethnicity, they eliminated this possible confound by selecting a sample of neighborhoods that were uniform in income and ethnicity. On the other hand, they were able to classify different levels of density in these financially homogeneous neighborhoods. Using this approach, they found no relation between density and infant mortality or venereal disease.

To the extent that these correlational studies are reporting unconfounded data (and this is a somewhat questionable assumption), they indicate that crowding in homes and in a variety of countries seems to have negative effects on health-related measures. If this is so, what stimuli lead to these negative effects?

One possible answer is that individuals are attempting to cope with a lack of privacy and a scarcity of resources.* Their inability to attain privacy and the adequate use of resources is likely to have general as well as specific consequences. At a general level, the individual is likely to experience a lack of control over outcomes in his or her environment,† with consequent feelings of helplessness and depression (e.g., Seligman 1975). These may sometimes be manifested in psychosomatic symptoms of the sort reported in the literature. The depression may lead to the need for psychiatric services also frequently reported in the literature. It should be noted, however, that these effects are certainly not the inevitable consequences of overcrowding. We believe that one critical mediator of the results of high-density living involves the way in which the living group organizes itself to deal with

---

*See Editors' Note on page 227.

†*Editors' Note:* The concept of *control* figures in all of the papers by social psychologists in this volume. The reader should compare discussions by Baron, by Freedman, and by Karlin. Epstein's reference to the association between lack of *control* and *learned helplessness* (which can be demonstrated in laboratory animals) suggests that the *control* concept be extended to animal studies, perhaps as a means of explaining the role of social rank in mediating density-related effects. The differential impact of high density on low- and high-ranking members of animal populations is discussed in various chapters of this volume (see especially Christian, Sade, and Packard and Mech). Moreover, there is some evidence that control per se is appreciated by animals other than man and the primates. In studies of the white-footed mouse (*Peromyscus*) these animals modified the illumination levels of their enclosures and counteracted nonvolitional changes in their environments by learning to operate complex switching systems in order to exert control over the environment. (Cf. J. L. Kavanau, Behavior of captive white-footed mice, *Science* 155 (1967):1623–39.)

the problems of crowding.* Cooperative efforts on the part of residents, for example, can help reduce the severity of a lack of privacy by developing and adhering to norms and procedures that allow one person to engage in private activities while others vacate the premises or move out of earshot or eyesight. Unfortunately, however, individuals who are crowded are frequently poor, and the additional strains of poverty can often weaken the quality of interpersonal relationships in the family, increasing the likelihood of competitive and individualistic efforts to cope with the problems of overcrowding. Under these conditions, ill effects can be expected.

At a more specific level, responses to overcrowded living conditions may include efforts to escape from the home. Persons doing so are likely to spend more time on the streets and in other locations where the possibility for getting into trouble is increased.

Evans (1978) has reviewed studies of crowding with nonhuman populations. We will not review these studies here. Suffice it to say that Evans finds considerable evidence of health-related impairment as well as maternal deprivation and heightened aggression among animals living under conditions of high density. Although it must remain a matter of speculation, it is quite conceivable that the two problems we have noted for humans living in overcrowded residences—lack of privacy and resource scarcity—are also playing a key role in the effects observed among nonhuman populations. Resource scarcity leads to competition, which may itself lead to somatic symptoms. It may also require the abandonment of normal maternal caretaking activities so that offspring who are less well cared for are less likely to survive to maturity. Finally, the competition for scarce resources may lead to aggressive behavior resulting in injuries that increase the death rate. The second problem, lack of privacy, may also be operating in that organisms are unable to avoid unwanted interaction with others. This higher probability interaction, especially when organisms are experiencing other problems, may promote antisocial behavior leading to injuries and death.

*Editors' Note: The role of social structure as a mediator of density perception is discussed further by Baron, by Karlin, and by Freedman. The possible effects of the evolution of social structure on the growth rate of the human population are discussed by Cohen. Similar social structural effects on density perception are implied in the experiments of Lloyd and Terman on laboratory rodents as well as in some of the observations of Packard and Mech on wolf populations and of Sade on rhesus monkeys.

Interview Studies

Several studies have assessed health-related problems of high-density living by means of interviews. Findings from these studies contradict those obtained through the use of aggregate data.

Booth (1975) interviewed over 500 husbands and wives living in Toronto and obtained blood and urine samples as well as health clinic records about the families. By and large, this research team found little evidence of density-related deficits in health, psychiatric functioning, or reproduction. The exception was that women who perceived their homes as crowded had more uterine dysfunction than women who perceived their homes as less crowded. No relation between actual crowding and uterine dysfunction was found.*

Mitchell (1971) studied what might well be one of the most crowded housing facilities in the world—the high-rise housing in Hong Kong. So crowded were these facilities that, on the average, 10 or more persons lived in an apartment having only 400 ft^2 of space. Moreover, 39% of these families shared their apartment with another unrelated family and 28% of these people slept three or more to a bed. Even under these extreme conditions of overcrowding, Mitchell failed to find evidence of deficits in emotional health. However, he did find a relation between the floor level that people lived on and stress. The higher the floor, the greater the stress experienced. This supports our earlier contention that high density creates a need to escape outside the home. Presumably, the greater distance from ground level decreased the ability of residents on high-level floors to escape, leading to increased stress.†

Rohe (1978) studied the reactions of a stratified random sample of small-city dwellers. The sample was composed of equal numbers of single students, married students, working people, and elderly individuals. No relation between number of people per room and numbers of visits to doctors or an index of poor health was found.

Several other interview studies, however, found what might be

---

Editors' Note: Interview studies, which are, of course, peculiar to the literature on contemporary human beings, create a class of data hard to compare to that relating to other species. These data may produce misleading results to the extent that verbal self-report conflicts with other (behavioral) measures of density as in the present example. The data also point to the importance of subjective evaluation of circumstances as a mediator of density-dependent responses, a phenomenon which may be more important for animal studies than we now recognize.

†*Editors' Note:* The Mitchell study is also cited by Karlin and by Freedman as are others of Epstein's examples. There are some important differences in emphasis and interpretation.

construed as evidence for health-related impairment in crowded residences. Dean et al. 1975) studied 938 men on 13 different naval ships and found that there was a significant positive correlation (albeit a very low one) between crowding and illness and accident rates. In another study, Gruchow (1977) surveyed 283 females in the midwestern United States. He found that physiological effects depended on a complex relationship of background, present living conditions, and the perception of how crowded present living conditions are. Women who grew up in households of low density and who later lived under high-density conditions were found to have the highest levels of VMA in their urine. However, the strongest correlations between crowding and VMA levels were found with perceived crowding rather than actual density. Finally, in a small-scale interview study, Stokols and Ohlig (1974) interviewed 27 women living in dormitories and apartments at the University of California–Irvine. They found a positive correlation between crowding and the number of visits to the University Health Service during the year.

Field Experiments

Two studies conducted in prisons have compared the health of prisoners living one or two to a standard cell with those sharing a dormitory-style cell. McCain et al. (1976) found that dormitory inmates had higher illness complaint rates than those housed in single cells. D'Atri (1975) found physiological data that are consistent with and support the complaints of the prisoners in the McCain et al. study. He examined the systolic and diastolic blood pressure of inmates and found that it was higher when they shared a dormitory-type cell with several others. Finally, Cox et al. (1978) found a positive correlation between density and palmar sweat for prisoners in a Texas County jail.

While crowded prisons seem to produce physiological impairment, two studies conducted in college dormitories found little similar evidence. Both of these studies compared students living two to a room with students living as a threesome in rooms originally designed to accommodate only two persons. In the first of these studies, Baron et al. (1976) found no differences in the number of visits to the college health clinic of crowded and uncrowded students. In the second study, Karlin et al. (1978b) collected unbound cortisol samples from tripled and doubled students several times during the course of the semester and failed to find any difference in cortisol levels. They did find that women who are tripled reported more symptoms of physical ailments on the Cornell Medical Index than did doubled women. However, doubled and tripled males did not differ. Moreover, using the SCL-90, an instrument frequently employed in epidemiological studies of mental health, and administering this instrument monthly over the course of the fall semester, they failed to find any differences in psychiatric symptoms.

In sum, crowded prisons appear to have negative effects while crowded dormitories have few such effects on physical or mental health. Findings for crowded apartments, the most common overcrowded residential setting, vary, depending upon the method of investigation.

We next consider crowding in laboratory settings. Some of these studies seem relevant to the problems posed by crowded mass transit facilities. Others, while not clearly analogous to any particular real-world setting, seem most relevant to the problems of crowded classrooms. Subjects in these studies work on tasks either individually or in groups in much the same way that students in the classrooms work at tasks. They are seated close together just as students in crowded classrooms are seated. There are, of course, several ways in which the situation differs from a classroom setting (e.g., no teacher and no competition for his or her attention). Nevertheless, because of the similarities mentioned above, we have described these studies as studies of "classroom" settings.

Crowding in "Classroom" Settings

One hypothesis frequently tested in "classroom" settings is that crowding is physiologically arousing. The studies conducted to date have tested this hypothesis using nonverbal behavior, task performance, and such physiological measures as pulse rate, skin conductance, and palmar sweating.

Arousal Assessed by Task Performance

The concept of arousal refers to a state of activation. When an individual is stimulated he or she mobilizes a series of neurological and metabolic processes that prepare him or her to respond to the stimulus.

There is a fundamental law in psychology, called the Yerkes-Dodson Law (Kahneman 1973), which relates arousal and cognitive performance. It states that the quality of performance on a task is an inverted U shaped function of arousal. For moderate to moderately high arousal levels, performance on simple tasks improves while performance on complex tasks deteriorates. Thus crowded environments would be considered at least moderately arousing if we could find data showing improvement in simple cognitive task performance and impairment in complex task performance under conditions of crowding. The studies are about evenly divided between those finding support and those failing to find task performance data supporting the arousal hypothesis. Let us first mention those studies supporting the arousal hypothesis.

By and large, the complex task performance data support the arousal hypothesis. Most studies comparing performance on complex tasks in high-density environments with performance in low-density environments find that there are performance decrements (Heller et al. 1977; Evans 1975; Paulus et al. 1976; Joy and Lehmann 1976; Judge et al. 1977; Worchel and Teddlie 1976; Worchel and Yohai 1979). However, a number of other studies failed to find complex task decrements associated witb high-density environments (Poe and Schiffenbauer 1976; Bergman 1971; Saegert 1974; Stokols et al. 1973; Freedman et al. 1971).

Results of studies assessing simple task performance are not as clear cut. While two studies (Hillery and Fugita 1975; and Judge et al. 1977) found improvements in simple task performance, a series of studies by Freedman et al. (1971) failed to find this effect.

Arousal Assessed by Physiological Measures

Three studies have assessed arousal directly using physiological measures. Two of these used palmar sweat, a measure somewhat related to skin conductance, to assess arousal. In the first of these two studies, Saegert (1974) assessed the relative contribution of room size and group size on palmar sweat for males and females in same-sexed groups. She found that palmar sweat was higher for both males and females as group size increased or room size decreased, thus supporting an arousal hypothesis. Bergman (1971), using male students only, found higher palmar sweat when members of a group were seated closer together. Evans (1975) used two other physiological measures:

heart rate and blood presure. He used mixed-sex groups of 10 persons and found higher blood pressure and more rapid heart rate after the students left the small experimental room.

Arousal Assessed through Nonverbal Behavior

A number of studies have used nonverbal behavior as an indication of crowding-related arousal. Perhaps this assessment is less justified than the others just discussed since there are few data relating nonverbal behavior and arousal. However, intuitively, it may be argued that behaviors such as fidgeting, avoiding eye contact, physical distancing, and turning one's body away from others may reflect discomfort, perhaps resulting from high levels of arousal. Further, these sorts of nonverbal behaviors in conjunction with physiological evidence might strengthen the argument that crowding in classrooms is arousing.

These nonverbal measures provide limited support for the arousal hypothesis. The strongest findings were obtained by Sundstrom (1975), who reported that compared to persons seated in large rooms, subjects in small rooms showed less facial regard and more object manipulation. Other marginal support comes from a study by Ross et al. (1973), who found a trend for lower facial regard by males in a small room than for males in a large room. These investigators, however, found the opposite pattern for females.

Three other studies report on nonverbal behaviors of subjects who, although not actually crowded, anticipated that they would be crowded later in the experimental session. In one of these studies, Baum and Greenberg (1975) found that subjects anticipating higher spatial density sat farther away from a confederate. In a second study, Baum and Koman (1976) found that subjects anticipating higher density either because of increased group size or because of decreased room size exhibited less facial regard toward a confederate. Finally, Greenberg et al. (1975) found a tendency for subjects anticipating crowding to make more head movements away from confederates.*

Editors' Note: The importance of anticipation in understanding human responses to crowding (as well as the importance of perceived ability to escape from crowded situations discussed earlier) is suggestive of the kind of displacement between actual and perceived density that is described by Baron. It is instructive to ask whether on the one hand such displacement is a distinguishing feature of human responses or whether, on the other hand, similar effects should be explored in animal studies. The literature on learned helplessness in animals (cf. Seligman 1972, referenced in Epstein's bibliography) suggests that anticipation is an important part of animal as well as human perceptions.

In sum, based on task performance and on physiological and non-verbal assessments, it is not unreasonable to suggest that subjects in laboratory analogues of crowded classrooms are aroused. But the evidence is somewhat mixed and it should be noted that, for the most part, these studies have involved groups of strangers who have been exposed only briefly to one another. It is impossible to determine, on the basis of these studies, whether with the passage of time and in the presence of others with whom a person is acquainted, the individual would adapt. An expectation of adaptation would be consistent with the findings of studies on reactions to other stressful situations (see Glass and Singer 1972).

"Transportation" Crowding

A second set of laboratory studies seems most relevant to the problems of crowding found in mass transportation. Our criterion for categorizing a laboratory study of crowding as a mass transit analogue requires that the degree of spatial density be so high that bodily contact between group members is forced to occur. In most of the studies to be summarized, space available to each person was less than 3 ft^2. This is roughly equivalent to the extreme of 2 ft^2 per person available to commuters on a New York City rush hour subway (see Freedman 1975). Laboratory research using this high degree of density investigated whether it is arousing. Two types of data are indicative of stress-related arousal. One type, perhaps an indirect measure, is reflected in task performance. A more direct measure is seen in psychophysiological measures such as increased levels of skin conductance, more rapid pulse, and higher levels of blood pressure.

Theoretically, there is reason to believe that mass transit crowding should be arousing. Zajonc (1964) has marshaled considerable evidence indicating that the mere presence of others is arousing. McBride et al. 1965) have demonstrated that GSR increases as interacting individuals move closer to one another. A mass transit type of crowding involves both the presence of many others and extremely close interaction distance and should, therefore, be arousing. What humans are responding to here, in contrast to the other settings described, is overly close proximity to others.

Epstein and Karlin (1975) found improvement in simple task performance following crowding but failed to find decrements in complex task performance. On the other hand, Aiello et al. (1977) found that after being crowded subjects performed more poorly on a complex creativity task when compared with noncrowded controls. When arousal was measured more directly with the use of skin conductance, support for the arousal hypothesis was obtained. Aiello et al. (1975) found that compared to noncrowded controls, crowded subjects showed higher conductance levels and a failure to adapt over the course of the session. Aiello et al. (1977) also found higher and more rapidly increasing levels of skin conductance among crowded than among noncrowded subjects. Finally, Epstein et al. (1978) found that crowded subjects had higher systolic and diastolic blood pressure than did noncrowded subjects. They also found that over three repeated exposures to crowding at 1-week intervals, systolic blood pressure of crowded subjects increased while for noncrowded subjects it remained the same. These investigators also found that over 3 weeks' time, vasoconstriction increased for crowded subjects but not for noncrowded ones. In all, this study showed that although noncrowded subjects habituate physiologically, crowded subjects do not.

Several studies attempted to determine some of the factors that mediate arousal in this form of crowding. Nicosia et al. (1979) assessed the effects of bodily contact on arousal and found that by using barriers which prevented bodily contact, they could decrease the level of arousal normally associated with crowding. Epstein et al. (in press) investigated whether the opportunity to read a newspaper or talk to others would reduce the level of arousal for crowded subjects. They failed to find evidence that these distractors reduced arousal. Karlin et al. (in press) used a variety of clincial interventions to reduce arousal in crowding. They found that any of the clinical interventions they used led to smaller increases in pulse rate than when no interventions were used. Finally, Aiello et al. (1977) found that personal space preferences mediated arousal in crowding. Crowded subjects who preferred to interact at further distances from others had higher skin conductance levels than crowded subjects having close distance preferences.

One transportation situation, the automobile traffic jam, gives rise to congestion but has no component of close physical proximity. In a field study, Stokols et al. (in press) studied Types A and B coronary-prone persons who commuted for long, moderate, and short distances. They found that diastolic and systolic blood pressure of Type B persons was highest in the long-distance conditions. For Type A persons, highest systolic and diastolic blood pressure occurred in the moderate distance condition. Stokols et al. suggested that at far distance, Type A people abandoned attempts to exert control over the environment.

Summary and Conclusions

We have examined the effects of crowding in residential, classroom, and transportation settings. The literature indicates that crowding in residences sometimes has negative health-related effects and sometimes does not. In prisons or on the upper floors of Hong Kong tenements there is evidence for stressful effects. In both these cases, the critical issue may well involve the inability to escape from the crowded environment. In "classroom" settings, although the evidence is somewhat mixed, many studies suggest that close proximity to others is arousing. Mass transit settings, where close proximity leads to bodily contact, seem to always be arousing. It is conceivable that the arousal may be due, in a large measure, to the bodily contact, since when it is removed or when subjects are effectively distracted from noticing it, the level of arousal is reduced. The usual caveat about generalizing from these results to behavior in other cultures seems especially relevant in this case. Anglo-Saxon cultures are nontouching cultures (see Jourard 1966), and arousal may result from violations of the touch taboo. Finally, it should be noted that perceived control over the environment appears to reduce arousal.

In general, for each of these settings, we are suggesting that the perception of control is a factor which may mediate the occurrence of stress-related arousal. When people are involved in a situation that is aversive, cognitive coping mechanisms are typically of great importance. When people envision a future in which they are locked into an increasingly negative situation, they are likely to despair and suffer concomitant stress reactions. Recent research in behavioral medicine suggests that under such circumstances the rate of stress-related illness increases and, in general, health suffers. Some crowded environments create such a feeling of inescapability and are thus likely to lead to stress. Alternatively, when people feel able to control the environment and escape its aversive impact, they will not be stressed.

Acknowledgment

Preparation of this paper was supported by a grant from the Rutgers University Research Council.

References

Aiello, J.; Epstein, Y.; and Karlin, R. 1975. Effects of crowding on electrodemal activity. *Sociol. Symp.* 14:43–57.

———; DeRisi, D.; Epstein, Y.; and Karlin, R. 1977. Crowding and the role of interpersonal distance preferences. *Sociometry* 40;271–82.

Baron, R.; Mandel, D.; Adams, C.; and Griffen, L. 1976. Effects of social density in university residential environments. *J. Pers. Soc. Psychol.* 34:434–46.

Baum, A., and Greenberg, C. 1975. Waiting for a crowd: the behavioral and perceptual effects of anticipated crowding. *J. Pers. Soc. Psychol.* 32:671–79.

———, and Koman, S. 1976. Differential response to anticipated crowding: psychological effects of social and spatial desntiy. *J. Pers. Soc. Psychol.* 34:526–36.

Bergman, B. A. 1971. The effects of group size, personal space, and success-failure on physiological arousal, test performance, and questionnaire response. Unpublished doctoral dissertation, Temple Univ. (Abstract, *Diss. Abstr. Int.*, 1971, 2319–3420-A.)

Booth, A. 1975. Final report: urban crowding project. Unpublished manuscript, Ministry of State for Urban Affairs, Canada, Aug. 1975.

Cox, V.; Paulus, P.; McCain, G.; and Schkade, J. In press. Field research on the effects of crowding in prisons and off-shore drilling platforms. In *Residential crowding and design*, ed. J. R. Aiello and A. Baum. New York: Plenum.

D'Atri, D. A. 1975. Psychophysiological responses to crowding. *Environ. Behav.* 7:237–52.

Dean, L.; Pugh, W.; and Gunderson, E. 1975. Spatial and perceptual components of crowding: effects on health and satisfaction. *Environ. Behav.* 7:225–36.

Epstein, Y., and Karlin, R. 1975. Effects of acute experimental crowding. *J. Appl. Soc. Psychol.* 4:34–53.

———, Lehrer, P.; and Woolfolk, R. 1978. Physiological, cognitive, and behavioral effects of repeated exposure to crowding. Unpublished manuscript, Rutgers Univ.

———; Teitelbaum, R.; Karlin, R.; Katz, S.; and Aiello, J. In press. An assessment of two tactics to reduce crowding related arousal in mass transit settings. *J. Appl. Soc. Psych.*

Evans, G. 1975. Behavioral and physiological consequences of crowding in humans. Unpublished doctoral dissertation, Univ. of Massachusetts.

———. 1978. Crowding and the developmental process. In *Human response to crowding*, ed. A. Baum and Y. Epstein. Hillsdale, N.J.: Erlbaum Associates.

Factor, R., and Waldron, I. 1973. Contemporary population densities and human health. *Nature* 243:381–84).

Freedman, J. 1975. *Crowding and behavior*. San Francisco: Freeman.

————; Klevansky, S.; and Ehrlich, P. 1971. The effect of crowding on human task performance. *J. Appl. Soc. Psychol.* 1:7–25.

————; Heshka, S.; and Levy, A. 1975. Population desntiy and pathology: is there a relationship? *J. Exp. Soc. Psychol.* 11:539–52.

Galle, O.; Gove, W.; and McPherson, J. 1972. Population density and pathology: what are the relations for man? *Science* 176:23–30.

Glass, D., and Singer, J. 1972. *Urban stress.* New York: Academic Press.

Greenberg, C.; Lichtman, C.; and Firestone, I. 1975. Behavioral and affective responses to crowded waiting rooms. Unpublished manuscript, Wayne State Univ.

Gruchow, H. 1977. Socialization and the human physiologic response to crowding. *Am. J. Public Health* 67:455–59.

Heller, J.; Groff, B.; and Solomon, S. 1977. Toward an understanding of crowding: the role of physical interaction. *J. Pers. Soc. Psychol.* 35:183–90.

Hillery, J., and Fugita, S. 1975. Group size effects in employment testing. *Educ. Psychol. Meas.* 35:745–50.

Hollingshead, A., and Redlich, F. 1958. *Social class and mental illness.* New York: Wiley.

Jourard, S. 1966. An exploratory study of body-accessibility. *Br. J. Soc. Clin. Psychol.* 5:221–31.

Joy, V., and Lehmann, N. 1976. The cost of crowding: responses and adaptations (revised version). Unpublished manuscript, N.Y.S. Department of Mental Hygiene.

Judge, L.; Cohen, S.; and Sherrod, D. 1977. Crowding and perceived control. Paper presented at the Am. Psychol. Assoc., San Francisco, Aug. 1977.

Kahneman, D. 1973. *Attention and effort.* Englewood Cliffs, N.J.: Prentice-Hall.

Karlin, R.; Epstein, Y.; and Aiello, J. 1978a. A setting specific analysis of crowding. In *Human response to crowding,* eds. A. Baum and Y. Epstein, pp. 165–79. Hillsdale, N.J.: Erlbaum Associates.

————; Epstein, Y.; and Aiello, J. 1978b. Strategies for the investigation of crowding. In *Design for communality and privacy,* eds. A. Esser and B. Greenbie. New York: Plenum Press.

————; Katz, S.; Epstein, Y.; and Woolfolk, R. In press. The use of therapeutic interventions to reduce crowding related arousal: a preliminary investigation. *Environ. Psychol. Nonverbal Behav..*

Lantz, H. R. 1953. Population density and psychiatric diagnosis. *Sociology and Social Research* 37:322–26.

Levy, L., and Herzog, A. 1974. Effects of population density and crowding on health and social adaptation in The Netherlands. *J. Health Soc. Behav.* 15:228–40.

————, and Herzog, A. 1978. Effects of crowding on health and social adaptation in the city of Chicago. Unpublished draft, Univ. of Illinois, Chicago.

McBride, G.; King, M.; and James, J. 1965. Social proximity effects on galvanic skin responses in adult humans. *J. Psychol.* 61:153–57.

McCain, G.; Cox, V.; and Paulus, P. 1976. The relationship between illness complaints and degree of crowding in a prison environment. *Environ. Behav.* 8:283–90

Marsella, A.; Escudero, M.; and Gordon, P. 1970. The effects of dwelling density on mental disorders in Filipino men. *J. Health Soc. Behav.* 11:288–94.

Mitchell, R. 1971. Some social implications of high density housing. *Am. Sociol. Rev.* 26:18–29.

Nicosia, O.; Hyman, D.; Karlin, R.; Epstein, Y.; and Aiello, J. 1979. Effects of bodily contact on reactions to crowding. *J. Appl. Soc. Psychol.*

Paulus, P.; Annis, A.; Seta, J.; Schkade, J.; and Matthews, R. 1976. Density does affect task performance. *J. Pers. Soc. Psychol.* 34:248–53.

Poe, D., and Schiffenbauer, A. 1976. A personal space interpretation of some crowding effects. Unpublished manuscript, Virginia Polytechnic Institute.

Rohe, W. 1978. Effects of mediating variables on response to density in residential settings. Paper presented at the Annu. Conv. Am. Psychol. Assoc., Toronto.

Ross, M.; Layton, B.; Erickson, B.; and Schopler, J. 1973. Affect, eye contact, are reactions to crowding. *J. Pers. Soc. Psychol.* 28:69–76.

Saegert, S. 1974. Effects of spatial and social density on arousal, mood and social orientation. Unpublished doctoral dissertation, Univ. of Michigan.

Schmitt, R. 1966. Density, health and social disorganization. *Am. Inst. Planners J.* 32:38–40.

Seligman, M. 1975. *Helplessness: on depression, development and death.* San Francisco, Calif.: Freeman.

Stokols, D., and Ohlig, W. 1974. The experience of crowding under different social climates. Paper presented at the Annu. Conf. Midwest. Psychol. Assoc., Chicago, May 1974.

———; Rall, M.; Pinner, B.; and Schopler, J. 1973. Physical, social, and personal determinants of crowding. *Environ. Behav.* 5:87–115.

———; Novaco, R.; Stokols, J.; and Campbell, J. In press. Traffic congestion, Type A behavior and stress. *J. Appl. Psychol.*

Sundstrom, E. 1975. A study of crowding: effects of intrusion, goal blocking, and density on self-reported stress, self-disclosure, and nonverbal behavior. *J. Pers. Soc. Psychol.* 32:645–54(a).

Ward, S. 1975. Methodological consideration in the study of population density and social pathology. *Hum. Ecol.* 3:275:–86.

Winsborough, H. 1965. The social consequences of high population density. *Law Contemp. Prob.* 30:120–26.

Worchel, S., and Teddlie, C. 1976. The experience of crowding: a two factor theory. *J. Pers. Soc. Psychol.* 34:30–40.

———, and Yohai, S. 1978. The role of attribution in the experience of crowding. *J. Exp. Soc. Psychol.*

Zajonc, R. 1964. Social facilitation. *Science* 149:269–74.

11

SOCIAL EFFECTS OF CROWDING ON HUMANS

Robert A. Karlin

This volume focuses primarily on three questions: What stimuli are perceived by crowded organisms? How are these stimuli processed? What responses result? In the case of human crowding these questions lead to extremely complex answers. Humans encounter and occupy many different settings, and the conditions that would prompt labeling them "crowded" differ widely across these settings.*

For example, subway cars and residences may both be labeled "crowded." In subway cars people may be in such close physical proximity that they are forced to touch strangers. In residential settings, however, a level of density that would result in such forced physical contact is almost inconceivable. Yet both situations may be labeled "crowded."

The literature on the effects of crowding on humans seems laced with contradictory findings, largely as a result of differing operational definitions of this sort. This chapter is a review of the literature on the effects of crowding on social behavior and affect. First, a model is presented for the perception, processing, and effects of crowding. The model is brief and still in a preliminary stage. Nonetheless, it distinguishes between different types of settings and events that may lead to the perception of crowding within each situation. Therefore, it allows us to classify studies as relevant to one or another setting rather than

Editors' Note: The discussion of setting-specific measurements of density and of different attributes of *crowding* as perceived in those settings by human beings is also developed by Epstein and by Freedman. This differentiation of the concept of crowding suggests refinements both of experimental design for testing the responses of laboratory animals to crowding and of field observations of natural populations. Compare the more general meaning of references to density and crowding in the animal literature.

attempt to reconcile the seemingly contradictory findings of studies that actually address entirely different problems. Then, a brief review is presented of the literature relevant to different types of settings— residences, means of transportation, classrooms, shopping facilities, and workplaces.

Toward a Model of Human Crowding

In each setting that humans may occupy, different goals may be viewed as paramount. At home one may wish to relax. In a car or subway the primary consideration is usually getting to a specific destination quickly and comfortably. In a store the speed and ease with which one can find needed goods is of most concern. *Restricted space and/or a surplus of occupants may block goal attainment in each setting and lead to the perception of crowding.*

For example, most employed urban residents get up in the morning, travel on mass transit, walk or drive to work, remain at work all day (except for a lunch break), and then return home in the evening. During evenings and weekends, they shop and use recreational facilities such as parks, restaurants, and theaters. On occasion, they may participate in a demonstration or a large meeting, or otherwise be part of a large public gathering. Their children attend school and play in nearby parks and streets. It appears that the majority of situations that people label as crowded occur in one of these contexts.

If we delineate the conditions in each of these settings that prompt the label "crowded,"* we may better understand what humans perceive. It may also be possible to distinguish between those data that are relevant to crowding in a specific setting and those that are not.

It is possible to identify several conditions that block goal attainment in crowded settings and subsequently result in occupants labeling a situation as crowded. The most salient factors include congestion, resource scarcity, inability to control and limit interactions with others, and close physical proximity to others (Karlin et al. 1978a).

Lack of control† over interpersonal interaction has been discussed

Editors' Note: Labeling or *attribution* which refers to categorization and interpretation of social events is an important topic for social psychologists. Its importance in the population density area is touched upon also by Freedman and by Baron.

†See Editors' Note on page 212.

extensively in terms of privacy needs (Altman 1975) and excessively frequent and unwanted interaction (Baum and Valins 1973). This condition seems most relevant to crowding in work and residential settings. For instance, a husband and wife may wish to argue without the concurrent problem of dealing with their children. Inadequate space makes such interaction control impossible. In other settings, the lack of control over interpersonal interaction is less important. In a crowded restaurant, patrons are not primarily concerned about interruption by the other people waiting in line for a table. Rather, the major problem is that a number of people wish to use the same set of limited resources simultaneously; therefore, the patron must wait.

Resource scarcity* is one of the most important effects of population growth. Although resource scaracity is hardly a new condition for humans, present concern is probably centered upon the fact that it can occur despite, or indeed because of, our increasingly sophisticated technology. One set of problems related to resource scarcity involves congestion. When many people attempt to use a scarce resource at one time, congestion may occur. Congestion in the context of crowding occurs when the presence of others impedes one's expected temporal flow or ease of progress toward a goal. The analogy here is the proverbial "theater on fire." Even though the theater may be half empty, the need for rapid access to the doorway may produce a traffic jam.

Congestion has an obvious role in crowding in residences, work settings, shops, and recreational facilities. It may play some role in mass transit when inability to find a seat elicits reactions to crowded buses or subways.

It should be noted that resource scarcity and congestion may give rise to the label "crowded" without the situation having an inherent spatial component. One instance involving congestion occurs when there is a shortage of roles or activities compared with the number of persons who wish to participate. Wicker (1972) has referred to this as

*Editors' Note: Resource scarcity is an important concept throughout this volume, but it is conceptualized in different ways by investigators from different disciplines. Its place among the variables relating to density and population regulation does not appear to be agreed upon. However, note that in the studies in this book, resource scarcity has not usually been implicated in the direct regulation of population. It is usually claimed that the population regulates itself below the carrying capacity of the habitat, implying that biosocial mechanisms operate to limit population density before resources become depleted. For expressions of this viewpoint see Terman, Tamarin, Sade, Cohen, and Lee. However, see also Packard and Mech and Hassan, who suggest a more important role for resource scarcity as a regulator of population.

"overmanning." Overmanning may be illustrated by the comment that the field of teaching is too crowded.*

Resource scarcity alone may also evoke the label "crowded." Although physical proximity may play a role in resource scarcity, it is not an essential element. For instance, classes may be called overcrowded. The central element in this "overcrowding" is probably the teachers' scarce time, energy, and attention—not lack of space. The situation is labeled "overcrowded" because of immediate scarcity of resources. In the same way, we might say the planet is overcrowded with respect to available food or energy resources. There has been a general neglect of this issue in the human crowding literature. As a result, crowding in the sense of pure resource scarcity resulting from group size lies outside the scope of this paper. It should be noted that in the animal literature, resource scarcity is often seen as central.

Finally, when people are forced into extremely proximate interaction with others, the situation is frequently labeled as being "crowded." In the city, such situations are found most clearly in mass transportation. In a rush hour subway people are clearly exposed to this aspect of crowding. Although this is an important aspect of some forms of crowding, it is largely irrelevant in other crowded settings. As noted above, in crowded apartments people may never have to approach one another very closely. Here other conditions, such as lack of control over personal interaction and congestion, determine that the situation is crowded.

A number of factors mediate whether these conditions succeed in blocking goal attainment and cause the perception and effects of crowding. These factors include culturally defined coping mechanisms and the individual's learning history of coping with such problems. Group composition variables, including such factors as similarity, role complementarity, and degree of interdependence among actors in the setting, are also involved.

Editors' Note: The idea of "undermanning" and "overmanning" refers to a theoretical position taken by Roger Barker and developed by Alan Wicker (1979; see Editors' Note on page xvii). The idea includes the notion of responsible roles (vs. nonresponsible roles) in a behavioral setting, and the idea that both the structure of the setting and the maintenance of the setting are related to population density on the one hand and behavior on the other hand. For a fuller discussion, see Baron. The implications of the manning concept for social evolution and human population growth in prehistory are discussed by Cohen. Compare the observation offered by Terman that laboratory rodents reach asymptote at unpredictable levels. The latter may suggest that "social" crowding or *overmanning* not unlike that which Karlin describes may be a factor in the stabilization of rodent populations.

Successful goal attainment becomes more probable the greater the promotive interdependence among actors, the greater the similarity between them, the more they have a history of successfully coping with the conditions described above, and the more their culture provides them with effective coping mechanisms.

However, when the conditions mentioned above do succeed in blocking goals, actors experience negative emotions and seek to explain the cause of these emotions. They can attribute their negative emotions either to situational factors or to dispositional properties of the other persons in the setting. If they make dispositional attributions, they are likely to experience anger and behave aggressively or withdraw from interactions with others. If, however, they make situational attributions, they may label the environment as crowded. They will then explain their responses and the responses of others in the situation as caused by crowding. They may then attempt to exert control over the situation by trying to change it or escape from it. If this cannot be done, the individual experiences a lack of control and may feel helpless and depressed. Under these circumstances, goal attainment becomes even more difficult. Consequently, the negative effects of crowding are likely to emerge.

It should be noted that this formulation makes clear that high density alone may well have few, if any, effects. Freedman, in this volume and elsewhere (Freedman et al. 1975), has carefully reviewed the evidence on this point. He concludes that high density alone does not reliably produce negative effects on humans.

It is when relatively high density in a given setting leads to goal blocking, especially when perceived loss of control ensues, that crowding is likely to result in negative consequences that are attributed by occupants to their being crowded. Thus, the model suggests that in each setting, high density must interact with the other factors noted above before we should expect negative consequences.

Residential Crowding*

Having specified a model for the effects of crowding on humans, we may now examine research relevant to each of the specific settings in

*Editors' Note: "Residential crowding" among human beings is also discussed by Epstein, by Freedman, and by Baron as are several of the other specific settings and specific studies discussed by Karlin. The reader should note important differences in emphasis and interpretation in the discussion of several of these settings.

which the urban dweller may be crowded. However, it should first be emphasized that most of the studies reviewed here, other than those dealing with residential crowding, have not attempted to simulate crowding in a particular real-world setting. Rather, they studied the effects of crowding per se. Nevertheless, it seems helpful to order them in terms of the setting-specific taxonomy. With this proviso, let us turn first to an examination of the social effects of residential crowding.

Animal analogue research bears mainly on the question of residential crowding, and major effects of crowding on animal populations are the rule (cf. Calhoun 1962; Christian et al. 1961). It is outside the scope of this paper to review such effects, however. The interested reader should consult reviews by Davis (1971) and Evans (1978) and other chapters in this volume.

In terms of the analysis proposed above, crowding in residences usually involves an inability to control and limit interaction with others, congestion, and resource scracity. These events may cause severe problems in goal attainment for residential occupants when (1) the structure of the crowded group is not cooperatively oriented, (2) cultural norms and individual learning histories do not dispose occupants toward effective coping, and (3) it is difficult or impossible to escape from or change the environment.

Three types of residential environments—crowded homes, dormitories, and prisons—have been studied, using different methods. We will look at the findings of each research method, then summarize the findings for each type of residential setting.

Ecological Correlational Data
Studies of residential crowding have employed the techniques of ecological correlation, interviews, or field experiments. The earliest studies of residential crowding utilized archival records of aggregate data and analyzed them using the ecological correlational technique. Easily available public information on census tract density and dwelling unit density was correlated with other public data, such as infant mortality, hospital admissions, and psychiatric impairment. Attempts were made to control statistically for the influence of such demographic variables as income, education, and ethnicity. The results of these studies can be considered a mixed bag, most often showing that crowding has negative effects, reflected in such variables as juvenile delinquency and the receipt of welfare (e.g., Schmitt 1966; Galle et al. 1972), but

at other times failing to show negative effects (e.g., Ward 1975; Levy and Herzog 1974). Since adequate statistical control of socioeconomic status is difficult, these results should be treated with caution. Freedman and his colleagues (Freedman et al. 1975), however, were able to eliminate the confounding effects of SES by studying neighborhoods similar in income but different in density. They found no relationship between density and juvenile delinquency or number of out-of-wedlock births. A mild relationship between crowding and psychiatric illness was found.

Three sets of investigators, using similar methods, have studied prison inmates. Paulus et al. (1978) employed archival data to study the effects of crowding on prison inmates. Again, crowding was related to higher levels of psychiatric commitments. Parenthetically, it was also strongly related to higher death rates. Nacci et al. (1977) found that as crowding increased, inmates in federal prisons assaulted each other more frequently. The relationship was strongest for younger inmates. Finally, Megargee (1977) found that prison crowding led to increased disruptive behavior and aggression.

Interview Studies
Booth (1975) interviewed over 500 married men and women living in Toronto. He found that crowded families used more physical punishment to discipline their children and tended to have more arguments than did noncrowded families. Crowded and noncrowded families did not differ on other measures of family relations or aggression within the family. Additionally, they did not differ on measures of aggression outside the family or on social participation or political activity.

Mitchell (1971) studied the extraordinarily crowded residents of Hong Kong tenements. Family functioning suffered moderately only among those families who shared a small room with unrelated others and could not conveniently escape into the streets because they lived on upper floors of high-rise buildings. The children of these families spent more time out of the house and parents were concerned that they had lost the ability to suprvise the activities of their children. Additionally, fewer persons visited these families.

Gruchow (1977) surveyed residents of a midwestern city in the United States. Those of higher socioeconomic status perceived their environments as more crowded than did those of lower socioeconomic status.

Rohe (1978) studied the reactions of a stratified random sample of residents of a small American city. He found that competitive group structure mediated feelings of interpersonal press in crowded households. In competitively structured households, feelings of interpersonal press strongly increased as number of persons per room increased. This effect was significantly weaker in cooperatively structured households. In addition, members of cooperatively oriented households were more likely to stay away from their homes, thus alleviating the density problem.

Stokols and Resnick (1975) studied college students. Those who lived in more crowded housing were more sensitive to crowding in classrooms and rated other people in general more negatively.

Finally, Zuckerman et al. (1977) compared residents of two college dormitories. Residents of the more crowded dorms were less involved with their roommate and exhibited poorer mood.

Field Experiments
The final approach to the study of residential crowding involves field experiments. This approach has been used to study the effects of crowding in homes, naval ships, and college dormitories.

Three studies assessed the effects of crowded family life on children. Rodin (1976) compared the behavior of black children who lived in crowded and noncrowded apartments on tasks performed in a psychology laboratory. Crowded children showed evidence of learned helplessness on these tasks.

McConahay and Rodin (1976) studied the social behavior of lower-class junior high school students who played a game in which they could either cooperate or compete. Students from crowded homes engaged in more competitive responses than did students from noncrowded homes. This was the case even when competitive behavior minimized their own rewards as well as the rewards of their partners. Shapiro (1975) studied the effects of crowding and socioeconomic status on Israeli children. Low socioeconomic status combined with crowding predicted poor task performance for boys but not for girls.

A number of studies have assessed the effects of crowding on the social behavior of college students in dormitory settings. Baum and Valins (1973, 1974) and Valins and Baum (1973) compared the social behavior of students who lived in traditional two-person rooms in corridor-style dormitories with the behavior of students housed in groups of six in suites. Students in the corridor dormitories were considered crowded because they were continually exposed to higher levels of unwanted interaction with others than were students in the suites. Suite residents tended to form cooperative, cohesive groups, while corridor residents tended to remain alone or to compete with each other. These effects appeared on measures of social and nonverbal behavior and in residents' reports about their perceptions of other occupants.

Baum and Valins (1977) investigated the effects of a slightly different architectural pattern: long versus short corridors. The architecture of the dormitories with long corridors was identical to that of the corridor-style dormitories in the series previously discussed. Short-corridor residents lived two to a room in units that housed between 6 and 20 students per floor. Baum and Valins (1977) considered the long-corridor residents crowded because the greater number of residents increased unwanted interaction with others. In this study, crowded subjects felt stressed and helpless and perceived a loss of control over their environment. Crowded subjects also avoided interaction and felt more uncomfortable in a waiting room than did noncrowded students. Bickman et al. (1974) used the lost-letter technique and questionnaires to assess the effects of high- and low-density dormitories on social behavior. Students in the high-density dormitory were less helpful and reported lower levels of trust, cooperativeness, and responsibility in their dormitory.

Baron et al. (1976) compared the reactions of students who lived two or three to a room originally designed to accommodate two in a traditional corridor dormitory. They found that students in triples, especially upperclassmen, felt less satisfied with their living conditions and said they experienced less control over them. They also formed coalitions that frequently excluded one of the roommates. Grades of tripled students tended to be poorer than those of students living two to a room, although high variability prevented this difference from reaching significance (Baron, personal communication). In addition, Baron et al. (1976) found that previous exposure to crowded living conditions aggravated the effects of dormitory crowding. The more crowded a student's home had been, the more cramped he considered his dormitory room.

Karlin et al. (1978b) also compared the responses of students living three to a room with those of students living two to a room in rooms designed to accommodate two persons. Tripled women spent more time in their rooms and seemed to suffer the most. They were most disappointed in their room and least satisfied with college life. In addition, tripled women disclosed less intimate information to their roommates than did women living two to a room.

Karlin, Rosen, and Epstein (in press) studied these same students 2 years later. The students had lived in uncrowded dormitories or apartments during their sophomore and junior years. It was found that crowded students remembered being more disappointed and more emotionally negative during their first year than did noncrowded students. These effects were less strong for students who had grown up in more crowded homes, a finding opposite to that of Baron et al. (1976). Further, while all students attained higher grades as sophomores and juniors than they has as freshmen, freshman grades were significantly more depressed for the tripled students. The latter effect was not ameliorated by a previous history of crowding.

Eoyang (1974) studied the effects of crowding on college students housed in trailer apartments. Each apartment housed between two and five students; all apartments were the same size. Satisfaction with housing decreased as density increased. As in the study by Karlin, Rosen, and Epstein, this effect was less pronounced for students who had grown up in high-density households.

MacDonald and Oden (1973) studied reactions to dormitory life of Peace Corps volunteer couples who lived in a 30 by 30 ft room with no partitions and one toilet. Controls lived in accommodations similar to motel rooms. Crowded subjects treated the experience as a challenge, evidenced highly cooperative behavior, and seemed to benefit from the experience.

Two investigations examined the effects of crowding in naval settings. Dean et al. (1975) found that as density increased, naval personnel considered their ship less habitable. However, according to the authors, the largest proportion of the variance having to do with complaints about ship habitability was attributable to general dissatisfaction with the Navy rather than to population density. As part of a larger program of naval research, a second investigation was conducted by Smith and Haythorne (1972; see also Haythorne and Smith 1972) in a simulated sea laboratory. Two- or three-man compatible or incompatible groups, led by high- or low-status officers, lived in either crowded or uncrowded conditions for 21 consecutive days. There were few main effects for crowding. Crowding in combination with some of these other factors, however, had important effects. For example, crowding has opposite effects on compatible and incompatible groups. When the crowded groups were incompatible, men spent time doing nothing; in crowded compatible groups, men spent time in recreation together.

In sum, crowding in family residences does not seem to cause major social pathology. Juvenile delinquency, adult crime, out-of-wedlock births, or noninvolvement in political activities do not result from residential crowding. But in some instances competitive orientations may result from competition for scarce resources in crowded homes. In addition, competitive orientations seem to aggravate the effects of crowded environments. Children who cannot easily control their environments may learn to be helpless or overly competitive in these circumstances. The finding that few people like crowded living conditions is scarcely a revelation.

At the onset, norms in dormitories are probably more individualistic. Architecture and the particular nature of the group (e.g., college students vs. Peace Corps volunteers) play an important role in determining whether competitive or cooperative norms will eventually evolve. In most studies, groups that endure higher levels of interpersonal interaction become competitive. Further, the grades of crowded students may be adversely affected.

Finally, in prison, norms are competitive and the situation cannot be escaped. Here the effects of high levels of interpersonal interaction may be severe, involving higher levels of psychiatric commitments and increased aggression and death rates.

Crowded Transportation Settings

The first set of studies to be reviewed assessed the effect of crowding in situations similar to those found on crowded subways. In these studies, density was high enough to cause touching, although it never reached the extremes of 2 ft² per person found on rush hour subways in New York City.

Thus, in these studies the environment impinges on the occupant largely through conditions of extremely close physical proximity. In reviewing the literature on the physiological effects of transportation crowding, Epstein (this volume) has pointed out that in all studies relevant to crowded mass transit settings, the results have consistently shown the situation to be stressful. It is useful to keep this in mind in considering the social effects of transportation crowding.

There are several common social effects found in studies of mass transit-type crowding. Unsurprisingly, compared to their noncrowded counterparts, subjects feel more uncomfortable, more confined, more in competition for space, and more generally negative about the environment (Epstein and Karlin 1975; Aiello et al. 1977; Nicosia et al. in press; Sherrod 1974). Further, Epstein et al. (1978) and Griffit and Veitch (1971) found that crowding resulted in more negative mood as measured by the Nowlis Mood Adjective Check List. Additionally, in the Epstein et al. study (1978), which is the only study to measure subjects during repeated exposure to transportation crowding, this more negative mood persisted over a 3 week period.

Several studies have also found that males and females react differently to others with whom they are crowded. Compared to their noncrowded counterparts, women feel more positive toward and become cohesive and cooperative with members of their group. The reverse is true for males (Epstein and Karlin 1975; Aiello et al. 1977). In the Epstein and Karlin (1975) study, there were several levels of crowding. The respective sex-specific positive and negative social behaviors were most pronounced for the most crowded subjects.

Additionally, Teitelbaum (1976) found that crowded men who could neither read nor talk with one another expressed a strong desire for social interaction with strangers after they left the crowded room. Karlin et al. (1976) found that these sex-specific reactions to crowding were, to some degree, attributable to the level of interaction in the group. Under conditions of decreased interaction, women liked each other less and found the environment more unpleasant. In a study of mixed sex groups, Griffit and Veitch (1971) found no effects for crowding on attraction to others with whom subjects were confined.

Several studies assessed the success of interventions to reduce the negative effects of crowding. One measure of the success of the interventions was the ability of subjects to tolerate frustrations. Sherrod (1974) gave subjects a button that, if pressed, summoned the experimenter who would take them out of the room. Although subjects never used the button, its availability increased tolerance for frustration. Nicosia et al. (in press) used Plexiglas barriers to prevent bodily contact and found that it increased tolerance for frustration. However, Karlin, Katz, Epstein, and Woolfolk (in press) found that clinical interventions did not increase tolerance for frustration. Similarly, Teitelbaum (1976) found that the opportunity to talk or read while crowded did not increase tolerance for frustration.

The effects of these interventions on subjects' moods was also assessed. Teitelbaum (1976) found that the ability to talk or read made subjects feel more in control and tended to make them feel more pleasant. Karlin et al. (in press) found that a cognitive manipulation modeled on procedures used in Rational Emotive Therapy (Ellis 1962) produced the most pleasant mood and enabled subjects to feel most in control. However, these results may have been mediated by demand characteristics. Nicosia et al. (in press) found that barriers preventing bodily contact improved mood among male subjects but worsened it for females.

In sum, mass transit crowding has been studied in settings in which crowding is operationalized as close physical proximity at a level that creates physical contact with strangers. These experimental studies support the popular belief that crowded mass transit facilities are disliked and worsen people's mood. In this setting, when individuals decrease interaction with one another, they develop a competitive orientation. It should be noted that low levels of interaction are characteristic of real-world mass transit crowding. Finally, interventions have been only moderately successful in reducing the negative social effects of mass transit crowding.

Finally, two studies have gone beyond the laboratory to examine transportation crowding in real-world settings. Singer et al. (in press) found that congestion and loss of perceived control were central to decreased rider comfort as a commuter train became crowded. Stokols et al. (in press) found that drivers' tolerance for frustration after exposure to crowded highways was jointly dependent on personality type and length of the drive.

Classroom Crowding

The largest number of experimental studies of crowding, although not intended as analogues of crowding in any specific crowded setting, are most relevant to crowding in classrooms. These studies have the following characteristics. Individuals are placed in a small room for a brief, usually one-shot, exposure. Although close together, they are not so close that they physically touch one another. They are usually seated at desks or in chairs with facilities for writing. They are asked to work on tasks, sometimes alone and sometimes as a group, and are not interrupted by others. The groups sometimes contain both males and females, but most typically are composed of members of the same sex. Some of these studies also assess the aftereffects of the time spent in this crowded room on subsequent task performance in an uncrowded room. In none of these studies do crowded persons have less than 5 ft^2 of space each. Only representative studies in this area will be reviewed.

As Epstein (this volume) has reported, students sitting fairly close to each other are probably aroused. This should be kept in mind when considering the social effects of classroom crowding. Most of these studies found that subjects are to some degree bothered by the crowded environment (cf. Evans in press; Ross et al 1973; Schopler and Walton 1974; Sommer and Becker 1971) or anticipate that they would be bothered (cf. Baum and Greenberg 1975).

Many classroom studies have found sex differences in social behavior. Most typically it has been noted that, compared to their non-crowded counterparts, crowded females like each other better, whereas crowded males like each other less (Stokols et al. 1973; Worchel and Teddlie, 1976; Freedman et al. 1972). Additionally, Freedman et al. (1972) found that crowded males were more aggressive than un-crowded males. Crowded females, however, were less aggressive. Worchel and Teddlie (1976) found males to be more punitive at close interaction distances than at far interaction distances, although the size of the room had no effect on the punitiveness of females. It is noteworthy that a study by Marshall and Heslin (1975) found reverse effects. Women liked each other less and men liked each other more when crowded than when not crowded.

The studies mentioned above used same-sex groups. In mixed-sex groups, Freedman et al. (1972) found essentially no social effects for increased density. Marshall and Heslin (1975) found that subjects liked each other better in crowded rooms. Evans (in press) found the reverse. In his study, crowded subjects showed hostility toward each other and lowered frustration tolerance when compared to their non-crowded counterparts. According to Freedman (1975), these exaggerated reactions, both positive and negative, were the result of the intensifying effects of high-density environments. High density intensifies social interaction, according to this view.

Freedman and his colleagues (Freedman 1975) tested this "density-intensity" hypothesis in a series of three studies. In the first of these, they asked subjects to read a short speech to others in a large or a small room. High school students were given either pleasant or critical feedback about their speech. Subjects in the small room who had been given pleasant feedback were more positive about the experience than were their counterparts in the large room, whereas the reverse was true for subjects given negative feedback. In a second experiment, Freedman and his colleagues created a situation in which male high school students succeeded or failed. Crowding intensified the positive reactions to success and the negative reactions to failure. Finally, a third study was conducted, in which a mixed-sex group of college students was used to assess whether the effects of success and failure would be intensified when feedback came from external observers. Results indicated that the intensification effect of high density is limited to feedback from those present in the room.

All the studies reviewed above involve basic research relevant to the classroom setting. To shift perspective, a study by Weldon et al. (1977) has examined the effects of crowded classrooms on achievement. Interestingly, using archival data, these researchers found that when standard-size classrooms contained greater numbers of students, SAT performance improved. However, Summers and Wolfe (1975) found that while children with average ability could tolerate large class size, children of below-average ability could not.

Finally, two studies involving young children (Hutt and Vaizey 1966; Shapiro 1975) have found some increases in aggression and disruptive behavior under more crowded conditions.

It may be observed that schools are used for recreation as well as for instruction. Several studies have investigated the effects of densely populated play areas on childrens' behavior. These studies have shown that high density, in and of itself, has mild effects on the play of normal young children. For example, P. McGrew (1970), W. McGrew (1972), Loo (1972), Price (1971), and Preiser (1972) have all reported lower levels of interaction and higher levels of solitary activity as amount of space per child decreased. Other mild alterations in the style of childrens' play, such as postural changes (Preiser 1972) and decreases in gross motor movement (McGrew 1972), have also been reported. However, no major maladaptive changes in the play behavior of normal children have been observed.

Overcrowded classrooms may also be short of available physical resources, such as play equipment. Under such circumstances, congestion may occur. When high density is accompanied by a scarcity of play equipment, increases in childrens' aggressive play were observed (Rohe and Patterson 1974). This is consistent with Freedman's (1975) suggestion that high density intensifies prevailing social behavior.* On the other hand, the role of density in these findings must be viewed with caution. Smith and Connelly (1972) found that even in the absence of high density, lack of sufficient play equipment increases aggressive play behavior.

Most of the studies on classroom crowding are consistent with a combination of the arousal hypothesis and Freedman's (1975) density-intensity hypothesis. As Epstein (this volume) has reported, students who sit closer to each other are probably somewhat more aroused. It is also likely that others become more important under these conditions and that prevailing group process is intensified. When the class is used for recreation or a relaxed convivial discussion, increased density may have desirable effects. However, when angry or disruptive students are placed in a densely populated classroom, they may behave more negatively than they would have had they been placed in a less densely populated room. Similarly, resource scarcity may prevent children from obtaining desired goals and thus make them unhappy. High density is likely to intensify this negative affect. However, the physical density of classroom settings may be only secondary to the major problem of classroom crowding: The limited ability of one adult to attend to, control, and structure the behavior of a large number of children. Large class size may necessitate new and sometimes cumbersome approaches to teaching. Yet studies of the effects of increasing class size have failed to find consistent evidence of deficits in learning. A more complete treatment of the effects of large class size is outside the scope of this chapter. However, it is clear that previous level of student achievement, student motivation, and pedagogical style all control more of the variance than does class size.

Let us turn now to a consideration of crowded stores, restaurants, and work settings.

Editors' Note: Freedman presents his intensification hypothesis more fully in his chapter in this volume.

Crowded Shopping Facilities

Three studies have investigated the effects of crowding on shoppers. In each of these studies, subjects experienced congestion. The investigators studied how such congestion affected subjects' mood and their ability to process information. One study was conducted in a simulated grocery store in the laboratory (Dooley 1974). The other two studies were conducted in real stores (Saegert et al. 1975; Langer and Saegert 1977). Both males and females disliked the congestion. The congestion interfered with females' ability to process information (Saegert et al. 1975; Langer and Saegert 1977) and the ability to shop efficiently (Langer and Saegert 1977). Congestion, however, did not affect males' ability to shop efficiently in a simulated store (Dooley 1974). Increasing perceived control over the environment by providing information seems to ameliorate the negative effects on women, however (Langer and Saegert 1977).

One additional problem confronted by shoppers in the necessity of waiting in lines. Stokols et al. 1975) examined the effect of placing wooden partitions between lines of people waiting to transact business in the Department of Motor Vehicles. The use of these partitions seems to have increased the anxiety of persons waiting in lines.

Crowded Working Conditions

Only one study has examined the effects of lack of privacy and congestion among workers. Sundstrom and Kamp (1977) examined the job satisfaction and work performance of secretaries in a large office. Higher levels of privacy afforded by greater distance between desks or by means of partitions resulted in increased job satisfaction and higher ratings by supervisors. A supervisory group was also asked about its job satisfaction. They, too, showed greater job satisfaction with increases in privacy. However, ratings of privacy did not differ between supervisors and secretaries even though physical qualities of the work space did. Sundstrom and Kamp (1977) suggested that people adapt to the level of privacy that is available in work settings. Further, secretaries who were isolated spent even more time than did their colleagues visiting with their neighbors. In addition, Sundstrom and Kamp (1977) suggest that too-high levels of privacy may adversely affect secretarial performance.

Wicker 1972) has approached crowded work conditions from the perspective of ecological psychology. He introduced the concept of "overmanning"—an extension of Barker's concept of "undermanning." Overmanning occurs when the supply of persons seeking work exceeds the number of available roles. When this occurs, entrance requirements for jobs should become more stringent and commitment to the work product should decrease. Although these suggestions have yet to receive empirical support, they are nonetheless intriguing.

Summary

We suggested that when goal attainment is blocked by lack of privacy, extremely close proxemic interaction, or resource scarcity/ congestion, a problem is created for the occupants of a setting. If because of group composition variables, individual learning history or cultural factors the problem is not solved, it will continue to block goal attainment. Under these circumstances, situational or dispositional attributions will be made. One possible situational attribution is that crowding is responsible for the negative effect resultant from having one's goals blocked. In this case, individuals will either escape from the situation or try to change it. If both are inconvenient or impossible, negative effects will ensue.

Our review suggests that the literature on human crowding is consonant with this view. In residences, the effects of crowding worsen as norms move from cooperation to competition, as escape becomes inconvenient or impossible, and when the population is especially vulnerable (i.e., constituted of poor children). In mass transit settings that involve inescapable touching of strangers, stressed subjects exbibit a variety of ill effects. These are most pronounced when low levels of interaction promote a competitive orientation—a situation more than familiar to the Manhattan subway rider. In classrooms, close distance intensifies prevailing interaction, while congestion and resource scarcity promote aggression among young children. In all settings, those negatively affected perceive the environment as more crowded.

In general, then, crowding has complex but predominantly negative effects on the social behavior of humans.

Acknowledgments

I am grateful to the Rutgers Research Council for its support of our research program, and I would also like to thank Anne Stanford for her help in preparing the original version of this chapter.

References

Aiello, J.; DeRisi, D.; Epstein, Y.; and Karlin, R. 1977. Crowding and the role of interpersonal distance preferences. *Sociometry* 40:271–82.

Altman, I. 1975. *The environment and social behavior: privacy, personal space, territory and crowding.* Monterey, Calif.: Brooks/Cole.

Baron, R.; Mandel, D.; Adams, C.; and Griffen, L. 1976. Effects of social density in university residential environments. *J. Pers. Soc. Psychol.* 34:434–46.

Baum, A., and Greenberg, C. 1975. Waiting for a crowd: the behavioral and perceptual effects of anticipated crowding. *J. Pers. Soc. Psychol.* 32:671–79.

———, and Koman, S. 1976. Differential response to anticipated crowding: psychological effects of social and spatial density. *J. Pers. Soc. Psychol.* 34:526–36.

———, and Valins, S. 1973. Residential environments, group size and crowding. *Proc. 81st Annu. Conv. Am. Psychol. Assoc.* 211–12.

———, and Valins, S. 1974. Architecture, social interaction and crowding. *Trans. N.Y. Acad. Sci. Ser. II*

———, and Valins, S. 1977. *Architecture and social behavior: psychological studies of social density.* Hillsdale, N.J.: Erlbaum Associates.

Bickman, L.; Teger, A.; Gabriele, T.; McLaughlin, C.; Berger, M.; and Sunaday, E. 1974. Dormitory density and helping behavior. *Environ. Behav.* 5:465–91.

Booth, A. 1975. Final report: urban crowding project. Unpublished manuscript, Ministry of State for Urban Affairs, Canada.

Calhoun, J. 1962. Population density and social pathology. *Sci. Am.* 206:136–48.

Christian, J.; Flyger, V.; and Davis, D. 1961. Phenomena associated with population density. *Proc. Natl. Acad. Sci. U.S.A.* 47:428–49.

Davis, D. 1971. Physiological effects of continued crowding. In *Behavior and environment,* ed. A. Esser. New York: Plenum Press.

Dean, L.; Pugh, W.; and Gunderson, E. 1975. Spatial and perceptual components of crowding: effects on heath and satisfaction. *Environ. Behav.* 7:225–36.

Dooley, B. 1974. Crowding stress: the effects of social density on men with close and far personal space. Unpublished doctoral dissertation, Univ. of California at Los Angeles.

Ellis, A. 1962. *Reason and emotion in psychotherapy.* New York: Lyle Stuart.

Eoyang, C. 1974. Effects of group size and residential crowding. *J. Pers. Soc. Psychol.* 30:389–92.

Epstein, Y., and Karlin, R. 1975. Effects of acute experimental crowding. *J. Appl. Soc. Psychol.* 4:34–53.

————; Lehrer, P.; and Woolfolk, R. 1978. Physiological, cognitive and behavioral effects of repeated exposure to crowding. Unpublished manuscript, Rutgers Univ.

Evans, G. W. 1978. Crowding and the developmental process. In *Human response to crowding*, ed. A. Baum and Y. Epstein. Hillsdale, N.J.: Erlbaum Associates.

————. In press. Behavioral and physiological consequences of crowding in humans. *J. Appl. Soc. Psychol.*

Freedman, J. 1975. *Crowding and behavior*. San Francisco: Freeman.

————; Levy, A. A. Buchanan, R.; and Price, J. 1972. Crowding and human aggressiveness. *J. Exp. Soc. Psychol.* 8:528–45.

————; Heshka, S.; and Levy, A. 1975. Population density and pathology: is there a relationship? *J. Exp. Soc. Psychol.* 11: 539–52.

Galle, O.; Gove, W.; and McPherson, J. 1972. Population density and pathology: what are the relations for man? *Science* 176:23–30.

Griffit, W., and Veitch, R. 1971. Hot and crowded: influences of population density and temperature on interpersonal affective behavior. *J. Pers. Soc. Psychol.* 17:92–98.

Gruchow, H. 1977. Socialization and the human physiologic response to crowding. *Am. J. Public Health* 67:455–59.

Haythorn, W., and Smith, S. 1972. Behavioral activities in isolated and confined groups. Unpublished manuscript, U.S. Army Research Institute.

Hutt, C., and Vaizey, M. 1966. Differential effects of group density on social behavior. *Nature* 209:1371–72.

Karlin, R.; McFarland, D.; Epstein, Y.; and Aiello, J. 1976. Normative mediation of reactions to crowding. *Environ. Psychol. Nonverbal Behav.* 1:30–40.

————; Epstein, Y.; and Aiello, J. 1978a. A setting specific analysis of crowding. In *Human response to crowding*, ed. A. Baum and Y. Epstein, pp. 165–79. Hillsdale, N.J.: Erlbaum Associates.

————; Epstein, Y.; and Aiello, J. 1978b. Strategies for the investigation of crowding. In *Design for communality and privacy*, ed. A. Esser and B. Greenbie, pp. 71–88. New York: Plenum Press.

————; Katz, S.; Epstein, Y.; and Woolfolk, R. In press. The use of therapeutic interventions to reduce crowding related arousal: a preliminary investigation. *Environ. Psychol. Nonverbal Behav.*

————; Rosen, L.; and Epstein, Y. In press. Three into two doesn't go: a two year follow up on the effects of crowding in a college dormitory. *Pers. Soc. Psychol. Bull.*

Langer, E., and Saegert, S. 1977. Crowding and cognitive control. *J. Pers. Soc. Psychol.* 35:175–82.

Levy, L., and Herzog, A. 1974. Effects of population density and crowding on health and social adaptation in The Netherlands. *J. Health Soc. Behav.* 15:228–40.

Loo, C. 1972. The effects of spatial density on the social behavior of children. *J. Appl. Soc. Psychol.* 4:372–81.

MacDonald, W., and Oden, C. 1973. Effects of extreme crowding on the performance of five married couples during 12 weeks of intensive training. *Proc. 81st Annu. Conv. Am. Psychol. Assoc.*, pp. 209–10.

McConahay, J., and Rodin, J. 1976. Interactions of long and short term density of task performance. Unpublished manuscript, Yale Univ.

McGrew, P. 1970. Social and spatial density effects on spacing behavior in preschool children. *J. Child Psychol. Psychiatr.* 11:197–205.

McGrew, W. 1972. *An ethological study of children's behavior.* New York: Academic Press.

Marshall, J., and Heslin, R. 1975. Boys and girls together. *J. Pers. Soc. Psychol.* 31:952–61.

Megargee, E. 1977. The association of population density, reduced space and uncomfortable temperatures with misconduct in a prison community. *Am. J. Commun. Psychol.* 5:289–98.

Mitchell, R. 1971. Some social implications of high density housing. *Am. Sociol. Rev.* 36:18–29.

Nacci, P.; Teitelbaum, H.; and Prather, J. 1977. Population density and inmate misconduct rates in the federal prison system. *Fed. Prob.* 151:6–31.

Nicosia, O.; Hyman, D.; Karlin, R.; Aiello, J. and Epstein, Y. In press. Effects of bodily contact on reactions to crowding. *J. Appl. Soc. Psych.*

Paulus, P.; McCain, G.; and Cox, V. 1978. Death rates, psychiatric commitments, blood pressure and perceived crowding as a function of institutional crowding. *Environ. Psych. Nonverb. Behav.* 3:107–16.

Preiser, W. 1972. Behavior of nursery school children under different spatial densities. *Man-Environ. Syst.* 2:247–50.

Price, J. 1971. The effect of crowding on the social behavior of children. Unpublished doctoral dissertation, Columbia Univ.

Rodin, J. 1976. Density, perceived choice and response to controllable and uncontrollable outcomes. *J. Exp. Soc. Psychol.* 12:564–78.

Rohe, W. 1978. Effects of mediating variables on response to density in residential settings. Paper presented at the Am. Psychol. Assoc. Meet., Toronto, 1978.

———, and Patterson, A. 1974. The effects of varied levels of resources and density on behavior in a day care center. Paper repsented at the Annu. Meet. Environ. Design Res. Assoc., Milwaukee, Wisc., 1974.

Ross, M.; Layton, B.; Erickson, B.; and Schopler, J. 1973. Affect, eye contact, are reactions to crowding. *J. Pers. Soc. Psychol.* 28:69–76.

Saegert, S.; Mckintosh, E.; and West, S. 1975. Two studies of crowding in urban public spaces. *Environ. Behav.* 7:159–84.

Schmitt, R. 1966. Density, health and social disorganization. *Am. Inst. Planners J.* 32:38–40.

Schopler, J., and Walton, M. 1974. The effects of structure, enjoyment and participants' internality-externality upon feelings of being crowded. Unpublished manuscript, Univ. of North Carolina.

Shapiro, S. 1975. Some classroom ABC's: research takes a closer look. *Elem. School J.* 75:437–41.

Sherrod, D. 1974. Crowding, perceived control and behavioral aftereffects. *J. Appl. Soc. Psychol.* 4:171–86.

Singer, J.; Lundberg, U.; and Frankenhaeuser, M. In press. Stress on the train: a study of urban commuting. To appear in *Advances in environmental psychology* ed. A. Baum.

Smith, P., and Connelly, K. 1972. Patterns of play and social interactions in preschool children. In *Ethological studies of child behavior*, ed. N. Jones. Cambridge, England: Cambridge Univ. Press.

Smith, S., and Haythorne, W. 1972. Effects of compatibility, crowding, group size and leadership seniority on stress, anxiety, hostility and annoyance in isolated groups. *J. Pers. Soc. Psychol.* 22:67–79.

Sommer, R., and Becker, F. 1971. Room density and user satisfaction. *Environ. Behav.* 3:412–17.

Stokols, D., and Resnick, S. 1975. The generalization of residential crowding experiences to non-residential settings. Paper presented at the Annu. Meet. Environ. Design Res. Assoc., Lawrence, Kans.

———; Rall, M.; Pinner, B.; and Schopler, J. 1973. Physical, social and personal determinants of crowding. *Environ. Behav.* 5:87–115.

———; Smith, T.; and Proster, J. 1975. Partitioning and perceived crowding in a public place. *Am. Behav. Sci.* 18:792–814.

———; Novaco, R.; Stokols, J.; and Campbell, J. In press. Traffic congestion, type-a behavior and stress. *J. Appl. Psychol.*

Summers, A., and Wolfe, B. 1975. Schools do make a difference. *Todays Educ.* 64:24–27.

Sundstrom, E., and Kamp, D. 1977. Crowding in workspaces: architectural correlates of satisfaction and performance. Paper presented at the Annu. Meet. Am. Psychol. Assoc., San Francisco, 1977.

Teitelbaum, R. 1976. The effects of increased perceived control and distractions on reactions to crowding. Unpublished undergraduate thesis, Rutgers Univ.

Valins, S., and Baum, A. 1973. Residential group size, social interaction and crowding. *Environ. Behav.* 5:421–39.

Ward, S. 1975. Methodological consideration in the study of population density and social pathology. *Hum. Ecol.* 3:275–86.

Weldon, D.; Winer, J.; Loehy, J.; and Elkin, D. 1977. Crowding and classroom learning. Paper presented at the NATO Conf. on Human Consequences of Crowding, Antalya, Turkey,

Wicker, A. 1972. Processes which mediate behavior-environment congruence. *Behav. Sci.* 17:265–77.

Worchel, S., and Teddlie, C. 1976. The experience of crowding: a two factor theory. 34:30–40.

Zuckerman, M.; Schmitz, M.; and Yosha, A. 1977. Effects of crowding in a student environment. *J. Appl. Soc. Psychol.* 7:67–72.

12

THE CASE FOR DIFFERENCES IN THE RESPONSES OF HUMANS AND OTHER ANIMALS TO HIGH DENSITY

Reuben M. Baron

Recent reviews of responses to density by humans and other animals suggest that the harmful effects of density (commonly referred to as *crowding* effects) are more strongly influenced by the number of animals present (social density) than by space per se (physical or spatial density). They suggest also that the significance of unit space per organism, although secondary, cannot be completely neglected, since with unlimited space social interactions may not occur. (See, e.g., Sundstrom 1978 and Bell et al. 1978 for humans; Freedman 1979 for animals.) These reviews, however, disagree sharply about the implications of such generalizations.

Freedman (1975, 1979), by restricting his definition of density to physical density or space, concludes that the crowding data may be interpreted to mean that (1) density per se does not produce harmful effects in *either* humans or other animals, and (2) there is no reason to postulate different mechanisms for human and nonhuman reactions to density. Freedman's initial interpretation can be disputed simply by emphasizing group size instead of space as the crucial defining property of high density (e.g., Sundstrom 1978). Once this is done one can conclude that both humans and animals have been demonstrated to show negative reactions to social density.*

---

*There is a reasonably strong consensus on the ability of high group size in enclosed or circumscribed spaces to produce harmful effects in both humans and other animals. There is, however, disagreement about whether humans exhibit greater variability than infrahuman species in response to such conditions (i.e., show harmful effects less uniformly). The argument in the present chapter provides a set of rationales for the variability position (which assumes a greater gap between density and crowding for humans than other animals), Freedman's (1979) comments, notwithstanding.

The more important question, however, and the one I choose to address, is whether Freedman (1979) is correct in concluding that there is nothing to suggest that human mechanisms of response to high density differ from those of other animals.* I propose to take issue with Freedman's conclusions at two levels. First, I will argue that even when the same general class of mediating mechanisms appears to be implicated—for example, if we assume that social organization is one mediator of density effects for both humans and other animals—the mode of operation of the mediator differs so much in complexity and flexibility that one can question the utility of assuming that the same mechanism is at work. Second, I will argue that the increasing importance of symbolic-intellectual mediation and cultural regulation as we ascend the phylogenetic ladder cannot help but introduce qualitative differences in how humans and other animals cope with density or any other significant environmental event.

Similar Mechanism, Different Meaning?

Within certain traditions in the ecological literature density effects are examined within the context of the concept of *carrying capacity*—the number of organisms that can be supported within a given environment or habitat given fixed resources such as the availability of food and space (e.g., Clarke 1972; Tamarin 1978). With humans real questions arise as to whether it is useful to think of fixed population ceilings related to the productive capacity of the environment (Cohen 1977). Specifically, with humans the traditional concept of carrying capacity has become increasingly less relevant because of the advent of powerful technologies to modify the resource productivity of any environment and because of the progressive shift from economies based on the local availability of food to industrially based, exchange economies. For example, as we move from subsistence economies to econo-

---

Editors' Note: Freedman's alternate interpretation of the relation between animal and human reactions to density is presented in his chapter in this volume. For further discussions of social organization as a mediator of density effects in animal populations, see Christian, Terman, and Lloyd as well as the field studies by Sade and by Packard and Mech. In light of the complex effects which social organization appears to exert on density perception in these animal studies, it is interesting to question whether some of the constructs by which Baron attempts to distinguish human from animal responses to density might not profitably be applied to the animal literature.

mies based on exchange-oriented industrial products, population density becomes progressively less dependent on the intensity of local agricultural production (Clarke 1972).

While there are examples within the animal literature of species such as locusts, which appear able to alter their environment to affect their productive capacity (Davis 1972), it appears unreasonable to claim that the alterations of any infrahuman species approach the scale of human modifications. Thus, although it might be possible to argue that we are talking about differences in degree as opposed to kind, it would appear difficult to avoid the conclusion that nonhuman animal species are more limited by carrying capacity than are humans. The relative absence of such resource constraints is likely, in turn, to affect the relationship between increases in density and mechanisms of population regulation. Specifically, it may be hypothesized that the greater the ability of a species to alter its resource environment, the less likely population size will be controlled by fixed, biologically based mechanisms.

This type of hypothesis can be tested across species by ascertaining whether species with greater capacity to alter their external resource environment do in fact have less biologically fixed, automatic reactions to increases in density than do species with less altering capability. Within species we can ask whether, with increased capacity to alter resource availability, reproductive behavior comes to be regulated less by automatic biological mechanisms such as amount of body fat and more by experience-based cognitive-social processes (see Cohen 1977).

The Role of Social Factors

First, there appears to be little question that social factors, or to use Lloyd's term, "social pressures," represent critical mediators of density effects for humans and other species alike (Lloyd, this volume). What is at issue, however, is whether the greater flexibility and complexity that is characteristic of human social behaviors in regard to social organization, spacing, and patterns of social interaction means that at a genotypic level we are dealing with fundamentally different mechanisms.

Social Organization: Dominance Hierarchies

There is a great deal of evidence in the animal literature that at least one factor in the mediation of density effects involves the preexisting position of animals in some dominance hierarchy. Specifically, it appears that animals lower in the dominance hierarchy are more vulnerable to stress effects when radical increases in social and/or spatial density occur: for example, if the average size of the adrenal glands under high density is larger for animals *low* in the dominance hierarchy (Davis 1972; Christian 1975). Similarly, at the human level it appears to be the powerless (e.g., persons of low socioeconomic levels) who are most vulnerable to the harmful effects of high density (Bell et al. 1978).

There are, however, many differences between humans and other animals in how dominance might relate to density effects. First, with animals such as primates, dominance is based largely on physical differences in size and strength and immutable social bonds such as kin relationships (see Altmann and Altmann 1970; Altmann and Altmann 1978). Human dominance, on the other hand, is based on more cognitive information-centered factors such as location in a communication network and the ability to "sell" a particular self-presentation (Goffman 1959; Shaw 1976). In general, it appears that dominance in humans is more a matter of greater access to and skill in using crucial information than of size or strength. It is also important to understand that with humans dominance hierarchies are likely to shift with various settings, tasks, and so on (see Davis 1969). For example, the person dominant on the basketball court is not necessarily likely to be dominant in the classroom or on a job.

If this line of reasoning is correct, we should be able to track this phenomenon developmentally among humans. For example, we expect increasing differentiation of dominance hierarchies (i.e., greater situational specificity) as we move from preschool to junior high school students; that is, with young children dominance is likely to be (1) based on size and strength, and (2) generalized across settings. With older children nonphysical factors such as intelligence and situation-specific skills should become operative, with different children becoming dominant in different settings. Although the increasing differentiation of dominance hierarchies with age has already been observed (e.g., Omark and Edelman 1976), cross-situational specificity has not yet been investigated developmentally. With adults, however, the general finding in human leadership research is that there is strong situational and task specificity (J. Davis 1969; Steiner 1972).

Complexity of Social Organization: Roles, Density, and Behavior Settings

One of the most basic factors differentiating human social behavior from that of other animals is the greater complexity of human social organization, demonstrable at a number of levels. One particularly important aspect of complexity is the degree of task specialization occurring within a social system; human social organizations appear to be characterized by highly differentiated role systems which are often highly specific to different settings.

In addition to being a basic parameter of complexity, role differentiation occupies a central place in a major theory of crowding—the Barker-Wicker theory of under- and overmanning (see Wicker 1973, 1979). The theory can be summarized as follows:

1. Significant human social interaction occurs within temporally and spatially bounded environments referred to as behavior settings. These settings can be viewed as social niches. Examples of behavior settings are classrooms, parks, and supermarkets.

2. For a given behavior setting to function effectively, certain roles pertaining to the basic goals or tasks of the setting (the "program") have to be carried out.

3. Settings have a maintenance minimum, which is the minimum number of people required to carry out the essential roles.

4. Settings have a maximum capacity; this refers to the maximum number of people the setting can physically accommodate.

Certain basic definitions are also introduced. First, people who seek to participate in the activities of a given setting and who meet the eligibility requirements for that setting (e.g., age, price of admission, education, etc.) are called applicants. In addition, a distinction is made between two types of occupants of a setting: performers and nonperformers. The maintenance minimum for performers is the smallest number of people required for carrying out the necessary tasks in proper sequence. The maintenance minimum for nonperformers is the smallest number of people who must be present as audience or as consumers in the setting for the setting to continue functioning. Capacity for performers is constrained by the physical size of the setting and the number of roles available for a given activity (e.g., five on a team in basketball). For nonperformers physical factors are the major constraint (e.g., number of seats in the setting).

This formulation allows one to specify the three major conditions of manning (undermanned, adequately manned, or overmanned). Whether a setting is undermanned, adequately manned, or overmanned depends primarily on the relation of the number of applicants (to be either performers or nonperformers) to the maintenance minimum and the capacity of the setting for performers and/or nonperformers: Thus, if the number of applicants falls below the maintenance minimum, the setting is defined as *undermanned*. If, on the other hand, the number of applicants falls somewhere between the maintenance minimum and capacity, the setting is *adequately manned*. *Overmanning* occurs when there are more applicants than can be accepted given the capacity of the setting (defined in terms of roles and physical limitations).

This approach is particularly helpful for establishing the point at which density will become excessive. Thus, *what is at issue from this perspective is not the sheer number of people present or the unit space per person but rather the maintenance minima and capacities of settings that are located within specific physical spaces. Stated more generally, what is crucial is whether the number of people present and the skills they possess are adequate, too little, or too much, for the effective utilization of a given behavior setting.**

The manning type of analysis can then be used to modify the concept of carrying capacity to include the availability of social resources. Such an extrapolation allows us to accomplish two important tasks. First, it allows us to modify the carrying-capacity concept to accommodate social organizational factors. Carrying capacity, if it is to be useful, has to be gauged against (1) the particular task roles that have

---

Editors' Note: For another brief discussion of the "manning" concept see Karlin and the Editors' Note on page 228. It is tempting to draw an analogy between performers (those who hold responsible behavior setting roles) and dominant individuals in those species displaying dominance phenomena. References to dominance occur throughout the volume. It might be interesting to apply Wicker's behavior setting arguments to dominance phenomena to see just how good the analogy really is. The manning concept might also be applied to other aspects of the composition of social groups of animals such as wolves, rhesus monkeys, and langur monkeys and to the changes which occur in these groups. For example, see Packard and Mech for their discussion of the factors which may cause dispersal of some individuals from a wolf pack. Similarly, see Sade's discussion of the dispersal of male rhesus monkeys from their natal groups and the correlations sought between rank of the male or his mother and his fate in his new group.

to be filled for a given setting to maintain itself, and (2) the availability of applicants to fill these roles; that is, are there enough, too many, or too few people to perform the roles necessary for that setting to function effectively? We can ask, for example, are there enough people available to maintain a stable family structure and to allow a division of labor in the supplying of food, be it a hunter-gatherer or an agriculturalist economy? Or in more contemporary terms, are there enough people with technological skills to staff the armed forces, a space program, and the computer-related needs of home and office?*

Further, and of crucial importance to the present argument, the manning type of analysis provides a way of demonstrating both the continuity and the discontinuity of human and nonhuman reactions to density. Specifically, the basic proposition that crowding can be defined in functional terms relevant to the roles that have to be performed for a setting to function effectively can easily be extended to animal behavior. Some indirect support for the present line of reasoning can be found in animal research which removes a dominant member of a group of animals. For example, it has been found that the removal of a dominant male turkey results in a dramatic change in the size of the particular turkey population (Davis 1978).

Within the human crowding literature, important differences between males and females in vulnerability to density (such as those found by Marshall and Heslin 1975) can also be interpreted in these terms. For example, if, as it appears, the males were more likely than the females to approach the group task as a team activity, it is not at all surprising that the same level of density produced differential crowding effects. Similarly, the greater vulnerability of females to high-social-density dormitory rooms (found by Aiello et al. 1975) may be viewed in these terms. Specifically, females tend to give dormitory rooms more of a niche-like quality; for example, they spend more time in their rooms than males do, and decorate them more extensively. Thus, *personalization* goals may set the maximum capacity of a dormitory room at a lower level for females than for males. In relatively direct support of this line of reasoning, Mandel et al. (in press) have recently found that males and females differ in their definitions of the

---

Editors' Note: For an application of the concept of the carrying capacity of social resources to human prehistory see Cohen.

primary dimensions of dormitory crowding. Specifically, females are more likely than males to focus on parameters of physical density and in general are significantly more sensitive to visual aesthetic factors in dormitory living (we also replicated the findings of Aiello et al. 1975, that females spent more time in their room than males).

While the modification of carrying capacity to include a social resource-manning analysis has broad applicability across species, it is likely to become increasingly relevant for species with flexible social arrangements. Specifically, the social organizations of all infrahuman species are more likely to be bound by immutable biological and geographical constraints. For example, with infrahuman species, once a particular mating, family, or community living pattern is fixed it is repeated with little variation *within a given habitat*; humans, on the other hand, seem to be able to change patterns of mating, family structure, communal living, and so on, even when the habitat remains constant (e.g., Kanter 1972).

Spacing Mechanisms
The importance of spacing mechanisms in mediating the effects of both group size and spatial density has been demonstrated for a wide range of species, including rodents (Calhoun 1962), primates (Southwick and Siddiqi 1977; Altmann and Altmann 1970), and humans (e.g., Altman 1975; Proshansky et al. 1976; Edney 1974). Specifically, a wide variety of crowding effects, including aggressiveness, loss of reproductive capabilities, and physiological stress effects, have been found to occur when species-specific spacing mechanisms break down. There are, however, important differences, which characterize the relationships among density, spacing mechanisms, and crowding for humans as opposed to other animals.

First, it is likely that learning is more important in human spacing needs than in animal spacing needs; for example, we would expect much greater intra species variations in optimal spacing need in humans than in all other animals. Among humans, differences in spatial needs have been obtained for different cultures and subcultures (Hall 1966). For example, in the United States, subculture differences have been found in regard to preferred interaction distances for blacks and whites and latinos and nonlatinos. Further, personality and sex differences have also been observed (see Bell et al. 1978 for an excellent review of the group- and individual-difference literature on preference for personal space). Further, with humans, reactions to violations of preferred interaction or personal space zones appear to be highly situation-specific. For example, whether a violation of a spacing requirement creates positive or negative reactions is not so much a function of the extent of the invasion but rather who did the invading (e.g., a friend, lover, or stranger). For humans there is some evidence that invasion simply creates increased arousal, which may then be labeled positively or negatively depending on whether a friend or stranger invades (see Patterson 1976).

Spacing needs in humans also tend to be more portable. Thus, in humans it is particularly important to distinguish between personal space and territorial space. Personal space refers to the preferred distance for social interaction involving a conspecific. Territory typically refers to a fixed piece of geography that an organism claims—that is, is willing to mark and defend. Even when territories are involved with humans, the reactions to invaders are more likely to be a matter of social learning than of biological regulation (Hall 1966). Perhaps because of this general lack of preprogramming, human reactions to invasion are more variable, particularly in regard to aggression. For example, whereas animals fight quite readily when invaded, evidence of humans responding with overt aggression to invasions of territory is quite rare (Edney 1974). Indeed, with humans, withdrawal seems to be easier to document than aggression (Sommer 1969) except in regard to group territories such as a gang's "turf." Further, the more important human territories tend to be symbolic. For example, we copyright ideas and patent inventions. It is unlikely that animals other than humans have symbolic territories of this type. (The interested reader is referred to Edney 1974 and Altman 1975 for reviews of human spacing needs such as privacy.)

Finally, the functional meaning of a territory may differ radically for human and nonhuman species. For example, Proshansky et al. (1976; also Altman 1975) emphasize that the critical function of territories for humans is to provide an area where high freedom of choice is possible in regard to the types of private activities one can perform. On the other hand, animal territories are much more closely tied up with biological functions relating to reproductive activities and the protection of feeding areas. Thus, whereas the collapse of a spacing mechanism under high density may produce crowding effects in both humans and other animals, the functions of spacing are likely to be quite different and much broader in humans.

Number and Predictability of Interactions

Several investigators in the crowding area have stressed the importance of the number of social interactions in mediating the effects of group size and/or availability of space (Freedman 1979; Calhoun 1962; Lloyd, this volume). Thus, all other things being equal for both human and other animals, the greater the number of interactions, the greater the likelihood of crowding effects. However, with humans there is at least some indication that the *predictability* of the interaction equals or perhaps exceeds in importance the frequency of interaction.* For example, Baum and Valins (1977) propose that their dormitory crowding effects are largely a function of the greater proportion of random social interactions occurring in corridor as opposed to suite dorm arrangements. Indeed, it is possible that there are more social interactions in suites even though they are more predictable in regard to time, person, and setting.

With a consideration of predictability, we introduce a theme that, with variations, will be the major focus of the rest of this chapter. Specifically, we will begin to consider the relevance of the informational properties of density and the information-processing capabilities of animals as major factors differentiating the responses of humans and other animals to density.

The Role of Control in Responses to Density†

The mediation of responses to density by control-type mechanisms provides an excellent example of how the same general category of mechanism may be important for both human and nonhuman responses, but operate very differently. Control at a very general level

---

Editors' Note: In this and many of the examples which follow, it is important to question whether the contrasts drawn by Baron reflect real differences in animals and human information processing or whether they reflect our greater access to and appreciation of the human process. Perhaps animals, too, anticipate and respond to predictability. The literature on learned helplessness, cited elsewhere by Baron, suggests that this is the case.

†See Editors' Note on page 212.

refers to the ability of one system through its actions to constrain the actions of another system. For example, it may be said that the brain controls the action of the heart by releasing various hormones. When applied at the level of organism, control typically refers to organism/ environment relationships relevant to the achievement of certain goals or outcomes. (The environment may include other organisms as well as the physical setting.) We may then differentiate between intra- and interorganism control orientations. As applied to humans, for example, we can distinguish between personal (or intraorganism) and interpersonal control orientations. In this regard interpersonal control involves the ability to influence the range of outcomes attainable by other people (commonly referred to as power), whereas intrapersonal or personal control focuses on issues of personal efficacy involving one's ability to influence the attainment of desired outcomes through one's own actions. With personal control it is not necessary to affect the outcomes of others to achieve one's own desired outcomes (e.g., raising one's control over grades through increased studying does not necessarily affect the outcomes of other people). Given these definitions, it is perfectly possible to have control without power (i.e., a person may be able to influence his or her outcomes but be unable to influence the outcomes of other people).

Within the domain of personal power, two types of control have generally been distinguished: decisional control and outcome control (e.g., Steiner 1970; Averill 1973; Baron and Rodin 1978). Briefly, *decisional* control involves freedom of choice—the ability of a given animal to affect the types of preferred means and goals that are available in a given setting. *Outcome control*, on the other hand, refers to whether a given animal possesses the response capability to achieve positive outcomes and/or avoid negative outcomes. A special case of outcome control is Seligman's analysis of learned helplessness effects (see Seligman 1975). Specifically, learned helplessness typically refers to a reduction in the efforts of animals to master a "learnable" task, following a prior "helplessness" experience on a task where there is a lack of covariation between what responses the animals made and the occurrence of aversive outcomes. Lack of a reliable response-outcome contingency is assumed to undermine both expectancies and motivation for outcome control.

Important distinctions have also been made between behavioral and cognitive modes of control (e.g., Averill 1973). When one talks of behavioral control, what is at issue is the existence of physical arrangements such as the availability of a button, lever, or switch which will allow an animal to affect behaviorally the onset or offset of a stimulus event (e.g., the occurrence of shock, food, etc.). Cognitive control, on the other hand, refers to the animal's perception, beliefs, and attributions about whether they possess control. For example, Glass and Singer (1972) have demonstrated that verbal instructions producing variations in subjects' beliefs regarding whether they *could* press a button to turn off unpredictable noise lessened the decremental delayed effects of noise on performance. Further, a number of investigators (e.g., Tennen and Eller 1977) have found that subjects' attributions concerning why they were unable to control outcomes had an important mediating effect on the strength of the learned helplessness effect. For example, if an inability to control outcomes is attributed to a lack of ability, greater decrements occur in performance than if an attribution to a lack of effort is made (Dweck 1975).

As applied to the density literature, one can adopt two lines of reasoning. First, it is possible to argue that loss of control as a mediator of harmful density effects is more important with humans than with other animals. A second possible thesis is that whereas a density-induced lack of behavioral control is likely to produce crowding in humans and nonhuman populations alike, considerations of cognitive control are more important for humans.

With regard to the first interpretation, we do know that learned helplessness effects have been obtained with both humans and other animals (see Seligman 1975). Further, there is some direct evidence with humans that a learned helplessness mechanism can mediate density effects (Rodin 1976; Baron and Rodin 1978; Schmitt and Keating, in press). In principle, Rodin's (1976) procedure of exposing subjects with histories of varying levels of high-density living to a learned helplessness paradigm and then measuring susceptibility to the helplessness transfer effect could easily be implemented with almost any species of animal. The relative robustness of the impact of density history on learned helplessness could then be compared across species.

Another possible tack is to hypothesize that certain features of control differ for humans and animals. For example, it may be argued following Wortman and Brehm (1975) that only humans go through an initial reactance or attempt to restore control phase before surrendering to the learned helplessness effect. That is, the relative importance of freedom of choice vs. outcome control may differ for humans and other animals. Similarly, the generality of learned helplessness to positive as well as negative events, as well as the relative importance of predictability vs. control, can be compared for humans and other animals in the context of density-dependent variables.

Finally, it seems reasonable to argue that even if there are no substantial differences between humans and other animals in the operation of behavioral control, there will be differences at the level of cognitive control. Specifically, it is likely that only with humans would we be able to find evidence that perceptions, beliefs, and attributions about control are highly effective in mediating the density-crowding linkage (see Schmitt and Keating, in press; Baron and Rodin 1978). While there are some direct tests with humans as to mediation of crowding affects by such cognitive processes (e.g., Sherrod 1974; Baron et al. 1976; Rodin and Baum 1978), there are perhaps even more compelling conceptual and metatheoretical reasons for believing that cognitive control is largely a human mechanism for mastering density effects. Specifically, such derivations fall out naturally from the general proposition that the superior cognitive-symbolic abilities of humans produce greater variability in the meaning of any objective parameter of density for humans as compared to other animals. This line of reasoning will now be elaborated for both individual information processing and cultural labeling.

The Case for Qualitative Differences

Up until now we have discussed classes of variables and mechanisms that could be considered important in the responses of *both* humans and other animals to density. Factors such as number of social interactions and various parameters of social organization clearly affect whether density will create crowding effects, be they aggression, interference with reproductive behavior, or physiological stress reactions, in both humans and other animals (see Lloyd, this volume; Freedman 1979; Terman 1974). The major burden of our argument thus far is that even when there are common mediators, the quantitative differences are sufficiently large that (1) they border on differences in kind as well as degree, and (2) the meaning of the same general category of mechanism may be very different in humans than it is in other animals. For example, while a breakdown in spacing mechanisms may lead to crowding effects in both humans and other animals, the spacing mechanisms in humans may very well serve symbolic, image-maintenance functions as opposed to appetitive-type biological functions in other species. Further, while a "manning"-type modification of the concept of carrying capacity may be useful in understanding the density-dependent behavior of both humans and other species, it is likely that social resource factors, because of their greater flexibility and variety in humans, will be an even more important regulator of population density for humans. Indeed, as we shall argue shortly, social norms at the level of cultural mores may be the most important factor in human population regulation.

At this point I would like to introduce two interrelated classes of mechanisms which appear to be responsible for producing qualitative differences in human and nonhuman reactions to density. Specifically, it will be argued that differences in *information-processing mechanisms* and in the role of *cultural* factors create conditions that promote a fundamentally greater variability in human as opposed to nonhuman reactions to high density (assuming that density will produce crowding effects).

Differences in Perceptual-Cognitive Mechanisms

In this section I focus on two major sets of problems: (1) What differences exist between human and nonhumans in what constitutes density-relevant messages; do different types of stimuli signal the existence of high density for human and nonhuman populations (e.g., are there differences in the relative importance of visual, olfactory, and symbolic messages)? (2) Are there differences between human and nonhuman species in regard to how this information is processed (e.g., is there a difference in the depth of processing in regard to density-related cues)?

Lurking behind such questions is a proposition that cuts to the core of the present argument for qualitative differences, that of the importance of distinguishing between density as an objective description of an environmental state of affairs (e.g., the number of organisms present, the unit space per organism, etc.) and the meaning that these events have for the perceiving organism. For example, the correlation between a given physical parameter of high density and a crowding-type effect is likely to be much more variable in humans than in other animals because of the greater ability of humans to cognitively transform physical events (e.g., Neisser 1966).

The Nature of Density-relevant Messages. At the outset it may be conceded that it is probably reasonable to assume that the survival and everyday well-being of all species requires that they be sensitive to various stimulus parameters of density (e.g., the number of conspecifics present, the availability of space for social interaction, etc.). The presence of mechanisms for space regulation across both nonhuman and human populations argues strongly for the general ecological significance of density. Similarly, the cross-species data on social facilitation effects (Zajonc 1965) suggests that a wide variety of species are sensitive to the presence of group-size variations.

If density-related parameters are likely to be high in attention-getting potential for both human and nonhuman populations, wherein does a basis for differences lie? First, although density increases may have high attention value for all species, the significance of a given attentional cue is more likely to be biologically determined in lower animals. For example, whether olfactory cues related to closeness of contact function as aversive stimuli for humans varies greatly between cultures (Hall 1966). Animals, on the other hand, either belong to a species that is highly sensitive to olfactory cues at a species level, or they do not (e.g., rodents vs. primates). Sensitivity to a particular class of cues appears more likely to be preprogrammed at the level of the fine tuning of the sensory apparatus in nonhuman animals than in humans. Further, cue sensitivity in nonhuman species is more likely to depend on hormonally regulated, cyclical mechanisms. Humans, on the other hand, appear to possess the capacity to respond sexually at almost any time (e.g., Ford and Beach 1951). This line of reasoning suggests an attempt to demonstrate that the reactions of nonhuman species to density are more affected by variations in hormonal concentrations (e.g., when they are "in heat") than is the case with humans.

A second basic difference can be adduced from the strong likelihood that humans are more likely to be sensitive to symbolic inputs related to density than are other species. This proposition is likely to be true on two levels. First, humans are the species most able to produce internal representations (e.g., visual images) which represent previously encountered or expected external environmental events. For example, simply thinking about a crowd may produce signs of stress in humans. On the other hand, when in a crowd, thinking (e.g., imagining oneself in a noncrowded situation) is likely to reduce crowding stress. (The success of researchers such as Cautela 1966 using covert conditioning to reduce various compulsive reactions provides indirect support for this line of reasoning which itself has never been directly tested in regard to crowding stress.)

Similarly, although it has never been tested in regard to density-type parameters, the recent work of Mischel and his associates (e.g., Mischel and Baker 1975) on the symbolic transformation of affectivity charged stimuli is highly suggestive. Specifically, these researchers were able to increase subjects' control over delay of gratification (pressing a button to signal the experimenter to come in) for preferred food objects such as marshmallows by having subjects think about the abstract, as opposed to the consumatory properties of this object. It is likely that a great deal of the variability of human reaction to density rests on this type of symbolic transformation (e.g., imagining people encountered during the rush hour in various roles such as lover, etc.). Thus, the existence of covert symbolic processes is likely to provide humans with much greater freedom from domination by external stimuli related to the objective parameters of high density.

Symbolic processes related to language provide another domain that is likely to create qualitative differences between the reactions of humans and other animals to density. For example, Baum and Koman (1976) have demonstrated that verbal instructions that lead human subjects to expect encounters with high-density groups will instigate behavioral avoidance reactions in a group setting. Further, Sherrod (1974) has found that verbal inputs regarding the possibility of control over the termination of a high-density encounter (one group was told they could leave a crowded room whenever they wanted) were sufficient to attenuate unfavorable delayed reactions to actual high-density encounters. This sensitivity to language-mediated symbolic messages also implicates a difference in sensitivity to temporal dimensions for humans and nonhumans—*human reactions to high density are likely to involve more extended time frames*. For example, being able to plan for a summer vacation may mitigate the current effects of high-density working conditions.

In addition to the greater importance of symbolically mediated density cues as we ascend the phylogenetic ladder, it also appears that another critical difference lies in the greater importance of visual messages. As with symbolic messages, visual mediation produces information at a *distance* and thereby allows for greater planning. It appears likely that density-relevant messages are more likely to be communicated by close-contact olfactory and/or kinesthetic cues in cognitivity less complex species. For example, olfactory cues appear to play a more significant role than do visual cues in the manner in which rodents, as compared to primates, communicate the presence of conspecifics (see Lloyd this volume; Sacket 1966). From an evolutionary perspective, a dependence on proximity cues is likely to make planning almost impossible, thereby putting the burden on species-level preparedness, that is, on genetically preprogrammed fixed action patterns as opposed to individual learning histories or social conditioning. This leads us to the general evolutionary hypothesis that species which are highly vision-oriented will be characterized by *fewer* fixed reaction patterns to spatial and social density. For example, it may be expected that increases in group size will be less reliably tied to immediate stress-type reactions in vision- than in smell-dependent species.

Finally, while vision vs. olfactory mediation is readily testable across species, the symbolic mediation hypothesis, particularly if linked to language communication, is obviously more difficult to test. This difficulty can be circumvented at two levels. First, we can substitute pictures for language and still be in the realm of symbolic communication. For example, different types of mammals, such as deer, apes, and wolves, could be shown large pictures (photographs or moving pictures) of high-density groups of conspecifics and their stress reactions observed in regard to latency, intensity, and so on. Comparative differences may also be simulated within a species by looking at developmental differences. For example, within a symbolic species such as humans we could compare the reactions of preschool, elementary, and junior high students to the Baum and Koman (1976) expectancy of density manipulation. In general, it would be expected that that expectancy-crowding effects will be more manifest with increasing age.

Differences in Stages of Information Processing before Action
Another way to distinguish the responses to density of humans and those of other animals is to describe the types of steps that are likely to

---

Editors' Note: This is an interesting addition to the discussion by Sade of possible differences between rodent and primate reactions to density.

intervene before an overt instrumental response occurs. Specifically, it is proposed that with humans, density-related cues go through more elaborate cognitive appraisal processes *before* instrumental actions occur. Another way to put this proposition is that the gaps among noticeability, evaluation, and action involve a greater number of decisional steps for human as opposed to nonhuman species. Although it was not originally intended as means of differentiating between human and nonhuman reactions to density, I find the distinctions made by Rapoport (1975) between objective and perceived density and between perceived density and affective density useful in regard to the line of reasoning I am developing.

Objective vs. Perceived Density. Consider the following situation. You are a guard at a museum or theater opening who is using a counter to enumerate the people who have arrived for the opening. The counter supplies an objective record of the number of people present. We may contrast this number with an estimate by an attendee of how many people are present. The subjective estimate of the number of people present is what Rapoport calls *perceived density*. The argument I wish to advance is that there is a greater gap between objective and perceived density for human as opposed to nonhuman populations. This proposition rests on the assumption that more potentially biasing associational factors enter into the human judgment of environmental conditions of density than is true on the average for nonhuman populations.

A quick recitation of the range of factors suggested by Rapoport as affecting human judgments of density is illustrative. Rapoport implicates in the perception of density the height of building, the level of noise, high artificial light levels, many cars, and so on (physical-perceptual factors); the height of buildings and the absence of private gardens and entrances (symbolic-associational factors); as well as fast tempos and rhythms of activity extending over the whole of 24 hours (temporal factors). Rapoport also suggests a wide range of sociocultural factors, including the presence or absence of fences, courtyards, meeting places, and places for privacy as well as the heterogeneity of

---

Editors' Note: The issue of subjective density (the organisms appraisal) is in part a psychophysical question (discussed briefly in the introduction) which asks about the shape of the function relating physical parameters to behavioral changes in the perceiving organism. While such data might appear basic to any study of density measurement it also appears to be very difficult to get; we do not seem to have much of it.

the population and the existence of norms regulating social interaction. Rapoport also considers the importance of personal feelings of control, choice, or freedom; he proposes that lack of control will lead to judgments of less space, larger group size, and the like.

To these factors we can possibly add a number of social psychological variables suggested by Eric Knowles. For example, Knowles (1973) has found that sensitivity to density parameters is affected by whether people expect to interact with others, and whether one encounters a group of strangers (an aggregate or crowd) or a closely bonded social grouping. However, since Knowles has by and large used noncognitive measures such as changes in walking path, speed of walking, and glance rate, we cannot be sure whether these effects are best categorized as relevant to perceived density or to affective density (see below).

Affective Density. While I believe that an important source of the variability in human reactions to density-relevant parameters lies in the gap between objective and perceived density for humans; that is, in the likelihood that humans will under- or overestimate density levels, it is likely that even greater differences exist in regard to affective density—the organism's judgment that a particular level of density is unfavorable (or favorable). Specifically, I believe it is much more likely that many of the factors listed above will bias *affective* as opposed to perceived density judgments. I propose that because reactions to high density along dimensions of desirability, favorability, or threateningness reflect a greater freedom from stimulus determination than do judgments of perceived density, there is a greater likelihood that differences between human and nonhuman species in symbolic capacity, social organization, cultural conditioning, and sensitivity to dimensions of control will become operative. These predicted differences in perceived and affective density all point in the same direction; the same physical condition of high social or spatial density is potentially able to take on a *much greater range of meaning* in humans than in nonhumans.

If this general line of reasoning is correct, it should be easier to demonstrate consistency of response to a given group size or unit space availability in nonhuman than in human species. This hypothesis can be tested in regard to consistency over settings and time. For example, once it is demonstrated that a given level of group size produces negative effects for specific samples of human and nonhumans, we can observe the impact of changing contextual factors, such as color of walls, dimness of lighting, object arrangement, and shape of room.* In general, we expect more dramatic changes for humans. Further, if the groups meet over time, we expect more successful adaptations by humans, to the point where a once-disruptive group size is no longer a problem.

To ensure some comparability of reaction, the foregoing types of reactions would have to utilize nonverbal indices of comfort and stress. For example, assessments of corticosteroid levels in the urine could be used with both animals and humans. Observational data involving fear and general emotionality reactions could also be readily obtained (e.g., observations of postural adjustments, self-touching behavior, tremors, etc.).

Finally, if it may be assumed that distal behavioral reactions to high density are mediated by the cumulative impact of perceived and affective density as well as by a wide range of attitudinal and normative factors specific to the *instrumental behavior* (Fishbein and Ajzen 1975), we have good reason to expect even greater variability in human than in animal instrumental coping reactions to high density. For example, consider a situation where people evaluate a certain size of group as being too large for the particular activities they wish to perform. Under such circumstances, direct hostile reactions are much less likely to be performed by humans than by any other species, including the higher primates, because human action is more constrained by appraisal processes (e.g., considerations of norms, the perceived purpose of the interaction, etc.). Further, there is reason to believe that the existence of language, a critical feature of human cognitive processes, can reduce the frequency of agonistic gestures and interpersonal conflict (De Vos and Hippler 1969; Washburn 1965).

In sum, it is proposed that as we move from perceived to affective to overt reactions to density there is so great a transformation of the meaning of the input that variability of reaction becomes progressively greater. These filtering processes reflect both personal history and, perhaps even more important, the impact of cultural conditioning.

---

*Alternatively, based on the work of Seligman and Hager (1972), we may observe species X cue interactions (e.g., dimness of light may be a more significant cue for rodents than for humans). Such effects would also be consistent with the present position.

The Impact of Culture on Crowding Effects

An understanding of the role of culture in human reactions to density represents a key link in the present line of argument, for a number of reasons. First, it is through the achievement of a culture that we see most clearly the importance of the differences in complexity and flexibility of social organization and cognitive processes to which we have previously alluded. Further, the operation of culture in regard to density provides a very strong set of reasons for our basic contention that important aspects of the responses of humans and animals to density are mediated by qualitatively different mechanisms.

To set the stage for this analysis, we draw on Triandis' (1964) overview of the nature of culture. In general, culture is the man-made part of the environment (Herskovits 1955). This definition includes both the material artifacts and the conceptual features—"the beliefs, science, myths, religions, laws, etc., held by a group of people" (Triandis 1964, p. 2). These conceptual features can, in turn, be thought of as serving two principal functions. First, they provide norms for modal patterns of behavior. Second, "culture consists of ideologies justifying or rationalizing certain ways of behaving" (Kluckhohn 1954; p. 925). Further, although language is a fundamental part of culture, it is not identical with culture. Culture as a whole is more manifold and less channeled than is language (Kluckhohn 1954).

The existence of culture differentiates human behavior from that of animals at a number of levels. First, very few animal species that have been utilized to study density effects have the capacity to acquire or utilize language. Second, even when a relevant species such as apes has demonstrated some ability to acquire certain aspects of language (Gardiner and Gardiner 1969), such animals appear unable to master the syntactical aspects of language (Hebb and Thompson 1954). Further, culture constitutes a uniquely human constraint on the basic response systems of learning, perception, cognition, motivation, and emotion. For example, although other mammals do generalize and differentiate, humans exhibit certain culturally influenced approaches to knowing the world that appear unique. As Kluckhohn (1954, p. 955) so eloquently states: "Time to other animals is presumably determined by biological processes such as rutting and by physical events such as night and day. Men, however, classify according to principles not immediately derivable from nature; they devise systems of relationships that have arbitrary or value elements in them; they explain phenomena from varying premises; they produce sequences of activity that arise as much from conventional conceptions, as from the processes of the biological and physical world."

Questions of what, how, and why to which all cultures attempt to give symbolic answers cannot be firmly traced to common biological and physical environmental conditions shared by humans and other animals (Kluckhohn 1954). It is the present contention that the answers given to such questions cannot help but affect (and differentiate) how humans and other animals react to density-dependent conditions.

The following lines of evidence appear especially relevant. First, with regard to emotion, culture represents one important situational source of labeling for undifferentiated emotional arousal. For example, if Patterson's (1976) recent analysis of the implications of interpersonal invasion is correct, the initial impact of close social contact is an undifferentiated increase in arousal. The nature of the emotional label attached to this state is assumed to be situationally determined. Research cited by Patterson (1976) on the differential reaction to invasions by friends and strangers, as well as Worchel and Teddlie's (1976) demonstration that density-dependent parameters are susceptible to situation labeling, support the application of Schachter and Singer's (1962) theory of emotion labeling to the crowding domain.

Given these assumptions, we may ask whether there is reason to expect to find a cultural influence on the types of situational cues that are available for labeling density-induced states of arousal. In partial answer to this question, it may be noted that Triandis (1964), in his review of cultural influence on cognitive processes, finds strong evidence that people's conceptions of appropriate social distance within a dominance hierarchy are strongly influenced by cultural considerations. Of even more direct relevance, Altman (1977) reviews evidence strongly suggesting that privacy norms are culturally regulated. Specifically, Altman concludes that (1) people in all cultures engage in the regulation of social interaction, sometimes being accessible to others and sometimes being inaccessible to others; and (2) the behavioral mechanisms by which accessibility is controlled appear to be unique to the particular physical, psychological, and social circumstances of a culture.

A good concrete example of this type of cultural regulation is provided by Rapoport's (1975, p. 151) description of Japan:

In Japan we find a clear separation of public and private domains both physically (a turning inward) and socially—very different rules apply in public and private realms. We find the city broken up into many small areas where people are well known (i.e., are not strangers). There is a clear hierarchical and predictable set of rules for behavior. The house-settlement system contains many stress-reducing elements—such as entertainment areas, inns, baths, and so forth. There are also psychological withdrawal devices (e.g., drunkenness) and physical withdrawal in the house and garden, and within the dwelling, an increase in the effective space available through time scheduling and many other devices.

Such observations strongly suggest that cultural mores (i.e., norms), by affecting both the meaning of "close encounters" and regulating the nature of social contact, provide powerful mechanisms that can buffer the effects of high density. Japan is a particularly good testing ground for the value of the present line of reasoning, since researchers who argue against the existence of any strong negative relationship between high density and incidence of pathology with humans are particularly fond of pointing out, for example, that "Tokyo, a vast city with high density, has a fantastically low rate of crime . . . " (Freedman 1975, p. 107). A cultural analysis provides a ready explanation for such situations.

Moreover, this type of relationship between cultural regulation and density appears to be highly systematic. Societies that have historically been faced with a scarcity of space (e.g., Japan or Hong Kong) are the ones most likely to have developed the most effective cultural traditions for coping with high density. Further, this relationship appears to hold for preliterate as well as for literate societies (Altman 1977).

In sum, the existence of culturally derived mechanisms regulating social contact is likely to provide greater flexibility and variety of response to high density than is possible with the biologically fixed space regulation mechanisms found in other animals. Such cultural mechanisms explain how humans are able to maintain "illusions of privacy" under the most intimate of circumstances (e.g., paper-thin walls, shared dormitory rooms, etc.). Taken together with the ability of humans to transform the meaning of physical events, almost endlessly, ample justification is provided for proposing that at least on occasion human responses to density rest upon very different mechanisms than do those of other species.

Lest the foregoing comments be misinterpreted, *I do not presume to say that different is better.* It is not at all clear that the symbolic-cultural self-regulation mechanisms used by humans to cope with high density are superior, or even as effective, as the physiological self-regulation mechanisms of other animals (Davis 1972). Further, the phrase "on occasion" means that we should begin the arduous but scientifically essential task of establishing the *conditions* under which the responses of humans and other animals to various density parameters rest on similar mechanisms as opposed to different mechanisms. For example, it may be possible to specify contexts wherein the pituitary-adrenal mechanism shifts from being a proximal to being an intermediate link in the causal sequence because of a cognitive override. Finally, at a more basic level it may be necessary, in Donald Campbell's (1975) challenging terms, to distinguish between the impact of biological evolution and cultural evolution.

Acknowledgments

I wish to thank Jeffrey D. Fisher and an anonymous reviewer for their critical reading of an earlier draft of this paper.

References

Aiello, J. R.; Epstein, Y. M.; and Karlin, R. A. 1975. Field experimental research in human crowding. Paper presented at the meeting of the East. Psychol. Assoc., New York, Apr. 1975.

Altman, I. 1975. *The environment and social behavior.* Monterey, Calif.: Brooks/Cole.

———. 1977. Privacy regulation: culturally universal or culturally specific? *J. Soc. Issues* 33:66–84.

Altmann, S. A., and Altmann, J. 1970. *Baboon ecology.* Chicago: Univ. of Chicago Press.

———, and Altmann, J. 1978. Demographic constraints on behavior and social organization. Paper presented at the Hudson Symp. Biosoc. Mechanisms of Popul. Regulation, Plattsburgh, N.Y., Apr. 1978.

Averill, J. R. 1973. Personal control over aversive stimuli and its relation to stress. *Psychol. Bull.* 80:286–303.

Baron, R. M., and Rodin, J. 1978. Perceived control and crowding stress. In *Advances in environmental psychology,* vol. 1, ed. A. Baum, J. Singer, and S. Valins. Hillsdale, N.J.: Erlbaum Associates.

———; Mandel, D. R.; Adams, C. A.; and Griffen, L. M. 1976. Effects of social density in university residential environments. *J. Pers. Soc. Psychol.* 34:434–46.

Baum, A., and Koman, S. 1976. Differential response to anticipated crowding: psychological effect of social and spatial density. *J. Pers. Soc. Psychol.* 34:526–36.

————, and Valins, S. 1977. *Architecture and social behavior.* Hillsdale, N.J.: Erlbaum Associates.

Bell, P. A.; Fisher, J. D.; and Loomis, R. J. 1978. *Environmental psychology.* Philadelphia: W. B. Saunders.

Calhoun, J. B. 1962. Population density and social pathology. 1962. *Sci. Am.* 200:139–48.

Campbell, D. T. 1975. On the conflicts between biological and social evolution and between psychology and moral tradition. *Am. Psychol.* 30:1103–26.

Cautela, J. R. 1966. Treatment of compulsive behavior by covert sensitization. *Psychol. Rec.* 16:33–41.

Christian, J. J. 1975. Hormonal control of population growth. In *Hormonal correlates of behavior,* vol. 1, ed. B. E. Eleftheriou and R. L. Sprott. New York: Plenum Press.

Clarke, J. I. 1972. Geographical influences upon the size, distribution and growth of human population. In *The structure of human populations,* ed. G. A. Harrison and A. J. Boyce. London: Oxford University Press.

Cohen, M. N. 1977. *The food crisis in prehistory: overpopulation and the origins of agriculture.* New Haven: Yale Univ. Press.

Davis, D. E. 1972. The regulation of human population. In *Challenging biological problems: directions toward their solution,* ed. J. A. Behnke. New York: Oxford Univ. Press.

————. 1978. Discussant's comments delivered at the Hudson Symp. Biosoc. Mechanisms of Popul. Regulation, Plattsburgh, N.Y., Apr. 1978.

Davis, J. 1969. *Group performance.* Reading, Mass.: Addison-Wesley.

De Vos, G. A., and Hippler, A. A. 1969. Cultural psychology: comparative studies of human behavior. In *The handbook of social psychology,* vol. 4, 2d ed., ed. G. Lindsey and E. Aronson. Reading, Mass.: Addison-Wesley.

Dweck, C. S. 1975. The role of expectations and attributions in the alleviation of learned helplessness. *J. Pers. Soc. Psychol.* 31:674–85.

Edney, J. J. 1974. Human territoriality. *Psychol. Bull.* 81:959–75.

Fischer, C. S. 1976. *The urban experience.* New York: Harcourt Brace Jovanovich.

Fishbein, M., and Azjen, I. 1975. *Belief, attitude, intention and behavior: an introduction to theory and research.* New York: Wiley.

Ford, C. S., and Beach, F. A. 1951. *Patterns of sexual behavior.* New York: Harper.

Freedman, J. L. 1975. *Crowding and behavior.* San Francisco: Freeman.

————. 1979. Reconciling apparent differences between responses of humans and other animals to crowding. *Psychol. Rev.* 86:80–85.

Gardiner, R. A., and Gardiner, B. T. 1969. Teaching sign language to a chimpanzee. *Science* 165:664–72.

Glass, D. C., and Singer, J. E. 1972. *Urban stress: experiments on noise and social stressors.* New York: Academic Press.

Goffman, E. 1959. *The presentation of self in everyday life.* New York: Doubleday.

Hall, E. T. 1966. *The hidden dimension.* New York: Doubleday.

Hebb, D. O., and Thompson, W. R. 1954. The social significance of animal studies. In *Handbook of social psychology,* ed. G. Lindzey. Cambridge, Mass.: Addison-Wesley.

Herkovits, M. J. 1955. *Cultural anthropology.* New York: Knopf.

272 *Biosocial Mechanisms of Population Regulation*

Kanter, R. M. 1972. "Getting it all together." Some group issues in communes. *J. Orthopsychiatr.* 42:632–43.

Kluckhohn, C. 1954. Culture and behavior. In *Handbook of social psychology*, ed. G. Lindzey. Cambridge, Mass.: Addison-Wesley.

Knowles, E. S. 1973. Boundaries around group interaction: the effect of group size and member status on boundary permeability. *J. Pers. Soc. Psychol.* 26:327–31.

Mandel, D. R., Baron, R. M., and Fisher, J. D. (In press). Effects of height and view on room utilization and dimensions of density. *Environment and Behavior.*

Marshall, J. E., and Heslin, R. 1975. Boys and girls together: sexual composition and the effect of density and group size on cohesiveness. *J. Pers. Soc. Psychol.* 31:952–61.

Mischel, W., and Baker, N. 1975. Cognitive appraisals and transformations in delay behavior. *J. Pers. Soc. Psychol.* 31:254–61.

Neisser, U. 1966. *Cognitive psychology.* New York: Appleton-Century-Crofts.

Omark, D. R., and Edelman, M. S. 1976. The development of attention structures in young children. In *The structure of social attention*, ed. M. R. A. Chance and R. R. Larsen. London: Wiley.

Patterson, M. C. 1976. An arousal model of interpersonal intimacy. *Psychol. Rev.* 83:235–45.

Proshansky, H. M.; Ittelson, W. H.; and Rivlin, L. G. 1976. Freedom of choice and behavior in a physical setting. In *Environmental psychology: people and their physical settings*, 2d ed., ed. H. M. Proshansky, W. H. Ittelson, and L. G. Rivlin. New York: Holt, Rinehart and Winston.

Rapoport, A. 1975. Toward a redefinition of density. *Environ. Behav.* 7:133–58.

Rodin, J. 1976. Density, perceived choice and response to controllable and uncontrollable outcomes. *J. Exp. Soc. Psychol.* 12:564–78.

———, and Baum, A. 1978. Crowding and helplessness: potential consequences of density and 100% control. In *Human response to crowding*, ed. A. Baum and Y. Epstein. Hillsdale, N.J.: Erlbaum Associates.

Sackett, G. P. 1966. Monkeys reared in isolation with pictures as visual input: evidence for an innate releasing mechanism. *Science* 154:1468–73.

Schachter, S., and Singer, J. E. 1962. Cognitive, social, and physiological determinants of emotional state. *Psychol. Rev.* 69:379–99.

Schmitt, D. E., and Keating, J. P. In press. Human crowding and personal control: an integration of the research. *Psychol. Bull.*

Seligman, M. E. P. 1975. *Helplessness.* San Francisco, Calif.: Freeman.

———, and Hager, J. L. 1972. *Biological boundaries of learning.* New York: Appleton.

Shaw, M. E. 1976. *Group dynamics: the psychology of small group behavior.* New York: McGraw-Hill.

Sherrod, D. R. 1974. Crowding, perceived control, and behavioral aftereffects. *J. Appl. Soc. Psychol.* 4:171–86.

Sommer, R. 1969. *Personal space.* Englewood Cliffs, N.J.: Prentice-Hall.

Southwick, C. H., and Siddiqi, M. F. 1977. Population dynamics of rhesus monkeys in northern India. In *Primate conservation*, ed. H. S. H. Prince Ranier and G. Bourne, pp. 339–62. New York: Academic Press.

Steiner, I. D. 1970. Perceived freedom. In *Advances in experimental social psychology*, vol. 5, ed. L. Berkowitz. New York: Academic Press.

————. 1972. *Group processes and productivity*. New York: Academic Press.

Sundstrom, E. 1978. Crowding as a sequential process: review of research on the effects of population density on humans. In *Human response to crowding*, ed. A. Baum and Y. Epstein. Hillsdale, N.J.: Erlbaum Associates.

Tamarin, R. 1978. Dispersal, population regulation, and K-selection in field mice. *Am. Nat.* 112:545–55.

Tennen, H., and Eller, S. J. 1977. Attributional components learned helplessness and facilitation. *J. Pers. Soc. Psychol.* 35:265–71.

Terman, C. R. 1974. Behavioral factors associated with cessation of growth of laboratory population of prairie deer mice. *Res. Popul. Ecol.* 15:138–47.

Triandis, H. C. 1964. Cultural influences upon cognitive processes. In *Advances in experimental social psychology*, vol. 1, ed. L. Berkowitz. New York: Academic Press.

Washburn, S. L. 1965. Conflict in primate society. In *Ciba symposium: conflict in society*, ed. A. V. S. de Reuck and J. Knight. London: Churchill.

Wicker, A. W. 1973. Undermanning theory and research: implications for the study of psychological and behavioral effects of excess populations. *Represent. Res. Soc. Psychol.* 4:185–206.

————. 1979. *An Introduction to ecological psychology*. Monterey, California: Brooks/Cole.

Worchel, S., and Teddlie, C. 1976. The experience of crowding: a two-factor theory. *J. Pers. Soc. Psychol.* 34:30–40.

Wortman, C. B., and Brehm, J. W. 1975. Responses to uncontrollable outcomes: an integration of reactance theory and the learned helplessness model. In *Advances in experimental social psychology*, vol. 8, ed. L. Berkowitz and E. Walster. New York: Academic Press.

Zajonc, R. B. 1965. Social facilitation. *Science* 149:269–74.

13

SPECULATIONS ON THE EVOLUTION OF DENSITY MEASUREMENT AND POPULATION REGULATION IN *HOMO SAPIENS*

Mark Nathan Cohen

Reconstructions of the early history of the human population customarily divide this history into two phases, a very long early period of very slow growth encompassing the Pleistocene and a brief recent period of more rapid growth beginning with the "Neolithic Revolution" or the onset of farming economies about 10,000 years ago. Estimates of the average or overall growth rate for Pleistocene populations are on the order of .001–.003% per year (Cowgill 1975; Hassan 1973, 1975, this volume; Dumond 1975; Polgar 1972), whereas those for the later period are on the order of .10% per year (Hassan 1973; Hole et al. 1969; Carneiro and Hilse 1966). (In contrast, modern human populations have been observed to grow at rates of 1–2% per year or more.)

The slow rate of growth in the Pleistocene and the acceleration of population growth at the beginning of the Neolithic have appeared to be something of a paradox in recent years, as evidence has accumulated suggesting that the human hunting and gathering populations of the Pleistocene, rather than being constrained by positive Malthusian checks as once thought, may in fact have been relatively healthy and relatively well and reliably nourished by an array of wild foods that rarely would have placed an absolute limit on population (even a population with only a simple technology). It is this paradox that has suggested reevaluation of the regulation of human population growth in the spirit of this volume, with an eye to the possible existence of regulatory mechanisms at least one step removed both from strict Malthusian controls and from technological determination.

Before proceeding, however, it is perhaps worth reviewing and evaluating the evidence upon which the apparent paradox is built: the parameters from which growth rates have been reconstructed and the evidence by which the Malthusian limitation of Pleistocene population has been called into question.

The estimates of population growth, especially for the Pleistocene, are admittedly crude. Very little is known about the growth rates or fluctuations in those rates for particular populations or regions, and the figures quoted above are necessarily nothing more than an estimate of *average* growth, the theoretical rate of increase necessary for some minimum pre-Pleistocene population (usually postulated to have been two persons for purposes of simple modeling) to have reached the level estimated for the end of the Pleistocene just prior to the emergence of farming. The terminal Pleistocene population has commonly been estimated to be on the order of 3 to 10 million persons worldwide; or it has been estimated to have been of an overall density of about .1 person per square mile, which suggests a similar total (Hassan 1973, this volume; Keyfitz 1966; Dumond 1975; Braidwood and Reed 1957; Deevy 1960). Such estimates are necessarily derived from one of two sources. First, it is possible to estimate the size and number of archaeological sites (or of some other, similar parameter) for the terminal Pleistocene relative to that of later periods and to use this as an index of relative population size and density. Second, it is possible to use modern ethnographic analogies as an aid in reconstructing Pleistocene population. The population densities of modern hunter-gatherer groups exploiting various environments can be used as a basis for estimating Pleistocene population by extrapolation. Both sources of estimate are potentially fraught with error. Archaeological samples, particularly those representing the temporary camps of hunting-gathering bands, are quite poor. Attempts to compare the number and size of such camp sites with those of more permanent sedentary occupations of the type accompanying the Neolithic Revolution are subject to a number of errors which may lead to systematic underrepresentation of hunter gatherers and underestimates of terminal Pleistocene population (Cohen 1975). In contrast, the permanent settlements from the Neolithic period onward are likely to be more evenly represented and more nearly comparable to one another. Hence, estimates of relative population size and therefore of growth rates based on this type of settlement are more likely to be reliable. The estimated rate of growth (.1%) per year for the Neolithic is likely to be a more reliable figure than those available for earlier periods.

Ethnographic analogies may also be misleading: they could result in serious overestimation of prehistoric population because contemporary hunter-gatherers are in fact technologically superior to their prehistoric counterparts or because they have been forced to accept densities that are "artificially" high because of the political pressure of surrounding neighbors. Conversely, they could be low because modern hunter-gatherers live in some of the world's poorest environments and may thus not accurately reflect the affluence and density of their predecessors or because modern hunter-gatherers comprise disorganized, displaced, and largely declining populations. The estimates could also be skewed either up or down because extrapolations from modern samples are biased by prevailing assumptions about the hunter-gatherer life-style or about the nature of technological "progress." Estimates made under the influence of Malthusian stereotypes of "primitive" man are likely to be low; those made recently in a period when images of hunter-gatherer affluence are in vogue are likely to be high.

In what has become a classic survey of contemporary hunters, Lee and DeVore (1968) offer a figure of one person per square mile as a usable *maximum* estimate of hunter-gatherer density—a figure 10 times greater than the figure usually applied to the terminal Pleistocene but one clearly not applicable everywhere. Bearing in mind the probable underrepresentation of Pleistocene archaeological sites and arguing that farming began precisely because hunter-gatherers were overcrowded, I have recently suggested that something closer to the upper limit suggested by Lee and DeVore should be applied: that given 50,-000 square miles of earth, outside the Antarctic, a terminal Pleistocene population on the order of 15,000,000 should be considered. It is even possible that the figure should range even higher than this. So far, however, the point is moot.

What is important for present purposes, however, is that it makes relatively little difference what reasonable terminal Pleistocene population is assumed. Even by the most optimistic appraisal, terminal Pleistocene population, representing 2 million years of prior growth, is unlikely to reflect a growth rate even remotely approaching that of later periods: it is clear that Pleistocene hunter-gatherers cannot have approached modern growth rates or even those suggested for the Neolithic. For example, our hypothetical population of two, growing at a modern rate of 1% per year for 2 million years or even at the much smaller Neolithic rate of .1%, would have achieved a terminal Pleistocene population impossibly beyond the present population of the earth. There can thus be little doubt that, on the average, population growth during this early period must have been quite slow even by the standards of more recent archaeological time.

The slow rate of population growth in the Pleistocene was easily comprehended as long as Malthusian constraints on "primitive" man could be invoked as an explanation. But a number of observations in recent years (admittedly themselves not free of interpretive problems) suggest that the problem is not so simple. For example, studies of human fossils suggest that if hunter-gatherer life expectancy was somewhat shorter than that of Neolithic farmers, it was not sufficiently so to account for the difference in growth (Howell 1976b; Hassan this volume).* Moreover, contemporary hunter-gatherers, if they display a life expectancy less than that of modern western man, often appear to equal or surpass other nonwestern populations in this respect (Dunn 1968). (Such observations do not correspond entirely with the estimates of life expectancy from skeletal populations cited above, and it is not clear which "sample" is likely to be subject to greater error. But using either set of data it is clear that the harshness and brevity of hunter-gatherer life has traditionally been overstated.)

In addition, there are a number of indications that modern hunter-gatherers can make a good living. Richard Lee (1968, 1969) has described such a contemporary group, the !Kung San of the Kalahari Desert, who are both qualitatively and quantitatively well nourished and who obtain their subsistence selectively with relatively little effort among resources which if anything appear to be more reliable than those of their agricultural neighbors. Since the publication of this study and of a similar study by McArthur (1960; McCarthy and McArthur 1960) on Australian hunter-gatherers, many comparable data on various historic and contemporary hunter-gatherers have been collected (cf. Sahlins 1972; Cohen 1977) which portray a pattern of relative affluence. There are admittedly contraindications: observations of relative hardship among hunter-gatherers are recorded (see Meggitt 1962; Steward 1938) and it is possible to argue, by Liebig's Law, that even periodic hardship would have provided an effective Malthusian limit on Pleistocene population growth. To some extent, then, one is left with the problem of determining which data samples are more accu-

---

Editors' Note: See Hassan and Lee for more detailed description of the quantitative variables governing hunter-gatherer population growth.

rately descriptive of Pleistocene conditions. It seems probable, however, that in the Pleistocene, when hunter-gatherers exploited environments of choice rather than the marginal habitats now available to
them, they would have fared relatively well.* Moreover, it must be
pointed out that, if periodic crises afflict hunter-gatherers, they are also
well known among farming groups (see Watson 1966). There are various theoretical reasons to expect periodic resource failure to be, if anything, more characteristic of early farming groups than of hunter-gatherers. Farmers, after all, build relatively simple ecosystems, often of
artificially selected imports, which should be less well buffered than
naturally selected, diversified natural plant communities.

In further support of the sense of hunter-gatherer affluence, I have
recently documented a selectivity in food choices among Pleistocene
hunters even more marked than that of their modern counterparts
(Cohen 1977). Their avoidance (until fairly recent prehistory) of various habitats and of various food sources, most notably of shellfish and
other aquatic resources, is an indication of this selectivity, and it is
also a suggestion that populations were not constrained by available
total food or by food available to a given technology. (Clearly, the
technology for capturing shellfish or land mollusks was never beyond
anyone's grasp, although such foods were neither widely exploited nor
exploited intensively until the end of the Pleistocene.) Using this and
similar observations, I have argued elsewhere (Cohen 1977) that
throughout the Pleistocene the rate of population growth may have
been as much or more a determinant of the rate of technological "progress" as it was a consequence of that progress.

We are left, therefore, with the problem of accounting for a slow
rate of growth among populations who can reasonably be argued to
have been well nourished and who seem not to have been constrained
by Malthusian limits on total available food (or even on the total food
available through existing technology). That they may have been constrained, in some sense, by cultural definitions of desirable foods is
another matter.†

*Editors' Note: Contrast the views of Hassan.

†Editors' Note: Here and in his discussion of disease (below) Cohen suggests that internal
population controls were operating in a situation of abundant food and relative absence of disease.
The conditions that he postulates parallel those of experimental populations in which food and
disease are controlled (cf. papers by Lloyd and by Terman) but also resemble those of some "free
living" primate populations (cf. Sade).

There are a number of possible approaches to this problem. One that almost certainly has some validity has been offered by W. W. Denham and others. Denham (1974; see also Bronson 1975; Yesner 1975; Ammerman 1975) emphasizes the idea that the average growth cited above for the Pleistocene is a composite of local episodes of relatively rapid growth, episodes of decline or stasis, and episodes of local group extinction. The slow overall growth rate is then a function of the balance of such events among hunter-gatherers, as opposed to the balance among farmers. There can be no argument, I believe, with the basic idea that growth was irregular. However, whether one can postulate a higher rate of population failure or extinction for the Pleistocene is a matter of some debate. I have already suggested that there is reason to believe that the resources of hunter-gatherers are, if anything, more stable than those of farmers, at least of early farmers. Also, I would argue that in the face of actual "crop" failure, hunter-gatherers may actually have had more social mechanisms of homeo-stasis than did early farmers. Hunting and gathering bands are characterized by mobility and fluid social organization (Lee and DeVore 1968; Turnbull 1968). Local bands, moreover, are typically part of relatively far-flung social networks of mutual obligation and affinal exchange, and there is evidence that such networks may have characterized Pleistocene populations as well (e.g., Cohen 1977; Wobst 1974, 1975, 1976; Isaac 1972). These networks, as well as the availability of unused space (Cohen 1977), would have provided them with a number of outlets for responding to local resource failure. In this respect they may have fared better than early farmers, who, sedentary and circumscribed by neighbors or by the limits of agricultural potential, may have been far more vulnerable to local crises (natural or social) until they developed extensive and efficient redistributive networks to cope with the irregularities of nature (Cohen 1978, 1979).

These same social networks, incidentally, would also have buffered local groups against the dampening effects of random demographic events. For example, although population growth in a very small group could theoretically be slowed or even threatened entirely by random variations in the sex ratio, this is unlikely to have been a major problem as long as groups were united widely by marriage networks.*

Editors' Note: Compare the views of Hassan and of Lee on the role of periodic crisis in governing Pleistocene population growth.

In addition, although the irregularity and harshness of Pleistocene environments is occasionally cited as a factor in differential group mortality for the populations of the period, it should be noted that post-Pleistocene time is of the same order of magnitude as interglacial periods within the Pleistocene and is generally considered to be climatologically comparable to those periods. Thus, there is little reason to suggest that climate and therefore local resources are inherently more stable now than during comparable periods in the Pleistocene.

There is at least one other point of view from which Pleistocene populations should be viewed as, if anything, less susceptible to periodic devastation than are their more recent counterparts: they should have suffered somewhat less from the depredations of epidemic infectious disease. Although there is room for considerable argument about the role that infectious disease played in regulating Pleistocene populations (see below), there is at least good reason to believe that the kind of acute epidemics capable of decimating local groups (and commonly recorded to have done so in the historic period) have *increased* in frequency since the Neolithic revolution. Many such acute, rapidly spreading infections require very large populations to sustain them (Fenner 1970). For example, within the historic period measles have been observed to be self-sustaining on island populations only when they exceed a critical size usually estimated as several hundred thousand people (Black 1966; 1975; Black et al. 1974). The critical size is that required to reproduce new members at a rate sufficient to guarantee the virus access to fresh victims as old ones die or become immune. In a period of relatively small, isolated populations, such diseases, if they occurred by mutation from related forms, would be rapidly self-eliminating. (This would probably have been true, incidentally, even if Pleistocene groups were not quite as isolated as once pictured because very rapid group turnover over very large areas would be necessary to create a disease reservoir of sufficient size to maintain an acute infection.) The implication is that, although new mutant strains might occasionally devastate Pleistocene populations as indeed new mutant strains of flu do today, they would only have been important on a very local scale and would not have posed the general threat that the same event would pose today. Moreover, there would not have been the additional threat of the spread of repeated waves of epidemic diseases derived from "reservoirs" in neighboring civilizations paralleling those which have done so much damage to contemporary "primitive" populations. Whatever the role of disease, therefore, it is likely to have involved either chronic diseases capable of surviving for long periods in human groups or zoonotic diseases whose life cycles are commonly supported by other animals, which would have been problematic. Neither of these categories is particularly likely to account for the pattern of crisis postulated by Denham and others, although both may have contributed to a dampening of population growth.

Whether chronic disease or zoonotic disease would have dampened growth rates in the Pleistocene more than they did in later periods, however, is also problematic. Parasite loads should, in fact, have been relatively light among Pleistocene hunter-gatherers, who moved periodically away from their own wastes and whose low population densities should have provided a less than optimal environment for the dissemination of parasites, whose transmission, whether by airborne droplets, by direct contact, or by vectors, should be facilitated by higher human densities (see observations on the Hadza of East Africa by Jelliffe et al. 1962 and on Kalahari hunters by Heinz 1961).

The zoonotic diseases provide more of a problem. Goodman et al. (1975) have speculated that zoonotic diseases could have exerted a relatively heavy dampening effect on hunter-gatherer populations: that although the incidence of such diseases would have been low, mortality from them would have been relatively high. They argue that these diseases, normally cycling among wild animals and only occasionally infecting human beings, could have been important for two reasons. First, because their natural cycles do not involve people, these diseases not only could exist in man's environment in the absence of dense human populations but could also exist without coevolutionary adaptation to human hosts. Hence, when contracted they would be likely to produce serious infection rather than the more chronic and less demographically significant stress associated with some of our own "domestic" diseases. Second, these diseases would have hit an economically and demographically more significant segment of the population than would either chronic or epidemic human diseases. The latter, they argue, primarily strike children whose economic contribution is slight and whose replacement is relatively easy. In contrast, the loss of reproductive adults through occupational exposure to the zoonotics could, they argue, be far more significant as a demographic damper.

Their argument is an intriguing one, but it turns on the assumption that zoonotic infections would have been somewhat greater in severity and frequency among hunter-gatherers. However, my own review (in progress) of zoonotic disease based on a number of recent medical surveys (cf. Hubbert et al. 1975; Top and Werhle 1976; Andrewes and Walton 1977; Marcial-Rojas 1971) suggests that a large proportion of these diseases would have increased in importance as a result of various aspects of the Neolithic Revolution: the concentration and stabilization of domestic ungulates and their intimate handling by man, the collection of domestic pets, the association of ungulates and canids, the agricultural manipulation of land and water, the concentration of domestic rodents, and other problems associated with food storage and accumulation of wastes. Moreover, the broadening of the spectrum of exploitation just prior to the Neolithic Revolution (see Cohen 1977) would have involved exposure to a whole array of new, or previously only incidental zoonotic infections. (On the other hand, the narrowing range of niches exploited by farmers and their tendency to homogenize the landscape may in fact have reduced the range of zoonotic diseases and some of the dangers of occupational exposure.) The issue is by no means decided. Before it can be determined, we need to have a good deal of information about the relative demographic impact of diseases such as tick-borne viruses and rickettsias which hunter-gatherers would be likely to contract by penetrating relatively unmodified environments as compared to those diseases responsive to the economic and ecological modifications of the landscape enumerated above.

Another possible explanation is that the low rate of population growth in the Pleistocene resulted from cultural controls on fertility: the application of infanticide and/or abortion to unwanted pregnancies (Divale 1972; Divale and Harris 1976; Hayden 1972; Birdsell 1968; Hassan 1973, 1975, this volume; Ripley this volume). Birdsell (1968) argues that 15–50% of all pregnancies may have been thus terminated during the Pleistocene; Hassan's estimate is 25–35%. Both argue that such controls were the major factor distinguishing Pleistocene and recent growth rates.

How the rate of abortion or infanticide is related to the carrying capacity of the environment or to other determinants is a matter of some debate. Divale has suggested that a whole complex of female infanticide in combination with patterns of warfare and supporting values would have provided effective population limitation only indirectly linked to measurement of the food supply. The theory, reminiscent of much recent work in ecological anthropology, suggests that cultural practices which nominally serve nonecological functions may in fact have hidden or latent homeostatic functions that ensure survival. Birdsell (1968) has suggested that artificial birth spacing may have been necessitated by the problems of transporting infants; hence birth spacing is determined by the ontogeny of the human infant and by the need of the mother not to produce a second child while she is still transporting the first. This argument assumes that carrying children is particularly stressful under the relatively great mobility that is necessary for hunter-gatherer subsistence. In a parallel vein, Sussman (1972) has argued that the more rapid growth of population in the Neolithic might have resulted from the decreasing requirement for mobility, which would diminish the stress of transport and permit narrower spacing of births. (A parallel argument, but one that emphasizes the role of a physiological spacing mechanism in the explanatory model, is offered by Lee, this volume.)

Hassan (this volume and earlier works cited above) is skeptical of the presumed stress on hunter-gatherers. He argues that cultural controls on fertility might have been relaxed with the onset of the Neolithic because the new farming economy restructured time and labor demands in a manner that made additional children economically beneficial from a relatively young age. Hence, in effect, more children were permitted to grow because their marginal utility had increased.

There is considerable justification for assuming that cultural controls played a significant part in limiting Pleistocene population and in fact for assuming that such controls reflected, at least indirectly, an awareness of the supply of (preferred) foods rather than the inherent exigencies of the hunger-gatherer life-style. There is evidence that modern hunter-gatherers, although their natural fertility seems to be somewhat less than that of other populations as discussed below, nonetheless are capable of growth rates in excess of that indicated for the Pleistocene (see calculations by Howell 1976b; Hassan this volume). There is also evidence that such populations, in prehistoric time, were capable of relatively rapid expansion when faced with open environments of high quality such that population growth could be absorbed by outmigration with a minimum loss in the quality of life (Birdsell 1968). The initial colonizers of the New World have been said to have colonized the Americas in as little as 350 to 1,000 years, implying a growth rate of 1–3% per year (Martin 1973; Haynes 1966). Even though these estimates are almost certainly too high (and may in fact postulate a rate of growth *beyond* the physiological capabilities of hunter-gatherers), the colonization of the New World on present evidence was in fact very rapid by Old World standards (Cohen 1977).

The general point that human populations could expand relatively rapidly in the New World environment suggests several things. It suggests that whatever limited Pleistocene growth in general was not *entirely* a natural physiological ceiling on population growth. Nor was it purely a spacing mechanism necessitated by the inherent exigencies of hunter-gatherer life nor one geared to the inherently low marginal productivity of hunter-gatherer children. None of these mechanisms could have been as flexible as the discrepancy between New World and Old World colonization rates seem to imply. In fact, the reason for this discrepancy is not clear. One possibility is that cultural controls on population growth were relaxed by New World groups enjoying the possibility of expansion into relatively hospitable and warm environments and therefore tolerating rapid growth because there was little resulting decline in their standard of living. Another possibility, harking back to the possible role of disease as a regulator of populations, is that the New World offered relatively little in the way of serious human parasites in comparison with the old (MacNeill 1976). Also, the ability of populations to expand relatively rapidly faced with an open and relatively inviting frontier (unlike the northern frontier on which population expanded in the Old World) may imply that cultural regulation systems mimicked some of the systems of other organisms described elsewhere in this volume in responding to the distribution and social organization of organisms over a landscape and in being capable of relatively rapid expansion whenever an open frontier undermined the rigidity of the local social order.

Although the postulation of cultural controls on populations is thus a necessary *part* of an explanation of the discrepancy between Pleistocene and recent population growth rates, there are also reasons for assuming that such controls are not the total answer. Purely cultural explanations have weaknesses that have led me to consider also a set of more biologically oriented explanations of Pleistocene population growth as a supplement to the cultural. One point to be made is that there are at least some data (Howell 1976a,b) to suggest that remnant hunter-gatherer populations are unable to match other modern populations in fertility and in fact cannot have as many babies as they wish even though they structure marriage rules to maximize mating potential and even when they practice no form of birth control, infanticide, or abortion. Nancy Howell's data on the !Kung lead her to conclude that !Kung women have a total fertility rate averaging about five children (for women maximizing, and living to complete, their reproductive period). As she notes, this rate is less than half of that of other modern populations who design their cultural choices to maximize reproductive potential (e.g., the Hutterites). From these data in combination with !Kung mortality rates (which are not particularly high—the !Kung have a life expectancy at birth of 30 years and a distribution of deaths normal for this expectancy), she calculates that long-term growth for the population could be no more than .5% per year, well below that of other modern populations, although well above that of the Pleistocene. (The last calculation is cited in Kolata 1974.) These data suggest that some physiological constraints may have influenced the rate of population growth in the Pleistocene, even if these constraints could not have been sufficient in themselves (i.e., unsupplemented by cultural controls) to account for the low growth rate observed.

It should be noted, however, that there is some room for debate about just how representative the !Kung are in this respect. Ripley (this volume) suggests that the low fertility of the !Kung is a function of special features of their environment and adaptive pattern. Moreover, Australian hunter-gatherers seem to enjoy greater natural fertility than the !Kung, leading Birdsell (1968) to place greater emphasis on their need to resort to cultural population controls. On the other hand, there are observations suggesting that hunter-gatherers do, in general, have more widely spaced births than do farmers, even if they are not entirely uniform in this respect (Carr-Saunders 1922).

John Whiting, in commenting on this manuscript, has recently suggested another line of argument that may bear on this point. Using data from the World Ethnographic Sample and from privately coded samples, Whiting notes (personal communication) that there are correlations between the kinds of subsistence economy which a group practices and the kinds of artificial birth-spacing techniques (if any) which they employ (whether infanticide or postpartum sexual taboos). In his sample, 28 of 48 hunting and gathering societies (58%) practiced neither form of control, whereas only 13 of 36 farming societies (36%)

used neither. (The difference is statistically significant on a chi-squared test of homogeneity at the $p < .05$ level and *may* thus indicate something of the greater need of farmers to exert artificial population controls.)

Possibly more important is the fact that among societies using only one of the two techniques, hunter-gatherers strongly preferred infanticide (14 societies as opposed to 3 practicing postpartum sex taboos) and shifting agriculturalists strongly preferred postpartum sex taboos (21 societies as opposed to none relying on infanticide. Three hunting and gathering societies and 2 shifting agricultural societies used both techniques in combination.) Again, the difference is significant by the chi-squared test, this time at the $p << .001$ level.

The important difference, according to Whiting, is that infanticide and sexual taboos have very different properties as birth-spacing mechanisms. Simply put, a postpartum sex taboo more generally operates as a systematic spacer of births; infanticide more often operates in a remedial fashion as a corrector of "mistakes." These two comparisons suggest that cultural birth control systems are both less widespread and less quantitatively powerful among hunter-gatherers than among farmers. This, in combination with the low growth rates of the hunter-gatherers, provides some support for the notion that wide spacing of births, and therefore low fertility, are common features of this group.

A second reason for tempering purely cultural explanations of Pleistocene growth rates with a study of physiology is the realization forced on us by the sociobiologists (and in fact by the theory of evolution itself) that whatever the cultural mechanisms of regulation that may have developed in the course of our history, they are likely to have replaced or supplemented precultural mechanisms already present in ancestral populations.* These precultural mechanisms may have been overridden or modified and subsequently culturally supplemented at some time during the Pleistocene.

A third reason for postulating physiological factors as *part* of the mechanism of Pleistocene population regulation is that we can see remnants of what might have been such a spacing mechanism in viewing modern populations.

Editors' Note: Note that Cohen assumes (as does Lee) that ancestral human populations were programmed for population regulation in relatively stable environments. For an alternative view see Ripley.

A Model of a Biological Spacing Mechanism and a Biocultural Transition

The mechanism and the transition in question revolve around three factors: (1) a complex of interrelationships among body fat composition, nursing behavior, and birth spacing that has been discussed by a number of scholars (Frisch, various; Mosley 1977b; Howell 1976b; Lee 1972b and this symposium; Knodel 1977; Kolata 1974; Habicht et al. 1975; Jelliffe and Jelliffe 1975); (2) the correspondence between this complex and a mechanism of population regulation postulated by David Lack (1954, 1966); and (3) the relationship between this complex and changes in human dietary economy that can be reconstructed from the archaeological record (Cohen 1977).

Several years ago, Lack provided an explanation for an evolutionary paradox. He explained, in effect, how natural selection, which works through differential reproduction, could nonetheless select for self-imposed limits on the reproductive behavior of potential parents. Distinguishing between an optimum reproductive rate and a maximum reproductive rate, Lack pointed that natural selection, at least among bird and mammal populations, could favor parents who could gauge accurately how many babies they could rear successfully. Such parents would actually produce more surviving offspring than parents who, lacking restraint, produced more babies but also lost more of them because of their inability to provide. As Richard Dawkins (1976) points out, this model provides a relatively simple and direct answer to a problem that forced British naturalist V. C. Wynne-Edwards (1962) to postulate a model relying on group selection to offset individual genetic greed.

What is intriguing is that the model expounded by Lack bears a surprising resemblance to a birth-spacing mechanism which may be part of the human condition, even though under modern conditions of civilization the mechanism is rarely operative and only partly effective, for reasons to be discussed. The mechanism in question can be reconstructed from a series of observations on physiology and fertility in contemporary populations. (These observations are, however, controversial in varying degree. I intend to utilize some observations that are controversial and others that appear well documented, attempting to distinguish between the two as I proceed. I believe that the use of these controversial observations is justified by the speculative nature of this

essay, by their apparent fit with data from prehistory, and by the difficulties that have surrounded efforts to resolve some of these issues in
either direction. The speculative nature of what follows must be emphasized, however.)

It is important to note, first, that the fat composition of the female
human body and the duration and extent of infant nursing have each
been claimed to exert an independent effect on the spacing of children.
According to Rose Frisch (various), body fat affects female fertility by
helping to determine the age of menarche, the length of the period of
adolescent subfecundity, the degree to which menstruation and ovulation are regular or irregular, the length of the period of postpartum
amenorrhea and postpartum sterility, the frequency of fetal wastage,
and the age of menopause, all of which are affected by the achievement
and maintenance of a critical weight/height ratio. Thus, according to
Frisch, women whose weight falls below this critical standard tend to
become fertile relatively late, to ovulate irregularly, to endure (or enjoy) a relatively long period of postpartum sterility, to experience a
higher frequency of fetal loss, and to undergo menopause earlier. Such
women, she argues, also tend to have babies with small birth weights,
a factor that correlates with high rates of infant mortality. Such women
should obviously tend to have a low total fertility. It should be pointed
out, however, that many of Frisch's conclusions have been challenged.
The correlation between body fat levels and the age of menarche seems
to enjoy widespread acceptance (Mosley 1977a; Chowdhury et al.
1977; Brasel 1977), but others of her stated correlations, especially
that between body fat and birth interval—a powerful determinant of
total fertility—are subject to question. Many studies of the effects of
nutrition on fertility demonstrate some correlation (see Mosley 1977b).
But the causative pathways are not always clear; the significant elements, scarce or abundant in the nutritive complex, are not always
identifiable. Few studies on modern populations demonstrate a quantitative relationships specifically supporting Frisch's studies, and some
appear to contradict it (see Mosley 1977a; Trussell 1978; Masnick
1977; Chowdhury 1977; Cantrelle and Ferry 1977; Huffman et al.
1978). Moreover, as Lee (this volume) has pointed out, contemporary
studies on nutrition and birth interval, which often involve famine or
pathological malnutrition (e.g., Stein and Susser 1977), are inappropriate models of the effects of normal or marginally normal nutrition
on fertility.

On the other hand, there is some recent empirical evidence suggesting that Frisch's mechanisms or something like them do work among contemporary hunter-gatherers (see Wilmsen 1978, discussed below) and there are theoretical reasons (discussed below) to argue that a mechanism which is observed purely as a pathological condition in modern populations may nonetheless have operated in a more normal manner in prehistory.

Nursing behavior also exerts an independent effect on child spacing by a mechanism that is at present more generally accepted than the critical fat hypothesis (see Mosley 1977b). Prolonged and heavy nursing tends to extend the period of postpartum sterility by stimulating the production of prolactin and other hormones that are secreted as a response to suckling and which tend to suppress ovulation. Various estimates of the extent of this effect have been offered. Habicht et al. (1975) estimate that the onset of ovulation is delayed about 1 month for each 2 months of lactation after an initial 6-week interval of postpartum sterility. Jelliffe and Jelliffe (1975) estimate that sterility may be extended for as much as 26 months if nursing is complete, successful, and unsupplemented by other foods. Knodel (1977) indicates that extensions of the period of sterility by an average of 18 months or more by nursing characterizes some populations but that most populations experience a shorter extension.

Nursing behavior may also interact with body weight (or other nutritional variables) as a determinant of birth intervals, and there is considerable evidence that nursing acts more effectively to extend postpartum amenorrhea in poorly nourished populations (see Delgado et al. 1977; Ridley 1977; Menken and Bongaarts 1977; Wray 1977). This may be a variation on the critical fat hypothesis. Nursing, which places a heavy caloric demand on the mother (Frisch, 1975, estimates the burden at about 1,000 cal/day), may tend to retard a woman's ability to regain levels of fatness necessary to restore fertility. Conversely, a woman who has marginal caloric intake and marginal fat stores in the first place will tend to be more severely sapped by the effects of prolonged nursing and her fertility more greatly impaired than a woman with better fat reserves or intake who follows a similar nursing practice.

However, other interactions of nutrition and nursing are also possible. On the one hand, a well-nourished mother may be capable of nursing without dietary supplement to the infant for a relatively long

period of time, thus possibly extending the postpartum period of amenorrhea (Wray 1977). Conversely, it has been suggested that a less adequately nourished mother producing less milk may actually stimulate
more sucking and hence more prolactin secretion because the infant
has to work harder to get the same milk (Tyson and Peres 1977; Stanbury 1977).*

It would appear from the discussion above that women whose
stores of body fat are low or marginal, and/or who practice prolonged
nursing, will tend to enjoy naturally wide spacing of infants; conversely, any change in diet or behavior that increases fat stores or decreases nursing in extent or duration will tend to shorten the birth interval and increase the natural birth rate. As Knodel (1977; see also
Wray 1977) points out, however, infants weaned early suffer a number
of disadvantages related to the relative nutritional inadequacy of almost
all substitutes for mother's milk, including the loss of maternal antibodies and the increased danger of infection resulting from the processing of other foods. The resulting higher mortality rate for infants
may offset population gains resulting from the shorter birth interval.

This complex of factors has been cited by various authors (Howell
1976a,b; Lee 1972b and this symposium; Kolata 1974) as explaining
the apparently low natural fertility of the !Kung, who, although otherwise well nourished and displaying no measurable dietary deficiencies,
are lean, and who under aboriginal conditions tend to nurse for prolonged periods. The same authors have pointed out that under conditions of acculturation where the !Kung are settled, exposed to new
foods, and where they tend to wean babies earlier, their birth intervals
shorten and birth rates go up. Lee has emphasized the importance of
better weaning foods, which permits earlier weaning (see also the discussion of these factors by Knodel). Howell, following Frisch, is inclined to emphasize the increase in body fat that accompanies sedentary life. My inclination is to continue to explore the critical fat
hypothesis for three reasons.

First, the critical body fat mechanism could act as a sensitive density-dependent indicator in a way that the suppression of ovulation by
nursing alone could not. Body fat in women is likely to be a measure

*Editors' Note: It is noteworthy that neither Cohen nor Lee, who also deals with nursing as
a mechanism of birth control, addresses the issue of social interaction and population density as
they affect prolactin secretion and lactation. Compare the discussion of such effects in the rodent
studies by Christian and Lloyd.

of the ratio of available nourishment to work effort, which is in turn likely to be density-dependent. (The suppression of ovulation by lactation alone *could* be density dependent if, as Skolnick and Cannings 1972 speculate, a declining food supply regularly caused mothers to nurse their infants for a longer period, but to my knowledge, we lack cross-cultural information on this point. In any case, during the Pleistocene, a relative shortage of food is likely to have necessitated greater labor investment or the acceptance of secondary food sources rather than absolute shortages. The effects of such shortage on weaning practices should vary from location to location, depending on the nature of the secondary foods utilized and the patterns of labor investment, particularly by women, involved in obtaining them.)

Second, there is some empirical data showing that body fat, as well as nursing pattern, is important to hunter-gatherer fertility. Wilmsen (1978) has recently documented a seasonality in births among Kalahari San which corresponds to seasonal variations in body weight.

Third, as discussed below, the body fat hypothesis fits the reconstructions of prehistoric dietary patterns that I and others have offered, whereas hypotheses about nursing behavior are harder to relate to prehistory.

Whichever of these factors is given most weight, the critical point to be made is the contrast between the reproductive behavior of the !Kung, who are relatively infertile although healthy and well nourished, and that of other modern populations, who, as suggested by Hytten (1975) and Jelliffe and Jelliffe (1975) can remain fertile despite relatively severe malnutrition. Other modern populations are not completely immune to the effects of nutrition on fertility as recently suggested by Frisch (1978a); but certainly the ability of modern third world populations to continue to conceive even when dietary deficiencies, particularly of protein, threaten all concerned is in striking contrast to the pattern of the !Kung. Moreover, the !Kung are not the only hunter-gatherer population who appear to display rates of fertility tightly geared to their nutritional status (see Carr-Saunders 1922). One gets a sense that the physiology of hunter-gatherers in general responds sensitively to variations in nutrition in a way that that of farmers does not.

Why should there be this difference? If humans have a natural mechanism of birth spacing related to the diet and nursing practices of the mother, why doesn't this mechanism respond to contemporary economic deprivation by slowing reproduction? The answer, I believe, has two parts. First, although maternal body fat is certainly of itself an important contributor to infant and maternal well-being (Frisch and McArthur 1974 estimate that 144,000 cal is necessary to cover the costs of pregnancy and 3 months of lactation), it may be necessary to view this single factor not simply as one necessary condition for child birth but rather as a sort of environmental signal of the type implied in Lack's model—a sensitive indicator which has evolved as a mechanism to enable a woman's body to measure the optimal spacing for healthy babies. Body fat acts as a signal which, in effect, "tells" the mother when her body is capable of supporting the demands of a new pregnancy; or, in ecological terms, the woman's body fat level is her way of estimating biologically whether the level of resources of the environment is sufficient in relationship to the population density to permit an additional birth. Such a mechanism would provide a reliable density-dependent regulator of population, since the distribution of body fat levels in the population should reflect the relative scarcity of food or the decreasing caloric returns for work effort that should accompany increased density.

The second part of the answer is that we have short-circuited or outwitted this particular feedback mechanism. For this mechanism to work, body fat must indeed be an accurate indicator not just of caloric sufficiency, but of overall environmental quality (i.e., of the availability of the full spectrum of dietary needs). This mechanism must have evolved under conditions when the ratio of calories to other necessary dietary elements was both healthy and relatively fixed—a condition approximated by the !Kung, who are lean but qualitatively well nourished. For such a population, where body fat levels are near the critical level even when health is good, births are widely spaced and spacing is sensitive to variations in the environment or the density of the population. More "civilized" populations appear to be relatively insensitive to the same mechanism primarily because we have overloaded and "fooled" the system. We provide so many "free" calories (in the form of processed starches) relative to other nutrients that shortage is not perceived and the spacing mechanism does not work except under the most extraordinary conditions. We have fooled the system by altering our diets—in response to crowding, or its economic equivalent, poverty—in precisely those ways in which the mechanism is blind. We have maintained or even increased the availability of calories at the expense of other qualitative ingredients in the diet. In effect, the more crowded we have become, the more substantially we have overloaded and bypassed a feedback system whose primary sensitivity is to stored calories.

The loss of this regulatory mechanism results from a series of ecological and dietary adjustments which human populations seem to have made to their own slow growth during the Pleistocene (Cohen 1975, 1977). In the Middle Pleistocene, ancestral human populations of the *Homo erectus* grade seem to have relied heavily on the meat of large mammals as their preferred source of protein. The distribution of their settlements suggests that the pursuit of this meat provided the behavioral focus, although not necessarily the caloric bulk, of the diets. In fact, the protein of large mammals, while apparently highly desirable, then and now, may never have been available easily enough to provide a rich and steady source of calories. (It should also be noted that the meat of wild animals is very lean, so that there would have been relatively little animal fat available in a hunter's diet even if a good deal of meat were available.) Vegetable foods would have provided supplementary calories and other nutrients. However, as long as vegetable foods were chosen for qualities other than the provision of starch per se (starchy staples seem to be relatively recent and low-priority "third-choice" foods; see Cohen 1977), and as long as these vegetable foods were eaten unprocessed, they were unlikely to have provided more than marginal levels of caloric intake even while providing a diet that was fully adequate in other respects. Under these conditions, any increase in population density should have resulted in decreasing caloric returns, resulting in turn in wider birth spacing. However, human populations (with some regularity, to judge from the archaeological remains) seem to have made a number of adjustments to their diets which bypassed this regulatory system. As the meat of large mammals became scarce (both because human populations grew in proportion and because many large mammals became extinct through some combination of human hunting and climate changes), humans shifted to other secondary sources of protein.

First, they utilized the protein of smaller fauna and aquatic animals, particularly shellfish, which, although less desirable and previously eschewed, may have been calorically less expensive to obtain. Second, they made increasing use of qualitatively imperfect but quantitatively abundant vegetable protein sources. Increasing population densities thus led first to a gradual broadening of the range of foods exploited to supplement the meat of mammals and the preferred vegetable foods. However, with further increases in the density of populations, human economies came increasingly to focus on the exploitation of vegetable foods, notably grain and tubers, chosen primarily for their ability to produce calories but often deficient in other necessary dietary elements. At the same time, techniques of food processing, particularly cooking and grinding, were being added to the dietary economy. A primary result of these new techniques was to liberate calories (particularly among the vegetable foods) that had previously been inaccessible to human digestion. A side effect of the same techniques, however, would have been the further elimination of many of the other nutrient qualities of the same foods. By the end of the Pleistocene these trends had culminated in a pattern of settlement and subsistence that focused on the gathering, processing, and (later) cultivation of a variety of vegetable foods chosen primarily for their caloric productivity. The poverty of these foods in other nutrients reduced the quality of the diet at the same time that their caloric productivity overrode the natural birth-spacing mechanism. As Howell (1976b) points out, citing Neel and Weiss (1975), the Yanomamo hunter-gatherers, who have recently supplemented their diets with bananas, now have a total fertility rate of about 8 (as contrasted with that for the !Kung of 5).

Sedentism (the necessity of settling in the vicinity of these once despised foods which now provide the caloric staple) exacerbated the combination of problems. It cut human populations off from mobile sources of animal protein and from the range of dietary nutrients provided by nomadic, eclectic economy. It may also have reduced one source of caloric drain on women that was inherent in mobile food gathering. I have argued elsewhere that I doubt whether the onset of farming reduced the overall caloric costs of obtaining food, and I think that the burdens of carrying children may have been overplayed in some of the literature (Sussman 1972). But, both Howell and Lee stress the importance of reduced stresses and caloric demand on women as part of the significant changes accompanying sedentism. Kolata (1974) also points out that the adoption of sedentary farming, at least among the contemporary !Kung, involves a shift in the role of women, diminishing their economic contributions (and caloric expenditure). It may well be, therefore, that this transition in life-styles, along with the shift to caloric-intensive foods, helped push human females well above the marginal levels of body fat that prevailed previously. A final factor may have been the eating of newly domesticated animals, which, because of their own sedentary habits and artificial feeding, would have been somewhat fatter than their wild ancestors.

A change in nursing patterns may also have been involved, but this is more problematic. Lee (1972b, this volume) in comparing !Kung hunter-gatherers with their counterparts who have recently adopted sedentary farming, notes that the nursing period is shorter among the new farmers, resulting in a shortened birth interval. It is not clear that this pattern can be extrapolated back into the past, however. As Lee notes, the significant fact in this pattern is the availability to the farmers of good weaning foods which the nomadic groups lack. In prehistoric times, the availability of grinding technology and the appropriate foods (cereals and tubers) to grind into gruel may in fact have made earlier weaning possible. Unfortunately, the archaeological record is silent on this problem. The archaeologists' usual method is to check across contemporary populations for recurrent patterns or regularities that support extrapolation back into the Pleistocene. Hence, a determination that, among modern populations, farmers typically wean their children at a younger age than do hunter-gatherers would greatly strengthen Lee's case. Unfortunately, the existing data do not seem to support this assumption. The data are poor because the reporting of weaning practices is very uneven in the literature and because estimating the ages of young children of cultures without calendars is notoriously difficult. However, using what data there were—the World Ethnographic Sample and unpublished data gathered by the Laboratory of Human Development at Harvard and provided me by John Whiting— I recently attempted a cross tabulation of subsistence economy and various indices of the age of weaning. The tabulation (Cohen n.d.) suggests that there is no relationship whatever (let alone a significant one) between the two sets of variables, making it seem relatively unlikely that there was a general shift in weaning practices with the beginning of farming.

In addition, the arguments of Knodel (1977, cited above) that a shortened nursing period might increase infant mortality, offsetting the effects of a shortened birth interval, seem particularly cogent with regard to the generally low hygiene levels that must have accompanied incipient sedentism. The rapid spurt in the birth rate in the Neolithic seems more likely to have resulted from higher body fat levels associated with the new diet and behavioral pattern *without* a change in nursing patterns but *with* a caloric buffer that prevented nursing from having as serious a suppressive effect on ovulation as it might otherwise have had.

The Neolithic Revolution and the Perception of "Crowding"

A number of contributions to this symposium (most notably that by Baron) lead me to suggest that there is at least one other important feature of the Neolithic Revolution that should be discussed at least briefly. The failure of modern human populations to display symptoms of "stress" (Christian this volume) associated with high densities has been commented on by several of the social psychologists present and the suggestion has been made (see Baron this volume) that this may be a result of the relatively great flexibility which humans display in restructuring the social organization through which density is mediated. It seems appropriate to ask therefore whether the social transformations accompanying the beginning of sedentary farming could not be viewed as restructuring human interactions in ways that not only minimized the stresses of existing crowding but also provided avenues through which future increases in population could be assimilated with relative ease, permitting more rapid growth.

Lee (1972a) suggested something of this sort several years ago when he called attention to social strife and conflict as factors tending to prevent larger aggregates of !Kung San from forming and pointed to the importance of political controls as a factor in the formation of recent aggregations. Fried (1968) has described the structural transformation between hunting-gathering ("egalitarian") societies and that of farmers ("rank") societies, pointing to the emergence of predetermined patterns of authority and centralized exchange as features of the new order. Baron's discussion (this volume) may aid us in understanding the mechanisms by which these social transformations helped mitigate the potentially stressful consequences of increasing density, eliminating both the "strife" of Lee and possibly the "stress" of Christian.

The key concepts, I believe, are "overmanning," "control," and "privacy." The concept of overmanning suggests that additional individuals are stressful not because they add to the absolute density of an environment but only when they exceed or overflow the number of positions socially defined in a situation. Hence, identical populations with identical densities can be under stress in one situation and not in another, depending on how the role structure is defined in each. The "control" concept argues in a similar fashion that it is not density per se but rather an individual's loss of control over the outcomes of his actions resulting from density (or from other conditions including low social status) that is stressful. A social system capable of making social niches for new individuals and/or arranging those individuals such that they facilitated rather than interfered with each other's goals might well tolerate ever-increasing densities without inducing stressful reactions. Finally, the "privacy" concept (Epstein, Karlin this volume) emphasizes the importance of control over interpersonal interactions, suggesting that it is lack of this form of control (which may be dependent on density and on other features of the milieu) rather than density per se that may be stressful to an organism.

It may well be that the size and density of hunter-gatherer groups was limited because their social organization, which at first appears so mobile and stress-free, is relatively inefficient at minimizing the impact of growing population on existing role definitions and on existing privacy and control needs. The very lack of formal structure may have failed to provide individuals with institutional buffers against the fact and perception of crowding. (Although hunter-gatherer societies are not completely without effect in this regard; see Draper 1973, who discusses the apparent insensitivity of Kalahari San to one measure of crowding.)

As hunter-gatherer populations approached saturation of their environments at the end of the Pleistocene and were forced to adopt social systems appropriate to sedentism, they apparently adopted modes of social organization that were highly efficient at placing new personnel in functional, nonstressful positions. To the extent that the rate of population growth went up at this time simply as a matter of cultural choice (Hassan 1973, this volume), this choice may reflect not only the marginal utility of children in farming but also a kind of social facilitation that bypassed stressful density perceptions by creating social access to privacy, control, and cooperation. It is, at one level, a measure of the efficiency of our social system as organizers of persons that we do not feel the stress of dense populations; but, at another level it is perhaps this very efficiency that prevents us from stabilizing at fixed densities and permits continuing growth in the face of diminishing resources.

References

Ammerman, A. J. 1975. Late Pleistocene population dynamics: an alternative view. *Hum. Ecol.* 3:210–34.

Andrewes, C. H., and Walton, J. R. 1977. *Viral and bacterial zoonoses.* London: Ballière Tindall.

Birdsell, J. B. 1968. Some predictions for the Pleistocene based upon equilibrium systems among recent hunters. In Lee and DeVore, eds., pp. 229–40.

Black, F. L. 1966. Measles endemicity in insular populations: critical community size and its evolutionary implications. *J. Theor. Biol.* 11:207–11.

———. 1975. Infectious diseases in primitive societies. *Science* 187:515–18.

———, et al. 1974. Evidence for persistence of infectious agents in isolated human populations. *Am. J. Epidemiol.* 100:230–50.

Braidwood, R. J., and Reed, C. 1957. The achievement and early consequences of food production: a consideration of the archaeological and natural historical evidence. *Cold Spring Harbor Symp. Quant. Biol.* 22:19–31.

Brasel, J. 1977. The impact of malnutrition on reproductive endocrinology. In Mosley, ed., pp. 29–60.

Bronson, B. 1975. The earliest farming: demography as cause and consequence. In *Population ecology and social evolution*, ed. S. Polgar, pp. 53–78. The Hague: Mouton.

Cantrelle, P., and Ferry, B. 1977. The influence of nutrition on fertility: the case of Senegal. In Mosley, ed., pp. 353–64.

Carneiro, R., and Hilse, D. 1966. On determining the probable rate of population growth during the Neolithic. *Am. Anthropol.* 68:177–81.

Carr-Saunders, A. M. 1922. *The population problem: a study in human evolution.* Oxford: Clarendon Press.

Chavez, A., et al. 1975. *Prognosis for the undernourished surviving child.* Proc. 9th Int. Congr. Nutr., Mexico, 1972. Basel: Karger.

Chowdhury, A. K. M. A. 1977. Effect of maternal nutrition on fertility in rural Bangladesh. In Mosley, ed., pp. 401–10.

———, et al. 1977. Malnutrition, menarche and marriage in rural Bangladesh. *Soc. Biol.* 24:316–25.

Cohen, M. N. 1975. Archaeological evidence of population pressure in preagricultural societies. *Am. Antiq.* 40: 471–74.

———. 1977. *The food crisis in prehistory.* New Haven: Yale.

———. 1978. General and local models of prehistoric change: their applicability to different periods of prehistory. Paper presented to Annu. Conv. Soc. Am Archaeol.

———. 1979. The ecological basis for new world state formation: general and local model building. Paper presented to Hamilton College Symp. State Form.

———. n.d. A cross tabulation of indices for subsistence behavior and nursing patterns as coded in the World Ethnographic Sample (1979).

Cowgill, G. L. 1975. Population pressure as a non-explanation. In *Population studies in archaeology and biological anthropology: a symposium*, ed. A. Swedlund. Soc. Am. Archaeol. Mem. 39.

Dawkins, R. 1976. *The selfish gene.* New York: Oxford Univ. Press.

Deevy, E. 1960. The human population. *Sci. Am.* 204:194–204.

Delgado, H., et al. 1977. Nutrition and birth interval components: the Guatemalan experience. In Mosley, ed., pp. 385–400.

Denham, W. W. 1974. Population structure, infant transport and infanticide among Pleistocene and modern hunter-gatherers. *J. Anthropol. Res.* 30:101–08.

Divale, W. T. 1972. Systemic population control in the middle and upper Paleolithic: inferences based on contemporary hunter-gatherers. *World Archaeol.* 4:222–43.

————, and Harris, M. 1976. Population, warfare and the male-supremacist complex. *Am. Anthropol.* 78:521–38.

Draper, P. 1973. Crowding among hunter-gatherers: the !Kung Bushmen. *Science* 182:301–03.

Dumond, D. E. 1975. The limitation of human population: a natural history. *Science* 187:713–21.

Dunn, F. L. 1968. Epidemiological factors: health and disease in hunter-gatherers. In Lee and DeVore, eds., pp. 221–28.

Fenner, F. 1970. The effects of changing social organization on the infectious diseases of man. In *The impact of civilization on the biology of man*, ed. S. V. Boyden, pp. 48–76. Canberra Australian National.

Fried, M. 1968. *The evolution of political society*. New York: Random House.

Frisch, R. E. 1975. Demographic implications of the biological determinants of female fecundity. *Soc. Biol.* 22:17–22.

————. 1977a. Food intake, fatness, and reproductive ability. In *Anorexia nervosa*, ed. R. A. Vigersky, pp. 149–61. New York: Raven.

————. 1977b. Nutrition, fatness and fertility: the effect of food intake on reproductive ability. In Mosley, ed., pp. 91–122.

————. 1978a. Population, food intake and fertility. *Science* 199:22–30.

————. 1978b. Response to Trussell. *Science* 200:1509–13.

————, and McArthur, J. W. 1974. Menstrual cycles: fatness as a determinant of minimum weight for height necessary for their maintenance or onset. *Science* 185:949–51.

Goodman, A., et al. 1975. The role of infectious and nutritional diseases in population growth. Paper presented to the 74th Annu. Meet. Am. Anthropol. Assoc., San Francisco.

Habicht, J. P., et al. 1975. Repercussions of lactation on nutritional status of mother and infant. In Chavez et al., eds., pp. 106–14.

Hassan, F. 1973. On mechanisms of population growth during the Neolithic. *Curr. Anthropol.* 14:535–42.

————. 1975. Determination of the size, density and growth rate of hunting-gathering populations. In *Population ecology and social evolution*, ed. S. Polgar, pp. 27–52. The Hague: Mouton.

Hayden, B. 1972. Population control among hunter-gatherers. *World Archael.* 4:205–21.

Haynes, C. V. 1966. Elephant hunting in North America. *Sci. Am.* 214:104–12.

Heinz, H. J. 1961. Factors governing the survival of Bushman worm parasites in the Kalahari. *S. Afr. J. Sci.* 57:207–13.

Hole, F., et al. 1969. *Prehistory and human ecology of the Deh Luran plain.* Mem. Mus. Anthropol. Univ. Mich. 1.

Howell, N. 1976a. The population of the Dobe area !Kung. In Lee and DeVore, eds., pp. 137–52.

————. 1976b. Toward a uniformitarian theory of human paleodemography. *J. Hum. Evol.* 5:125–40.

Hubbert, V. T., et al., eds. 1975. *Diseases transmitted from animals to man.* Springfield, Ill.: Thomas.

Huffman, S. L., et al. 1978. Post partum amenorrhea: how is it affected by maternal nutritional status. *Science* 200:1155–57.

Hytten, F. E. 1975. Nutritional implications of maternal physiological adjustments in pregnancy. In Chavez et al., eds., pp. 66–70.

Isaac, G. 1972. Early phases of human behavior: models in lower Paleolithic archaeology. In *Models in archaeology*, ed. D. Clarke, pp. 167–99. London: Methuen.

Jelliffe, D. B., and Jelliffe, L. F. P. 1975. Interrelationships of lactation, conception and the nutrition of the nursing couple. In Chavez et al., eds., pp. 11–15.

Jelliffe, D. B., et al. 1962. The children of the Hadza hunters. *J. Pediatr.* 60:907–13.

Keyfitz, N. 1966. How many people have lived on earth? *Demography* 3:581–82.

Knodel, J. 1977. Breast feeding and population growth. *Science* 198:1111–15.

Kolata, G. B. 1974. !Kung hunter-gatherers: feminism, diet and birth control. *Science* 185:932–34.

Lack, D. 1954. *The natural regulation of animal numbers.* Oxford: Clarendon Press.

————. 1966. *Population studies of birds.* Oxford: Clarendon, Press.

Lee, R. B. 1968. What hunters do for a living or how to make out on scarce resources. In Lee and Devore, eds., pp. 30–43.

————. 1969. !Kung bushman subsistence: an input-output analysis. In *Ecological studies in cultural anthropology*, ed. A. Vayda, pp. 47–79. New York: Natural History Press.

————. 1972a. The intensification of social life among the !Kung Bushmen. In *Population growth: anthropological implications*, ed. B. Spooner, pp. 342–50. Cambridge, Mass.: MIT Press.

————. 1972b. Population growth and the beginnings of sedentary life among the !Kung Bushmen. In *Population growth: anthropological implications*, ed. B. Spooner, pp. 329–42. Cambridge, Mass.: MIT Press.

————, and DeVore, I. eds. 1968. *Man the hunter.* Chicago: Aldine-Atherton.

————, and DeVore, I. 1976. *Kalahari hunter gatherers.* Cambridge, Mass.: Harvard University Press.

McArthur, M. 1960. Food consumption and dietary levels in groups of aborigines living on naturally occurring foods. In *Records of the custodian—American scientific expedition to Arnhem Land*, ed. C. P. Mountford. Melbourne: Melbourne Univ. Press.

McCarthy, F., and McArthur, M. 1960. The food quest and the time factor in aboriginal economic life. In *Records of the Australian-American expedition to Arnhem Land*, ed. C. P. Mountford. Melbourne: Melbourne Univ. Press.

MacNeill, W. H. 1976. *Plagues and peoples.* Garden City, N.Y.: Anchor Press.

Marcial-Rojas, R. A. 1971. *Pathology of protozoal and helminthic diseases*. Baltimore: Williams & Wilkens.

Martin, P. 1973. The discovery of America. *Science* 179:969–74.

Masnick, G. S. 1977. Fecundability and contraceptive opportunities. In Mosley, ed., pp. 313–24.

Meggitt, M. 1962. *Desert people*. Chicago: Univ. of Chicago Press.

Menken, O., and Bongaarts, J. 1977. Reproductive models in the study of nutrition-fertility interrelationships. In Mosley, ed., pp. 261–312.

Mosley, W. H. 1977a. Nutrition, fertility and infant mortality: introductory statement. In Mosley, ed., pp. 87–90.

———, ed. 1977b. *Nutrition and human reproduction*. New York: Plenum Press.

Neel, J. V., and Weiss, K. M. 1975. The genetic structure of a tribal population, the Yanomamo Indians. *Am. J. Phys. Anthropol.* 42:25–52.

Polgar, S. 1972. Population history and population policies from an anthropological perspective. *Curr. Anthropol.* 13:203–09.

Ridley, J. C. 1977. Introductory statement. In Mosley, ed., pp. 175–78.

Sahlins, M. 1972. *Stone age economics*. Chicago: Aldine.

Skolnick, M. H., and Cannings, C. 1972. Natural regulation of numbers in primitive populations. *Nature* 239:287–88.

Stanbury, John. 1977. Nutrition and endocrine function: introductory statement. In Mosley, ed., pp. 9–10.

Stein, Z., and Susser, M. 1977. Famine and fertility. In Mosley, ed., pp. 123–46.

Steward, J. 1938. *Basin plateau aboriginal sociopolitical groups*. Bur. Am. Ethnol. Bull. 120.

Sussman, R. M. 1972. Child transport, family size and increase in human population during the Neolithic. *Current Anthropol.* 13:258–59.

Top, F. H., and Werhle, P. F., eds. 1976. *Communicable and infectious diseases*. St. Louis: Mosby.

Trussell, J. 1978. Menarche and fatness: Reexamination of the critical body composition hypothesis. *Science* 200:1506–09.

Turnbull, C. 1968. The importance of flux in two hunting societies. In Lee and DeVore, eds., pp. 133–37.

Tyson, J. E., and Perez, A. 1977. The maintenance of infecundity in post-partum women. In Mosley, ed., pp. 11–27.

Watson, P. J. 1966. Clues to Iranian prehistory in modern village life. *Expedition* 8:31.

Wilmsen, E. N. 1978. Seasonal effects of dietary intake on Kalahari San. *Fed. Proc.* 37:65–72.

Wobst, H. M. 1974. Boundary conditions for paleolithic social systems: a simulation approach. *Am. Antiq.* 39:147–77.

———. 1975. The demography of finite populations and the origin of the incest taboo. *Am. Antiq.* 40:75–81.

———. 1976. Locational relationships in Paleolithic society. *J. Hum. Evol.* 5:49–55.

Wray, M. D. 1977. Maternal nutrition, breast feeding, and infant survival. In Mosley, ed., pp. 197–230.

Wynne-Edwards, V. C. 1962. *Animal dispersion in relation to social behavior*. Edinburgh: Oliver & Boyd.

Yesner, D. R. 1975. Nutrition and population dynamics of hunter-gatherers. Paper presented to the 74th Annu. Meet. Am. Anthropol. Assoc., San Francisco.

14

THE GROWTH AND REGULATION OF HUMAN POPULATION IN PREHISTORIC TIMES

Fekri A. Hassan

> From the age of gods
> Man has continued,
> Men in their myriads
> Fill the land.
> Like flights of wild duck
> Bustling, they come and go.*

During most of the prehistoric past, people subsisted on hunting and food gathering. By approximately 10,000 years ago, food production began to supplement and replace hunting-gathering in many places, leading to a considerable increase in the size of world population. Prior to the transition, the world population was perhaps no larger than 10 million persons (Hassan 1978). During the early period of food production it soared to five times that size (Brothwell 1971; Deevey 1960); see figure 14.1.

The small size of world population by the close of the Pleistocene reflects a very slow average rate of growth, considering the span of more than 2 million years over which it had taken place. The rate is estimated at well below .001% per year (Polgar 1972; Hassan 1973). During the early period of food production, the annual rate accelerated to about .1% on the average (Carneiro and Hilse 1966; Hassan 1973; Cowgill 1975).† Although this is very modest compared with the

---

*Empress Saimei (a.d. 594–661), in *The Penguin Book of Japanese Verse*, trans. and ed. Geoffrey Brownas and Anthony Thwaite (Harmondsowrth, England: Penguin Books, 1974), p. 11.

†*Editors' Note:* These figures are the same as those cited by Cohen, who provides a brief description of how they are derived.

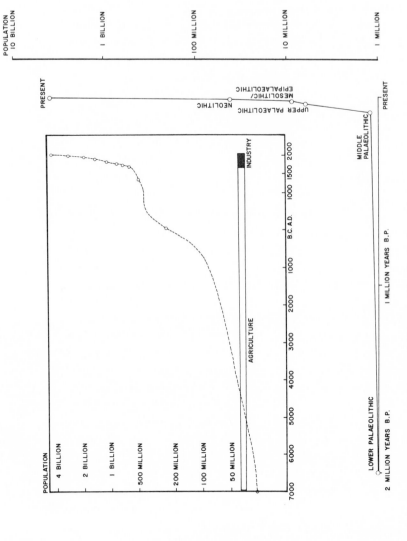

Figure 14.1. Pattern of population growth over the last 9,000 years. Shown clearly are the remarkable acceleration in population growth rate and the dramatic increase in world population size over the last few centuries (data from Hassan 1978; Thomlinson 1965).

2–3% rates of many contemporary populations, it was far greater than that of the Paleolithic. The causes for this slow growth during the preindustrial period might have been either biological or cultural regulation. This paper deals with some probable regulatory mechanisms, and it employs two conceptual models. The first, shown graphically in Figure 14.2, hinges on the biocultural determinants of the net reproductive rate, which included three key variables: survivorship to childbearing age, length of reproductive span, and child-spacing period. The second model takes into account the variables that are likely to influence the long-term pattern of population growth (Figs. 14.3 and 14.4).

Hunter-Gatherers

Some demographers have viewed prehistoric populations as characterized by uncontrolled high mortality and high fertility (Bogue 1969). Anthropologists, on the basis of paleodemographic analyses of collections of human skeletal remains and comparative studies of contemporary nonindustrial populations, have provided a data base that could be used to illuminate the nature of demographic processes in prehistory. Weiss (1972, 1973, 1976) suggests that the growth of prehistoric populations was checked more by mortality than by low fertility. Howell (1976), struck by paleodemographic evidence for high adult mortality in prehistoric groups and limited fertility among contemporary hunting-gathering populations (as a result of long child spacing), suggests that extinction of prehistoric populations is a distinct possibility. She also remarks that life expectancy at birth of 20 years would have led to rapid population decline. Henneberg (1976), in contrast, argues that the capacity for reproduction in most prehistoric populations was great.

I turn now to the first of the models mentioned above to discuss how the key variables might have affected the reproductive potential in prehistoric times.

Survivorship to Childbearing Age. Survivorship to nubility in the United States today is .938 (Coale 1974). This is a phenomenal rate compared with estimates of .550 for Upper Paleolithic populations (Weiss 1973) and .460 for the Maghribian Epipaleolithic peoples (Acsádi and Nemeskéri 1970). These figures are close to the .450 fig-

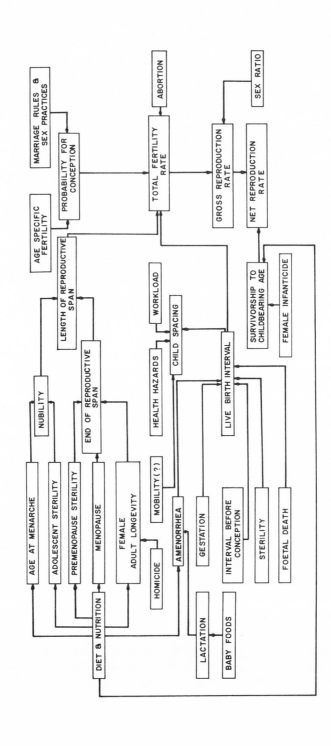

Figure 14.2. Biocultural determinants of net reproduction. Key variables include the length of the reproductive span, the child-spacing period, and survivorship to childbearing age.

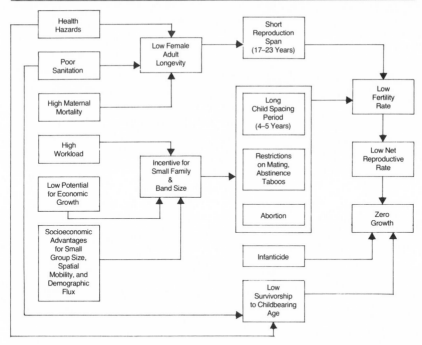

Figure 14.3.   The interplay between ecologic factors and the demographic characteristics of hunting-gathering communities.

ure cited by Pressat (1972) as characteristic of populations with high mortality. Howell (1976) reports a higher figure of .600, which we will use for hunter-gatherers enjoying, like the Bushmen, a healthy diet.

The Length of the Reproductive Span. The length of the reproductive span is delimited by the initiation of the capacity for conception (nubility) and the termination of the capacity by menopause or death. On the average, adult females in hunting-gathering communities did not live to menopausal age, dying at 30–35 years of age. Weiss (1973), on the basis of paleodemographic data and with the help of constructed life tables, estimates life expectancy at age 15 for the Australopithecines at 12.7 years, for the Neanderthals at 17.5 years, and for Upper Paleolithic populations at 16.9 years. He also estimates an average of 16.5 years for seven of the hunting-gathering populations living today.

The average age at death of all persons dying at age 15 or older for prehistoric populations (excluding the Australopithecines) was thus about 32–35 years. This is very similar to the average of 36 years for many populations from the Middle Bronze age to A.D. 1740 (Thomlin-

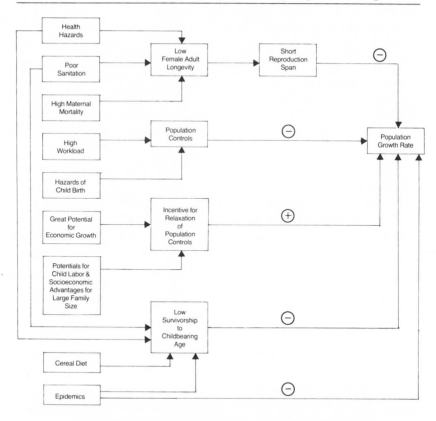

Figure 14.4   Mechanisms involved in the demographic transition from hunting-gathering to agriculture, which led to a noticeable increase in world population. Note that the
increase occurred despite the negative effect of the short reproduction span, low
survivorship to childbearing age, and cultural birth controls dictated by the work
regime and poor health conditions among early farmers.

son 1965, p. 77). It should also be noted that adult females in many
prehistoric populations died 2–4 years younger than did adult males
(Brothwell 1971; Angel 1972; Birdsell 1972).

The beginning of the reproductive period is determined by age at
menarche and the length of the period of adolescent sterility. The age
at menarche, which during the nineteenth century was about 15–16
years, coupled with a period of adolescent sterility of 1–4 years (Nag
1968; Tanner 1955; Frisch 1977), provides a reasonable estimate of
about 18 years as the probable age at nubility for prehistoric populations. In recent times, the age at menarche has been dropping. Pearl in
1939 estimated a world average of 15.2. Campbell (1966), 40 years
later, reports an average of 13.4 years.

Child Spacing. Child spacing is an important determinant of the fertility rate. The natural live birth interval for human populations is 27–28 months (Wrigley 1969; Barret 1972). This includes about 9 months for gestation, 10 months for amenorrhea, and 3 months for the period before conception, and allows for sterility and fetal death. Ethnographic observations (Krzywicki 1934; Carr-Saunders 1922; Howell 1976) indicate that hunter-gatherers have a long spacing period of 3–5 years.

Lee (1972) and Sussman (1972) link this long spacing period with the frequent spatial mobility of hunter-gatherers. Howell (1976) suggests that the long spacing is linked with a long period of breast feeding, which suppresses ovulation, as argued by Frisch (1977). Weiss (1976, p. 359) suggests that lack of baby or weaning food may be the cause for a lengthy lactation period. Hassan (1973, p. 535) has argued that a long child-spacing period would be favored among hunter-gatherers because it reduces the risk of health hazards to the mother and her children, given high work load and the young age of mothers. Whatever the reasons for a long spacing period, we may make use of about 40 months as an estimate of child spacing among hunter-gatherers (about 4 years, with allowance for resumption of conception for those females who lose an infant during the first year following birth).

Reproductive Potential and Potential Rate of Intrinsic Increase
Among hunter-gatherers, as noted above, the length of the reproductive span is shortened by the premature death of adult females at age 32 or younger and an age at nubility of 18 years. The natural live birth interval in human populations is about 28 months, and survivorship to childbearing age under preindustrial conditions could be placed at .600. Under these natural conditions, the average number of children per female (total fertility rate) would come to 6 children, of which 2.928 are likely to be females (assuming 48.8% female live births after Pressat 1972). The net reproductive rate (R_0), given these figures, would be 1.758, and the Lotka rate of natural increase would be 20 per 1,000 females as calculated from "$28/R_0 - 1$" (Pressat 1972, pp. 350–51).

This natural birth interval is less than the long child-spacing period, which we may estimate at 40 months. This prolonged spacing reduces the total fertility rate to 4.2 children and the net reproductive rate to 1.230, with a potential growth rate of 7.4 per 1,000 females. Under such conditions hunter-gatherers are capable of rapid and healthy growth, despite the short life span, a low rate of survivorship, and the prolonged child-spacing period.

It should be obvious that this potential for growth could be depressed by a variety of cultural controls, ranging from restrictive marriage and mating rules, through sex practices inhibitive to conception, abortion, and infanticide, to homicide (figs. 14.2 and 14.3). The universal presence of one form or another of cultural population controls among hunter-gatherers does indicate that hunter-gatherers are more often than not faced with the potential or the reality of excess offspring.

The impact of food shortage and a deterioration in diet, however, might have catastrophic consequences because of its adverse effect on female adult longevity and survivorship of infants to childbearing age. If the average age at death of adult females falls to 30 years and that of survivorship to .500, the net reproductive rate suffers a drop below 1 (.880). The impact could be still worse if menarche is delayed under poor nutritional conditions (Frisch 1977). A reduction of the child-spacing period may militate against such conditions, but since this would increase the work load on the mother (who is already suffering from poor health), this may serve only as a short-term solution. Under such conditions, whether by choice or by natural selection, only hunting-gathering population with an adequate diet are likely to survive.

The population growth of hunter-gatherers is essentially regulated by low survivorship to childbearing age, relatively high premenopausal death of adult females, and long child spacing. The low survivorship of children is characteristic of most human populations in preindustrial conditions. The premenopausal death of adult females is both a function of the higher mortality rates for preindustrial populations resulting from poor sanitation and lack of effective health care. The long child-spacing period, on the other hand, is most likely a phenomenon related to the high work load on mothers and the relative scarcity of baby foods. The population growth of hunter-gatherers may not thus reflect conditions of high fertility and high mortality as in standard demographic transition theories, but a condition of low fertility and high mortality. Weiss (1972) has already emphasized the role of mortality in regulating prehistoric hunting-gathering populations. The importance of the limited fertility of these populations has also been pointed out by Howell (1976).

Hunting-gathering populations are small. Regional units rarely ex-

ceed 1,000 persons (Wobst 1974). This implies that changes in populations size as a result of random change must have been very frequent
and sometimes even quite violent (Kunstadter 1972). Ammerman
(1975) has corroborated this view by a simulation study on the stochastic change of small populations. The frequent changes in age and
sex composition in a small group, which are due in part to shuffling of
individuals among and between groups, accentuates the fluctuations in
population size. Accordingly, it would seem that cultural and natural
selection will be in favor of a group size that is well below the carrying
capacity of the environment, as well as cultural population controls
that can be lifted or enforced, depending on the perception and anticipation of severe population fluctuations. The intergroup movement of
mates and exogamous relations would also have a selective advantage
as a regulatory mechanism if structured to ensure elimination of excess
mates in times of rapid population growth and recruitment of outside
mates when the population is undergoing a recession. Considering the
limited potentials for economic development under hunting-gathering
conditions and the spatial and seasonal distribution of wild food resources, the chances for remedying population problems by technological or economic improvement must have been very limited and
could not have been relied upon as a secure and reliable strategy to
cope with the endemic conditions of population fluctuations.*

Early Farming Populations

The relatively rapid fivefold increase in world population following
the adoption of early food production has been the subject of numerous
discussions (Sussman 1972; Hassan 1973; Lee 1972; Sengel 1973).
Sussman (1972) and Lee (1972) have suggested that the transition from
hunting-gathering to food production was associated with a reduction
in spatial mobility and hypothesized that this presumed reduction in
mobility permitted a reduction of child spacing.†

This argument is difficult to support, because although there is a
reduction in long-distance mobility, short-range daily mobility does

*Editors' Note: Compare the view of Cohen and of Lee on the importance of population
fluctuations and on the relation between human populations and carrying capacity in the Pleistocene.

†Editors' Note: Compare Lee's estimate of the stresses of hunter-gatherer mobility.

not seem to have been reduced, especially during the earliest periods of food production when food gathering was still widely practiced. Moreover, the work load per female does not diminish by the reduction in mobility, and it is the high work load per female that directly affects her ability to meet the nutritional demands of the fetus and newborn infant. More important than the figures that Lee (1972) shows on the increase in work load per female as a result of transporting children is the nutritional cost of closely spaced pregnancies. Sedentariness would not have altered that cost. Another factor which would tend to discourage frequent childbirth is that of birth hazards, which were only diminished in modern times. These hazards were not eliminated by a sedentary mode of life. The high ratio of women who died during the ages 20–30 compared to that of men of the same age category (Brothwell 1971) is an indication of the toll of birth hazards.

That sedentariness is not necessarily associated with a child-spacing period shorter than that for hunter-gatherers is documented by periods of 3–4 years among settled groups (Carr-Saunders 1922, pp. 166, 175; Krzywicki 1934, p. 178; Birdsell 1972, p. 357).

It seems thus that to explain population increase during the periods of early food production by reference to reduction in long-distance mobility and sedentariness is to lose sight of other crucial factors, such as high work load (which is not diminished by the reduction in long-distance mobility), birth hazards, and the nutritional cost of closely spaced births.

Sengel (1973) has hypothesized that population increase during the period of early food production is related to an increase in the intake of protein with the exploitation of cereals and the concomitant decrease in the age at menarche, extending the reproductive span. Hassan (1975, 1976) has suggested that despite the relatively high protein content of cereals, the quality of the protein is inferior to that of meat, and since the dietary changes during the period of early food production were toward a progressive reduction in the amount of meat consumed, the effect of the dietary change was probably to retard rather than to extend menarche to an earlier age. Esche and Lee (1975), however, link a high intake of carbohydrate with a decrease in the age at menarche.* The effects of low-quality protein foods and a carbohydrate-

*Editors' Note: The possible effects of altered carbohydrate intake on female fertility are discussed in greater detail by Cohen and by Lee.

based diet might have thus canceled each other out, leading to no significant change in the age at menarche. If the diet were improved as a result of an adequate diet of cereals, legumes, meat, and milk, the menarche could then be reached earlier, assuming that such a link between diet and menarche is indeed at work (Frisch 1977).

Determining the causes for population increase during the Neolithic, however, does not lie in just exploring the direct biocultural mechanisms by which the populations were capable of increasing their number, but mostly in finding out why such an increase was permitted at all by agricultural populations. We should recall here that hunting-gathering populations are capable of rates of increase that are equal to those under farming conditions. An average .1% annual rate of increase, reported for the Neolithic (Carneiro and Hilse 1966; Hassan 1973 and Cowgill 1975), is well within the capability of hunter-gatherers if cultural population controls were only partially relaxed. The reasons for this attitude should be sought in the changing economic conditions and the ecology of agricultural activities. Among the new factors that could have provided an incentive for a relaxation of population control are the socioeconomic potential of large families and groups for producing greater yield per capita and for effective defense. The scheduling of agricultural activities and the high demand for labor in certain peak periods (harvesting, sowing, processing) and the possibilities for child labor should have placed a higher value on offspring. Agricultural activities also require sustained, full-day input of labor in certain periods, which is unlike the more irregular work schedule of hunter-gatherers (Lee 1969). Addition of other members to the family could have reduced the length of the workday and allowed for skipping a workday or two by some members of the group while others carry on with the tasks. We should also note that early farmers did not abandon hunting and gathering altogether, and thus the demand for more people to solve the spatial conflict between hunting and cultivation is another motivating factor for permitting more offspring to survive.

The rewards for enlarging family and group size, coupled with the great economic growth potentials of agricultural systems (not the availability of surplus), could have minimized the economic cost of children. The value/cost ratio for children would thus have increased as a result of a reduction in the cost of children, at the very time when their value was enhanced.

It should be noted that a shift toward a cereal diet could have led to

an increase in the mortality of infants and children (Cook 1975; Wetterstrom 1975; Hassan 1976). Also, the impact of infectious diseases
on infants in agricultural systems is greater than that in hunting-gathering systems (Armelagos and McArdle 1975).* This might have led
to additional relaxation of population controls as a countermeasure. It
may also be noted that the availability of milk and cereals might have
provided substitutes for breast feeding (Weiss 1976) and could have
permitted a reduction in child spacing.

Summary

Population growth in preagricultural prehistoric times was on the average very slow. This was not a result of a biological low reproductive
potential, but a consequence of the low potential for economic growth
under hunting-gathering conditions. The hunters were not as much limited by their technology as by the limited yield of wild resources and
the spatial scatter and seasonal variations in the availability and abundance of wild game and plants. Not only was there a limit on the size
of regional groups, but there were also limits on the family and local
group size that would have favored the zero population growth ethic.
The limits for economic growth leave the hunter-gatherers with the
need for self-imposed controls if a boom-and-crash population growth
pattern is to be prevented. Such a pattern would have been deleterious
because of its disruptive impact on culture. Cultural controls, on the
other hand, could have been selected because they would have allowed
for cultural continuity and hence greater adaptive success. The flexible
character of these controls also means that a group could (1) relax or
totally lift such controls in the face of stochastic, or ecologically induced, plummeting of population size, or (2) take advantage of new
opportunities as during the transition from hunting-gathering to agriculture (see Cole 1957).
    The increase in population size during the Neolithic was motivated
on the local scale by the changes in the optimum economic group and
family size and by the great potentials for economic growth. As soon
as man switched from depending upon the natural yield of wild re-

---

Editors' Note: A further discussion of the impact of infectious diseases before and after the
Neolithic revolution is provided by Cohen.

sources to controlling the yield of resources by cultivation and herding, the potentials for multiplying the yield by innovations were almost beyond any limit. Even now, the increase in yield via human intervention has not abated. The recent "green revolution" has its roots in the first "green revolution," the Neolithic.

Acknowledgement

I wish to dedicate this essay to the memory of Steven Polgar, whose untimely death shortly before this symposium was held is a serious loss to his friends and to demographic anthropology.

References

Acsadi, G., and Nemeskeri, J. 1970. *History of human life span and mortality*. Budapest: Akademiai Kiado.
Ammerman, A. J. 1975. Late Pleistocene population alternatives. *Hum. Ecol.* 3(4):219–33.
Angel, J. L. 1972. Ecology and population in the Eastern Mediterranean. *World Archaeol.* 4:88–105.
Armelagos, G., and McArdle, A. 1975. Population, disease and evolution. In *Population studies in archaeology and biological anthropology: a symposium*, ed. A. C. Swedlund, pp. 1–10. Soc. Am. Archaeol. Mem. 30.
Barret, J. C. 1972. A Monte Carlo simulation of reproduction. In *Biological aspects of demography*, ed. W. Brass. London: Taylor and Francis, Ltd.
Birdsell, J. 1972. *Human evolution*. New York: Rand McNally.
Bogue, D. J. 1969. *Principles of demography*. New York: Wiley.
Brothwell, D. R. 1971. Palaeodemography. In *Biological aspects of demography*, ed. W. Brass. London: Taylor and Francis.
Campbell, A. A. 1966. *Human evolution*. Chicago: Aldine.
Carneiro, R. L., and Hilse, D. F. 1966. On determining the probable rate of population growth during the Neolithic. *Am. Anthropol.* 68:177–81.
Carr-Saunders, A. M. 1922. *The population problem*. London: Oxford Univ. Press.
Coale, A. 1974. The history of human population. *Sci. Am.* 231(3):41–51.
Cole, L. C. 1957. Sketches of general and comparative demography. *Cold Spring Harbor Symp. Quant. Biol.* 22:19–31.
Cook, D. C. 1975. Changes in subsistence base: the human skeletal evidence. Paper delivered at 74th Annu. Meet. Am. Anthropol. Assoc., San Francisco.
Cowgill, G. L. 1975. Population pressure as a non-explanation. *Am. Antiq.* 40(2):1277–31.
Deevey, Edward S., Jr. 1960. The human population. *Sci. Am.* 203:195–204.

Esche, H., and Lee, R. 1975. Is maximum optimum in human physiology? Paper delivered at 74th Annu. Meet. Am. Anthropol. Assoc., San Francisco.

Frisch, R. E. 1977. Population, food intake, and fertility. *Science* 199:22–30.

Hassan, F. A. 1973. On mechanisms of population growth during the Neolithic. *Curr. Anthropol.* 14(5):535–40.

———. 1975. Determinants of the size, density and growth rate of hunting-gathering populations. In *Population, ecology and social evolution*, ed. Steven Polgar. The Hague: Mouton.

———. 1976. Diet, nutrition, and agricultural origins in the Near East. In *Origine de l'élévage et de la domestication*, ed. E. Higgs, pp. 227–47. Nice: IXe Congr. Union Int. Sci. Préhist. Protohist.

———. 1978. Prehistoric demography. In *Advances in archaeological method and theory*, vol. 1, ed., M. Schiffer, pp. 49–103. New York: Academic Press.

Henneberg, M. 1976. Reproductive possibilities and estimation of the biological dynamics of earlier populations. In *The demographic evolution of human populations*, ed. R. H. Ward and K. M. Weiss, pp. 41–48. New York: Academic Press.

Howell, N. 1976. Toward a uniformitarian theory of human paleodemography. In *The demographic evolution of human populations*, ed. R. H. Ward and K. M. Weiss, pp. 25–40. London: Academic Press.

Krzywicki, L. 1934. *Primitive society and its vital statistics*. London: Macmillan.

Kunstadter, P. 1972. Demography, ecology, social structure, and settlement patterns. In *The structure of human populations*, ed. G. A. Harrison and A. J. Boyce, pp. 313–51. Oxford: Clarendon Press.

Lee, R. B. 1969. !Kung bushmen subsistence: an input-output analysis. In *Environment and cultural behavior*, ed. A. P. Vayda, pp. 47–49. New York: The Natural History Press.

———. 1972. Population growth and the beginnings of sedentary life among the !Kung bushmen. In *Population growth: anthropological implications*, ed. B. Spooner, pp. 327–50. Cambridge, Mass.: M.I.T. Press.

Nag, M. 1968. *Factors affecting fertility in non-industrial societies: a cross-cultural study*. New Haven: Human Relations Area File Press. (Reprinted from a 1962 edition.)

Pearl, R. 1939. *The natural history of population*. London: Oxford University Press.

Polgar, S. 1972. Population history and population policies from an anthropological perspective. *Curr. Anthropol.* 13:203–11, 260–62.

Pressat, R. 1972. *Demographic analysis*. Chicago: Aldine-Atherton.

Sengel, R. A. 1973. Discussion and criticisms. *Curr. Anthropol.* 14(5):540–42.

Sussman, R. M. 1972. Child transport, family size, and increase in human population during the Neolithic. *Curr. Anthropol.* 13:258–59.

Tanner, J. M. 1955. *Growth at adolescence*. Springfield, Ill.: Thomas.

Thomlinson, R. 1965. *Population dynamics*. New York: Random House.

Weiss, K. M. 1972. A general measure of human population growth regulation. *Am. J. Phys. Anthropol.* 37:337–44.

———. 1973. Demographic models for anthropology. Mem. Soc. Am. Archaeol. 27. Issued as *Am. Antiq.* 38(2), part 2.

———. 1976. Demographic theory and anthropological inference. *Annu. Rev. Anthropol.* 5:351–81.

Wetterstrom, W. E. 1975. Nutrition and paleodemography at Pueblo Arroyo Hondo. Paper delivered at the 74th Annu. Meet. Am. Anthropol. Assoc., San Francisco.

Wobst, H. M. 1974. Boundary conditions for Paleolithic social systems: a simulation approach. *Am. Antiq.* 39(2):147–78.

Wrigley, E. A. 1969. *Population and history.* New York: McGraw-Hill.

15

LACTATION, OVULATION, INFANTICIDE, AND WOMEN'S WORK: A STUDY OF HUNTER-GATHERER POPULATION REGULATION

Richard B. Lee

How do human hunter-gatherers regulate their numbers? Most observers have agreed that some form of population regulation is essential, simply because humans share with all successful species an "inherent excessive fertility," to use Birdsell's phrase (1968), while hunter-gatherer population densities remain strictly limited. Hunter-gatherers throughout prehistory have therefore had to tread the fine line between too much regulation of fertility, which could result in extinction (Schrire and Steiger 1974), and too little regulation, which could achieve the same effect by the too rapid expansion of the population and the exhaustion of resources. We have little knowledge of those who failed, but the fact that humans expanded to occupy six continents before the advent of agriculture is testimony to the degree of their success in treading this line.

In thinking about the ways that hunters have regulated their numbers, a wide variety of mechanisms have been suggested, including warfare, migration, starvation, and, paradoxically, local extinction. Undoubtedly, each of these scenarios has been played out at various times and places in humanity's long prehistory. But to invoke these mechanisms as the major explanations is like invoking catastrophism to explain the evolution of species.* I favor the search for a mechanism or mechanisms that arise out of the basic adaptation of the hunter-gatherers, a mechanism or mechanisms that can be calibrated or fine-tuned to respond to minor fluctuations in resources long before the thresholds of disaster are reached—in other words a self-regulating system.

*Editors' Note: Alternative views of the roles played by each of these mechanisms are offered by Cohen and by Hassan.

321

This line of inquiry has focused attention on two major mechanisms: systematic infanticide and the control of ovulation by lactation. Both kinds of mechanisms—one cultural, the other physiological—offer the possibility for modifying fertility in such a way that the reproductive success of the individual and the overall survival of the group are brought into congruence. Periodic warfare and starvation, by contrast, seem a more expensive and risky way in the short run of ensuring group survival in the long run.

Those who see infanticide as the primary regulating mechanism and those who credit suppression of ovulation by lactation have differed over the relative weight of each mechanism in determining family size. Birdsell (1968) has postulated a 15–50% rate of infanticide for all human births in the Pleistocene, and notes that "medical science has not yielded accurate information on the relationships between nursing and ovulation needed to fix the figure more accurately."

In the decade since Birdsell's excellent paper, a great deal of research has been conducted on the relation of lactation to ovulation and on the duration of the anovulatory period in nursing mothers. We are now in a much better position to evaluate the cultural and physiological mechanisms that regulate fertility in human hunter-gatherers and in humans in general. Recent evidence enables us now to make a clearer statement of how early human populations may have regulated their numbers, and how this situation changed dramatically with the onset of the Neolithic Revolution.

The argument is presented in the form of a case study of the !Kung San, a nomadic hunting and gathering people of northern Botswana who were in the process of settling down during the period of the research (1963–73).* The chapter starts with an analysis of the dual role of women in the productive and reproductive spheres and traces the points of articulation between the two spheres by means of a quantitative model of work. Nomadic !Kung women have an average interval between live births of almost 4 years. This shortens dramatically with the onset of sedentary life. Next, we examine the physiological

Editors' Note: There is considerable debate in anthropology about the use of the !Kung as a model for understanding Pleistocene hunter-gatherers. Both Lee and Cohen extrapolate !Kung data to the Pleistocene, albeit with some reservations. Ripley argues that the !Kung are atypical and cannot be used as a basis for extrapolation. She offers specific hypotheses to account for their anomalous condition.

mechanisms underlying long birth spacing and the reasons for its shortening with sedentarization.

Two main causal explanations are considered: the critical fatness hypothesis (Frisch and McArthur 1974; Howell 1976a) and the nursing stimulus hypothesis (Kippley 1975; Knodel 1977); both the !Kung evidence and the comparative data seem to favor the latter hypothesis. The conclusion briefly spells out the implications of this case study for human psychosocial development.

Production and Reproduction

Women play a dual role in !Kung society: as producers of food and the necessities of life, and as reproducers, to whom falls the major task of bearing and raising the next generation of gatherers and hunters. This dual role, which !Kung women share with women in all preindustrial societies, places them in a strategically central position, since for the !Kung the work of subsistence and of child rearing forms a very large proportion of the total work carried out by the society. This is in marked contrast to the situation in industrial societies, where women are often marginalized by being excluded from the labor force and confined to the home or concentrated in menial jobs of low productivity.

Like the men, !Kung women range widely through the countryside to find food. This necessity for mobility is a key factor in the foraging mode of production. Against this are the demands placed upon women in their other role, reproduction: pregnancy, childbirth, lactation, and the necessity to care for and carry the young infants tend to draw a woman toward the home and to reduce her mobility. Women are thus at the intersection of two critical systems within the foraging economy: the productive system and the reproductive system, each with its conflicting demands.* The one necessitates mobility and the other penalizes it. In hunting and gathering societies there is a tight articulation between these two systems, so that a change of the variables in one system leads to adjustment of the variables in the other.

Editors' Note: See Ripley for a further discussion of the possible consequences of focusing both productive and reproductive roles and choices on women.

Given this articulation, what are the factors that regulate !Kung fertility under traditional hunting and gathering conditions, and how might these factors be altered in a shift from a nomadic to a sedentary life? The predictive model of changing !Kung fertility was originally presented at a conference on population growth in 1970 and published 2 years later in a paper entitled "Population growth and the beginnings of sedentary life among the !Kung Bushmen" (Lee 1972). Pages 324–34 are a recapitulation of the argument in Lee 1972. Data to test the predictions of the model against actual birth statistics were collected in a restudy of the Dobe !Kung in 1973. These are presented in pages 334–38 (see also Lee 1979).

The Role of Women in the !Kung Economy

Woman's work—gathering wild vegetable foods—provides well over half of all the food consumed by a !Kung camp. Men's hunting activities and gifts of food from other camps makes up the remainder. Subsistence work occupies 2 or 3 days of work per week for each adult woman. On each workday a woman walks from 3 to 20 km (2–12 miles) round trip, and on the return leg she carries loads of 7–15 kg. Subsistence work, visits, and group moves require an adult woman to walk about 2,400 km (1,500 miles) during the course of an annual round. For at least half of this distance she carries substantial burdens of food, water, or material goods.

Of course, the major burden carried by women has yet to be mentioned. On most gathering trips and on every visit and group move, a woman has to carry with her each of her children under the age of 4 years. Infants and young children have an extremely close relationship with their mothers (Draper 1976; Konner 1976). For the first few years of an infant's life mother and child are rarely separated by more than a few paces. Although solid foods are introduced at the age of 6 months or earlier, breast feeding continues into the third or fourth year of life. For the first year or two, infants are carried on the mother's back in the special baby carrier. Then from 2–4 years of age they are carried in the kaross or straddling the mother's shoulder. For the first 2 years of life, a child is carried everywhere. In the third year some babysitting occurs, and this increases in the fourth year. For each of the first 2 years of life, a child is carried by the mother for a distance of 2,400 km; in the third year this decreases to about 1,800 km; and in the fourth year to about 1,200 km. Over the 4-year period of dependency, a !Kung mother will carry her child a total distance of around 7,800 km (4,900 miles).

The Reproductive System

The onset of puberty in girls is late compared to western standards, usually occurring between the ages of 15 and 17. First pregnancies are further delayed for several years by postmenarcheal adolescent sterility (Howell 1976b). Thus, a woman does not bear her first child until she is between 18 and 22 years of age. The first pregnancy is followed by four to eight others spaced 3–5 years apart until menopause occurs after age 40. Howell has noted that !Kung fertility appears to be lower than among other populations (Howell 1979).

What is critical to the present analysis is not the overall fertility picture as expressed in birthrate but the frequency with which successive births occur to individual women—that is, the interval between births or birth spacing, expressed in months or years.

The Economic Consequences of Birth Spacing

Since every child has to be carried, it is fortunate that generally the birth interval among the !Kung is as long as it is. The advantage of long birth spacing to hunter-gatherers is obvious. A mother can devote her full attention to caring for an offspring for a longer period, and the older the offspring is when his mother turns to the care of the subsequent young, the better are his chances for survival.

There is also the matter of the sheer weight of an infant to be carried by the mother. A woman whose children are spaced 4 years apart will have only one child to carry at any one time. By the time the next infant is born, the older child is mature enough to walk on his own. On the other hand, a woman whose births are spaced only 2 years apart will have to carry two children at once; a newborn to 2-year-old on the back and a 3- to 4-year-old on the shoulder. No sooner is the older child "weaned" from the shoulder when yet another newborn arrives. The !Kung San of the Dobe area recognize the plight of the woman with high fertility and express it in the saying: "A woman who gives birth like an animal to one offspring after another has a permanent backache."

The actual work involved in raising young children in a hunting

Table 15.1. Average Weight in Kilograms and Pounds by Age for 40 San Children from Birth to 8 Years

Age (years)	kg	Range (kg)	lb	Range (lb)	Number of observations	Number of individuals
0–1	6.0	3.1–8.7	13.2	7–19	32	12
1–2	8.8	7.3–11.8	19.4	16–26	21	12
2–3	11.6	8.2–14.1	25.6	18–31	15	9
3–4	12.4	10.9–15.0	27.4	24–33	15	7
4–5	13.4	9.5–15.9	29.6	21–35	31	11
5–6	14.7	12.3–16.8	32.3	27–37	20	10
6–7	15.3	11.8–17.7	33.8	26–39	13	7
7–8	17.6	12.7–19.5	38.7	28–43	17	5
Total					164	73[a]

[a]A number of individuals appear in two or more age categories.

and gathering society is in large part a function of three variables: weight of children, the distance to be traveled, and the frequency with which children are born to a given woman. Fortunately, each of these variables can be precisely quantified, and from their interaction a simple calculus can be developed to show more precisely the relationship between birth spacing and woman's work—that is, between the reproductive system and the productive system.

Women's Work

The Weights of Infants and Children. !Kung adults are small in stature and light in weight by western standards. Birth weights and rates of infant growth for the first 6 months of life are comparable to western standards. Thereafter, children grow more slowly than do western children. The weights of the former at each age run about 75–80% of the latter. For example, a 3½-year-old American child weighs about 16.0 kg, while a !Kung child of about the same age weighs 12.5 kg (Truswell and Hansen 1976).

The average weights of !Kung infants and children from birth to 8 years are shown in table 15.1. The figures are based on 164 observations on 40 children weighed during field work in 1967–69. The values vary from 6.0 kg in the first year of life to 17.6 kg in the eighth year. Note that these figures represent average weight during the year, not

Table 15.2.   Work Load of Women with Children of Various Ages

Child's Age (Years)	Average weight of child		Average annual distance to be carried		Work load for the mother (kg/km)
	kg	lb	km	miles	
0–1	6.0	(13.2)	2,400	1,500	14,400
1–2	8.8	(19.4)	2,400	1,500	21,120
2–3	11.6	(25.6)	1,800	1,125	20,880
3–4	12.4	(27.4)	1,200	750	14,880
4–5	13.4	(29.5)	—	—	—
5–6	14.7	(32.3)	—	—	—
6–7	15.3	(33.8)	—	—	—
7–8	17.6	(38.7)	—	—	—

the weight attained at the end of the year. Presenting the data in this form enables us to calculate the average burden to be carried by the mother during each year of the child's life.

In the first year children weigh from 3.1 kg at birth to a high of 8.7 kg for an exceptionally fat older infant, with the average weight of infants being 6.0 kg. In the second year of life the mother's burden is 8.8 kg, with a range of 7.3–11.8 kg. By the fourth year this average has increased to 12.4 kg, with a range of 10.9 to as high as 15.0 kg.

The Distance to be Traveled. I have estimated that a woman walks about 2,400 km during a year's activity. Apart from the food, water, and personal belongings, a woman will carry each of her children under the age of 4 for all or much of this distance. The weight she actually carries is determined by the age of the child and its rate of growth. Table 15.2 shows the different burdens of women with children of various ages. I introduce the useful, although somewhat cumbersome, measure of the "kilogram/kilometer," which is simply a product of weight times distance; that is, a load of 1 kg carried a distance of 1 km.

The Interval between Births. Given a mean birth interval among nomadic San of 4 years (for women of normal fertility), the work load of an average woman's reproductive career can be estimated. Her first baby is born in year 1, her second baby in year 5, her third in year 9, and so on. Each year she will have a variable weight of child to carry, depending on the age of the child. For a 10-year period her work effort will be as shown in table 15.3.

Table 15.3. Average Daily Burden over a 10-Year Period for a Woman
with 4-Year Birth Spacing

	Year	Kilograms to carry
First baby	1	6.0
	2	8.8
	3	11.6
	4	12.7
Second baby	5	6.0
	6	8.8
	7	11.6
	8	12.7
Third baby	9	6.0
	10	8.8

During the 10-year period the average woman will raise three children and will have carried an average burden of 9.2 kg/day. Her burden will be least during the years when she is carrying a newborn (6.0 kg/day) and greatest when she is carrying a 3-year-old (12.4 kg/day plus the burden of being pregnant at the same time).

With shorter birth spacing, both the number of children and the weight of children to be carried will go up. Table 15.4 shows the work load required of mothers with four different birth intervals: 2, 3, 4 and 5 years. The table shows the number of babies and the weight in babies for each year of a 10-year period of the reproductive career.

As one moves from longer to shorter birth spacing, the work required of the mother progressively increases. At one extreme, a mother with 5-year spacing will at the end of 10 years have raised two children and will have carried an average daily burden of only 7.8 kg (17.2 lb). At the other extreme, a woman with 2-year spacing will, after the same time period, have five children, and her average daily burden will have been 17.0 kg (37.4 lb), and for 4 of the 10 years will have been as high as 21.2 kg (46.6 lb). Two-year birth spacing would, in fact, represent a theoretical upper limit of birth frequency for San women living under hunting and gathering conditions, since to carry more than two babies would be beyond a woman's capabilities.

For the majority of fertile women living as foragers, the intervals between live births varies between 5 and 3 years (see below). Shortening the birth interval from 5 to 4 years adds a daily burden of 1.4 kg to a woman's work load. Shortening the interval further from 4 to 3

Table 15.4. Effect of Different Birth Intervals on Work Effort of Mother

	Birth interval							
	2 years		3 years		4 years		5 years	
Year	Weight (kg)	Baby no.	Weight (kg)	Baby no.	Weight (kg)	Baby no.	Weight (kg)	Baby no.
1	6.0	1	6.0	1	6.0	1	6.0	1
2	8.8	1	8.8	1	8.8	1	8.8	1
3	17.6	1 & 2	11.6	1	11.6	1	11.6	1
4	21.2	1 & 2	18.4	1 & 2	12.4	1	12.4	1
5	17.6	2 & 3	8.8	2	6.0	2	—	2
6	21.2	2 & 3	11.6	2	8.8	2	6.0	2
7	17.6	3 & 4	18.4	2 & 3	11.6	2	8.8	2
8	21.2	3 & 4	8.8	3	12.4	2	11.6	2
9	17.6	4 & 5	11.6	3	6.0	3	12.4	2
10	21.2	4 & 5	18.4	3 & 4	8.8	3	—	—
No. of children at end of 10 years	5		4		3		2	
Average weight of baby per annum	17.0 kg (6–21.2)		12.2 kg (6–18.4)		9.2 kg (6–12)		7.8 kg (0–12)	
No. of years carrying 2 children	8		3		0		0	
No. of years carrying 1 or 0 children	2		7		10		10	

Table 15.5. Work per Mother per Year According to Birth Spacing (kg/km)

	Birth interval			
	2 years	*3 years*	*4 years*	*5 years*
Average kg/km per year	32,064	22,824	17,808	14,256

years more than doubles the increase in burden to 3.0 kg, for a total weight of 12.2 kg.

We have noted how actual work for the mother is a product of weight carried times distance traveled. To carry a child for 1 year requires between 14,000 and 21,000 kg/km of effort by the mother. To carry one child for the full 4 years requires a total of 72,280 kg/km and the average per year of 17,820 kg/km.

Table 15.5 shows how the amount of work is affected by different lengths of birth spacing. The curve of increased work effort rises slowly as the birth interval shortens from 5 to 4 years; it rises more steeply as the birth interval reduces to 3 years, and extremely sharply as the interval is further reduced to 2 years. This table indicates some of the "costs" in work effort of raising children under nomadic hunting and gathering conditions, and it also shows the added costs of an increase in the birth rate.

A mother with 5-year birth spacing will have two children at the end of 10 years. To add a third child during the same period (by lowering the birth interval to 4 years) will add only 3,500 kg/km to a mother's work load. To add a fourth child (by further lowering the birth interval to 3 years) will "cost" 40% more than the cost of adding a third child—5,016 kg/km as opposed to 3,542 kg/km. And to add a fifth child (by lowering the birth interval even further to 2 years) would "cost" over 2½ times as much per child as adding a third.

Given these "high costs" of short birth spacing, it is not surprising that under nomadic conditions the birth intervals average close to 4 years, and this is maintained even in the absence of contraceptive measures; the !Kung practice postpartum sex taboos, but only during the first year of the baby's life. This long birth spacing is adaptive both at the individual level and at the level of population. The individual woman is better equipped to care for each of her children if births do not follow too closely one after another, and this long birth spacing lowers overall fertility so that the population does not grow so rapidly that it threatens the food supply. Long birth spacing alone is not sufficient to keep the population in long-term balance with resources, but the modest amount of excess fertility of the !Kung is readily absorbed by infant mortality, occasional infanticide, and outmigration.*

In this context it is worth noting that the slow rates of growth of !Kung children, mentioned earlier, are also adaptive. For people who have to walk a lot, small babies are easier to carry than large babies. This is another way that smallness makes sense in terms of the nomadic foraging way of life. If the !Kung children grew as fast as they should according to western standards (see Truswell and Hansen 1976), an intolerable burden would be imposed on the parents, who would have to do the carrying, thereby reducing the survival chances of both generations. It is also worth noting that among adult !Kung, shorter men are more successful hunters than are taller men (Lee 1979).

Mobility, Birth Spacing, and Population Growth

I have examined the implications of higher and lower fertility levels for the economic adaptation of the hunting and gathering San. More babies and/or greater distances to travel mean more work for San mothers. Similarly, work effort would decline with fewer babies and/ or less walking. It is the latter possibility—less walking or reduction of mobility—that is of interest here. This is precisely what happens when hunters and gatherers shift to agriculture. Even partial agriculture allows more food to be grown closer to home, allowing the population to maintain the same level of nutrition with much less walking.†

What are the consequences for a !Kung mother's work load of a partial shift to food sources closer to home? To raise one child to the point where he can walk by himself requires four years of carrying, for an average annual work load of 17,820 kg/km. This average is based on 1,200–2,400 km/year of walking. If walking is reduced by a third—to 800–1,600 km/year—the annual work load falls to 11,880 kg/km.

Table 15.6 sketches the implications of reduced work effort for birth spacing. Formerly, the mother with 5-year birth spacing had an

Editors' Note: Note that Lee, Ripley, Hassan, and Cohen all agree that physiological birth spacing mechanisms are inadequate to account for low hunter-gatherer growth rates. The disagreement among them is largely one of emphasis.

†*Editors' Note:* Both Hassan and Cohen question Lee's emphasis on the reduction of physical stresses which accompanies sedentism.

Table 15.6. Effect of Reduced Mobility on Fertility

| | kg/km Work per year for women with various birth intervals | | | |
	2 years	3 years	4 years	5 years
Under nomadic conditions:				
1,200–2,400 km/year	32,064	22,824	17,808	14,256
Under more sedentary conditions:				
800–1,600 km/year	21,376	15,216	11,872	9,504

annual work load of 14,256 kg/km. Under the more sedentary conditions, this falls to 9,504 kg/km. A mother with 4-year birth spacing used to work 17,808 kg/km per year. Now she works only 11,872 kg/km, which is less than that of a mother with 5-year birth spacing under the nomadic conditions.

What this means in practical terms is that with reduced mobility a woman may shorten the interval between successive births and continue to give each child adequate care while keeping her work effort a constant. To put it another way, a mother can have more children with no increase in work effort. Table 15.6 shows how a mother may now have babies every 3 years with slightly less work effort than having babies every 4 years required under nomadic conditions (15,216 kg/km vs. 17,800 kg/km). Shortening the mean birth interval results in a general rise in the level of fertility, which, in turn, leads to an upswing in the rate of population growth.

I do not intend to imply that sedentarization alone causes population growth. In the first instance, reduction of mobility may produce a situation where the number of children remains the same but there is more leisure time. What I am suggesting here is that settling down removes the adverse effects of high fertility on individual women. Among hunters and gatherers high natural fertility is maladaptive: even with 3-year birth spacing the mother's work load may be great enough to endanger her own fitness and affect the survival chances of her offspring. With sedentary life these restraints are removed: 3-year birth spacing becomes no more strenuous to the mother than was 4-year birth spacing to mothers under nomadic conditions.

Thus, for the population as a whole, sedentarization may lead to the upsetting of the hunting-gathering low-fertility adaptation and trig-

ger population growth, even in the absence of any expansion in the
food supply. The cause of the sedentarization need not be the shift to
agriculture, although such a shift is occurring among the !Kung San.
It is apparent that any change in the subsistence economy that allows
reduced mobility may be sufficient to increase fertility. Such preagricultural examples of sedentarization as the exploitation of wild grains
with a milling technology or the exploitation of coastal and riverine
resources may have had a similar effect of increasing fertility by reducing mobility.

The relation between nomadism and long birth spacing has been
known at least since 1922, when Sir Alexander Carr-Saunders referred
to "the problem of transportation in nomadic societies." He pointed out
that the necessity of carrying children for the first few years of life
sharply limited the number of children a woman could successfully
rear during her reproductive span (Carr-Saunders 1922). J. B. Birdsell
speaks of at least a 3-year birth interval among Australian aboriginal
women (Birdsell 1968). To my knowledge the first person to pinpoint
live birth spacing as a key variable in the shift from hunting and gathering to sedentary life was Lewis R. Binford, as quoted by John Pfeiffer in *The emergence of man* (1969, p. 218):

Binford suggests that one result (of a more reliable food supply at the end of
the Pleistocene) may have been a increased trend toward year round settlements reducing the need to pack up and move on to new hunting grounds,
and permitting an adjustment of primitive birth control measures. As long as
mothers had to keep on the move, they were limited to one child every three
or four years because that was all they could carry but infanticide could be
relaxed in more settled times with fish and fowl to supplement basic supplies
of reindeer meat.

Note that unlike the present theory, Binford points to infanticide as the
key mechanism of hunter-gatherer population control. Sedentarization
in his view triggers population growth through a reduction of infanticide and not through a shortening of the birth interval. Birdsell (1968)
also sees infanticide as the key mechanism, arguing that "difficulties
of nursing and mobility in the Pleistocene may have made necessary
the killing of 15–50% of children born, since lactation alone would not
have provided sufficient spacing of births to provide equilibrium" (p.
243).

My own view is that such a level of infanticide is *not* a necessary component of hunter-gatherer population control. (It should be added, however, that this low level could easily rise should the need come about.) Under most foraging conditions the !Kung are able to maintain very low fertility through long birth spacing with a rate of infanticide of less than 2% (Howell 1976b). In fact, we are now in a position to specify precisely how long the birth intervals are under hunting and gathering conditions and how these birth intervals change when the !Kung settle down to village life.

!Kung Birth Spacing: A Test of the Hypothesis

Starting with July 1963, our research project has maintained a registry of births (and deaths) in the Dobe population. During field work birth dates were recorded by direct observation. These dates are usually accurate ±5 days. When there was no observer in the field, birth dates were reconstructed through interviews. These dates are usually accurate to ±30 days. In all we followed the reproductive lives of 256 adult women over the 10-year period 1963–73.

A process of sedentarization was going on in the Dobe area, but this had a markedly differential effect on groups at different waterholes. At one eastern waterhole (!Goshe), the San had built a village of mud huts in the early 1960s and essentially occupied this same site throughout the study period. They continued to hunt and gather on short trips, but an increasing proportion of their subsistence came from cows' milk and cultivated grains. At the other extreme of mobility were the /Du/da subpopulation 60 km south of the Dobe area, who moved camp five or six times a year in a classic foraging pattern. The remainder of the population exhibited patterns intermediate between these two poles. This varied situation offered the investigator a natural laboratory for testing hypotheses about the social, economic, and demographic effects of sedentarization.

After the original study appeared in print (Lee 1972), I returned to the Dobe area the following year to complete the 10-year record of births and deaths and to provide data for testing the hypothesis about the relationship between birth spacing and sedentarization. The 256 adult women included virtually all the resident women of reproductive age (15–59) in the population. Basically, there were two sets of cross-cutting variables characterizing the women in the sample: the stage of

Table 15.7. Women of Reproductive Age in the Dobe Area, 1963–1973

Stage of reproductive career	Number of pregnancies 1963–73			
	None	One	Two +	Total women
Early[a]	24	22	16	62
Middle[b]	63	19	73	155
Late[c]	32	2	3	37
Total	119	43	92	254[d]

[a] Women for whom menarche occurred during period 1963–73.
[b] Postmenarcheal women between the ages of 15 and 59.
[c] Women who underwent menopause during the period 1963–73.
[d] For two women of total 256, data were insufficient.

the reproductive career and the number of children born; this yielded the nine categories of women in table 15.7. Of the total, 119 women had no pregnancies during the period 1 July 1963–30 June 1973. Forty-three others had only one pregnancy, and for two women the data were insufficient, leaving 92 women with two or more births and hence with one or more measurable birth intervals.

The first step was to consider all the birth intervals while acknowledging that infant mortality could shorten the interval considerably. The average interval between successive births was 37.23 months for all 92 women (165 intervals). That means that over 3 years elapsed between births, whether or not the first baby died. This figure varied from a low of 11 months in a woman whose infant died in the first week of life and who conceived soon after, to a high of over 8 years in a woman of very low fertility. This figure is very high for a population in which no forms of contraception are practiced.

To eliminate the effects of infant mortality, I abstracted from the data those birth intervals in which the first child survived to the birth of the second. I further divided the population into two groups: women at *more nomadic* foraging camps and women at *more sedentary* non-foraging villages. Finally, I divided the 10-year run of data into two 5-year periods. This last division yielded three temporally related sets of data: (1) intervals falling within the period 1 July 1963–30 June 1968, (2) intervals falling within the period 1 July 1968–30 June 1973, and (3) intervals straddling the mid-1968 boundary. By comparing period 1 with period 2 we could discern possible secular trends through the 10-year period.

Table 15.8. Intervals in Months between Successive Live Births to !Kung
Women during the Period 1963–1973

	Mean Length of Birth Interval in Months (n)			
	1963–68	*1968–73*	*1963–73*	*Mean of all three periods*
More nomadic women	42.27 (11)	36.42 (12)	47.63 (32)	44.11 (55)
More sedentary women	38.35 (17)	29.82 (22)	40.12 (26)	36.17 (65)
All women	39.89 (28)	32.15 (34)	44.26 (58)	39.81 (120)

The results are set out in table 15.8. The mean birth interval for
nomadic women was 44.11 months and for sedentary women 36.17
months, indicating that throughout the period sedentary women tended
to reconceive about 8 months earlier than did nomadic women. This 8-
month difference would significantly increase both the birth rate and
completed family size for the sedentary women.

The difference between more nomadic and more sedentary women
comes into even sharper contrast when we examine the time dimension. The entire population was undergoing sedentarization during the
period 1963–73, and this is reflected in the fact that the birth interval
for all women dropped from 39.89 months in period 1 to 32.15 months
in period 2. This shortening of the birth interval was particularly
marked for more sedentary women, with a drop of 8.53 months, but
the process is apparent in the more nomadic women as well, who exhibited a decrease of 5.85 months. The increase in fertility was most
marked at the most settled village of !Goshe, where there were four
young women each of whom in the period 1968–73 had had two successive live births spaced 22, 23, 21, and 20 months apart, respectively.

To illustrate the effects of birth spacing on actual people, here are
case histories of several women, representing first the more nomadic
and then the more sedentary categories.

1. /Twa (born 1933) is a married woman who alternates between
!Kubi and /Xai/xai waterholes, spending a large proportion of her time
with her group foraging in her husband's n!ore in the southwestern Aha
hills. In 1968, /Twa had three well-spaced children: //Koka (born c.

1960), !Xam (born 2/63), and N!ai (born 3/68). She had a fourth birth
9/71 and when interviewed in 8/73 she was about 3 months' pregnant.
Three of her birth intervals fall roughly within the study period:

2/63–3/68	61 months
3/68–9/71	42 months
9/71–c. 1/74	28 months

The average birth interval was 43.67 months, with clear evidence of a
shortening of the interval through the 10-year period.

2. N ≠ isa (born c. 1941) has lived with her husband at cattle posts
at Mahopa and Bate. In addition to an older son by a previous husband,
N ≠ isa has had five pregnancies since the early 1960s, a girl //Kushe
(born 1962), a boy /Tishe (born 2/65), a boy Bo (born 10/68, de-
ceased), and another boy /Twi (born 3/71). She was in the middle
stages of pregnancy when observed in July 1973. Her three birth intervals within the study period are as follows:

2/65–10/68	44 months
10/68–3/71	29 months
3/71–c. 10/73	31 months

The average birth interval was 34.67 months and there was some evidence of shortening through the period, although N ≠ isa does not approach the very short intervals (20–24 months) of some of the !Goshe
girls.

3. An example of the latter is N!uhka (born 1947), who has spent
most of her life at cattle posts north of the Dobe area and who married
a !Goshe man in the mid 1960s. She had one stillbirth prior to 1968
(undated) and a pregnancy that spontaneously aborted in 9/68. She had
a baby girl in 4/70 and 23 months later a boy in 3/72 for a birth interval
of only 23 months and a period between birth and reconception of only
14 months.

The data presented in table 15.8 are specific to the period 1963–73,
a time of increasingly rapid change for the !Kung. We have no way of
knowing what the birth intervals might have been 10, 25, or 100 years
ago when the !Kung were leading more nomadic lives. However, the
data presented here convincingly demonstrate that the actual interval
between live births continues to be well over 3 years for nomadic
!Kung even under present circumstances, and that this long birth spacing is achieved without recourse to infanticide or to other forms of
contraception. Howell recorded only six cases of infanticide in the 500
live births to the 165 women in the Dobe !Kung population (1976a).

In fact, methodologically the technique tends to underestimate the mean of the birth intervals. Because only a 10-year time period is considered, the cutoff of July 1973 gives us a truncated distribution of the full range of birth intervals and tends to overrepresent shorter intervals and underrepresent longer ones. For example, we do not know how many of the 43 women with only one birth in the 10-year period have ceased to be fertile and how many will give birth again after intervals of 60, 70, or 80 months (Sheps and Menken 1973; Howell personal communication). If these longer intervals were added into the sample I believe that the mean birth interval for nomadic women would fall between 4 and 5 years, as postulated by the model. Unfortunately, the termination of fertility by gonorrhea is a factor in many of the cases of women of midreproductive age who had no pregnancies during 1963–73. Gonorrhea thus could be reducing overall !Kung fertility, even as sedentarization could be increasing the fertility of nongonorrheal women (cf. Howell 1979).

A second point brought home by the data in table 15.8 is the rapidity of change during the decade. There is no statistical reason why the birth intervals in 1968–73 should be 7.75 months shorter than the intervals in 1963–68. The difference suggests that a change in the means of production toward reduced mobility can rapidly alter the balance in the system of reproduction and release, in effect, a flood of suppressed fertility. Schaefer (1971) and Freeman (1971) have observed a similar burst of fertility among the recently settled Inuit and other Canadian native people.

Lactation and Ovulation: The Causal Links

Two additional questions can now be asked. First, by what mechanism is long birth spacing maintained under foraging conditions, and second, what factors in the productive system could underlie the shortening of birth spacing when the shift to sedentary life is made? To the first question the answer is that long lactation appears to suppress ovulation in !Kung women. The mothers are observed to nurse their children for the first 2–3 years of the child's life. Nursing is vigorous, frequent, given on demand, and spaced throughout the day and night. During the latter half of the nursing period the mother's sexual life is active, yet conception does not occur. Although the exact mechanism is still in dispute, it seems clear that it is the long period of vigorous continuous nursing that suppresses ovulation in enough women enough of the time to produce an average birth interval in Nomadic !Kung women of about 3.7 years (44.11 months).

The data on the relation between lactation and ovulation in other populations were at first difficult to interpret, but more recently the relationship has become increasingly clear. Carefully studies have shown a marked suppressant effect in third world populations where nursing mothers show much longer birth intervals than do nonnursing mothers. These studies include Rwanda (Bonte and van Balen 1969), India (Tietze 1961; Peters et al. 1958; Potter et al. 1965), Egypt (El-Minawi and Foda 1971), and Taiwan (Jain et al. 1970) as well as among native North Americans, including Indians in New Mexico (Gioisa 1955) and Alaskan Eskimos (Berman et al. 1972). The data have led the demographer John Knodel to conclude that "There is ample evidence that lactation inhibits conception through prolonged post-partum amenorrhea" (Knodel n.d.; see also Van Ginneken 1974; Knodel 1977).

The fact that studies from urban western populations have shown the suppressant effect to be present but in a weaker form has led some western authorities to express doubts that lactation has any contraceptive value beyond the first few months of the child's life (e.g., Guttmacher 1952). In a recent study of American nursing mothers Kippley and Kippley have argued that cultural factors such as nursing schedules, the early use of pacifiers, midnight bottles, and supplementary feedings have tended to greatly reduce the effectiveness of lactation as a suppressor of ovulation in western societies (1975). For western mothers who are committed to a program of what the Kippleys call "natural mothering"—no pacifiers, bottles, or solid foods used for first 5 months, plus 24-hour feeding on demand—much longer periods of lactational infertility have been achieved. In a survey of 22 American La Leche League Mothers who breastfed their children from 12 to 37 months, the Kippleys found the mean length of breast feeding to be 22.8 months and the mean period of amenorrhea to be 14.6 months (Kippley and Kippley 1975). These values are, of course, short by !Kung standards but they are very long by western standards, where most bottle-feeding mothers are observed to resume menstrual cycles within 90 days of giving birth.

Although data on the incidence of postpartum amenorrhea are not yet available for the !Kung, we can infer from the length of the birth intervals and from the absence of evidence for the use of contraceptive devices or for postpartum sex taboos after 12 months that the !Kung women experience much longer periods of infertility following parturition and that their strong continuing lactation is probably involved in the persistence of the infertile period.

How does lactation suppress ovulation? Two kinds of related explanations have been offered. The first, called the critical fatness hypothesis, was originally developed by the Harvard biostatistician Rose Frisch to account for the timing of menarche in adolescent girls. Frisch found that the onset of menses was correlated with the attainment of a critical level of fatness, a level that was in fact a better predictor of the timing of menarche than was a girl's chronological age (Frisch 1974; Frisch and McArthur 1974). She has also suggested that a critical threshold of fatness may control the cessation and resumption of menstrual cycles in adult women (Frisch 1975). Citing evidence for amenorrhea in poorly nourished wartime populations, Frisch has directed attention to fat loss as a possible way of controlling menses and ovulation. Howell has applied this hypothesis to the !Kung data seeking to determine whether the caloric demands of lactation are so great that fat stores in nursing mothers are reduced below a critical threshold to the point where menses and ovulation cannot resume. She also considers the possibility that the gradual shift of the older nursing child to solid foods may permit the mother's fat levels to rise sufficiently to the point where menstrual cycles and ovulation are triggered (Howell 1976b, 1979; see also Kolata 1974).

There are three problems with the critical fatness hypothesis as an explanation of the !Kung womens' long postpartum infertility. First, nutritional amenorrhea is a usually serious condition of ill-health and reduced fitness; it seems unlikely that !Kung fertility would be regulated by a mechanism that routinely reproduces wartime conditions of semistarvation. Second, the clinical evidence for the nutritional status of lactating !Kung mothers indicates adequate levels of such key nutrients as vitamin B_{12}, folates, and iron (Truswell and Hansen 1976; Metz et al. 1972).* Third, Howell in a study (1979) of the weights of preg-

Editors' Note: Compare the treatment of the critical fat hypothesis by Cohen, who offers a hypothesis by which a critical fat threshold need not be inconsistent with good nutrition and attempts to explain why a mechanism which appears under pathological conditions among modern populations could have worked among healthy Pleistocene populations.

nant !Kung women found a wide scatter of weight levels for women around the time of conception, with thinner women conceiving as frequently as fatter women.

Other studies have also failed to show a correlation between weight gain and the timing of conception. For example, nursing mothers in a Guatemalan rural study population were actually found to be *losing* weight at reconception, not gaining it (Bongaarts and Delgado 1977).

Given these problems, attention has turned to alternative explanations. The second possible mechanism relating lactation to suppression of ovulation concerns the strength and persistence of the sucking stimulus itself. In a paper entitled "Effects of suckling on hypothalamic LH-Releasing factor and prolactin inhibiting factor," Minaguchi and Meites (1967) reported that follicular growth and ovulation were inhibited by the suckling act itself, a finding that confirmed earlier observations by other researchers (e.g., McKeown and Gibson 1954; Udesky 1950; Keettel and Bradbury 1961; Topkins 1959).* Topkins (1958; quoted in Kippley 1975, pp. 149–50) has stated:

Recent evidence indicates that it is the stimulus of sucking of the infant rather than lactation which acts on the pituitary gland probably by way of the mid-brain. The decrease in the frequency of feedings and the cessation of nursing result in the re-establishment of ovarian function, the reappearance of menstruation and ultimately ovulation. Complete breast-feeding in the early months of life is a fairly effective method of suppressing ovarian function and conception.

Subsequent research has confirmed this finding. In 1977, Mosley, drawing on the work of Tyson and Perez (1978) and others, could state (Mosley, 1977, pp. 8–9):

It is now well-established that lactation and post-partum amenorrhea rely heavily upon the effectiveness of the nursing stimulus which in turn causes secretion of the pituitary hormone prolactin. This hormonal reflex system has even been demonstrated in normally menstruating women who induce lactation simply by nipple stimulation.

Editors' Note: Although suppression of ovulation by lactation is not discussed by Christian, his review of the interaction of the adrenal cortex, hypothalamus, pituitary, and gonads will provide the reader with an appreciation of the complexity and sensitivity of the endocrine systems feedback control mechanism. Lacking from Lee's discussion is consideration of other density-related or socially induced effects on lactation similar to those discussed for rodents by Christian or by Lloyd.

In other words, vigorous sucking—of a kind that is regular, frequent, and occurs round the clock—seems more likely to be responsible for the persistence of amenorrhea during lactation than does the falling of a woman's fat levels below a critical threshold (see Huffman et al. 1978, 1979). A number of studies, including work in Indonesia, Bangladesh, and among the !Kung San (Konner personal communication), are currently exploring the relative weights of these two kinds of factors, and we can look forward to some exciting results in the near future.

Whatever the mechanism (and the interactions between the two are complex; see Frisch and McArthur 1979), the !Kung appear to be able to achieve periods of lactational amenorrhea that are two to three times longer than that of other populations of breast-feeding noncontracepting mothers. The mean birth interval of 39.8 months (table 15.8) for !Kung mothers would imply a mean period from birth to conception of 30.8 months. If we assume that a woman's menstrual cycles resume on the average 3–6 months before she becomes pregnant again, that would place the mean length of the period of amenorrhea in the range 24.8–27.8 months, compared to figures of 10–12 months for native populations in India, Alaska, and Rwanda (Berman et al. 1972).

How are we to account for this persistence? If vigorous, persistent sucking stimulus is the causal mechanism, the !Kung present a good case. Observers of !Kung nursing mothers have been struck by the high frequency with which the children take the breast and the vigor with which the older children especially stimulate the nipples. In fact, the !Kung are quite striking in the degree to which they accept as the cultural norm the continued nursing of older children with full sets of teeth and fully developed sucking muscles. It is common to see 2- and 3-year-olds standing to nurse at a seated mother's breast. In fact, the primary reason for weaning appears to be a following pregnancy; when a woman becomes sure she is pregnant she quickly withdraws the breast, saying to the child: "Look this milk is no longer for you, it is for your younger sibling" (see Shostak 1976). But in the absence of a pregnancy a child may continue to nurse to age 5 or more. Only when the child is as old as 6 and the mother is still not pregnant are steps taken to wean the child with social pressure and mild ridicule ("You are too old for baby stuff like that"). This kind of late weaning is almost always confined to the last child of a mother in her forties. Here we have the interesting (but not uncommon for the !Kung) situation of a lactating mother undergoing menopause while still nursing. We do not know how much nourishment the 3-year-old or 5-year-old child is actually getting from the breast, probably not very much; but if the sucking stimulus itself proves to be instrumental in inhibiting ovulation, !Kung child-rearing practices offer an ideal milieu to maximize its effectiveness.

Of course the 3-year-old child running with his play group does not nurse as frequently as the 1-year-old who is carried on the mother's hip, but the vigorousness of the stimulus may compensate for the decline of nursing frequency.

The emphasis the !Kung place on carrying the younger child may now be more clearly understood since the constant stimulation of the breast by the carried child may contribute significantly to the birth control effect, rather like carrying your contraceptive on your hip. If the infant were left at home with babysitters for a 6-hour working day, the contraceptive effect might be reduced.

Australian aboriginal women in Arnhem Land organize their work groups differently from the !Kung. They leave their children in camp in the charge of older cowives or other babysitters while they go out to gather. It is worth considering whether this fact alone may not account for the much shorter birth intervals and higher rates of infanticide that have been observed among Australian aboriginal women compared to !Kung women (McCarthy and McArthur 1960; Rose 1960; Birdsell 1968; Lancaster-Jones 1963).

Finally, we can ask why this system of long lactational amenorrhea breaks down when the shift to sedentary life is made. The rapidity of the change makes it unlikely that "removing the adverse effects of high fertility" will account for the change, since we see birth intervals shortening from one pregnancy to the next in the same women. It is more likely that some more proximate or immediate cause is at work. The probable mechanism is not too hard to discern. The nomadic !Kung diet, although rich in nutrients, is deficient in suitable weaning foods, that is, soft foods such as milk and porridge, which are easily digested by infants and toddlers. As a result, although infants are introduced to solid foods by 6 months of age, mother's milk continues to be an important part of the child's diet into the third year of life. At !Goshe and the other more settled !Kung villages there is a more plentiful supply of cows' milk and cultivated grains. This availability of alternative foods lessens the child's need for breast milk, and this may lower the level of lactation and the frequency of nipple stimulation. The result of the infants' reduced demands is that a woman's lactational amenorrhea may cease and her ovulation may resume as early as 11–14 months after she has given birth, a situation that would lead to the 20- to 23-month birth intervals actually observed at !Goshe.

It must be emphasized that these are not either/or propositions. When you have a variable such as diet, it will affect different women differently. In some women it may lead to an earlier conception; in others it may not. The net statistical effect, however, would be a shorter birth interval and a rise in the birth rate.

The Emotional Economy of Reproduction

The more rapid succession of births is not an unmixed blessing. Quite apart from the long-term consequences of population growth and shrinking food supply, this sudden embarrassment of riches in terms of births is already imposing hardships on !Kung mothers and children alike. This degree of stress reveals the existence of a third system interlocked with production and reproduction, a system I will call the emotional economy of the San. Long birth spacing for the !Kung has meant that a great deal of energy, both physical and emotional, has gone into the raising of each child. For the nomadic !Kung each child got her mother's exclusive attention for 44 months, a period that included 36 months of breast feeding. By the time the child was weaned, she entered the world with the teeth, motor development, language, and social awareness of a 3-year-old. The weaning transition was not without difficulties. The child would cry for the breast and to be carried in the back pouch, and she would throw tantrums if she did not get her way. But after a few months the child usually adjusted to her new status of older sibling as her mother turned her attention to the new arrival. For the child who is weaned at 12 months instead of 36 months, the trauma of separation becomes much more severe. Remember that the year-old child under traditional !Kung circumstances was carried full time by the mother, was nursed on demand, and probably obtained a large proportion of her calories from the breast milk. From the point of view of the culture, the year-old child was just a third of the way toward the point at which she would have to give up breast and back.

When the mother of such a young child becomes pregnant, the effects are striking. The most miserable children I have observed among the !Kung are some of the 1.5- to 2-year-old youngsters with younger siblings on the way. Their misery begins at their weaning and continues to the birth of their sibling 6–8 months later and beyond. The mother for her part has not only a demanding newborn to care for but the constant intrusions of an angry, sullen 2-year-old. A grandmother or aunt may do her best to feed and cheer up the child and to give the overworked mother some relief, but it is clear to the observer that something is out of kilter. The scene is in marked contrast to the relatively placid scenes of infant care in the nomadic camps documented by Draper (1976) and Konner (1976). In light of the emotional stress brought on by their short birth spacing, it is not surprising that several of these women have asked for birth control assistance. The Dobe area has never had a regular medical presence until the last few years, but the !Kung women had heard rumors of a European pill that would make them stop having babies and they sought this as a way out of their problems.

The unhappiness of the prematurely weaned !Kung babies and their mothers brought home to me how closely the emotional and psychological dynamics of life are tied into the productive and reproductive systems. The long birth spacing, which makes such good sense for hunter-gatherers in economic and health terms, also provides the opportunity for a high parental investment in each child, making possible the raising of what might be called fewer children of higher quality. The children's personalities were moulded by this system of exclusive attention for the first few years. The emotional security that !Kung adults display may be related to the security they experienced in early childhood. With short birth spacing the circle is broken and the emotional economy is put under stress, even though the nutritional and health needs of mother and child may be adequately met. Clearly, marked changes in the patterns of child care and maternal behavior will be required before the !Kung can adjust emotionally to their new economic and demographic realities. In the interim a generation of !Kung children may be growing up bearing the psychological scars of the rapid transition.

Acknowledgements

Financial support for the present research from the following is gratefully acknowledged: the National Science Foundation (U.S.), the National Institute of Mental Health (U.S.), the Wenner-Gren Foundation, and the Social Sciences and Humanities Research Council of Canada. A version of this chapter also appears in Lee 1979.

References

Berman, M. L.; Hanson, K.; and Hellman, I. L. 1972. Effect of breast-feeding on postpartum menstruation, ovulation, and pregnancy in Alaskan Eskimos. *Am. J. Obstet. Gynecol.* 114:524–34.

Birdsell, J. B. 1968. Some predictions for the Pleistocene based on equilibrium systems among recent hunter-gatherers. In *Man the hunter*, ed. R. B. Lee and I. DeVore, pp. 229–40. Chicago: Aldine.

Bongaarts, J., and Delgado, H. 1977. Effects of nutritional status on fertility in rural Guatemala. Paper presented at the Seminar on Natural Fertility, Institut National d'Études Démographiques, Paris, Mar. 1977.

Bonte, M., and van Balen, H. 1969. Prolonged lactation and family spacing in Rwanda. *J. Biosoc. Sci.* 1:97–100.

Carr-Saunders, A. 1922. *The population problem: a study in human evolution.* Oxford: Clarendon Press.

Draper, P. 1976. Social and economic constraints on child life among the !Kung. In *Kalahari hunter-gatherers*, ed. R. B. Lee and I. DeVore, pp. 199–217. Cambridge, Mass.: Harvard Univ. Press.

El-Minawi, M., and Foda, M. 1971. Postpartum lactation Amenorrhea. *Am. J. Obstet. Gynecol.* 111:17.

Freeman, M. R. 1971. The significance of demographic changes occurring in the Canadian East Arctic. *Anthropologica* 13:215–36.

Frisch, R. E. 1974. Critical weight at menarche: initiation of the adolescent growth spurt and control of puberty. In *Control of onset of puberty*, ed. M. M. Grumbach, G. D. Growe, and F. E. Mayer. New York: Wiley.

———. 1975. Demographic implication of the biological determinants of female fecundity. *Soc. Biol.* 22:17–22.

———, and McArthur, J. 1974. Menstrual cycles: fatness as a determinant of minimum weight for their maintenance or onset. *Science* 185:949–51.

———. 1979. Difference between postpartum and nutritional amenorrhea. *Science* 203:921–22.

Gioiosa, R. 1955. Incidence of pregnancy during lactation in 500 cases. *Am. J. Obstet. Gynecol.* 70:162.

Guttmacher, A. F. 1952. Fertility of man. *Fertil. Steril.* 3:281–89.

Howell, N. 1976a. The population of the Dobe area !Kung. In *Kalahari hunter-gatherers*, ed. R. B. Lee and I. DeVore, pp. 137–51. Cambridge, Mass.: Harvard Univ. Press.

————. 1976b. Toward a uniformitarian theory of human paleodemography. *J. Hum. Evol.* 5:25–40.

————. 1979. *Demography of the Dobe area !Kung.* New York: Academic Press.

Huffman, S. L.; Chowdhury, A. K. M. A.; and Mosley, W. H. 1978. Postpartum amenorrhea: how is it affected by maternal nutritional status? *Science* 200:1155–57.

————. 1979. Difference between postpartum and nutritional amenorrhea. *Science* 203:922–23.

Jain. A.; Hsu, T.; Freedman, R.; and Chang, M. 1970. Demographic aspects of lactation and postpartum amenorrhea. *Demography* 7:255–71.

Keettel, W., and Bradbury, J. 1961. Endocrine studies of lactation amenorrhea. *Am. J. Obstet. Gynecol.* 82:995.

Kippley, S. 1975. *Breast-feeding and natural child spacing.* New York: Penguin Books.

————, and Kippley, J. 1975. The relation between breast-feeding and amenorrhea: report of a survey. In S. Kippley, *Breast-feeding and natural child spacing,* Appendix II, pp. 163–78. New York: Penguin Books.

Knodel, J. 1977. Breast-feeding and population growth. *Science* 198:1111–15.

————. n.d. *The influence of child mortality on fertility in European populations in the past: results from individual data.* Mimeographed.

Kolata, G. 1974. !Kung hunter-gatherers: feminism, diet, and birth control. Science 185:932–34.

Konner, M. 1976. Maternal care, infant behaviour and development among the !Kung. In *Kalahari hunter-gatherers,* ed. R. B. Lee and I. DeVore, pp. 218–45. Cambridge, Mass.: Harvard Univ. Press.

Lancaster-Jones, F. 1963. *A demographic survey of the aboriginal population of the Northern Territory with special reference to Bathurst Island Mission.* Canberra: Australian Institute of Aboriginal Studies.

Lee, R. 1972. Population growth and the beginning of sedentary life among the !Kung bushmen. In *Population growth: anthropological implications,* ed. B. Spooner, pp. 329–42. Cambridge, Mass.: M.I.T. Press.

————. 1979. *The !Kung San: men, women, and work in a foraging society.* New York: Cambridge Univ. Press.

McCarthy, F., and McArthur, M. 1960. The food quest and the time factor in aboriginal economic life. In *Records of the American-Australian scientific expedition to Arnhem Land,* ed. C. P. Mountford, pp. 145–94. Melbourne: Melbourne Univ. Press.

McKeown, T., and Gibson, J. 1954. A note on menstruation and conception during lactation. *J. Obstet. Gynecol. Br. Emp.* 61:824.

Metz, J., et al. 1972. Iron and folate nutrition among the !Kung bushmen. *J. Clin. Nutr.*

Minaguchi, H., and Meites, J. 1967. Effects of suckling on hypothalamic LH-releasing factor and prolactin inhibiting factor, and on pituitary LH and prolactin. *Endocrinology* 80:603.

Mosley, W. H. 1977. The effects of nutrition on natural fertility. Paper presented at Seminar on Natural Fertility, Institut National d'Etudes Demographiques, Paris, March 1977.

Peters, H.; Israel, S.; and Purshottam, S. 1958. Lactation period in Indian women—duration of amenorrhea and vaginal and cervical cytology. *Fertil. Steril.* 9:134.

Pfeiffer, J. 1969. *The emergence of man.* New York: Harper & Row.

Potter, R. G.; New, M.; Wyon, J.; and Gordon, J. E. 1965. Application of field studies to research on the physiology of human reproduction. *J. Chronic Dis.* 18:1125–40.

Rose, F. G. G. 1960. *Classification of kin, age structure and marriage amongst the Groote Eylanot aboriginies: a study in method and a theory of Australian kinship.* Berlin: Akademie-Verlag. (London: Pergamon.)

Schaefer, O. 1971. When the Eskimo comes to town. *Nutr. Today* 6 (6).

Schrire, C., and Steiger, W. 1974. A matter of life and death: an investigation into the practice of female infanticide in the Arctic. *Man* 9:161–84.

Sheps, M., and Menken, J. 1973. *Mathematical models of conception and birth.* Chicago: Univ. of Chicago Press.

Shostak, M. 1976. A !Kung woman's memory of childhood. In *Kalahari hunter-gatherers*, ed. R. Lee and I. DeVore. Cambridge, Mass.: Harvard Univ. Press.

Tietze, C. 1961. The effect of breastfeeding on the rate of conception. Paper presented at the Int. Popul. Conf., New York.

Topkins, P. 1958. Letter to the editor. *J. Am. Med. Assoc.* 167:144.

Topkins, P. 1959. The histologic appearance of the endometrium during lactation and its relationship to ovarian function. *Am. J. Obstet. Gynecol.* 77:921.

Truswell, A. S., and Hansen, J. D. L. 1976. Medical research among the !Kung. In *Kalahari hunter-gatherers*, ed. R. B. Lee and I. DeVore, pp. 166–94. Cambridge, Mass.: Harvard Univ. Press.

Tyson, J. E. and Perez, A. 1978. The maintenance of infecundity in postpartum women. In *Nutrition and human reproduction*, ed. W. H. Mosley, pp. 11–27. New York: Plenum Press.

Udesky, I. 1950. Ovulation in lactating women. *Am. J. Obstet. Gynecol.* 59:843.

Van Ginneken, J. K. 1974. Prolonged breastfeeding as a birth spacing method. *Stud. Fam. Plann.* 5:201–06.

16

INFANTICIDE IN LANGURS AND MAN: ADAPTIVE ADVANTAGE OR SOCIAL PATHOLOGY?

Suzanne Ripley

We have reached a crucial time in the sequence of efforts to understand and control the growth of human populations. A new picture of human history and prehistory is emerging, the result of important new insights from anthropology, ethnology, and biology. We can now begin to see archaeologically that human populations grew very slowly and remained at relatively low densities during the time—approximately 99% of its duration as a species—that all members were exclusively foragers (Swedlund and Armelagos 1976; Hassan this volume). We can examine ethnologically how specific intervals between births to one female and specific completed reproduction for one female can differentially affect both female fertility and population density in economies of varying productivity. That is, we can examine these variables in low to moderately productive cultures (primarily mobile foragers and nomadic pastoralists), where maximum effective fertility of females and optimum population density may favor limitation of population growth through regulation by controls of various sorts (Lee this volume). We can also examine moderately to highly productive cultures (primarily sedentary foragers and shifting/agrarian cultivators), in which the same two factors (maximum effective fertility of females and optimum population density) may conversely favor rapid population growth through the *defeat* of previously effective controls. We can determine empirically the nature of the controls (ecological, physiological, cultural) that maintain demographic variables (especially births) at specific levels in various populations. Finally, we can view these controls comparatively in an evolutionary perspective provided to anthropologists by primatology.

This chapter views the operation in humans of one such control—

infanticide—from the perspective of another primate species, the leaf-eating gray langur, *Presbytis entellus*, of South Asia in the attempt to frame a hypothesis for future testing.

1. Focusing first on the original and primary adaptation of humans as generalist foragers (hunters and gatherers), I set this adaptation into comparative perspective among patterns of primate foraging in the order as a whole, highlighting the importance of the shift from female to male as major provider of post-weaning nutrients in some, but not all, hunters.

2. Given that among mammals most primates, and especially man, are premier foraging generalists as individuals and as populations, and given that this individual behavioral flexibility is largely learned and can probably be reliably reproduced by monomorphic genetic programming, I note that by contrast leaf-eating colobines are largely specialized foragers, morphologically and behaviorally, and presumably genetically homogeneous. The gray langur, however, is an outstanding exception among leaf-eaters. I outline the peculiar adaptive nature of this foraging generalist, a species that occupies an extremely broad range of habitat types, and I conjecture about the ecological and genetic conditions behind its undoubted success in seasonal, chancy, high risk habitats such as the high Himalayas and Rajasthani desert.

3. Generalists of this sort require high reproductive rates and broad phenotypic variability as individuals and as populations to succeed in difficult habitats. Thus they occasionally require a means of population limitation and ensurance of outbreeding insofar as phenotypic variability (including behavior) is due to genetic polymorphism in such species.

4. Infanticide is one means of ensuring both genetic variability and limitation of population growth in multimale as well as unimale langur troops. Adult male reproductive competition is a peculiarly apt means of effecting such infanticide, but the feedback link is circuitous and costly because of special problems of adaptive compromise by which colobine generalists resolve their evolutionary dilemma.

5. In human foraging generalists (low density, low productivity, mobile hunters and gatherers), as in some other carnivorous species, outbreeding is effected by incest inhibitions, and thus only population limitation results from infanticide, largely instigated by females acting in their own individual best reproductive interest, thus providing an

immediate direct feedback loop between primary reproducer and support provider.

6. In post-Neolithic, preindustrial agrarian economies for which relatively high population densities are advantageous, the coalescence of a congeries of factors (economic and social structural complexity, a long generation time, a common shift from female to male as focus of a network of support providers, etc.) lengthens the chain of links in the feedback loop between primary reproducers and support providers, effectively defeating the very ancient system of limitation. Industrialized societies are in a position to reinstate a system of limitation of growth (leading to the third stage of the demographic transition) through the use of sophisticated means of conception control.

The widespread cultural practice of infanticide as one of the most important forms of population control has received little study (despite Carr-Saunders 1922; Krzywicki 1934; and a few others). The exclusion of male ethnographers, along with male parents and male medical practitioners, from the perinatal scene in many societies (Miller and Newman 1978; Newman personal communication) apparently accounts for a large part of our ignorance. Selective inattention (Dickeman 1975) and the antistatistical, antibiological, antievolutionary biases of cultural anthropology in the middle years of this century have also blinded us to the now obvious messages regarding this and other controls (postpartum sex taboos, contraceptives, and abortions) in the demographic tables.

The problems with various recent analytical models for humans (i.e., Divale and Harris 1976, 1978; and critics Lancaster and Lancaster 1978; Hirschfeld et al. 1978) may well be resolved through closer examination of aspects of the intersection of the productive and reproductive spheres. Those aspects requiring investigation include the following: (1) long-term optimum carrying capacities (including total population, local densities, mobility, and ratio of primary food producers to secondary producers and nonproducers) achieveable through different modes of subsistence production in various types of habitat; (2) allocation of age and gender roles in different cultural versions of such subsistence modes; and (3) the social structure of knowledge about carrying capacity (sensors) and authority for making decisions affecting population size (effectors) in societies of varying complexity.

Dickeman (1975) points out that the reproductive unit (the mother-family, or the biparental family) and successively higher levels of societal integration, especially the productive units supporting the reproductive units, may be at odds regarding these sensing and effecting roles in their population policies. She notes that the larger the society is, the longer the period of time necessary to establish an adaptive relationship between growth rates and carrying capacity, a relationship primarily thought to be mediated in humans by cognitively structured processes (including prestige exchanges, rituals, and chronic warfare) reverberating among these societal levels.* In the highly complex "modern world system" (Wallerstein 1974), the institutionalization of change effectively prevents stabilization.

Anthropological analyses, using the method of controlled comparison, can clarify such situations in at least two ways: (1) by examining the adaptations of human foraging societies—the fundamental socio-ecological situation for the species in evolutionary terms—and later transformations of foragers into food-cultivating societies, and (2) by examining the nonhuman primates as background context from which the fundamental human foraging adaptation emerged in remote past time.

Clues from Human Foragers

Following the first of these two approaches in nicely quantified approximations for one population of recent foragers (the !Kung San, or Bushmen, of the Dobe area of Botswana), Lee (this volume) shows the relationship between mobility of females and optimal birth spacing operating as consciously experienced work loads on women in a rich "emotional economy" of child-rearing characterized by long lactation. Women are the key figures in both the productive and reproductive spheres because of their control of mongongo nut supply (the staple food) during their years of childbearing.

Editors' Note: A similar point is made by Lee, who stresses the dual role (production and reproduction) played by !Kung women and the importance of this dual role for population regulation. Ripley's emphasis on the relative insensitivity of larger social units to density should also be compared to Baron's discussion of factors affecting the quality and flexibility of human density perception.

Lee questions the nature of the mechanisms for controlling population growth in foragers. He objects to the characterization of infanticide and other "catastrophic means" (such as warfare, starvation, and
migration) as primary. Since the San did not practice infanticide,* yet
did not have an overpopulation problem, he prefers to relegate these
means to secondary status, or "backup means." Like Carr-Saunders
(1922) and Sussman (1972) before him, Lee finds that, given the availability of weaning foods, sedentarization of previously mobile food-
gathering, burden-bearing females is a key cause of the defeat of a
"natural" system of population regulation operating in the !Kung San,
and in other populations of foragers for whom the San are often made
to serve as model. The defeat is caused by the collapse of the constraints that resulted in long interbirth intervals, which in precontact
times had functioned to equalize from year to year the loads (of large
unweaned young and mongongo nuts) routinely carried by females
over long distances.

Among the San and other foragers the proximate causes of female
sedentarization may be many. If we group together hunters and fishers
living north of the climatic limits for cultivation along with any other
human forager societies in which a greater dependence for primary
subsistence effort falls on males, we find that in such societies females
are, or can easily be, effectively sedentarized. Among foragers, such
dependence on males can occur for many proximate reasons, including
harshness of climate for infants, or limitation of subsistence resources
to a few types of large prey, and so on. Wherever weaning foods are
available as well, fertility resulting from such female sedentarization
is potentially high (Birdsell 1968). But unless the carrying capacity is
also locally high (as in ecosystems with a Mediterranean-type climate
DiCastri and Mooney 1973, or at rich biome junctures such as riverine
and marine coastal margins, or in ecosystems with both these special
conditions in combination—the Mediterranean itself, the Canadian
Northwest coast, California, the Chilean coast, northern Japan, and
southwest Africa [Ripley 1979]), we can perhaps predict that the incidence of infanticide (directly, or indirectly by neglect or abuse) and

---

*Recent data indicate that an infanticide rate of 6 per 100 births has been found in the San,
and that these deaths are the result of maternal decisions at a perinatal scene from which males
are excluded (Lee personal communications).

other culturally mediated means will assume a more important role (Balikci 1967; Meggers 1971).*

A dependence on male subsistence effort and relative female sedentarization are characteristic features of many, although by no means all, post-Neolithic food-producing cultures as well. Such sedentarization, as well as the availability of weaning foods, an artificially raised productivity (Hyams 1952), and resulting population growth are all characteristics of one exceedingly important post-Neolithic culture: the Old High Culture area of western Eurasia with its large stock animals, plow cultivation of grains, and milking complex (Lomax and Arensberg 1977). This fact is of special significance for the modern global dilemma, since it was from this cultural area that the worldwide colonization effort of the past half millennium was launched under the soul-hungry crusading and commercializing Christian aegis. Hence, as Dickeman (1975) has stressed, there is no reason to expect that the operation of cultural controls on population growth ceased during the transition from foraging to food-producing economies simply because the carrying capacity was raised by developing (or switching to) tillage, a more productive, although more vulnerable, subsistence mode classifiable ecologically at the primary consumer (herbivore) trophic level. Cultural controls may indeed continue to be practiced, as in non-Christian Japan (Dickeman 1975), in conjunction with higher carrying capacities made feasible by Neolithic techniques.

Lee's chapter is a key quantitative formulation of the existential situation confronting the provider/decision makers (the females) in one of the few foraging societies still available to us for study, and thus valuable heuristically regardless of the status of the San as representative or not of human foragers in general (Dickeman 1975). The major gap in Lee's analysis is its incomplete exploration of the nature of the *non*catastrophic controls that render the long (4-year) interbirth interval possible in the San without culturally mediated contraceptive measures, thereby giving the strong impression to Lee's readers that some humans have an effective "natural" (i.e., physiological) means of limiting conception, a means that is somehow lost once civilization

Editors' Note: Ripley, like Hassan, assumes an important role for local carrying capacity in the regulation of Pleistocene populations. Contrast the view of Cohen, who points to the selective use of resources by Pleistocene hunter-gatherers and questions whether absolute limits on local food supply would have provided a significant limit on population growth.

strikes. It sounds as if some magical antifertility potion is circulating, a potion that disappears once the San become sedentary cattleherders. Cohen's chapter picks up this loose thread.

Cohen suggests the operation of the fat deposit hypothesis (Frisch and MacArthur 1974), which, if true, should work among foragers in a nicely density-dependent fashion. That is, the closer such a population grows to the carrying capacity of a particular habitat, the leaner the individuals will be under an egalitarian ethic of food sharing, an ethic now seen as generally characteristic of human foragers (Bicchieri 1972; Damas 1969a, 1969b; Lee and DeVore 1968; Leacock 1974); thus the leaner the females the later the onset of breeding.

A major understated aspect of the combined Lee/Cohen model, but one stressed by Dickeman (1975), is the neat concordance effected in the San between individual reproductive strategies of average females (each attempting to maximize her own effective fertility in classical Darwinian fashion), and the work requirements of the type of subsistence mode by which offspring must be supported in this particular ecosystem (especially the mutually exclusive nature of gathering plant foods and small prey on the one hand and hunting large prey on the other). Both of these factors favor long interbirth intervals and small completed family size, and thus favor regulation of reproduction by any means, "natural" or cultural. A key feature of the system's success for the traditional San was the participation of females of reproductive age in both spheres (productive and reproductive). As a result, the ecological pressures indicating a need to exert limitations on population growth can be sensed directly, simultaneously, and cognitively by the very figures who, in exerting such controls, would be acting in their own best reproductive interest as well as that of the larger society. We would not be surprised, therefore, if it were found that San females did in fact occasionally practice infanticide.

The fact that the San (and perhaps the pygmies, Turnbull 1961) could achieve such limitation on growth, apparently without resort to infanticide (but see note on page 353), is perhaps explainable on nutritional grounds (see below). If so, the "naturalness" of the "noncatastrophic" noninterventionist system in the San, insisted upon by Lee, would be a red herring. That is, avoidance of infanticide to achieve regulation is possible only if fertility is being reduced by other means, one of which could be indeed a circulating antifertility potion: namely, dietary secondary compounds (see below).

Clues from Nonhuman Primate Foraging Societies

The type of human foragers represented by the San (primary subsistence dependence on female effort) may well not be typical of human foragers of the past, as maintained by Dickeman (1975) and others, but the San *are* comparable in this respect to nonhuman primates, among whom a female foraging for herself and all her offspring in their immature stages, primarily on plant products, also serves as the keystone for the control of population growth (Clark 1978). Thus, these primate females, too, serve as direct sensors of the carrying capacity of the habitat (through quality of food obtained) as well as effectors of population regulation, a control role that probably does operate physiologically (Klein 1978) as well as behaviorally (Sade et al. 1977; Sade this volume) via nutritional effects on the estrous cycle in most nonhuman primates. In this particular problem we may find among foraging primates further clues to the lack of need among the San for secondary, artificial (i.e., cultural) forms of conception control, a need that is otherwise characteristically human (Dickeman 1975). Here we can use the second anthropological analytical strategy mentioned earlier and attempt to trace the primate roots from which the human species emerged in its fundamental condition as gatherer-hunter, or hunter-gatherer, foragers.

The work on antiherbivore protective strategies of plants originally done by insect ecologists (Price 1975) showed that some plants produce secondary compounds mimicking hormones that can delay maturation and can have other depressing effects on the reproduction of plant-eaters (heterotrophs).* This work has strongly influenced the research of many primatologists, especially those studying the foraging behavior of folivores of various kinds (i.e., Glander 1975; Milton 1977; McKey et al. 1978; Ripley 1970, 1977a, 1977b, 1978; Oates 1974). Such investigations among primates (Clutton-Brock 1977) as well as other mammals (Montgomery 1978) reveal the existence of complex strategies to avoid toxic substances and still achieve balanced diets.

Natural selection in plants for such secondary compounds is expected to be greater wherever grazing and browsing pressures (pri-

---

*Editors' Note: The role of a prey species in regulating the fertility (rather than the mortality) of its predators as suggested here is largely ignored elsewhere in the volume but might be profitably explored in the ecology of other species discussed.

marily by insects) are high or very detrimental. Thus, the evolution of such compounds in the flora should be especially rapid in outer tropical and subtropical habitats (such as low-stature monsoon and woodland forest, savannah, and grassland/steppe) with typical summer-wet, winter-dry seasonality (Walter 1973), since such habitats support many large macroherbivores in addition to insects, and since some of the latter exhibit devastating periodic population booms (Hemming 1978). Significantly enough, not only is this the kind of environment in which the San have persisted, but also these seasonally dry habitats are the very places where many anthropologists believe that hunting first appeared and became common among proto-humans. In fact, one probable reason for the increasing dependence on vertebrate predation/ hunting on the part of hominids (and chimpanzees and baboons) in such habitats and not in others, such as the rain forest west of the 29th meridian (Kortlandt and Kooij 1963; Teleki 1975), was to utilize the guilds of grazing and browsing mammals as necessary prior links in the food chain. Such links serve to convert a rich (Bourliere and Hadley 1970), but unassimilable (silica, cellulose, toxic compounds) primary production into secondary production, that is, to convert it to a form that is assimilable by hominids and other carnivores and scavengers. Necessarily, this secondary production was less abundant than primary production because of energy-conversion inefficiencies. Hence the price paid by hominids for occupancy of this type of habitat as predator/hunters was a biomass density significantly less than an occupancy based on direct consumption of primary production such as roots and tubers (Isaac 1978).

Thus, this type of typical subtropical (seasonally winter-dry) ecosystem, important in the origins of hunting hominids, joins certain types of ecosystem into which hunting hominids subsequently spread (harsh climate, few large prey species), types that were discussed above. All are ecosystems in which, for different reasons, the hunter subsistence role (predominantly male) may tend to rise in significance and even overshadow the gathering role (predominantly, but not exclusively female). Among the San, of course, Lee found that the abundant and reliable staple protein source was not in hunted meats but in the gathered mongongo nuts. Thus, this shift in balance of preponderant subsistence role from female to male has not occurred in this population of foragers. It is the lack of such a shift that may indeed render the San atypical of the few extant foraging populations—that is, to those still remaining because they were pushed into marginal (noncultivable) areas. But the San are then perhaps more typical of foragers previously occupying richer lands, ones that are today farmed. It is also the lack of such a shift that may account for low San fertility without the use of infanticide.

Thus, with the help of the San, we arrive more generally at a spectrum of simple models for human and nonhuman primate foragers in which, for whatever reasons, at one extreme gathering/collecting outweighs hunting/predation in overall subsistence effort, as measured in calories and essential nutrients supplied, and at the other extreme the opposite relationship prevails (Lee and DeVore 1968; Teleki 1975; Rose 1978). Both extremes and all intermediates are represented among human foragers known to ethnology (Lee and DeVore 1968). Only the first-noted extreme of the spectrum in humans, however, is directly comparable to apes and monkeys, even the partially hunting chimpanzees and baboons reported recently (Teleki 1973, 1974; Harding 1975; Hausfater 1975a; Strum 1975). These two meat-eating nonhuman primate species are an important demonstration to anthropologists of how a vertebrate hunting/predation component can enter into higher primate foraging strategies at all, even if they cannot yet show how this component can have become predominant.

What is common to both extremes of this spectrum in humans is that they are alternatives facultatively available to a generalist (eurytrophic) foraging species (MacArthur 1972). A generalist forager utilizes many food types from many resource species and has a number of alternative foraging substrategies organized into a complex multiseasonal schedule that may extend over several years in response to longer climatic cycles. The term here applies both to individuals and to populations. It is a relative term used ecologically in comparing such an eurytrophic species with another (often closely related) taxon that has a narrower subsistence niche (oligotrophic, monotrophic).

The essence of the evolutionary meaning of a generalist foraging strategy is either to do well in environments with fluctuating abundances of resources (often ones experiencing seasonality of various kinds), or to coexist sympatrically with a dominant oligotrophic specialist congeneric species by taking seasonal products scattered patchily and unpredictably over a wide area in a habitat rich enough to sustain two intercompeting species of somewhat similar subsistence mode and body size (see literature references listed in Ripley 1977a, 1979). Although perhaps rare, such habitats are important as likely sites for the speciation events separating foraging specialists and generalists (Levins 1968; Cody 1974), in itself possibly a rare evolutionary event. Although foraging specialists seem to predominate in tropical communities (Cain 1969), once generalists have evolved, in these rare tropical habitats or elsewhere, they can then migrate and expand their geographic range of distribution to include a wide variety of high-risk habitats.

High *r* among Generalists

Generalist species can exploit habitats susceptible of turbulence and resource fluctuation, as noted above. Since mortality in such places is likely to be high, a compensatorily high reproductive capacity is adaptive (Wilson 1975; Conaway 1971; Orians 1969) in order to recover as rapidly as possible from local population losses.

Only in this light can we understand the presence in the human species, the generalist foragers *par excellence*, of such a high maximum potential reproductive rate (Birdsell 1968; Dickeman 1975; Lorimer et al. 1954), a capacity that is higher than that found in any other living hominoids. This *potential* capacity for annual reproduction must be carefully ditinguished from the *practice* of permitting any such offspring as may be produced circannually to "survive" by withholding alternative disposal through abortion, infanticide, or adoption. It is this potential capacity, even with nursing, that makes humans as a species much more comparable in this respect to macaques (1-year interbirth interval generally) than to baboons or to langurs (2-year interval generally), let alone to any other of man's closer living relatives, even the generalist chimpanzee (3- to 4-year interval). This capacity for successful annual reproduction without the loss of the previous infant is undoubtedly connected evolutionarily with the loss of the estrous period in the human menstrual cycle.

Resistance is frequently shown to the idea that man's reproductive capacity is indeed high for a primate of ape grade, no doubt because a long potential life span, slow maturation, and a characteristic generation structure (Ripley in preparation) make *Homo sapiens* appear slow in comparison with the species usually cited as having a high *r*. Models of human population growth start by taking as a given the need for regulation of growth (Dickeman 1975) but do not attempt to account for the prior conditions leading to that given, namely, the presence in man of this remarkable potential capacity for annual successful reproduction.* It is this relatively high primary reproductive capacity (a necessary feature in any opportunistic generalist species for rapid recovery of population levels following the inevitable pessimum cycles that occur in fluctuating environments),† that creates, in and of itself, the need for countervailing controls of some sort, natural or artificial. Such controls are necessary when conditions favorable for reproduction lead to a growth in population density that threatens to overstep locally optimal saturation levels, optima that will be different for different habitats over the distributional range.

A good example of a high reproductive capacity in another large (nonprimate, non-eutherian) mammal is the gray kangaroo (Dawson 1977), a terrestrial generalist folivore of some 67 kg or more, whose allegedly "primitive" reproductive system in fact turns out to be a beautifully effective adaptation for rapid recovery of numbers from population downturns, a frequent occurrence in its arid, inhospitable habitat. Rapid recovery of population levels under favorable moisture and foraging conditions is possible because the kangaroo maintains three offspring in various stages of extreme immaturity, all simultaneously: one resting blastocyst in embryonic diapause, one joey in the pouch, and one joey at the knee. The delayed maturation of the embryo, made possible by a gestation period shorter than one estrous cycle, and immediate postpartum estrus and fertilization, are insurance against the loss of either of the older joeys. Thus, limitation of maximal population growth in this marsupial is by endogenous controls— embryonic diapause.

Countervailing Controls: Infanticide

Given the need for countervailing control of local density accumulations in rapidly reproducing generalist species, there are several possible corrective means, of which dispersal is perhaps most common. Other means come into play only when, for some reason, dispersal is blocked (Tamarin this volume; Packard and Mech this volume) and

---

Editors' Note: However, see Hassan, who cites references that give the natural birth interval for human populations as 27–28 months.

†*Editors' Note:* Compare the arguments of Lee and of Cohen who appear to assume that human hunter-gatherer populations were naturally programmed for a spacing of births appropriate to relatively stable environments.

infant mortality from disease and predation do not take sufficient toll.*
One such possible mechanism is infanticide, already known to occur
in many populations of gray langurs over the major part of the species'
range of distribution (Sugiyama 1965; Mohnot 1971; Parthasarathy and
Rahaman 1974; Hrdy 1974, 1977a; Ripley in preparation) as well as in
a few other species of primate (see citations in Angst and Thommen
1977).

Since general Darwinian views of biological fitness require that
intraspecific infanticide ordinarily be classed as a pathological behavior (as maintained by the Berkeley group: Dolhinow 1977; Curtin and
Dolhinow 1978; but see criticisms by Hrdy 1977b, Hausfater 1977;
Ripley in preparation) there must be very strong adaptive pressures in
effect for it to emerge at all, let alone become a "normal" or adaptive
behavior pattern, and the appearance and maintenance of the trait in
this species must result from severe constraints (Chapman and Hausfater 1976). I will suggest below that infanticide by adult males becomes a likely pattern for a generalist folivore species, in that it combines a device for preserving genetic polymorphism and defeating
inbreeding with a means for control of population growth via the species-level mechanism, on which selection can act, of reproductive advantages for the competing adult males.

Male Reproductive Strategy. Hrdy (1977a) has elaborated one basic model for a sociobiological interpretation of infanticide. In gray
langurs she sees the pattern as an adaptive aspect of adult male reproductive strategy, part of a cycle in which infant deaths (some of which
are known to result from adult male attacks) follow closely upon takeovers of troops from resident adult males by nonresident, previously
nonreproductive, males in areas where the one-male social group
structure is the norm.† Thus, Hrdy refines and considerably extends
earlier suggestions by Sugiyama (1965) and by Thompson (1967). She
reviews all known, reported, and suspected instances of infanticidal
behavior in langurs and other primates (Hrdy 1974, 1977a, 1977b).

Struhsaker (1977) apparently accepts Hrdy's hypothesis in repeat-

---

Editors' Note: Compare the view of hunter-gatherer infanticide offered by Cohen suggesting
that infanticide is more often used as an adjuster of occasional mistakes than as a major controller
of population.

†*Editors' Note:* Langur infant mortality caused by strange males has its analogue in some
rodents in the Bruce effect, in which the presence (or urine odor) of a strange male mouse will
cause pregnancy blockage in the female. (See H. M. Bruce. An exteroceptive block to pregnancy
in the mouse, *Nature* 184(1959):105.

ing it for *Cercopithecus ascanius*, and in extending it to predict that most primates for whom unimale groups are the norm will be found to exhibit infanticide as a normal aspect of adult male reproductive competition once longitudinal studies of such species are undertaken.

Neither Hrdy nor Struhsaker, however, attempt to specify the conditions under which the unimale troop becomes more common than the multimale troops, nor why troop takeovers and infanticide occur in multimale langur troops as well as one-male troops. These crucial matters are taken into consideration at some length in the following explanation.

Device That Ensures Genetic Polymorphism. Ripley (1979) hypothesizes that the ultimate cause of intraspecific adult male infanticide following troop takeovers in langurs lies elsewhere, specifically in the role played by behavioral variability in the adaptive strategy of this unusual folivore species, an adaptive strategy that is the most generalist of the colobines. Among the higher primates, who are on the whole foraging generalists, colobine leaf-eaters are relatively specialized, both morphologically and behaviorally. Given a prior commitment *as colobines* to their phylogenetically characteristic social structure and breeding pattern, both of which favor ecological specialization, behavioral monomorphism, and inbreeding (Seger 1977) gray langurs should face difficulty in retaining a genetic basis for such variability.

Seger (1977) has shown that close inbreeding (and by implication genetic homogeneity) rapidly becomes characteristic of breeding groups with unimale structure such as are found in most populations of gray langurs. Yet Hrdy et al. (1975) have found considerable polymorphism in a variety of blood proteins in 26 specimens of *Presbytis entellus*, a finding they note is in remarkable contrast to the monomorphic character of many other species of leafmonkey. Such a finding is suggestive if not conclusive.

Infanticide following adult male replacement is one means (however costly and indirect [Gould 1978]) of preserving a polymorphic potential which is likely to be at least partly responsible for the maintenance of phenotypic flexibility and variety in this monomorphic-tending colobine. Flexibility and variety characteristic of generalist species can apparently be reliably reproduced (genetically) in two ways: either by retaining a polymorphic potential leading to greater individual phenotypic variability than the demands of any one habitat can select for (Levins 1968), or by a complex genetic monomorphism that produces the kind of labile, educable, open behavioral program that is characteristic of humans—and to a lesser extent of other higher primates—but is otherwise rare (Slobodkin personal communication). Whether reproduced by either of these means or by a mixture of them, flexibility and variety at the individual level and between populations are necessary prerequisites for acquiring, maintaining, and regularly switching among foraging substrategies, capacities that are crucial for the adaptive success of an ecologically generalist species. Given known clear-cut behavioral differences, such as tail-carriage, between populations of langurs, it should be possible to conduct cross-breeding and cross-fostering experiments that would reveal whether any genetic basis is responsible for such behavioral differences.

Male reproductive strategy as an explanation for the troop takeover and infanticide cycle in langurs (Hrdy 1974) itself then becomes simply one of several possible enabling mechanisms: a comprehensible, acceptable, likely, species-level efficient cause, primarily significant, however, for its role in ensuring outbreeding in the biogram of an obligate generalist. From this point of view the situation of infanticide and outbreeding in langurs is comparable to Wilson's (1975) startling parable of the ultimate altruist as one who cannibalizes his own species in times of declining carrying capacity and one who thereby conserves his own species biomass. Comparably, the adult male langur who eliminates his rival's offspring, for whatever motivation, in a situation of environmental flux, high reproductive rate, and detrimental inbreeding, contributes positively, if unwittingly, to his own species viability.

There is no logical reason why "altruism" at the species level should be congruent with "altruism" at the level of individual interaction, or vice versa. This important point is often missed in heated criticisms of sociobiological analyses of reproductive strategies (Sahlins 1976). In fact, sociobiology concerns itself with much more than individual reproductive strategies, even though such strategies are the narrow gate through which the evolution of all forms of higher sociality must pass.

Population Control Device. If we accept (following Hrdy's and Struhsaker's reasoning) that the proximate cause of infanticide lies in adult male reproductive strategy but recognize (as argued here) that its ultimate biological value lies in retaining polymorphism of genotypes for populations of an ecological generalist reproducing within a type of social structure that otherwise rapidly leads to inbreeding (Hrdy 1977a;

Seger 1977), there is no reason why both proximate and ultimate explanations for langur infanticide cannot also operate in concert to control population growth (Rudran 1973) in *some* habitats.

In the highly seasonal outer tropical and subtropical habitats (and
a few atypical inner tropical ones as well) in which gray langurs are
found most abundantly (Ripley 1970, 1977a,b, 1979), some critical
season of at least 1–2 months' duration is normally encountered* in
the annual round (Yoshiba 1967, 1968). During this period food shortages and competition are maximal, creating a temporary population
bottleneck. As has been shown in general theoretical terms by Simon
(1973) and Levins (1973), there is no way for prenatal forms of population control to be selected for, other than the only partially effective
device of mild birth seasonality, since the remaining "good" part of the
year (10–11 months) is longer than the periodicity of the entire reproductive cycles of langurs (1–2 months of estrous cycling plus 6.5
months of gestation). Birth seasonality in the form of birth peaks does
in fact occur in most populations (Prakash 1962; Jay 1963; Ripley
1965; Hrdy 1977a; Sugiyama 1965, 1976; Mohnot 1971; Vogel 1971),
although the causes for the timing of the various reproductive events
have not yet been specified for primates in general (Lancaster and Lee
1965) or for langurs in particular.

Under these conditions we might expect a pattern to evolve in
which the most rapid possible maturation of neonates from infantile to
adult diet within the first year would be advantageous, combined with
large natal size and rapid growth, as perhaps occurs in the squirrel
monkey, *Saimiri*. Such a pattern would free the mother metabolically
and take advantage of seasonally limited resources. But such rapid
growth would conflict with the essential generalist strategy among
higher primates of slowly learning the various foraging subroutines,
acquired as they are encountered while living in relatively large heterogeneous social groups within which the routines are transmitted by

---

*Hrdy (1977a) notes that for the langurs she studied at the top of Mt. Abu (c. 1,200 m
altitude), where water is usually more abundant than at lower levels, and where the pods of the
legume *Bauhinia* are eaten by langurs during the dry season, relatively high individual and biomass densities are normal, and food shortages result only during an extremely dry year, such as
1975. Thus, somewhat paradoxically, we can expect *more* competition between *smaller* troops
and among *fewer* males at the *lower* locations, where periodic food shortages are more common,
and lower saturation densities are normal. In short, the top of Mt. Abu is more comparable to
distant areas which are enriched both naturally and artificially than it is to the plains areas immediately adjacent to this isolated hill station.

observation along existing social networks (Ripley 1970). This process has been described most clearly for Japanese macaques (*Macaca fuscata*), who undergo not rapid but slow maturation. In some extreme environments Japanese macaque infants even return to nursing during winter after having stopped, their mothers in effect becoming "wet-nurses." A long nursing period also occurs in some langurs living in a temperate Himalayan habitat (Bishop 1975). Both are solutions to the problem of supporting slow-maturing infants found among generalists living in extreme habitats of their respective distributional ranges.

Infanticide in Langurs and Man

It must be remembered that infanticide in langurs is a fundamentally different sort of infanticide from that found in humans. The extraordinary nature of human infanticide resides in the fact that it is exercized in large part by *females* (with or without male parental concurrence) on their *own* progeny as a means, when absolutely necessary, of maximizing the female's own effective fertility, whenever this conflicts with maximizing her own fecundity. It does this by permitting *post hoc* correction of reproductive errors such as (1) foreshortened optimal spacing jeopardizing parental investment (Trivers 1972), (2) undesirable sex ratios or birth orders, (3) too large a completed family size for optimal parental care (Trivers 1972), and (4) defectives and twins (Dickeman 1975).

Since many human reproductive units are polygynous, reproductive strategies of males can be expected to differ from those of co-reproducing female partners. As such, it is probable that the sorts of human maternally instigated infanticide just noted will often be opposed by their male partners in any society in which such males suffer less competitively from the consequences of these reproductive errors; this is especially likely to occur in lineally organized, polygynous, post-Neolithic societies. Hence, the exclusion from perinatal scenes of male ethnographers, along with male social parents and male medical practitioners in many such societies (Newman personal communication), noted earlier, becomes an expectable outcome.

Infanticide in langurs (and lions, Bertram 1976), by contrast, is practiced by *males* on the offspring of other males, (the latter two both potentially inbred [Seger 1977]), following the group takeovers by which reproductively excluded males gain access to females. Thus, it is not surprising to find that in langurs, infanticide by males is opposed by female counterstrategies (Hrdy 1974, 1977a, 1977b) since competing females suffer reproductively more than do males by the loss of *any* infant, inbred or not. One such counterstrategy of exceptional interest is postconception estrus, a pattern that is *functionally* similar to the human condition of frequent mating by females at all stages of the reproductive cycle.

One additional by-product of the whole complex pattern for langurs is the ouster from the recently taken over troop of a group of closely related males (including the previous resident alpha and his postweanling male offspring), who then join, or form, an all-male or mostly male group. In time these ousted males may themselves form the core of a successful takeover party. As very close relatives (Seger 1977) these ousted males will therefore suffer less genetically when, during the course of such a subsequent takeover, all but one of *them* are ousted in turn. Thus, provided that the ousted males and the takeover party form an enduring social unit, the cooperation necessary to take over a troop may not require intermale deception, contrary to Hrdy's theoretical prediction (1974).

Just as human and langur infanticide are formally quite dissimilar, although they may share some similar biological values, there is no a priori reason to expect that the social patterns involving infanticide found in some other species (chimpanzees: Goodall 1977; *Cercopithecus ascanius:* Struhsaker 1977; macaques and baboons: Angst and Thommen 1977) can all be accounted for by the same processes, alone or in combination.

Direct Competition among Generalists

It is essential to the enlargement of the Darwinian perspective, under healthy pressure from sociobiological analyses, to recognize that a large amount of intraspecific *sturm und drang* accompanies the appearance and maintenance of a generalist species. This social turbulence is in addition to the interindividual competitive nature of mammals generally (Wilson 1975). Such turbulence exists between age grades, genders (Hrdy 1977a), and groups (Ripley 1967b) as well as within these social units. The overt expression of social turbulence is controlled somewhat by the balanced pressures existing in more complex social structures typical of the cercopithecines and hominoids.

This social turbulence contrasts markedly (Ripley 1970) with the behavioral synchrony and quietude characteristic of one-male groups of foraging specialists (Sussman 1977; *Lemur fulvus*: Poirier 1970: *Presbytis johnii*; Curtin 1976: *Presbytis obscura*), all species likely to be the inbred, genetically monomorphic type.

Generalist folivores therefore represent a kind of intermediate condition between morphologically and behaviorally specialized colobines (with whom they share anatomical similarities) and primarily generalized cercopithecines (with whom they share behavioral similarities).

Among generalists social competition in a group is particularly well developed within and between male and female reproductive classes (Hrdy 1977a). It is somewhat less pronounced in females than in males, apparently because females remain in their natal group and are therefore more closely related than are males (Seger 1977). The individual advantages that males in particular may be seen to "strive for" (always modified by the sociobiological "as if" caveat clearly stated by Barash 1977) come to be "sacrificed" in the process of repeated "political" changes (resident male replacement in langurs; rank order changes in baboons and macaques). Thus, the apparently self-defeating, or futile, nature of these takeovers when repeated *ad infinitum* (noted by Angst and Thommen 1977), which is difficult to explain as a normal process for those who leave the analysis at the level of intermale competition, now becomes understandable. The process is driven not merely by the energy generated by sexual competition but also by the sociogenetic conditions for the continued existence of generalist species: namely, a broad behavioral flexibility at both individual and population levels.

Infanticide actuated by males, each acting in his own best reproductive interest, contributes to a genetic flux remarkable for leaf-eaters (Hrdy et al. 1975) that facilitates the exercise of a broader range of behavioral potentials in some component populations of the species over a wide range of habitat types. Favored in the selection processes for generalist primates is the capacity to utilize locally appropriate subroutines and to coordinate them in complex situations involving large face-to-face gatherings with well-defined properties (Goffman 1961, 1967, 1969; Ripley 1965, 1970). For, as we noted above, to remain a generalist species requires that there be broader individual variation than the demands of any one habitat type can select for (Levins 1968; MacArthur 1972).

It is this feature of generalists that makes the identification of species-specific behaviors notoriously difficult to establish in most primates, as difficult as is the separation of phylogenetic from ecological influences on social organization (Crook 1970; Crook and Gartlan 1966; Struhsaker 1969; Eisenberg et al. 1972; Clutton-Brock 1974; Gartlan 1973). In spite of such academic difficulties, generalist strategies are essential to the nature of higher primate adaptive modes in particular and thus are worthy of our attention. Component features of the respective strategies are easier to identify when one can compare generalist and specialist congeners (Ripley and Wells 1977), hence the major theoretical advantage of "leaf-eaters" when analyzed from this perspective. Given the subtleties of the differences in one behavioral domain, positional behavior (Ripley 1967a, 1970, 1977a, 1977b, 1979), leaf-eaters are further valuable heuristically because the nature of their diet favors populations that successfully economize on all behavioral expenditures, especially including, but not limited to, those for routine positional behaviors.

Lability in Social Organization: Unimale and Multimale Troops
Next to chimpanzees and man, gray langurs have the widest latitude in species-typical form of social grouping (Vogel 1971), a feature that argues for low genetic selection (Slobodkin, personal communication). This remarkable lability, especially in a morphologically specialized folivore, is left unexplained by the primatological theorists of infanticide considered above, although it is as crucial to their arguments as it is to this one (Hrdy 1977a).

Curtin and Dolhinow (1978) state that the multimale troop form is "normal" and the unimale pattern a "pathological response" to crowding and harrassment by men and dogs dating only from historical times. If so, the crowding response, if it can continue for so long a time, should be maximal at the Kaukori village, where 98% of the land is cultivated (Dolhinow 1977). The Kaukori troop, however, has the multimale form alleged by Curtin and Dolhinow to be found only in relatively "undisturbed" sites. On the other hand, the study sites that these authors consider as "normal" (Orcha, Junbesi), because human influence is much less, are actually quite marginal areas characterized by densities (1–2.7 individuals/km^2 or 12–42 kg/km^2)* that are extremely

---

*Biomass densities for the various sites at which studies of langurs have been conducted were crudely calculated from data supplied in Hrdy (1977a, table 3.4 and appendix 2).

low for a folivorous primary consumer for whom 4 + kg/hectare (400 kg/km^2) was found to be appropriate by Hladik (1975). Curtin and Dolhinow (1978) themselves show this in their chart of superimposed home range sizes in which their own sites (Junbesi; Orcha and Kaukori) are clearly at the outer limits of the range of distribution for langurs, not central to it.

If, in contrast, the two forms of social organization (unimale and multimale) are both normal and evolutionarily old (Hrdy 1977a, 1977b), and if the hypothesis outlined by Ripley (1979, and above) is valid, there must be an internally consistent accounting not only for how polymorphisms are maintained in multimale as well as unimale troops, but also for the predominance of one or the other type of social organization in the different areas. We must search beyond the "human disruption hypothesis" for the socioecological causes of this widespread structural dualism in this "weedy" species that so obviously has thrived until recently (Oppenheimer personal communication) as a commensal of man.

In attempting to understand the socioecological correlates and causes of this structural dualism, it helps to recall that multimale troop organization is common among cercopithecines. Indeed, Struhsaker (1969) convincingly argues that it is a phylogenetically conservative trait in this subfamily. Multimale troop structure may be common in this subfamily because cercopithecines are mainly foraging generalists, and the trait is being implicated increasingly in the foraging strategies of generalist species (Sussman 1977; Curtin 1976; Ripley and Wells 1977). It is possible that the outbreeding essential for a variable behavioral repertoire among generalists of monkey grade is accomplished in the largely terrestrial cercopithecines by the sociogenetic features of dominance-oriented rank orders, intertroop transfers by males, and intralineage mating inhibitions (Sade 1968).

For the few arboterrestrial generalist species that have evolved among the predominantly specialist folivorous colobines, whose phylogenetically conservative group structure is unimale (Struhsaker 1969), outbreeding is necessarily accomplished by other devices, namely, male takeovers and infanticide, given the opportunism of evolution (Gould 1978) and the prior existence of these fundamental features in colobines (Ripley 1979). It follows that in certain habitats that can, and do, support a high *proportion* of multimale troops (for reasons to be explained shortly), populations of generalist colobines (in this case gray langurs) behave more like cercopithecines and undergo fewer takeovers and infanticidal events (Ripley in preparation). It is paradoxical, but nonetheless comprehensible, that such habitats include the *two* extremes of biomass density: the highest (Polonnaruwa) and the lowest (Orcha, Kaukori, Junbesi, Melemchi).

Multimale troop structure is atypical and may be expected to appear only in generalist folivores (suggested at present to include some other colobines, such as *Presbytis melalophos* and *Colobus badius*, Ripley 1979), and some prosimians (*Propithecus verreauxi:* Richard 1977) under only two special conditions.

1. Wherever potential carrying capacity, and therefore achieved densities in conditions undisturbed by human activity, are locally quite high and *a critical season of food supply is not experienced*, intermale competition is reduced, or at least deferred to a higher level of population density, and multimale troops can predominate. This type of situation for folivores occurs naturally in the rare tropical and subtropical locations with reversed seasonality of precipitation (summer-*dry*, winter-*wet*) that have high proportions of trees with multilayer leafing strategy but no season of synchronized deciduousness (see references and discussion in Ripley 1977a, 1979), as well as artificially for successful commensals of man (religious provisioning; crop-, stores-, and bazaar-raiding).

2. Multimale troop structure may also appear at the other (low) end of the range of biomass densities (Hrdy 1977a p. 44), where distances between troops are extreme (Bishop 1979) and ousted males can and must associate with one male troops in the non-breeding season. These situations occur at the outer limits of the range of tolerance for extreme conditions of moisture (Orcha), human density (Kaukori; Ahmedabad City, personal observation), altitude and temperate seasonality (Junbesi, Melemchi, Simla, Bhimtal) and where predation by carnivores and humans is heavy. These populations are not, therefore, the "typical" ones for generalist folivores, contrary to the claims of Curtin and Dolhinow (1978).

The "multimale troop" is thus a heterogeneous category within which finer distinctions must be made. Those multimale troops that grow by internal recruitment (resident male tolerating his son's presence and breeding activity) into "age-graded" troops (Eisenberg et al. 1972) are highly inbred (Seger 1977). Other multimale troops, of whatever origin, in which only one male breeds successfully (Boggess 1976) are also highly inbred and are genetically equivalent to one-male troops. Indeed, the latter appear from some descriptions to be more a close association between a small all-male band and a one-male troop outside the breeding season. Thus, some populations with troops that are demographically multimale, but are sociogenetically unimale, behave like specialists, adapting genetically to local situations that represent the extreme outer limits of the species' range of distribution. As possible examples, researchers report the loss of the female head-flag as a sexual solicitation, and the loss of male whooping chorus, simplifications that repeatedly occur only in marginal high-altitude habitats (Bishop 1979) and could possibly reflect genetic losses.

Despite the prominence of multimale troop structure in some populations of the generalist folivore gray langur under the few special conditions noted above, unimale troop structure remains the phylogenetic norm for most genera in the subfamily Colobinae. The unimale troop structure is indeed more favorable for the evolution of successful, inbred foraging specialists (Levins 1968; Seger 1977) such as the "typical" colobine leaf-eaters mostly are (Hladik and Hladik 1972; Hladik 1975; Ripley 1970, 1977a, 1977b, 1979). In fact, such specialist folivores are only "typical" because in terms of absolute numbers *many* such species are generated, each of which is adapted genetically to each local situation, and hence monomorphic locally as well (Hrdy et al. 1975).

Eventually, with more precise ecological data, it may be possible to define a discontinuous spectrum of sociogenetic types of troop structure for gray langurs along a gradient of potential biomass density per unit of appropriate habitat, instead of actual densities without regard to local human density, as is now given by investigators (Hrdy 1977a, table 3.4). Using the distinction between types of multimale troops just made, such a spectrum could run as follows: (1) multimale troop structure (demographically *and* sociogenetically) predominating in certain rare natural habitats with *very* high normal biomass density (outer tropical Polonnaruwa: 25 kg/hectare of *two* species of folivores); (2) unimale troop structure predominating in the widespread typical subtropical habitats (with one critical season of winter-dry synchronized deciduousness) potentially supporting 1–9 kg/hectare of only *one* species of folivore (Sariska, Dharwar), actually less if human densities are high (Abu, Jodhpur, and Singur area); and (3) multimale troop structure (demographically but not sociogenetically) in difficult habitats with very low biomass densities (less than 1 kg/hectare: Orcha, Junbesi, Melemchi), apparently excepting two sites that have moderate densities (Simla, 2.6 kg/hectare; Bhimtal, 8.9 kg/hectare, based on only 17 data days). I will shortly elaborate on this spectrum, moving from focal adaptation ("normal")—that is, (2) on the spectrum—to peripheral adaptation ("abnormal")—that is, (1) and (3) on the spectrum.

Lessons from Langurs: Sympatry of Generalist and Specialist Foragers

The gray langur (*Presbytis entellus*) of South Asia is an eurytrophic folivore that lives sympatrically with an oligotrophic folivore congener, the purple-faced langur (*Presbytis senex*, = *P. johnii* of South India) in only one area; the north-central dry zone of Sri Lanka, where both of these species as well as the sympatric macaque and loris were studied at Polonnaruwa by the Smithsonian Primate Ecology Survey (1967–71). This site lies in a vegetationally unusual area of the dry zone (Mueller-Dombois 1969). The mixed semideciduous/semievergreen forest at Polonnaruwa supports an extremely high density of primates, especially folivores (25 kg/hectare contributed equally by both colobines, Hladik 1975), apparently without exceeding the carrying capacity of the vegetation (Hladik and Hladik 1972). Ripley (1979) suggests that this high biomass density is possible and normal at this site because of a specific kind of vegetational response to climatic conditions that are unusual in the tropics.

The contrast in adaptive strategies between these two folivorous species of *Presbytis* permits us to learn valuable lessons about the evolution of generalist strategies, ones that are commonly found among higher primates (cercopithecines and hominoids).

As a *folivore*, the gray langur is localized in home ranges somewhat larger than those of the sympatric purple-faced langur (Hladik 1975) and has similarly limited powers of dispersal, often blocked because of saturation densities, leading to direct (territorial) intertroop encounters in which "spacing mechanisms" (whooping vocalizations, jump displays, sentinel staring) seem to serve as attractants, not dispersants (Ripley 1967b). As a *generalist* forager the gray langur is obliged to maintain greater behavioral flexibility in somewhat larger groups (Ripley 1970, 1977a, 1977b) probably by preserving relatively high levels of genetic polymorphisms already shown for blood proteins (Hrdy et al. 1975). However, as a fellow *colobine*, the gray langur's phylogenetically characteristic troop structure is unimale (Struhsaker 1969), the type best suited to generate the highly inbred, genetically monomorphic, locally adapted foraging specialists (Levins 1968) typical of this subfamily of leaf-eaters. Thus, the gray langur is in an evolutionary dilemma requiring a variety of compromise solutions, some of which have been sampled by studies conducted in various habitats over the past 20 years.

Most habitats for gray langurs lie in the northern subtropical summer-rain zone (between 10′ and 30′N latitudes) of South Asia. A study made in India (Walter 1973) shows the following relationships between mean annual rainfall plus maximum number of months of drought and kinds of forest vegetation, all of which are tolerant of some degree of climatic seasonality: (1) semievergreen tropical rain forest (1,000–2,000 mm plus 4–7 drought months), (2) moist to dry (deciduous) monsoon forest (500–1,000 mm plus 5–8 drought months), and (3) thorn bush forest (250–500 mm plus 7–11 drought months). Densities of gray langurs can range from 1 to as much as 9 kg/hectare. As is normal for the subtropics (Walter 1973), all these habitat types have in common a season that is "bad" for folivores (synchronized deciduousness as well as cold and drought stress during the leafless winter dry period). Hence, competition at all social levels is accentuated because of the food and moisture supply "bottleneck" of this critical leafless, cold, dry season. Indeed, it is only because of their generalist foraging strategy that *entellus* leaf-eaters can survive at all in these seasonally dry habitats.

At these sites the phylogenetically characteristic group structure is realized: one-male troops of small size (12–21 individuals). Male reproductive competition is enhanced and troop takeovers plus consequent infant deaths (at least some of which are direct infanticides) are found, as we now expect, to be routine and chronic (Dharwar: c. 1,000 mm rainfall, Sugiyama 1965; Mt. Abu: c. 2,000 mm rainfall, Hrdy 1974, 1977a). Even with trophic enrichment (religious provisioning by Hindus and some crop raiding) only the *size* of the one-male troop increases in regions of extreme seasonal aridity (Jodhpur: c. 280 mm rainfall, with biomass density in the lower portion of the range of variation about 1.26 kg/hectare, Mohnot 1971), or where some essential resources are widely separated (Sariska: c. 800 mm with biomass density about 7–9 kg/hectare and mean troop size, at 64, in the upper part of the species range of variation).

In locations in which seasonal contrasts of climate are more moderate, or its effects on vegetation and food supply are somehow tempered, the multimale troop structure in larger groups (20–60 + individuals) can be realized, particularly where predation may be heavy (Gir Forest: 1,080 mm, Kurup 1970; Starin 1978; Kanha: 1,524 mm, Nagel and Lohri 1973). In areas of milder seasonal effects and topography, where agriculture is more secure, sites are often patchily enriched artificially (by crop raiding and bazaar pilfering as well as religious provisioning), a situation some five millennia old. Despite such local enrichment and high potential density, present actual densities (as calculated by researchers) may be quite low, because troop core areas (usually village shrines and firewood commons containing trees with interconnecting crown canopies) are widely separated by cultivated fields (Kaukori: 1,000 mm, Jay 1963).

In the tropics (between 10′N and 10′S latitudes) certain locations supporting quite dry semideciduous forests are naturally enriched; that is, they have no critical season for synchronized leaflessness due to winter-*wet* climatic conditions, but have complex unsynchronized phenological patterns due to early spring-dry and summerlong-dry climatic conditions. Given such trophic enrichment, very high normal saturation densities of folivores are possible (two species, together reaching 25 kg/hectare). Multimale troop structure is common in one of these species, the *generalist* folivore gray langur. Many troops contain several breeding males, organized into a dominance oriented rank order, from among whom females select and solicit mating partners, sometimes presenting persistently to low-ranking males (Polonnaruwa: 1,750 mm, Ripley 1965, 1967a, 1967b, 1970, 1977a, 1977b, 1979). Even in this enriched area, however, troop takeovers (accompanied by infant mortality and ouster of males into mostly male groups) occur in *both* one-male and multimale troops of gray langurs, although perhaps at lower frequencies than elsewhere (Ripley in preparation). They also occur in the unimale troops of purple-faced langurs at high frequencies (Rudran 1973).

A source of confusion for students of the behavior of gray langurs has been the fact that multimale troop structure is also found where individual densities are quite low (below the 20 per km² found at

Kanha: Nagel and Lohri 1973 and Simla: Sugiyama 1976). Thus far such sites are known to include those (1) at the outer limits of ecological tolerance for gray langurs close to the 2,000-mm isohyet (Walter and Lieth 1960) as at Orcha (Jay 1963), and in high-altitude sites with pronounced winter-cold climates and vegetational seasonality as at Junbesi (Curtin 1975; Boggess 1976), Melemchi (Bishop 1977), and Bhimtal (Vogel 1971); or (2) in subtropical habitats where predation (by humans as well as other carnivores) is commonly heavy as in Gir Forest (Kurup 1970), Kanha (Schaller 1967), and Orcha (Jay 1963).

If, as a rough rule of thumb, about 1–4 hectares per langur of medium size (12–15 kg) is required for calculating "supplying area" (Hladik 1975) at moderate densities (25 to 50 per km^2), it is clear that any area may be judged marginal for this species—even allowing for a near doubling of body weight in continental higher latitudes—in which 8 (Melemchi), 15 (Orcha), 30 (Kaukori), or even 50 (Junbesi) times this amount of supplying area is required per langur, as was acknowledged by Curtin and Dolhinow (1978) for Junbesi. However, "supplying area" for langurs living in areas of high human density (Kaukori, Mt. Abu, Jodhpur, Singur, Simla, and Bhimtal) should not be compared without correction with that for langurs living in areas of low (Kanha, Gir, Orcha, Melemchi, Sariska) or moderate (Polonnaruwa, Dharwar, Junbesi) human density.

Since one male may be responsible for most of the breeding in at least some of the low-density "multimale" troops (Junbesi: Boggess 1976), the latter may be genetically equivalent to unimale troops and hence more monomorphic, like the foraging specialists. Thus, it is crucial to distinguish between social structure and sociogenetic breeding structure in the different populations in which multimale troops are found. This distinction can only be made after *intensive* long-term study of individually identified animals over several breeding seasons, not by *extensive* survey-census techniques, which can sometimes fail to separate multitroop aggregations (which often occur during intertroop encounters) from very large (100 +) troops. Only in some populations of gray langurs with multimale troops is the necessary genetic polymorphic potential preserved either by male takeovers and ousters plus infanticide, or, alternatively, in ways that are typical of macaques and baboons (rapid cycling of rank orders controlling breeding performance by males, intertroop transfer by males, and intralineage mating inhibitions). Actual, or virtual (sociogenetically) one-male troops that lack a means of assuring polymorphism are as much evolutionary sinks for the obligate generalist gray langur as are closed breeding groups for man. I propose that extremely low density (peripheral) populations of langurs are evolutionary sinks.

Implications for Early Hominids

As we saw in langurs, it is often the presence of an adaptively superior specialist species dominating the optimum resources of a habitat that relegates the leftovers (including suboptimal habitat) to a canny sympatric generalist (Levins 1968; Cody 1974) in areas rich enough to support two closely related species of similar body size. However, there must be sufficient differentiation in "grain of resources" (MacArthur 1972) from which generalists can carve such additional niches.

Thus, the baffling presence (Leakey and Walker 1978), until 1 million years ago, of two (or more) species of Australopithecine man-apes makes good ecological sense; one was a foraging specialist (*Australopithecus robustus*) and the other was a foraging generalist (*A. africanus/Homo habilis*), as read recently from their dentitions (du Brul 1977). The exploitation of seasonally dry savannahs, grasslands, and woodlands can then be seen as the conquest of very difficult aspects of a habitat that was clearly suboptimal for a forest living ape, a conquest in which small seeds (Jolly 1970) or roots and tubers (Isaac 1978) may have played important roles (Dunbar 1976). The eventual success of the generalist over the specialist, however, was associated with the slow painful evolution of a new adaptive mode: predatory hunting. One problem for anthropologists lies in recognizing that whereas dry savannahs were suboptimal habitat for the forest-dwelling arboterrestrial generalist ancestors of the man-ape *Australopithecus africanus*, these same dry savannahs became optimal habitat for the fully human generalists (*Homo habilis*) once the new adaptive plateau (bipedal terrestrial carnivory) was mastered, a plateau that Napier (1970) termed a "breakaway exception" for primates. It was at this point that the specialist species of the sympatric congeneric pair (*Australopithecus robustus*) was outcompeted.

It was at this point in the transition made by early hominids from lower (herbivore) to higher (carnivore) trophic levels that behavior patterns less profligate of species biomass than those possible for primary consumers like the gray langur were favored. Thus, it is at this point in our interpretations that analogies from the more conservative non-primate carnivores (lions, wolves, dogs, hyaenas, etc.) became apt (Schaller and Lowther 1969; King 1975, 1976; Rose 1978). Of paramount interest in the area of population control is the pattern of incest avoidance (Sade 1968; Ripley, in preparation), in which intergenerational mating restrictions within a long-lived minimal reproductive and productive unit can operate not only as a means of population regulation but also as a device to ensure polymorphism through outbreeding (Packard and Mech this volume). This pattern defeats the inbreeding and genetic homogeneity, fatal to generalists, which is otherwise inevitable in such groups. In both wolf packs and human nuclear families only one breeding pair is tolerated in the group: fertile juveniles must either defer breeding, helping the breeders until generational succession occurs, or leave the pack/family.

There are other consequences that followed upon the move from a lower to a higher trophic level. One consequence is that saturation densities for partial and fully carnivorous hominids (secondary consumers) are far lower than for all other higher primates, who are all herbivorous primary consumers of various kinds. Saturation densities of hunting hominids would have been particularly far below those of folivores, both generalist and specialist. In addition, densities of individual predatory hominids would have been lowered still further because the reduction in total species biomass at the higher trophic level was packaged into larger individual body sizes.

Thus, this hunting hominid became an exceptional primate species with a peculiar population dilemma. It was an aberrant ape that had to remain a genetically polymorphic, ecologically generalist species in order to compete successfully with its sympatric specialist congener. As a generalist and a hunter, it had to maintain *simultaneously* both a high r and a low population density. With high mortality, this result would be simple. But it would have been a problematic achievement in any habitat in which (1) postnatal mortality from exogenous causes was not severe enough to stabilize the population density at a stationary (low) profile safely enough below carrying capacity for a large-bodied species at the secondary consumer level, or (2) prenatal fertility depressants were *not* operating (*un*like the atypical !Kung San discussed above). Since for a carnivore such a "safe" density is quite low, it is likely that the problem applied to all or most habitats occupied by this species.

Two solutions were possible for the continued success of populations of this species of ape-man in such habitats. (1) They could practice two types of infanticide, either by mothers out of reproductive self-interest as primary investing parent, and/or by males competitively, through casualties followed by rape in attacks in a permutation of the langur pattern. Such infanticide would occur in richly endowed centers of rapid population accumulation from which dispersion was somehow blocked (*K* selection locations). (2) The ape-men could experience out-migration by small colonizing founder groups in less well endowed, unimpacted habitats (*r* selection locations). However, since optimal group sizes (10 to 100) and optimal population densities (c. 1 per 2 km², Lee and DeVore 1968) in both *K* and *r* types of location were quite similar, and *low, wherever hunting was an important part of the adaptive mode* (Ripley 1976), the two situations are not easy to distinguish in the field ethnologically (as among the Yanomamö, Neel 1970), let alone archaeologically.

Summary and Conclusions

As Dickeman (1975) has shown, control of population growth by infanticide commonly occurs in foraging as well as in food-cultivating populations of human beings, the generalist species *par excellence*. (The aboriginal !Kung San and the Pygmies may be exceptions, a circumstance that, if true, may be attributable in part to plant-produced secondary compounds in their diets helping to depress fertility.) Is this widespread infanticidal behavior adaptive or pathological in man?

To answer this question, we looked for comparison and contrast at another foraging generalist primate, the gray langur (*Presbytis entellus*) of South Asia, in which infanticidal behavior has also been found common. As a colobine and folivore this species is morphologically highly specialized among primates generally. However, in contrast to most other colobines its behavior is flexible, variable, and multiphasic, enabling it uniquely to occupy high risk habitats that are too extreme in drought, temperature, altitude, and human density for any other colobine as well as for most other higher primates.

Data from field studies which have sampled populations of this species were arrayed along a gradient of biomass density, a gradient confounded only in areas of intense human agricultural activity where potential biomass density is assumed to be higher than reported actual densities. Demographically, multimale troop structure was found to be common at both ends of the density spectrum. It is argued that both unimale and multimale troop structures are adaptive, or "normal," and evolutionarily old for this variable generalist species and that this structural dualism is attributable to specific habitat characteristics. It is further argued that the analytic category "multimale" is a heterogeneous one, and care must be exercised in its use. It follows that explanations of infanticidal behavior of adult males are insufficient insofar as they assume only unimale troop structure to be the species norm.

The generalist nature of the gray langur's adaptive strategy is clearly revealed in the one area of South Asia where this species lives sympatrically with a foraging specialist congener, the purple-faced langur (*Presbytis senex*): the north-central dry zone of Sri Lanka. The peculiar circumstance of a species pair of colobines, one a foraging generalist relative to the other, leads us to inquire into the ecological (Cody 1974) and genetic (Levins 1968) conditions rendering such a situation of sympatry possible, particularly in a rather dry habitat that nevertheless supports without difficulty a record primate biomass density (Ripley 1977a,b, 1979).

Such an inquiry seems to show that the gray langur experiences an evolutionary dilemma in *some* ways similar to one probably experienced by early hominids. Although phylogenetically remote, gray langurs make a good heuristic model in this respect for early hominid adaptation not only because infanticide plays a role in the resolution of the population dilemma in both species but also because both are very successful widespread species in drier seasonal habitats, species who are foraging generalists relative to congeners and whose basic adaptations date from Pliocene times.

The evolutionary dilemma for langurs and for human foragers in each case lies in the opposition of fundamental conditions for continued existence. For both species their adaptation as foraging generalists in risky habitats requires (1) a high reproductive rate to overcome losses and (2) a means of ensuring behavioral variability. For the langur these requirements are in direct opposition to its phylogenetic status as a morphologically specialized colobine folivore. For the human hunting forager these requirements are in direct opposition to its phylogenetic status as a large-bodied frugivorous/omnivorous ex-ape whose nearest relatives maintain a low to moderate population density by reproducing only once every 3–5 years without practicing pre- or postconception controls.

In order to exploit the sort of fluctuating resources in the environments in which behavioral generalists are successful, a high reproductive rate seems essential as a means of rapid recovery from population downturns resulting from a run of particularly unfavorable seasons. With sufficient mortality from these causes, infanticide is rare. During favorable times some sort of countervailing controls must be applied to prevent intolerable local density accumulation, and if dispersal is blocked, infanticide is more common. For the folivore primary consumer gray langur, "intolerable densities" are quite high, whereas for the large-bodied secondary consumer *Homo sapiens* "intolerable densities" are quite low and the control must be sensitive.

The second requirement for the continuing success of a generalist species is that individual variation, however it is produced, be greater than the demands any one habitat can select for. This phenotypic variability must be maintained in spite of social structures in which inbreeding and/or behavioral monomorphism is a likely outcome for both species.

In langurs, the phylogenetically characteristic breeding structure may be a one-male troop or a multimale troop in which only one male breeds (Boggess 1978) or a multimale troop that grows by internal recruitment into an age-graded troop (Eisenberg et al. 1972). In all of these sociogenetic structures, inbreeding results rapidly unless counteracted (Seger 1977). In langurs, infanticide by sexually competing adult males achieves both the defeat of such inbreeding and also population limitation.

Foraging humans must achieve genetic variability despite living in bands which are comparably small (20–60 individuals) but which, in contrast to all but peripherally adapted langurs, are widely spaced out from one another. Like wolves, hunting humans conservatively substituted mating inhibitions within the minimal productive unit (the nuclear family/pack); thus inbreeding is defeated under *all* environmental and density conditions. The two functions that are joined in langurs are split in humans: for *Homo*, inbreeding is controlled by incest inhibitions, and infanticide serves primarily to control only the excess breeding success of a high-r generalist faced with a low feasible overall density as a secondary consumer.

Hominids evolved as secondary consumers, frugivore-omnivores, and generalists with a potentially long individual lifespan and a generational structure that facilitates cultural transmission by observation and limitation (Ripley in preparation). This complex nexus of features placed humans in a double bind; it required them to have a high intrinsic reproductive rate to achieve rapid recruitment in the face of high natural losses of infants *per reproductive unit* yet low supportive ability *per productive unit*. Whenever such infant mortality did not hold population levels sufficiently well below the low carrying capacity, local densities could be regulated through the process of pairs of spouses "selfishly" correcting reproductive errors after the fact, as needed individually, by behavioral means, of which the most flexible and biologically multivalued are *post*natal ones: adoption and infanticide (Davis and Blake 1955). This direct feedback is possible because productive and reproductive units are one and the same in foragers.

In the monogamous bilateral and ambilateral (or cognatic) societies especially characteristic of foraging cultures such decisions, and responsibility for them, involve both parents. As a cooperating minimal productive unit their interests in limiting reproduction to a supportable number are likely to coincide, and to be similar (two to three) and traditional for all parental pairs in part because of interdependence among nuclear family units resulting from egalitarian exchanges. Although decisions may involve both parents, the goals guiding spacing of offspring and total completed family size should accommodate the optimum capacity of females, sedentarized or not, as primary investing parent in economies of low per capita productivity. Ideal birth orders and sex ratios relate to other biocultural matters.

The Neolithic transition is in a complex mutually causative relationship with relatively high population density. The increase may be seen as cause, effect, or both. Cohen (1977) sees a rise in population pressure among Mesolithic foragers as partly responsible for the implementation of the domestication procedures constituting the Neolithic revolution itself. Ripley (1977a, 1979) suggests bioclimatic reasons why it should have occurred first in a Mediterranean-type ecosystem. During the Neolithic transition, whatever its causes, the new techniques permitted the ceiling on tolerable local density accumulation to rise. Some of the factors contributing to a de facto rapid growth in preindustrial agrarian society (stage two of the demographic transition model [Swedlund and Armelagos 1976]) seem to be consequences of the increase in scale and complexity of state-level society. Such factors include the uncoupling of reproductive decisions from economic decisions affecting the ability of parents to provide support throughout maturation; the possible erosion of parental ability to provide such support after the reproductive decision has been taken; the high value of contributions immature offspring make to already existing domestic units in need of helping hands. Religious and legal sanctions can preclude parental decisions not to bear already conceived young, and certain theologies (such as Catholic Christianity, especially in its aggressive phase as a state religion) can heavily support unlimited production and conversion of new "souls" and the bodies that go with them. Such a stage two growth has even been seen as favored by the occasionally expansionist policies of some state-level societies and ethnic groups within plural societies (Harris 1975).

The increase in scale and complexity of post-Neolithic societies has permitted partial defeat of the prior system of regulation among foragers. In the lineally organized, often polygamous, kin-group-structured societies especially characteristic of post-Neolithic (food-cultivating) labor-intensive preindustrial cultures such reproductive decisions may precipitate interparental conflict. In fact it is a conflict between the growth-fostering policy of the supporting corporate kin group of one parent and the growth-limiting policy of the in-marrying spouse when the latter is the female, a conflict for which the compound plural family is a partial answer. As primary investing parent the female, frequently but not always the in-marrying spouse, is better able to exercise her options if the male parent or his representatives (sometimes including male medical practitioners) are excluded from the perinatal scene. Such exclusion is facilitated wherever gender subcultures are well differentiated ("schismogenesis"; Bateson 1935), as is apparently common in these preindustrial agrarian cultures (Newman personal communication).

The most favorable population-to-resource relationships are achievable when the party (individual, spouse pair, or kin group) making the reproductive decision also has the responsibility for supporting the results of that decision and the ability to predict its future capacity to do so, or if rapid feedback occurs to the party who does. This is a relatively simple achievement in small-scale societies, in which all (or most) relevant parties interact on a daily face-to-face basis, are familiar with one another, and are self-supporting egalitarian exchangers. It is not simple, however, in state-level, urbanized, agrarian societies. In such complex societies the reproductive decisions of large numbers of parents are severed by time, space, weather, productive organization, and social class, from the economic decisions affecting their ability to provide support for their slow-maturing young. In addition, in such societies the period of maturation and dependency is often progressively and expensively extended well into adulthood by the demands of advanced education and/or temporary unemployment.

An important potential contrast exists between preindustrial and industrialized agrarian societies, however. In mature industrialized societies the reproductive and supportive units tend to be reduced once again to the mobile nuclear family, dependent as much upon female as upon male employment. That is, they become similar to the earlier units among foragers. Sophisticated means of conception control and prenatal testing now exist which permit these small units some selection of birth orders, spacing, total numbers, and sex ratios, as well as avoidance of defectives. Failing adoption, however, such selectivity depends upon abortion rather than infanticide, as was pointed out by Davis and Blake (1955). Although conception control, prenatal diagnosis, and abortion provide the potential for regulation, the use of such means is not always possible. Even in modern democratic nation-states the reproductive decision can be preempted by law and/or religion; the long-term supportive ability of the primary parents can be undermined by occasionally deteriorating economic processes, leaving ultimate responsibility for support in cases of parental default to functionally specialized bureaucratic institutions.

All these factors are intimately involved in the "modern" dilemma, which in fact is as old as the species itself. Those factors in complex agrarian societies which have permitted realization of the rapid growth potential of the human population as a whole date only to the Neolithic revolution, and they can be mitigated in technologically advanced industrial societies. Given their common dependence upon relatively high population density per se, however, both preindustrial and industrial agrarian societies stand in direct contrast to mobile foragers, an adaptation of incomparably greater antiquity, smaller scale, and socioecological continuity. It seems that the possibility of adaptive infanticide is an inevitable accompaniment of the status of an ecologically generalist species and is simply a price our species had to pay in the process of becoming, and remaining, human. It is the interplay of carrying capacity (a variable resultant of soil and climatic influences on vegetation) and combinations of evolutionary strategies (generalist or specialist, folivore or frugivore-omnivore, primary or secondary consumer, etc.) that determines the biological value of infanticide in *both* human and nonhuman primate species populations.

Acknowledgments

The author's field studies on which this chapter is based in part were supported by National Institutes of Health fellowship MF1273, research grant supplement M-5542, during 1962–63, and by Smithsonian Foreign Currency grant SFC-9-7004, and National Institutes of Health grant 1 RO1 MH15673-01 in 1968–1971. Essential assistance in the field was provided by M. Lockhart in 1962–63, and by V. Nugegoda and D. Thomas in 1968–72. Logistical support was provided by K. D. David. The cooperation of the Sri Lankan Government Departments of Wildlife, Agriculture, and Archaeology as well as the zoo and its director, L. de Alwis, is much appreciated. The National Geographic Society provided vehicles.

For the opportunity to observe langurs and other species in other areas, thanks are due to Y. Sugiyama and the late K. Yoshiba, to S. M. Mohnot and M. L. Roonwal, to Gerald Berreman, to D. Chivers and Lord Medway, and to A. Janeway and T. Zopf. Thanks are also extended to S. Blaffer Hrdy, N. Bishop, and L. Slobodkin for their criticisms of the manuscript. The impetus to write the analysis is due to the energy generated by this unique conference and its participants.

References

Angst, W., and Thommen, D. 1977. New data and a discussion of infant killing in Old World monkeys and apes. *Folia Primatol.* 27:198–229.

Balikci, A. 1967. Female infanticide on the Arctic coast. *Man* 2:615–25.

Barash, D. P. 1977. *Sociobiology and behavior.* New York: Elsevier.

Bateson, G. 1935. Culture contact and schismogenesis. *Man* 35.

Bertram, B. 1976. Kin selection in lions and in evolution. In *Growing points in ethology*, ed. P. P. G. Bateson and R. A. Hinde. Cambridge, England: Cambridge Univ. Press.

Bicchieri, M. G. 1972. *Hunters and gatherers today.* New York: Holt, Rinehart and Winston.

Birdsell, J. B. 1968. Some predictions for the Pleistocene based on equilibrium systems among recent hunter-gatherers. In *Man the hunter*, ed. R. B. Lee and I. DeVore, pp. 229–40. Chicago: Aldine.

Bishop, N. H. 1975. Social behavior of langur monkeys (*Presbytis entellus*) in a high altitude environment. Ph.D. dissertation, Univ. of California, Berkeley.

———. 1977. Langurs living at high altitudes. *J. Bombay Nat. Hist. Soc.* 74(3):518–20.

————. 1979. Himalayan langurs: temperate colobines. *J. Human Evol.* 8:251–81.

Boggess, J. 1976. The social behavior of the Himalayan langur (*Presbytis entellus*) in eastern Nepal. Ph.D. dissertation, Univ. of California, Berkeley.

Bourliere, F., and Hadley, M. 1970. The ecology of tropical savannahs. *Ann. Rev. Ecol. Syst.* 1:125–52.

Cain, A. J. 1969. Speciation in tropical environments: a summing up. *Biol. J. Linn. Soc.* 1:233.

Carr-Saunders, A. M. 1922. *The population problem: a study in human evolution.* Oxford: Clarendon Press.

Chapman, M., and Hausfater, G. 1976. Infanticide in langur monkeys (Genus: *Presbytis*): a computer analysis. Unpublished manuscript.

Clark, A. N. 1978. Sex ratio and local resource competition in a prosimian primate. *Science* 201:163–65.

Clutton-Brock, T. H. 1974. Primate social organization and ecology. *Nature* 250:539–42.

————, ed. 1977. *Primate ecology.* New York: Academic Press.

Cody, M. L. 1974. Optimization in ecology. *Science* 183:1156–64.

Cohen, M. N. 1977. *The food crisis in prehistory: overpopulation and the origins of agriculture.* New Haven: Yale Univ. Press.

Conaway, C. H. 1971. Ecological adaptation and mammalian reproduction. *Biol. Reprod.* 4:239–47.

Crook, J. H. 1970. The socioecology of primates. In *Social behavior of birds and mammals*, ed. J. H. Crook, pp. 103–66. New York: Academic Press.

————, and Gartlan, J. S. 1966. Evolution of primate societies. *Nature* 210:1200–03.

Curtin, R. 1975. The socioecology of the common langur (*Presbytis entellus*) in a high altitude environment. Ph.D. dissertation, Univ. of California, Berkeley.

————, and Dohlinow, P. J. 1978. Primate social behavior in a changing world. *Am. Sci.* 66:468–75.

Curtin, S. Hunt. 1976. Niche differentiation and social organization in sympatric Malaysian colobines. Ph.D. dissertation, Univ. of California, Berkeley.

Damas, D., ed. 1969a. *Band societies.* National Museum of Canada 228. Ottawa: National Museum of Canada.

————, ed. 1969b. *Ecological essays.* National Museum of Canada 230. Ottawa: National Museum of Canada.

Davis, K., and Blake, J. 1955. Social structure and fertility: an analytic framework. *Econ. Dev. and Cult. Change* 4:211–35.

Dawson, T. J. 1977. Kangaroos. *Sci. Am.* 237(2):78–89.

DiCastri, F., and Mooney, H. A., eds. 1973. *Mediterranean type ecosystems.* New York: Springer-Verlag.

Dickeman, M. 1975. Demographic consequences of infanticide in man. *Ann. Rev. Ecol. Syst.* 6:107–37.

Divale, W. T., and Harris, M. 1976. Population, warfare, and the male supremicist complex. *Am. Anthropol.* 78:521–38.

————, and Harris, M. 1978. Reply to Lancaster and Lancaster. *Am. Anthropol.* 80:117–19.

Dolhinow, P. J. 1972. The north Indian langur. In *Primate patterns*, ed. P. J. Dolhinow, pp. 181–238. New York: Holt, Rinehart and Winston.

———. 1977. Normal monkeys? Letter to the editor. *Am. Sci.* 65:266.

du Brul, E. L. 1977. Early hominid feeding mechanisms. *Am. J. Phys. Anthropol.* 47:305–20.

Dunbar, R. I. M. 1976. Australopithecine diet based on a baboon analogy. *J. Hum. Evol.* 5:161–67.

Eisenberg, J. F.; Muckenhirn, N. A.; and Rudran, R. 1972. The relation between ecology and social structure in primates. *Science* 176:863–74.

Frisch, R. E., and MacArthur, J. W. 1974. Menstrual cycles: fatness as a determinant of minimum weight for height necessary for their maintenance or onset. *Science* 185:949–51.

Gartlan, J. S. 1973. Influences of phylogeny and ecology on variations in the group organization of primates. *Symp. IVth Int. Cong. Primatol.* 1:88–101. Basel: Karger.

Glander, K. 1975. Habitat and resource utilization: an ecological view of social organization in mantled howler monkeys. Ph.D. dissertation, Univ. of Chicago.

Goffman, E. M. 1961. *Encounters.* Indianapolis: Bobbs-Merrill.

———. 1967. *Interaction ritual.* Chicago: Aldine.

———. 1969. *Strategic interaction.* Philadelphia: Univ. of Pennsylvania Press.

Goodall, J. 1977. Infant killing in chimpanzees. *Folia Primatol.* 28:259–82.

Gould, S. J. 1978. The panda's peculiar thumb. *Nat. Hist.* 87(9):20–30.

Harding, R. S. O. 1975. Meat-eating and hunting in baboons. In *Socioecology and psychology of primates.* ed. R. H. Tuttle, pp. 245–58. The Hague: Mouton.

Harris, M. 1975. *Culture, people, and nature.* 2d ed. New York: Crowell.

Hausfater, G. 1975a. The predatory behavior of yellow baboons. *Behaviour* 56(1–2):44–68.

———. 1975b. *Dominance and reproduction in baboons (Papio cynocephalus): a quantitative analysis.* Contributions to Primatology 7. Basel: Karger.

———. 1977. Letter to the editor, *Am. Sci.*

Hemming, C. F. 1978. A new plague of locusts. *Nat. Hist.* 87(10):6–18.

Hirschfeld, L. A.; Howe, J.; and Levin, B. 1978. Warfare, infanticide, and statistical inference: a comment on Divale and Harris. *Am. Anthropol.* 80:110–5.

Hladik, C. M. 1975. Ecology, diet, and social patterning in Old and New World primates. In *Socioecology and psychology of primates*, ed. R. H. Tuttle, pp. 3–35. The Hague: Mouton.

———, and Hladik, A. 1972. Disponibilités alimentaires et domaines vitaux des primates à Ceylan. *Terre et la Vie* 26:149–215.

Hrdy, D. B.; Barnicot, N. A.; and Alper, C. A. 1975. Protein polymorphism in the hanuman langur (*Presbytis entellus*). *Folia Primatol.* 24:173–87.

Hrdy, S. Blaffer-, 1974. Male-male competition and infanticide among the langurs (*Presbytis entellus*) of Abu, Rajasthan. *Folia Primatol.* 22:19–58.

———. 1977a. *The langurs of Abu.* Cambridge, Mass.: Harvard Univ. Press.

———. 1977b. Infanticide as a primate reproductive strategy. *Am. Sci.* 65:40–49.

Hyams, E. 1952. *Soil and civilization.* London: Thames and Hudson.

Isaac, G. 1978. The food-sharing behavior of protohominids. *Scientific American* 238(4):90–109.

Itani, J. 1972. A preliminary essay on the relationship between social organization and incest avoidance in non-human primates. In *Primate socialization*, ed. F. Poirier, pp. 165–71. New York: Random House.

Jay, P. 1963. The social behavior of the langur monkey. Ph.D. dissertation, Univ. of Chicago.

Jolly, C. 1970. The seed-eaters: a new model of hominid differentiation based on a baboon analogy. *Man* 5:5–26.

King, G. E. 1975. Socioterritorial units among carnivores and early hominids. *J. Anthropol. Res.* 31(1):69–87.

———. 1976. Society and territory in human evolution. *J. Hum. Evol.* 5:323–32.

Klein, D. 1978. The diet and reproductive pattern of a population of *Cercopithecus aethiops*. Ph.D. dissertation, New York Univ.

Kortlandt, A., and Kooij, K. 1963. Protohominid behavior in primates (preliminary communication). *Symp. Zool. Soc. Lond.* 10:61–88.

Kurup, G. U. 1970. Field observations on habits of Indian langurs, *Presbytis entellus* (Dufresne), in Gir Forest, Gujarat. *Records of the Zoological Survey of India* 62(pts 1 & 2):5–9.

Krzywicki, L. 1934. *Primitive society and its vital statistics*. London: Macmillan.

Lancaster, C., and Lancaster, J. B. 1978. On the male supremicist complex: a reply to Divale and Harris. *Am. Anthropol.* 80:115–7.

Lancaster, J. B., and Lee, R. B. 1965. The annual reproductive cycle in monkeys and apes. In *Primate behavior*, ed. I. DeVore, pp. 486–513. New York: Holt, Rinehart & and Winston.

Leacock, E. B. 1974. The structure of band society. *Rev. Anthropol.* 1(2):212–22.

Leakey, R. E., and Walker, A. 1978. The hominids of East Turkana. *Sci. Am.* 239(2):54–66.

Lee, R. B. 1972a. Population growth and the beginning of sedentary life among the !Kung Bushmen. In *Population growth: anthropological implications*, ed. B. Spooner, pp. 329–42. Cambridge, Mass.: M.I.T. Press.

———. 1972b. The intensification of social life among the !Kung Bushmen. In *Population growth: anthropological implications*, ed. B. Spooner, pp. 343–50. Cambridge, Mass.: M.I.T. Press.

———, and DeVore, I. 1968. Problems in the study of hunters and gatherers. In *Man the hunter*, ed. R. B. Lee and I. DeVore, pp. 3–12. Chicago: Aldine.

Levins, R. 1968. Evolutionary consequences of flexibility. In *Population biology and evolution*, ed. R. C. Lewontin, pp. 67–70. New York: Syracuse Univ. Press.

———. 1973. The limits of complexity. In *Hierarchy theory*, ed. H. H. Pattee, pp. 109–27. New York: Braziller.

Lomax, A., and Arensberg, C. M. 1977. A worldwide evolutionary classification of cultures by subsistence system. *Curr. Anthropol.* 18(4):659–79.

Lorimer, F., et al. 1954. *Culture and human fertility*. Zurich: UNESCO.

MacArthur, R. A. 1972. *Geographical ecology*. New York: Harper & Row.

McKey, D.; Waterman, P. G.; Mbi, C. N.; Gartlan, J. S.; and Struhsaker, T. T.

1978. Phenolic content of vegetation in two African rain forests: ecological implications. *Science* 202:61–64.

Meggers, B. 1971. *Amazonia: a counterfeit paradise.* Chicago: Aldine.

Miller, W. B., and Newman, L., eds. 1978. *The first child and family formation.*
Carolina Population Center, Univ. of North Carolina at Chapel Hill.

Milton, K. 1977. The foraging strategy of the howler monkey in the tropical forest of
Barro Colorado Island, Panama. Ph.D. dissertation, New York Univ.

Mohnot, S. M. 1971. Some aspects of social change and infant killing in the Hanuman
langur (*Presbytis entellus*) (primates: Cercopithecidae) in western India. *Mammalia* 35:175–98.

Montgomery, G. G., ed. 1978. *The ecology of arboreal folivores.* Washington:
Smithsonian Institution Press.

Mueller-Dombois, D. 1969. Ecogeographic analysis of a climate map of Ceylon with
particular reference to vegetation (with map). *Ceylon For.* 8(3–4):1–20.

Nagel, U., and Lohri, F. 1973. Die Languren der Kanha-Wiesen. *Vierteljahrsschrift
der Naturforschenden gesellschaff in Zürich.* 118:71–85.

Napier, J. R. 1970. Paleoecology and catarrhine evolution. In *Old World monkeys*,
ed. J. R. Napier and P. Napier, pp. 55–95. New York: Academic Press.

Neel, J. V. 1970. Lessons from a "primitive" people. *Science* 170:818.

Oates, J. F. 1974. The ecology and behavior of the black and white colobus monkey
(*Colobus guereza* Rüppell) in East Africa. Ph.D. dissertation, Univ. of London.

Orians, G. H. 1969. On the evolution of mating systems in birds and mammals. *Am.
Nat.* 103:589–603.

Parthasarathy, M. B., and Rahaman, H. 1974. Infant killing and dominance assertion
among the hanuman langur. *Proc. 5th Int. Congr. Primatol. Soc.*

Poirier, F. 1970. The Nilgiri langur (*Presbytis johnii*) of South India. In *Primate
behavior*, ed. L. A. Rosenblum, 1:251–383. New York: Academic Press.

Prakash, I. 1962. Group organization, sexual behavior, and breeding season of certain
Indian monkeys. *Jap. J. Ecol.* 12:83–86.

Price, P. W. 1975. *Insect ecology.* New York: Wiley.

Richard, A. 1977. The feeding behavior of *Propithecus verreauxi*. In *Primate ecology*, ed. T. H. Clutton-Brock, pp. 71–96. New York: Academic Press.

Ripley, S. 1965. The ecology and social behavior of the Ceylon Gray langur, *Presbytis entellus thersites.* Ph.D. dissertation, Univ. of California, Berkeley.

———. 1967a. The leaping of langurs: a problem in the study of locomotor adaptation. *Am. J. Phys. Anthropol.* 26:149–70.

———. 1967b. Intertroop encounters among Ceylon gray langurs, *Presbytis entellus
thersites.* In *Social communication among primates*, ed. S. Altmann, pp. 237–53.
Chicago: Univ. of Chicago Press.

———. 1970. Leaves and leaf-monkeys: the social organization of foraging in gray
langurs, *Presbytis entellus thersites.* In *Old World monkeys*, ed. J. R. Napier and
P. Napier, pp. 483–509. New York: Academic Press.

———. 1976. Anthropology. In *Encyclopedia Brittanica book of the year for 1975*,
pp. 125–27. Chicago: Encyclopedia Brittanica.

———. 1977a. Gray zones and gray langurs: is the "semi-" concept seminal? In
Yearb. Phys. Anthropol. 20:376–94. See the notation for Ripley 1978.

————. 1977b. Crossing the arbo-terrestrial rubicon: etic dimensions of a habitat boundary transition. In *Yearb. Phys. Anthropol.* 20:395–407.

————. 1979. Environmental grain, niche diversification, and positional behavior: an evolutionary hypothesis. In *Environment, behavior, and morphology: dynamic interactions in primates*, ed. M. E. Morbeck and H. Preuschoft, with N. Gomberg, pp. 37–74. New York: Gustav Fischer. This paper and Ripley 1977a contain important errors resulting from editorial processes beyond the author's control. Interested readers should request the corrected version directly from the author.

————, and Wells, J. 1977. Introduction: kinetics, kinematics, and context II. *Yearb. Phys. Anthropol.* 20:371–75.

Rose, M. R. 1978. The roots of primate predatory behavior. *J. Hum. Evol.*

Rudran, R. 1973. Adult male replacement in one-male troops of purple-faced langur (*Presbytis senex senex*) and its effect on population structure. *Folia Primatol.* 19:166–92.

Sade, D. S. 1968. Inhibition of mother-son mating among free-ranging rhesus monkeys. *Sci. Psychoanal.* 12:18–38.

————; Cushing, K.; Cushing, P.; Dunaif, J.; Figueroa, A.; Kaplan, J. R.; Lauer, C.; Rhodes, D.; and Schneider, J. 1977. Population dynamics in relation to social structure on Cayo Santiago. *Yearb. Phys. Anthropol.* 20:253–62.

Sahlins, M. 1976. *The use and abuse of biology.* Ann Arbor: Univ. of Michigan Press.

Schaller, G. B. 1967. *The deer and the tiger.* Chicago: Univ. of Chicago Press.

————, and Lowther, G. R. 1969. The relevance of carnivore behavior to the study of early hominids. *Southwest J. Anthropol.* 25(4):307–41.

Seger, J. 1977. A numerical method for estimating coefficients of relationship in a langur troop. In *The langurs of Abu*, S. B. Hrdy, Appendix III, pp. 317–26. Cambridge, Mass.; Harvard Univ. Press.

Simon, H. A. 1973. The organization of complex systems. In *Hierarchy theory*, ed. H. H. Pattee, pp. 1–28. New York: Braziller.

Struhsaker, T. T. 1969. Correlates of ecology and social organization among African Cercopithecines. *Folia Primatol.* 11:80–118.

————. 1977. Infanticide and social organization in the redtail monkeys Cerpithecus ascanius schmidti of Kibale Forest, West Uganda. *Z. Tierpsychol.* 45:75–84.

Strum, S. 1975. Primate predation: interim report on the development of a tradition in a troop of olive baboons. *Science* 187:755–57.

Sugiyama, Y. 1965. On the social change of Hanuman langurs (*Presbytis entellus*) in their natural conditions. *Primates* 6:381–418.

————. 1976. Characteristics of the ecology of the Himalayan langurs. *J. Hum. Evol.* 5:249–77.

Sussman, R. W. 1972. Child transport, family size, and increase in human population during the Neolithic. *Curr. Anthropol.* 13(2):258–59.

————. 1977. Feeding behavior of *Lemur catta* and *Lemur fulvus*. In *Primate ecology*, ed. T. H. Clutton-Brock, pp. 1–36. London: Academic Press.

Swedlund, A. C., and Armelagos, G. 1976. *Demographic anthropology.* Dubuque, Iowa: Wm. C. Brown.

Teleki, G. 1973. *The predatory behavior of wild chimpanzees*. Lewisburg, Pa.: Bucknell Univ. Press.

———. 1974. Chimpanzee subsistence technology: materials and skills. *J. Hum. Evol.* 3:575–94.

———. 1975. Primate subsistence patterns: collector-predators and gatherer-hunters. *J. Hum. Evol.* 4:125–84.

Thompson, N. S. 1967. Primate infanticide: a note and a request for information. *Lab. Primate Newsl.* 6:18–19.

Trivers, R. L. 1972. Parental investment and sexual selection. In *Sexual selection and the descent of man*, ed. B. Campbell, pp. 136–79. Chicago: Aldine.

Turnbull, C. M. 1961. *The forest people*. New York: Simon and Schuster.

Vogel, C. 1971. Behavioral differences of *Presbytis entellus* in two different habitats. Proc. 3d Int. Congr. Primatol. 3:41–47.

Wallerstein, I. 1974. *The modern world system: capitalist agriculture and the origins of the European world-economy in the 16th century*. New York: Academic Press.

Walter, H. 1973. *Vegetation of the earth*. Heidelberg Science Library, vol. 15. London: The English Universities Press; New York: Springer-Verlag.

———, and H. Lieth, 1960. *Klimadiagram-Weltatlas*. Jena: VEG Fischer Verlag.

Wilson, E. O. 1975. *Sociobiology: the new synthesis*. Cambridge, Mass.: Harvard-Belknap.

Yoshiba, K. 1967. An ecological study of Hanuman langurs, *Presbytis entellus*. *Primates* 8:127–54.

———. 1968. Local and intertroop variability in ecology and social behavior of common Indian langurs. In *Primates*, ed. P. C. Jay, pp. 217–42. New York: Holt, Rinehart and Winston.

INDEX

Abortion, 359, 383; in Pleistocene populations, 283–84

AC. *See* Adrenocortical activity

Acetylcholine, 63

ACTH. *See* Adrenocorticotropins (ACTH)

Adaptations: to density (humans), 266; in foraging generalist hominids, 376; in gray langurs, 362; in higher primates, 368; of human foraging societies, 352–55

Adaptive strategies: of gray and purple-faced langurs, 372, 379

Adolescent sterility, 310, 325

Adoption, 359, 383

Adrenal gland enlargement: density and, 190

Adrenal response: affected by social interactions (mice), 11

Adrenal weight, 56–58, 129

Adrenocortical activity (AC), 56–57, 85; correlation with population density, 58

Adrenocorticotropins (ACTH), 61, 62, 99–100; and agression in animals, 90–91; in tbe anterior pituitary, 64–67; inhibits reproductive function directly, 91; nature of, 58–60; in the intermediate lobe of the pituitary, 62–64

Age composition: and population growth (mice), 5, 6; and territorial system (mice), 3

Aggression, 37, 56, 85; in deermice, 15, 17, 29; density and, 190, 198; effect of dispersal on, 124; and genetic change in population, 129; in house mice, 4, 5, 6; in humans, 255; as mechanism of inhibition of reproduction and growth, 90–91; relation of gonadotropins to (house mice), 13–14;

relation of, to mortality (mice), 3; in rhesus monkeys, 164, 174–75; and spacing mechanisms, 254–249; testerone required for (mice), 12, 14T

Aiello, J., 220

Alaska, Game Management Unit 13, 136

Alaskan Eskimos, 339

Albrecht, E. D., 42

Algonquin Park, Ontario, 136

Aligarh district (India): rhesus monkey populations in, 153–55, 156T, 157–58

Allen, D. L., 142

Alouatta palliata. *See* Monkey, howler

Altman, I., 268

Altmann, J., 152, 165

Altmann, S. A., 152, 165

Altruism: and population control, 363

Amboseli, 165, 171

Amenorrhea: nutritional, 340; postpartum, 290–91, 339, 340, 341, 342

Ammerman, A. J., 313

Andervont, H. B., 41

Androgens, 56–57, 92; relation of, to aggression and social rank (mice), 12, 13

Animal populations: studies of, xvi, xviii

Animals: effects of crowding on, 230; information-processing capabilities of, 256, 259–66; response difference to density from humans, 247–73; significance of density cues biologically determined in, 261; social organization of, bound by biological constraints, 254

Anthropology, xix

Anticipation: in human response to crowding, 218

391